MASCULINE FIGURES

MASCULINE FIGURES

Fashioning Men and the Novel in Nineteenth-Century Spain

NICHOLAS WOLTERS

VANDERBILT UNIVERSITY PRESS

Nashville, Tennessee

Library of Congress Cataloging-in-Publication Data

Names: Wolters, Nicholas Alexander, 1986– author.
Title: Masculine figures : fashioning men and the novel in
    nineteenth-century Spain / Nicholas Wolters.
Description: Nashville, Tennessee : Vanderbilt University Press, [2022] |
    Includes bibliographical references and index.
Identifiers: LCCN 2022011170 (print) | LCCN 2022011171 (ebook) | ISBN
    9780826505170 (paperback) | ISBN 9780826505187 (hardcover) | ISBN
    9780826505194 (epub) | ISBN 9780826505200 (pdf)
Subjects: LCSH: Men—Spain—History—19th century. |
    Masculinity—Spain—History—19th century. | Spain—Social life and
    customs—19th century. | Men—Spain—Fiction.
Classification: LCC HQ1090.7.S7 W65 2022 (print) | LCC HQ1090.7.S7
    (ebook) | DDC 305.310946—dc23/eng/20220406
LC record available at https://lccn.loc.gov/2022011170
LC ebook record available at https://lccn.loc.gov/2022011171

I dedicate this book to the memory of my brother, Jared "Jay" Wolters (1995–2019): one of the coolest guys I have ever known.

CONTENTS

Acknowledgments

I owe thanks to so many folks who have supported me and this project over the years, and I will try my best to acknowledge them all here in one way or another.

First, my manuscript would not have become a book without the steadfast work of Vanderbilt University Press. I owe special thanks to Zack Gresham, Joell Smith-Borne, and Gianna Moser, as well as the Press's anonymous reviewers, whose feedback undoubtedly helped to improve the manuscript.

The research undertaken to write *Masculine Figures* would have been impossible without the resources available to me at Wake Forest University. My yearly research trips to Madrid and Barcelona, as well as to conferences in the US and abroad, were made possible by generous funding from the Archie Fund for the Humanities, the Humanities Institute, the Offices of the Dean and Provost, and the Department of Spanish at Wake Forest University.

In the Departments of Spanish and Italian, I am especially thankful for the collegiality, generosity, and kindness of Jane Albrecht, Alison Atkins, Corey Cantaluppi, Margaret Ewalt, Luis González, Anne Hardcastle, Linda Howe, Kathy Mayers, Carmen Pérez Muñoz, Irene Picconi, Sol Miguel-Prendes, Silvia Tiboni-Craft, José Luis Venegas, and John Welsh. Throughout the writing process I was also constantly inspired by colleagues from other departments at Wake Forest University. Dean Franco, Claudia

Kairoff, Stephanie Koscak, Morna O'Neill, Jessica Richard, and Mary Wayne-Thomas have been amazing colleagues whose encouragement of interdisciplinarity has enriched my own work and made for wonderful conversations over the years. I also have to thank my seminar and honors thesis students, especially Lydia Milhoun, whose astute observations about and engagement with topics related to gender and dress provided regular encouragement to me as I finished writing *Masculine Figures*.

I owe a special debt to those who graciously volunteered their time to read and comment on so many drafts of chapters and translations from Spanish and Catalan to English. Laureano Bonet, Carlos Ferando Valero, Leslie Harkema, Toni Maestre Brotons, Sarah Sierra, Jennifer Smith, and José Luis Venegas gave careful and thoughtful feedback during critical stages of the writing process. If a "thank you" in this category was measurable, though, the biggest one I could offer would undoubtedly go to Gaby Miller. Her abilities as reader and editor are only equaled—if not exceeded—by her compassion and generosity as a pal and a confidant. I also offer a heartfelt *merci/gràcies* to Montse Prats and Laura Masforell, who taught me to speak, read, listen, and write in Catalan and who inspired me to continue studying it.

Several colleagues in modern Spanish and Iberian studies (including some already named above) also assisted with various stages of the book-writing process and have continued to instill in me an appreciation for and enriched understanding of Spanish cultural studies and literature. *Masculine Figures* would not be what it is without their generosity and feedback during (and in between!) conferences and research trips in the US and abroad. Those scholars include Elena Cueto-Asín, Julia Chang, Stacy Davis, Toni Dorca, Fran Fernández de Alba, Marcela Garcés, David George, Hazel Gold, María Luisa Guardiola, Cathy Jaffe, Colin McKinney, Leigh Mercer, Gaby Miller, Sara Muñoz, Lisa Nalbone, Wadda Ríos-Font, Erika Rodríguez, Ana Rueda, Alan Smith, Wan Sonya Tang, Erika Sutherland, Sarah Thomas, Akiko Tsuchiya, Aurélie Vialette, and Linda Willem. Many thanks, as well, go to Irene Gómez-Castellano and Isaac García-Guerrero, who invited me to give book-related talks to their generous students and colleagues at the University of North Carolina at Chapel Hill and Virginia Military Institute, respectively.

The archival component of this project was facilitated by the expertise and kindness of dozens of archivists and librarians in Madrid and Barcelona. Artifacts and texts that I studied with assistance provided by Elisa Regeiro of the Arxiu Històric in Barcelona, as well as Cristina Jiménez of the Museo Cerralbo and Juan Gutiérrez of the Museo del Traje in Madrid, are this book's warp and weft.

Though Chapter 2 of this book is the only section related in any significant way to the work I did at the University of Virginia, I am grateful to several mentors, peers, and friends I met there. Randolph Pope and David Gies read early drafts of essays that would later become or inspire chapters in this book, and they buoyed me in my professional endeavors in ways that exceeded the duties of an adviser or reader; I can only hope to aspire to the scholarly model they first set for me in graduate school. I would also like to thank Andrew Anderson, Allison Bigelow, Eli Carter, Shawn Harris, Stephanie Knecht Gates, Cheryl Krueger, Gaby Miller, Carmen Moreno Díaz, Elena Neacsu, Tally Sanford, Paula Sprague, Jennifer Tsien, and Miguel Valladares for their friendship and generous support during my time in Charlottesville. Huge thanks also go to Nora Benedict, who constantly shared her experience and expertise on all things book-related (and who only made fun of me a little bit for my absurd orders during our coffee dates).

I owe so much to my parents, John and Brenda, and to my younger siblings, Kait, Jay, Rachel, and Tommy. My family and friends have showered me with a seemingly endless supply of love and laughter over the years, reminding me that there is much more to life than deadlines and the ticking tenure clock. I thank my barber, Tim Parker, for making me look cooler than I am and for his insightful comments (and for listening to me ramble more than once about the contents of this book). I am thankful to my closest friends in Winston-Salem, especially Andrew Johnson; they all celebrated, hugged, and uplifted me when I needed it the most.

An earlier version of Chapter 1 appeared as "Secondhand: The Used Clothing Trade and Narrative Ragpicking in Galdós's *El Doctor Centeno*" in *Anales Galdosianos*, no. 53 (2018), 55–75; an earlier version of Chapter 2 appeared as "'Debajo de la sotana': (Re)Dressing Clerical Masculinity in *La Regenta*" in *Revista de Estudios Hispánicos*, 53, no. 1 (2019), 329–52.

FIGURE 0.1. Advertisement for tailor services from the last third of the nineteenth century. The caption reads, "Latest novelties in boys' suits in all shapes, sizes, and tastes with an eye to elegance and economy. Special made-to-measure section for gentlemen." Image courtesy of the Arxiu Històric de la Ciutat de Barcelona, Barcelona, Spain.

INTRODUCTION

In a late-nineteenth-century advertising card (see fig. o.1), a father appears to oversee his son while a tailor or journeyman kneels to take the boy's measurements. Depicting one of many steps in crafting a made-to-measure suit, the illustration's iconography demarcates a clear hierarchy.[1] Whereas the father's broad shoulders, dark suit, top hat, cane, and solid stance bespeak his status as an affluent and gentlemanly client, the tailor's crouched position, worker's cap, and tape measure signal the deferential respect of a trustworthy craftsman. Stationed between the father's walking stick and the tailor's tape, the boy submits obediently to the measure of paternal and societal expectations. An ephemeral reminder of nineteenth-century advertising and commerce, the all-male scene focuses on both fashionable production and consumption while also illustrating a common transaction between men who represent different but complementary spectrums of the middle class. It also hints at a male homosocial rite of passage in the shepherding of young boys to adulthood. Perhaps indirectly, the promotional illustration reflects the existence of multiple configurations of middle-class masculinity produced and made visible by interactions between men in nineteenth-century Spain's culture of consumption. Like many other advertisements of its kind, the card promises "Economy, Elegance, and Careful Tailoring" to the faithful clients of Pantaleoni Hermanos (see fig. o.2), values and virtues that were capitalized upon by advertisers, tailors, and department store owners alike in order to appeal to aspirants to, or members of, Spain's bourgeoisie or "dominant groups."[2]

Not unlike the images used in advertising cards and other commercial ephemera, memoirs and realist literature commemorate and fictionalize the role of sartorial craftsmen in ferrying young men to adulthood during the final decades of the nineteenth century in Spain. While domestic seamstresses were responsible for outfitting sons, brothers, nephews, lovers, and husbands alike, bourgeois men's autobiographical writings offer evidence of their reliance on sartorial professionals in their own maturation and self-fashioning. Nobel-prize winning neuroscientist Santiago Ramón y Cajal (1852–1934), for example, struggled at times to meet demanding paternal expectations and spent a period of his young adult life as an apprentice and journeyman to various shoemakers, who represented a trade identified by his father as a respectable (if temporary) alternative to the academic vocation eventually pursued by the Aragonese youth.[3] Eusebio Güell y López (1877–1955), son of the wealthy industrialist Joan Güell i Bacigalupi and the heiress to Antonio López y López's fortune, Luisa Isabel López Bru, cites having frequented "a tailor named Pantaleoni" once he was of age.[4] In his memoirs, politician and writer Joaquín María de Nadal (1883–1972) also recalls his childhood in Barcelona, commenting on "that ample first floor apartment, the home of the wise Verdereaux, the seamstress who clothed [him] until [he was] handed over to the tailor."[5]

Novelists build further upon these stories, perhaps unsurprisingly since, as middle-class professionals and observers of contemporary social reality themselves, they were—along with their work—also entangled in consumer culture, masculinity, and male homosocial networks. In José María de Pereda's local-color sketch "A las Indias" (1864; To the Indies), a mother scoffs at the delusions of grandeur of her son: a future emigrant with his eyes set on making a fortune in the Americas and whose desire to emulate a local gentleman informs his preference for a bespoke city suit. The boy, perhaps modeled after Pereda's oldest brother or any number of other men who left for the Americas during this time, derides the handiwork of the women in his rural Cantabrian family, symbolized by the apparent crudeness of his "mother's scissors and his sister's needlework."[6] Emblematizing the classic city/country divide, as well as the supposed superiority of a craftsman over his female counterparts, the boy fantasizes instead about the silhouette a professional in Santander would be able to achieve for him, also recalling the values marketed by Pantaleoni Hermanos (see fig. 0.1).

Male characters in Benito Pérez Galdós's novels—from *Lo prohibido* (1885; Forbidden fruit) to the *Torquemada* tetralogy (1889–1895) and the *Episodios nacionales* (1872–1912; National episodes) rely on the handiwork of tailors

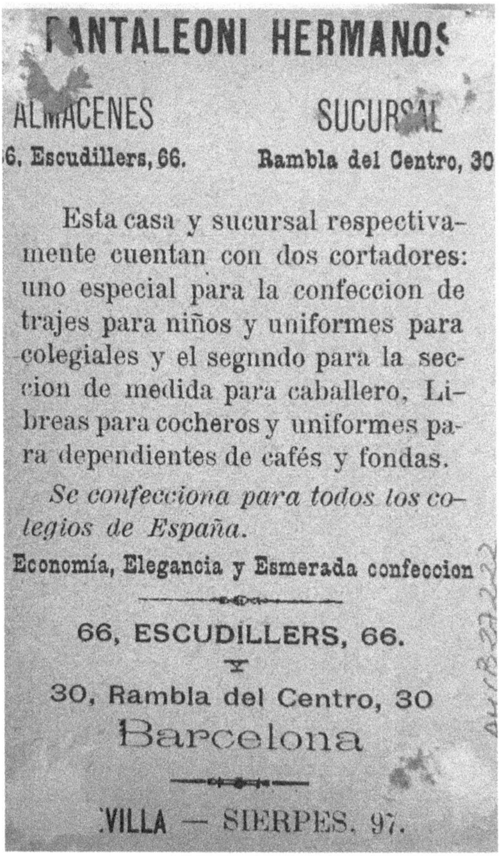

FIGURE 0.2. Reverse of Figure 0.1. The description reads, "These establishments have two cutters: the first specializes in the crafting of suits for boys and uniforms for students, and the second in the made-to-measure section for gentlemen, livery for coachmen, and uniforms for the employees of cafés and inns. Tailoring available for all schools in Spain. Economy, Elegance and Painstaking Craftsmanship." Image courtesy of the Arxiu Històric de la Ciutat de Barcelona, Barcelona, Spain.

to match their changes in fortune and subsequent attainment of bourgeois polish. For example, in Galdós's *Mendizábal* (1898)—the second installment in the Canarian writer's third series of episodes devoted to telling the story of modern Spanish history via the novel—introduces Fernando Calpena, a young man recently settled in Madrid and who is the recipient of a surprise visit from a cloth-cutter in the employ of the Romantic-era tailor Juan Utrilla. Sent by a mysterious benefactor, the craftsman takes Calpena's measurements and is explicit in his plans to style the client after Juan Álvarez

Mendizábal, the titular prime minister whose liberal political agenda—partially informed by his travels to Great Britain—is matched by a penchant for traditional English and Scottish fabrics and prints.[7]

As storytellers and spinners of tales, novelists were acutely aware of the affinities weaving through their own cultural production and, for example, that of the tailors who outfit the characters inhabiting their fictional worlds. As a figure of speech, Leopoldo Alas "Clarín" often alluded to his novels awaiting revision or publication as in "the loom."[8] Additionally, the language of plot shared seemingly natural connections to vocabulary used in the production of textiles, since words like *trama* meant both plot and weft, the threads that, together with the warp, constitute the structure of a length of cloth. In Benito Pérez Galdós's 1897 acceptance speech to the Spanish Royal Academy, the author discusses the exigencies of his realist agenda, which for him involved aestheticizing the human character down to the "the very garments tailoring the external traits of one's personality."[9] By the end of the century, Galdós would even characterize the "capricious and fugitive" nature of aesthetic opinion, realism included, "to the flashing by of fashion trends (*modas de vestir*)."[10] To be sure, these writers embraced literary realism as the primary brand of their publishing agendas, but the genre's unabashed capitalization on the conventions of other aesthetic modes in Spain—from the local color sketch and melodrama to decadence and naturalism—perhaps justifies Galdós's comparisons of aesthetic or literary whims to those who thought to coincide with changing fashions, while also emphasizing the kinship between the novel and fashion.[11] Men's fashion—from its production and distribution by craftsmen and advertisers, to its consumption, use, and display by men of all socioeconomic stripes, along with its representation in art, ephemera, and literature—was just one of a number of industries responsible for manufacturing a variety of patterns or styles of mainstream masculinity in Spain during the nineteenth century.

Masculine Figures presents the reader with a gallery of male social types—the student, the priest, the businessman, and the heir—that showcases the multiple ideals of middle-class masculinity that had become increasingly visible in fin-de-siècle Spain. During this time, upwardly mobile boys and men from Madrid and Santander to Barcelona and Oviedo had increasing access to plural models of behavior to which they could aspire in the construction of their identity and public personas. By situating representative novels against the backdrop of previously unstudied archival materials like tailoring journals, department store catalogs, fashion advertisements, and photographs, this book also argues that fictional masculinity—or the artistic representation of men and their defining characteristics—performs a symbolic role in negotiating the challenges and contradictions male authors often encountered in their own fraught attempts to succeed not only as professional artists and novelists, but also as businessmen, professors, lawyers, husbands, and fathers. On the one hand, writers still wished to transform the Spanish novel into a work of art worthy of comparison to international paragons like Balzac, Flaubert, Zola, and Tolstoy.[12] On the other hand, they struggled to make a comfortable living from the novelistic craft, which they blamed on low literacy rates, unfavorable market circumstances associated with publishing practices they considered arcane, and an inferiority complex related to the belief that the national model most worthy of imitation was Miguel de Cervantes (1547–1616). Because literacy rates in Spain lagged significantly behind those of other industrial and industrializing Western nations, as we will see later, nineteenth-century Spanish novelists only marginally benefitted from what Pierre Bourdieu refers to as "a constant growth of a public of potential consumers, [and] of increasing social diversity, which guarantee the producers of symbolic goods," like art and novels, "minimal conditions of economic independence and, also, a competing principle of legitimacy."[13] As we will see, these tensions come to light in male novelists' contradictory framing of their novels as, on the one hand, works of art, and, on the other, as fashionable merchandise, secondhand acquisitions, speculative enterprises, canonical objects, or cultural inheritances.

Through their literary output, writers like Benito Pérez Galdós, Leopoldo Alas "Clarín," Narcís Oller, and José María de Pereda took on the task of representing both real and imagined anxieties and issues related to modern manhood relevant to their own lives and work. Through recurring masculine figures from the precarious student to the affluent heir, both artists and novelists represent an increasingly middle-class world that saw itself at odds with the traditional values and virtues it inherited from a more storied, imperial past—represented by the long shadow cast by Golden Age paragons like Cervantes's *Don Quixote*—and those it imported from more industrialized nations like England and France. With the object of identifying and analyzing nineteenth-century Spain's masculine figures, this book contends that both complementary and competing configurations of middle-class masculinity were capitalized upon as artists, novelists, and other Spanish intellectuals sought to cut and brand for themselves a modern, national image from the cloth of a waning empire.

Visualizing the Manly Body in Nineteenth-Century Spain

During at least the second half of the nineteenth century in Spain, perhaps the most immediately recognizable way a man demonstrated his manliness was through the display of outwardly visible bodily signs that included physical beauty, physique and stature, facial hair, deportment, and dress, all of which had the potential to contribute to (or detract from) a man's social capital and privilege. Some of the elements that came to denote manliness during this time were inherited, such as impressive height or stature. Others were attainable through the consumption of conduct manuals, cosmetics, and fashion. Informed by patriarchal imperatives, however, nineteenth-century intellectuals seeking to institutionalize differences between the sexes relied on pseudoscientific discourses, like hygiene and physiognomy, which resulted in the naturalization and reification of gender stereotypes.[14] Whereas men were characterized by their "hardness and imperviousness to change," women were viewed as soft, "changeable and malleable."[15] As elsewhere in industrializing Europe, manly ideals took shape in opposition to "negative stereotypes," which, in Spain, were represented as non-Catholic, racialized, and effeminate others.[16] By contrast, the dominant model of masculinity as it related to the male body coalesced around classical paradigms of male beauty, a robust and hirsute physique, tidy self-presentation, and whiteness.[17] Masculinities studies theorist R. W. Connell calls this configuration of gender and power "hegemonic masculinity," which she defines as "the configuration of gender practice which embodies the currently accepted answer to the problem of the legitimacy of patriarchy, which guarantees (or is taken to guarantee) the dominant position of men and the subordination of women."[18] As this section will show in the example of king Alfonso XII, the hegemonic bodily ideal was itself a fantasy that even one of the most powerful Spaniards failed to embody for everyone at all times.[19]

The gendered expectations of men appear monolithic thanks in large part to the apodictic registers adopted by many cultural commentators and hygienists who wrote about them. Pedro Felipe Monlau, for example, took part in discursively constructing the dominant ideal, itself a fiction to which many would aspire but few or none would (or could) embody fully. According to one of his most popular publications, *Higiene del matrimonio, o, El libro de los casados* (1853; Marital hygiene, or, The book of husbands and wives), Monlau substantiates the theory of essential differences by first describing in detail the physiological and intellectual attributes of the so-called "sterner sex," a model against which he later measures women:

> Man is fervent, proud, vigorous, hirsute, daring, prodigious and domineering. His character is ordinarily expansive and bustling; his texture is fibrous, resilient, and compact; his muscles are sturdy and angular; his thick mane, his dark and full beard, and his hairy chest are exhalations of the flames that fuel him; his sublime and impetuous mind launches him upward and makes him aspire to immortality.[20]

According to Monlau's prescriptive and essentializing account, manliness is that which issues from a male body ideally exhibiting all or at least some of these attributes to some unspoken degree. As the wide-ranging number of approved masculine types makes clear, many men deviated from this aspirational rubric. However, what made men manly in the court of popular opinion was hardly bound to physiological treatises, such as Monlau's, even if they were reprinted in several editions throughout the nineteenth and early twentieth centuries.[21]

Prescriptive texts including *Higiene del matrimonio* should not be assumed to be reflective of what the majority of middle-class men experienced or recognized, since "normative definitions [of masculinity] allow that different men approach the standards to different degrees."[22] Still, even kings were not exempt from the kinds of bodily ideals disseminated in a variety of discursive contexts. During the first half of the restoration of the Bourbon monarchy, Spaniards in rural and urban areas alike were witnesses to sweeping political, economic, and social changes following a string of civil wars, initially spurred on by cultural and dynastic disputes between conservatives and liberals. The relative economic and political stability that ensued in the metropole was signaled primarily by the return of a male heir to the throne in the person of the prince of Asturias—Isabel II's oldest son, Alfonso—and his subsequent overseeing of the end of the final Carlist war and embrace of the 1876 constitution architected by Antonio Cánovas del Castillo. At least initially, there seemed to be widespread optimism surrounding Alfonso XII's masculine potential as a constitutional monarch. On the occasion of his eighteenth birthday in November 1875, moderate Alfonsine journal *La Época* (The epoch) extols the youthful king's virile bearing, emblematized for the writer by his "robust hand" and "manly stamina," before explicitly remarking upon the parliamentarianism, peace,

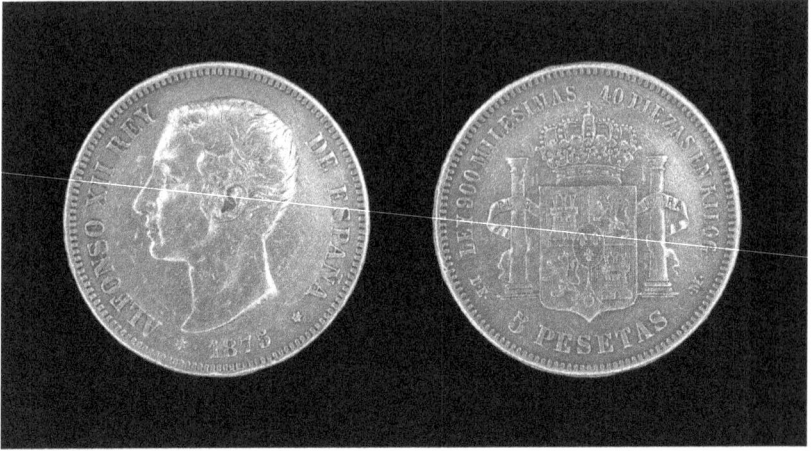

FIGURE 0.3. Five-pesetas coin from 1875 featuring a beardless Alfonso XII, who was only seventeen upon his coronation. Image courtesy of Wikimedia Commons.

and clemency that supporters thought his reign would herald.[23] The conflation of masculine attributes and political prowess in the eyes of an ideologically sympathetic magazine corroborates Mosse's assertion that positive stereotypes of masculinity in the West were "a motor that drove the nation and society at large."[24]

Official images of the king naturally mirror this idealized description, and his embodiment of the paradigm expounded upon by Monlau. For example, coinage circulating during Alfonso XII's short reign betokens his transition from boy to man with recourse to bodily signifiers that reflect aesthetic conventions dating back to Greco-Roman antiquity, but that also recall Monlau's physiognomy of the perfect man. In the five-peseta coin from 1875, the royal teenager's cleanshaven face is an idealized stamp of his boyish innocence, a reminder of the king's young age during the first year of his reign (see fig. 0.3).

Providing a stark contrast with the example from early on in the king's tenure, the five-peseta coin from 1885 lionizes the monarch—still a young man at the age of twenty-six—by way of physical features that symbolize his authority, maturity, and solidity: a thickset neck, defined mustache and mutton chops, and a formal comb over. As Collin McKinney summarizes from his survey of portraits of bourgeois men from around this time, "although specific styles may have varied, [. . .] beards," and, I would add, mustaches and facial hair in general, "had [. . .] become the mark of manliness."[25] According to biographers, the new Spanish king did sport such gendered symbols by the late 1870s, following the fashion of Austrian emperor Franz Joseph I, with whom Alfonso XII came into contact during his education at the Theresianum in Vienna.[26]

Enthusiasm and hero worship in loyalist newspaper columns and enshrined in legal tender notwithstanding, the king's actual physiognomy hardly met expectations, at least according to some critics. One foreign diplomat went as far as to comment on the king's short stature, the only characteristic that apparently prevented him from being a "particularly strapping lad."[27] Carrying this appraisal to its extreme, a political cartoon published as a centerfold image in *El Loro* (1879; The parrot) depicts a partially hidden prime minister Cánovas, who worriedly observes a skinny, boyish and intimidated Alfonso XII. The latter's ineptitude is symbolized here by a cowering posture, a dainty mustache and a broken lance with which he appears to have crippled his own mount. Jeered by a raucous crowd of bourgeois onlookers, the satirized monarch might have summoned for viewers the image of Cervantes' Alonso Quijano: the errant hidalgo and protagonist of *Don Quijote*, a novel in which the lofty and erstwhile ideals of medieval chivalry are often undermined by the main character's questionable mental state and physical frailty. Similarly negative stereotypes were passed down from father to son. Alfonso XIII, who only came of age as king around his sixteenth birthday in 1902, was often emasculated and infantilized, for example, by North American satirists at the height of the Spanish American War of 1898. In one cartoon from 1898 (see fig. 0.4), the boy-king—attired in the classical dress of the *majo* or bullfighter—is depicted playing with his toys on Cuban soil; his bent-over stance and the phallic missile clearly evoke the emasculation of Spain by the superior forces of the United States of America.

However, for Alfonso XII, what was an unfortunate reality had potential remedies in the form of a number of cultural practices with which the king was already very familiar. Since his youthful years spent in England, France, Switzerland, and Austria, Alfonso XII participated in a number of activities meant to bolster his physical health and virility in the public eye. For example, royal advisers and physicians would submit him to further regimes of gymnastic exercises, regular visits to baths and springs, as well as sports in order to invigorate his otherwise sickly constitution.[28] In articles he wrote for a journal devoted to exercise and gymnastics during the 1880s, Miguel de Unamuno corroborates wider societal belief in the benefits of such a regime: "Gymnastics not only provides us with strength, but it distributes and regulates it and teaches us how to understand and manage it. The man who understands the limits of his physical vigor, who considers his forces and becomes master over them, has an appreciable advantage over other men."[29] Absent in Monlau's medico-literary portrait, coins bearing the king's manly aegis, and caricatures, of course, are indications of the many cultural producers and products responsible for constructing, marketing, and normalizing nineteenth-century patterns of masculinity to men representing (or who sought entry to) the bourgeoisie.

"The Gentlemen's Paradise": Producing and Consuming Middle-Class Masculinity

Autobiographical and fictional depictions of nineteenth-century men's commercial and consumerist habits were commonplace and point to shopping and fashionable self-display as central to the enterprise of middle-class self-fashioning and masculinity. When close friends and cousins Narcís Oller and Josep Yxart traveled to Paris and Geneva together in 1878, the latter's travelogue unabashedly records repeat visits to French and Swiss department stores and shops (in between visits to expositions and museums) to browse and purchase souvenirs and toys for family members, as well as novels and photographs for themselves.[30] During the 1888 Universal Exposition in Barcelona, novelist José María de Pereda set up shop in the Cantabrian pavilion not to advertise his regionalist novels, which had already made him a national literary celebrity, but rather to show off and sell the new colognes, perfumes, and soaps produced by the Santander-based factory of which he was a proprietor.[31] Male protagonists in realist novels offer additional evidence of men's interaction with commodity culture within the nineteenth-century cultural imagination, as well as middle-class masculinity's constitutive reliance on consumerism. Galdós's *Lo prohibido* recounts José María Bueno de Guzmán's upwardly mobile trajectory—a result of the wealth generated from his speculative business ventures—granting him access to a lavish lifestyle that allows him to purchase tailor-made shirts, lunches in posh locales like Lhardy, as well as gifts for his many female love interests; even Bueno de Guzmán's less financially successful rivals, like Constantino Miquis, still embrace middle-class culture through the masculine-coded consumption of athletic paraphernalia as well as highly stylized photographic portraits.[32] Alas's *Su único hijo* (1890;

FIGURE O.4. 1898 cartoon by Victor Gillam for American weekly satirical magazine *Judge*. Image courtesy of Cornell University–PJ Mode Collection of Persuasive Cartography.

His Only Son), to provide yet another example, often alludes to office clerk Bonifacio Reyes's expenditures on his extramarital love interest—which include "a Regency corset, a pair of chinoiserie vases, [. . .] rings and flowers and ladies' pantaloons."[33]

Even though Monlau, along with other nineteenth-century hygienists like Amancio Peratoner, viewed manliness as coterminous with, or naturally arising from, a male body, the reality was more complex, as indicated by the king's example, Unamuno's commentary, and the autobiographical and fictional evidence surveyed earlier. Caricatures satirizing men who unabashedly participate in nineteenth-century commodity culture (see fig. 0.5) were reminiscent of the frequent censure of women who spent too much time or resources on shopping, as is evident in Galdós's depiction of Isidora Rufete in *La desheredada* or Alas's characterization of Obdulia Fandiño in *La Regenta*.[34] However, men wishing to advance socially were still very much encouraged to behave according to an increasingly capitalistic cosmovision that conditioned the proper enactment or performance—or, in

¿EL SEXO ¿FUERTE?

FIGURE 0.5. Satirical illustration ("The 'Sterner' Sex?") of a male window-shopper in the November 6, 1897, issue of *Madrid Cómico*. The caption reads, "Good gracious! I simply must have a dozen ties and I do not know which styles to choose . . . Good God! They've sent us quite a selection from Paris this year . . ." Image courtesy of the Hemeroteca Digital of the Biblioteca Nacional de España, Madrid, Spain.

Judith Butler's well-known phrasing, the "repetition of stylized acts"—of middle-class masculinity in public and in private.

Loosened from the rigid hierarchies of the Ancien Régime, social status no longer depended solely on one's birthright or title, but rather, it was acquired in the form of what Pierre Bourdieu calls economic, cultural, and symbolic capital, or "material wealth in the form of money, stocks and shares, property, . . . knowledge, skills and other cultural acquisitions, . . . [and] accumulated prestige or honor."[35] A man's ability to possess culture—in the form of art, literature, fashionable objects, and spectacles (e.g., universal expositions, theater)—was central to middle-class manhood, as it signaled one's embrace of artistic, economic, and industrial modernity, not to mention adjacent values like respectability.[36] Despite its frequent elision in studies on consumerism from the twentieth century and beyond, masculine consumerism was "a vital component of middle-class identity."[37] Men interested in obtaining such forms of capital took part in activities increasingly associated with the middle class or bourgeoisie, which ranged from practicing sports to working, shopping, collecting (e.g., antiques, art), gambling, and, as we will see later, writing. Such activities became part and parcel of the middle-class masculine habitus, particularly at a time during which Spanish intellectual elites—including artists and novelists—sought to consume and imitate English and French cultural models in their work to fashion and restore prestige to the Spanish novel.

While men were encouraged to exercise supposedly manly virtues of self-control and restraint by moral authorities, other values like comfort, elegance, and adventurousness—particularly in specific contexts—provide additional keys to understanding the various ways men lived gendered lives "within the rules" during the nineteenth century.[38] Because even during this time the dominant patterns of gender looked differently according to one's position within culture and society, masculinity is best understood as relational and plural in its configuration.[39] Shopping for themselves, friends, children, or significant others in the department store, the tailor's boutique, or secondhand markets was an integral part of what it meant to be a middle-class man. The consumption and display of certain products became dependable ways for men to broadcast their acknowledgment, if not total embodiment, of masculine aesthetics and ideals ranging from cleanliness and tidiness to comfort, efficiency, and careful self-presentation, not to mention the values they were capable of signaling.

Drawing on the title of Émile Zola's naturalist novel *Au bonheur des dames* (1883, The ladies' paradise), this section sheds light on how the makers of what I call a "Gentlemen's Paradise"—artists, advertisers, clothiers, entrepreneurs, journeymen, tailors, and shoppers—contributed to the consolidation of bourgeois, masculine identities through the manufacture, consumption, use, and display of clothing and other fashionable merchandise. Visual cultural evidence like tailoring journals, department store catalogs, chromolithographic advertising cards (*cromos*), and promotions in popular newspapers reveal an ideal masculinity that was not figured exclusively through the austere "man in black," as described by Harvey and McKinney and ubiquitous in formal portraiture, but rather an ideal that was kaleidoscopic in the shapes and shades of gender it represented.[40] Understood as a system of production and consumption, as well as stylish clothing and other merchandise more broadly, fashion offers a heretofore overlooked but significant key to understanding how bourgeois men constructed and displayed their public personas, since it constituted the "paraphernalia of gentility" necessary to achieve increasingly commodifiable virtues such as "cleanliness, order, [and] organization," together with the embrace of commercial and technological progress.[41] Shopping for a constellation of fashionable goods (and knowing how and when to use or wear them correctly) was part of the construction of middle-class masculinity during the nineteenth century, which is made most visible by visual cultural ephemera connected to the fashion industry.[42] The "Gentlemen's Paradise"—an image that evokes both a fantasy of masculine commerce and gentility as well as the modern Spanish novel, inspired as it was by those of French paragons like Zola—will also serve as a suitable metaphor for the generative relationship between cultures of capitalistic production and consumption and the multiple patterns of middle-class masculinity they engendered. As we will see, this consumerist metaphor will also contribute to our understanding of the literary output of a predominantly male homosocial coterie of writers invested in bringing their novels to a market and realizing their own self-fashioning as modern masculine figures.

Given that it was central to Spanish elites' embrace of commercial and industrial modernity, men's marketing, display, and use of fashionable commodities and the related values they helped to visualize also threaded through ideas about masculinity, national identity, and empire.[43] A fulcrum in the relationship between male producers and consumers of clothing, tailoring journals and menswear catalogs, for example, manufactured values such as professional association, high-quality craftsmanship, and faith in national commerce and local industry, which make them constitutive cultural products in the "field of meanings and symbols associated with national life."[44] Representing a significant if forgotten or overlooked discursive terrain in narratives of national identity formation in the modern Spanish context, sartorial ephemera and the fashionable discourses they gloss can also be said to function as signposts for what Homi Bhabha calls "national life" since, as Jo Labanyi importantly reminds her readers about the nineteenth-century novel, "any cultural form appealing to a nationwide mass public can be said to contribute to nation formation."[45] While marketing materials were in many ways fictions of their own—their self-interested raison d'être was at least twofold: first, to increase sales, and second, to churn out lucrative fantasies capable of fortifying the brand they represented—commercialized images in advertisements, fashion plates, and catalogs add yet "another layer to the imagined nation, according to which, at least in theory, the whole country had access to the same merchandise."[46]

In the context of nineteenth-century Spain, the idea of multiple masculinities within an increasingly capitalistic cosmovision must also account for rival political ideologies, which offered competing visions of the shapes that Spanish masculinity needed to take in order to overcome a perceived "deficit" in the nation's virility. Referring to this tension as a crisis, Nerea Aresti summarizes that, according to the "modernizing vision" of liberal reformers:

> it was a matter of deficit in relation to the qualities that defined hegemonic masculinity in fin-de-siècle Europe, inasmuch as they were operative. For traditionalists, the idea of a deficit [of virility] referred to the lack of legendary values of the Spanish gentleman-knight, and the solution to the problem would result from the recuperation of virtues lost in time.[47]

For many liberals, then, including both moderates and progressives, the deficit could be overcome by more closely aligning Spanish masculinity to English and French models, whereas for some conservatives, a perceived deficit of virility could only be overcome by recuperating erstwhile values like honor and martial valor, associated during the Golden Age with "military service, financial aid to the Crown, diplomatic cooperation, [...] forging alliances," and "sociability" or "the art of pleasing others," all of which once "served to publicize the nobleman's collaboration with the powers at court."[48]

The representation of fashionable patterns of masculinity through racialized figures in visual cultural ephemera demonstrates that mainstream menswear, along with the values that came to be associated with it, was also relevant to motifs of empire that continued to inform the construction of Spain's modern national image.[49] On the cover of an April 1878 issue of political, scientific, and literary magazine *El Globo* (The globe), an illustration depicts a predominantly male throng attired in traditional Japanese dress and European-style formalwear as they cross paths around a bustling corner of Tokyo (formerly Edo, or *Yeddo* in its transliteration to Spanish; see fig. 0.6). Evoking the modernizing efforts that followed in the wake of Japan's Meiji Restoration (1868), the image's corresponding caption juxtaposes the embrace of technological advancements like the railway and German weaponry with Japanese men's adoption of European formalwear which included "the black frockcoat and white bowtie."[50] In so doing, and

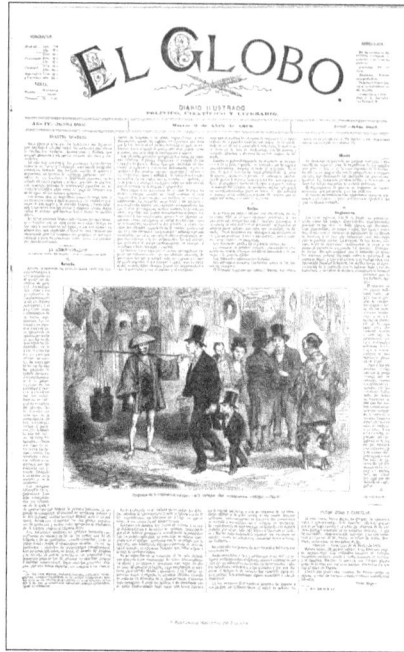

FIGURE 0.6. *El Globo* cover page with illustration of men in Tokyo (formerly Edo), who wear traditional Japanese dress and European-style suits. The caption reads, "The progress of European civilization. Formal dress." Image courtesy of the Hemeroteca Digital of the Biblioteca Nacional de España, Madrid, Spain.

by insisting on the importance of such reporting "for the progress of *our* contemporary moment and for the relations among all peoples of the civilized world," the columnist conceives of Spain within the wider context of nineteenth-century Europe's "civilizing" discourse.[51] Spanish bourgeois men's obsession with Japanese art, cultural artifacts, and imports—part of the wider European craze for such paraphernalia known as *japonisme* that extended to contexts like menswear catalogs (see fig. 0.9)—manifests in a number of examples including the Marquis of Cerralbo's Arabesque Parlor or Galdós's depiction of a similar room in the summer home owned by the banker Pedro de Fúcar in *La familia de León Roch* (1878).[52]

These examples offer telling evidence of the reliance of masculine self-fashioning on the possession of exotic (and exoticizing) cultural products, while also corroborating Anne McClintock's assertion that race, gender, and class "come into existence *in and through* relation to each other—if in contradictory and conflictual ways."[53] Even though its imperial claims

FIGURE 0.7. Cover image of the El Águila (The eagle) department store's menswear catalog for the 1898–99 winter season. The illustration by M. Prats depicts a woman in Japanese ceremonial dress and a parasol. El Águila had chain locations in Madrid, Barcelona, Valencia, Seville, Cádiz, and Valladolid. Image courtesy of the Biblioteca Nacional de España, Madrid, Spain.

paled in comparison to those of England and France during this time, Spain continued to constitute an "imperial nation," which sought to transform "the old empire into a liberal capitalist society with the aim of participating in divvying up the world."[54] Colonial expansion was viewed by figures like Restoration politician Cánovas del Castillo as a potential solution for Spain's declining status as an imperial power, a cause for anxiety among the nation's elites.[55] However, unlike in Italy, Álvarez Junco summarizes, Spanish expansion in Africa, for example, "was a mimetic operation induced by some governmental factions that saw in imperial expansion a way to redirect or tranquilize chronic, internal political tensions."[56] As is evident in a variety of contexts explored in this book—from the stalls of Madrid's second-hand market (e.g., El Rastro, also known as "the Americas" [las Américas]) to the posh interiors of industrial Barcelona—mainstream patterns of masculinity in nineteenth-century Spain often emerged from dialogues between race, gender, and class even at a time when the mainstream ideal represented in visual culture and realist fiction was an almost exclusively white one.

According to George Mosse, "the image of man" has been shaped largely by positive and negative stereotypes, the former of which became closely attached to Western patriarchal structures of power that rewarded productivity, self-control, and risk-taking. For Mosse, positive stereotypes contributed to abiding ideals of modern masculinity, the ubiquity of which is made apparent by their deployment and occasional weaponization by historical agents spanning political ideologies: "willpower, honor, and courage," "self-restraint," "standards of classical beauty," "self-control," "strong sense of liberty, a commitment to freedom," "fair play, harmony, and order," "physical skill and dexterity," and "love of work, moderation, and cleanliness."[57] Corroborating the extension of Mosse's analysis of stereotypes to the literary field, Franco Moretti has shown that novelistic depictions of the nineteenth-century gentleman—from Victorian England and Second Empire or Third Republic France to Restoration Spain—relied on notions of "self-restraint; intellectual clarity; commercial honesty; [and] a strong sense of goals."[58] In Moretti's reading of novels from Balzac's Le Père Goriot (1835; Old Goriot) to Galdós's Torquemada tetralogy (1889–1895), fictional men, too, are shown to aspire to or embody a number of keywords like "useful," "efficiency," "comfort," "serious," "influence," and "earnest."[59]

It is not that such values (and anxieties about their proper performance among men) did not exist prior to the nineteenth century, but rather that in Restoration Spain they were produced and commercialized in the form of self-help texts and advertisements related to social conduct and work, fields that were central to bourgeois self-fashioning.[60] José Rementería y Fica's immensely popular conduct manual *El hombre fino* (1829; The refined man), an adaptation of French source material that was revised and reprinted in twelve editions throughout the nineteenth century, invites men to act and dress so as to not draw excessive attention to themselves, thus encouraging middle-class men and aspirants to walk a fine line between stylish self-display and moderation or self-control.[61] Cleanliness and good hygiene were great levelers, as even one's servants could appear refined so long as they kept their clothing in a tidy manner and paid some degree of attention to sartorial practices associated with particular events or changing seasons: "Always dress tidily. A man's white clothes should signal the attention he pays to himself, and he should always take care to brush his hat and frock-coat; nothing should display a sense of negligence or indifference. One need not be rich to dress well and be admitted into society."[62] As Cruz remarks, the major contribution and novelty of the nineteenth-century conduct manual to conversations about urbanity was its assurance that any boy or man—at least in the ideal worlds in which such texts traded—could enter into polite society should he learn to live within its rules.[63] Similar texts—like Francisco Castaño's popular *Guía-manual del comercio y de la banca* (1860; Guide to commerce and banking), published in over a dozen editions—existed for aspiring or established bankers, businessmen, and entrepreneurs who needed to acquire or keep up with the modern financial system's codes and vocabulary if they wished to succeed as bourgeois professionals, thus demonstrating that the comportment of the refined, working man was only part of the prescription for success. The behavioral tightrope Rementería y Fica recommended to readers notwithstanding ("let only he who has no other way to distinguish himself invent when it comes to fashion"), self-help literature was only a portion of a much larger tapestry of men's consumerism that encouraged and promoted the commodification of middle-class masculinity's values and virtues discussed at the beginning of this section.[64]

Alongside the recommendations proffered by conduct literature, men were also encouraged to consult a range of sartorial professionals whose products and services were sold under a bourgeois aegis constituted by elegance, tidiness, thrift, as well as homosocial camaraderie.[65] Tailors and their professional organizations, for example, along with the visual cultural evidence they left to posterity, were responsible for the production and distribution of a variety of journals in order to assist in the professionalization and modernization of their craft. *El Arte Español* (The Spanish art), *La Moda de Madrid* (Madrid fashion), and *El Genio y el Arte* (Genius and art)—inspired by similar titles in England and France—sought to defend the interests of Spanish-speaking craftsmen, while at the same time promoting national commerce and standardizing "bourgeois self-refinement" to outfit both liberal and conservative elites eager to embrace economic and industrial reform in the interest of bringing Spain into wider circuits of modernity.[66] The importance of such reform and its relationship to male homosociality was enshrined formally in the professional societies that tailors founded in Madrid and Barcelona during the 1860s and 1870s: La Confianza (Madrid, 1865), which continues to operate today, and La Confiança (Barcelona, 1876), both of whose names translate to "trust" or "confidence."

While the aforementioned values were part and parcel of bespoke, ready-made, and made-to-measure offerings, they were also distributed in the form of fashion plates and concomitant textual descriptions. Shifting according to each season, fashion plates gave illustrators the opportunity to display men donning lighter fabrics for spring and summer, fur-lined

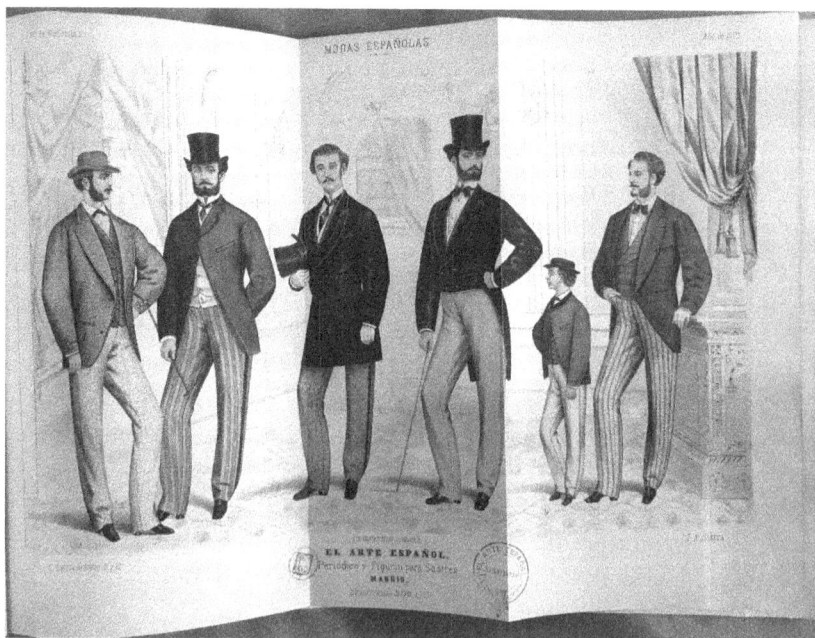

FIGURE 0.8. Fashion plate from an 1871 issue of *El Arte Español*. Image courtesy of the Biblioteca Nacional de España, Madrid, Spain.

jackets for the winter months or whimsical costumes for festive occasions and masquerade balls. In an issue of *El Arte Español* from September 1871, for example, five men and one boy stand around an elegantly wallpapered foyer or hallway (see fig. 0.8).

Each member of the stylishly bedecked coterie wears items of men's dress designed for consumption by the affluent: pants in striped and checkered patterns in shades of beige, gray and peach; top hats made with beaver pelts and silk; jackets with fur-lined lapels; gloves in shades of white, lavender or peach; richly dyed ties. Prose descriptions accompanying the plates foreground the materials to be used as well as the recommended structural elements.[67] Even though the production, distribution, and consumption of fashionable garments were only a few among a number of ways in which the contours of bourgeois masculinity were defined, this image also demonstrates that the "man in black" historicized by John Harvey and Collin McKinney was hardly middle-class masculinity's only avatar during the *fin de siècle*.

Literary representations confirm that a man's stylish silhouette was the synthesis of the authoritative voice of the tailor and the specific interests of the consumer, whose agency in such transactions also guaranteed him a certain amount of autonomy and individuality. As a sign of his recently reacquired purchasing power, the blind gentleman Rafael del Águila in Galdós's *Torquemada en el Purgatorio* (Torquemada in Purgatory), for example, provides cheeky instructions to a tailor who visits his Madrid home: "Well, since my sister here said I needed more clothes, Mr. Balboa, I would also like a three-piece suit for the change of seasons, an overcoat, you know, like the one Morentín wears? Add to that three or four light pairs of pants for summer. What do you think, dear sister?"[68]

Tailors and their employees—as well as their analogues in men's sections of department stores—also promised the ability to suit all bourgeois clientele, regardless of their shape or size, thus demonstrating their desire to produce a comfortable and elegant silhouette for a broad range of consumers, as well as the elasticity of the manly body ideal described earlier by Monlau's treatise.[69] In an advertisement culled from a series of cards that exemplify this desire on the part of sartorial professionals (see fig. 0.9), a tailor or journeyman measures the waist of a client whose robust physique is attired in a style typical of the 1860s–1870s.[70] The image also illustrates tailors and marketers' own role in creating and perpetuating the tropes about menswear that would later become associated with the iconography of parody and satire, including overt feminization, which is indicated here by rouged lips and the exaggeratedly sentimental gaze the two men share. Reflecting the content of columns in tailoring journals about how professionals could adapt or "correct" paper patterns to suit a variety of body shapes, such cards were one of the many ways tailors and the lithographers they entrusted with the promotion of their services created and branded the bourgeois gentleman's behavioral and sartorial regimes, as well as the values of craftsmanship, fit, comfort, and polish they signaled. The idea that a man's body could be adjusted or corrected by the tailor also offers evidence of the multiple ways a man could fit into masculinity's multiple patterns during the nineteenth century in Spain.

Frequenting and shopping in department stores (whether on site or remotely) were other activities in which masculine identity and its concomitant values like athleticism, efficiency, tidiness, and thrift were branded, marketed, and sold to metropolitan and rural consumers alike. While male window shoppers were sometimes at the receiving end of satirical caricatures (see fig. 0.5), advertisers used the same imagery to appeal to customers in earnest, while also gesturing to the interconnectedness of commercial and technological progress. As studies have shown, the consumption of fashionable goods was particularly encouraged when it also supported national and local economies.[71] Visual representations of male window-shoppers made by renowned illustrators like Apel·les Mestres and Josep Lluís Pellicer—both of whom were much sought after by novelists wishing to have their volumes illustrated—gesture to this flexibility, while also demonstrating that the department store was also a site for the construction of middle-class masculinity.

In one image from the 1884 catalog (*almanaque* in Spanish) (see fig. 0.10) of the El Siglo (The Century) department store, a man attired in working-class apparel stands in contrapposto while staring at El Siglo's window displays from its central location on the Rambla dels Estudis in Barcelona's Gothic quarter. Cigarillo in hand, he admires the emporium's newly installed electric lighting, inaugurated with much fanfare in October 1884. The image's exclamatory caption, written in Catalan, reflects the point of view of the coolly astonished young man and captures the novelty electric lighting would have represented for passersby more accustomed to the diffuse illumination afforded by gas lamps: "Mother of God, how bright! Just for that they should call it the Century of Lights!" Perhaps because of the caption's simultaneously self-aggrandizing and tongue-in-cheek confusion with the eighteenth-century Enlightenment, Pellicer's visual effectively

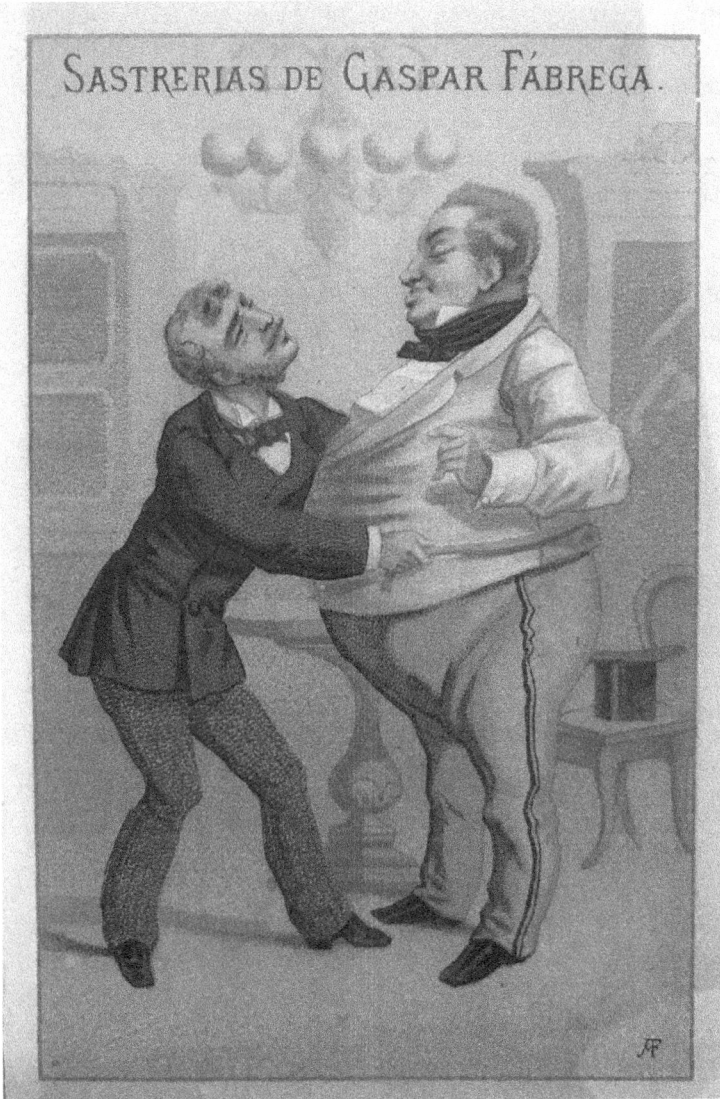

FIGURE 0.9. Advertising card for the Gaspar Fábrega tailoring shop in Barcelona. Image courtesy of the Arxiu Històric de la Ciutat de Barcelona, Barcelona, Spain.

bolsters the link between consumer culture and scientific or technological progress. In a similar illustration (see fig. 0.11), a coterie of fashionably attired men surrounds a woman crossing the threshold of El Siglo, and the caption evokes the woman's desirability as "the best El Siglo has to offer." The image's function seems to be twofold: on the one hand, the representation of a banner advertising the department store's photography section signals its embrace of modern photographic merchandise, and, on the other, it fashions the department store itself as a propitious meeting point for eligible bachelors and bachelorettes.[72] Since artists like Mestres and Pellicer were also responsible for illustrating novels by Spain's preeminent novelists Benito Pérez Galdós and José María de Pereda, not to mention popular periodicals like *La Ilustració Catalana* (The Catalan illustrated) and *La Vanguardia* (The avant garde), the inclusion of their work in commercial materials simultaneously legitimizes them while further blurring

—¡Mare de Deu quina claror! per xo dehuen dir al SIGLO DE LAS LUCES

FIGURE 0.10. "Electricity in the El Siglo Department Store" (1884) by Josep Lluís Pellicer. Image courtesy of the Arxiu Històric de la Ciutat de Barcelona, Barcelona, Spain.

the boundaries separating high and low culture during the turn of the century. Department store catalogs like this one for El Siglo blended Catalan- and Spanish-language content to appeal to both cosmopolitan Barcelonans—whose adhesion to or use of Castilian was often framed as a sign of their cultural capital or as a pretentious badge of honor—and men and women from the provinces who would travel by train to make purchases in the regional capital. Commercial images such as those examined here and throughout this book sought to normalize shopping among men from across the working and middle classes. However, they also betokened promotion and support of local industries and the regional and national

—Ahora sale lo mejor de EL SIGLO.

FIGURE 0.11. Illustration by Josep Lluís Pellicer for El Siglo. The caption reads, "Here comes the best part about El Siglo." Image courtesy of the Arxiu Històric de la Ciutat de Barcelona, Barcelona, Spain.

economy, even when raw materials were sometimes imported from the Americas or elsewhere in Europe.

Central to men's embrace of bourgeois fashionability, the material world of sport offered a prime arena for the cultivation of manly values and virtues including adventurousness, mobility, dexterity, technical skill, and leisure. Different fashions, of course, had different use values, and a diversifying leisure industry resulted in a number of kits and outfits specific to new masculine-coded hobbies like gymnastics and cycling. While many sports—like cycling—were practiced or spectated by men and women alike, as Ramon Casas's genre paintings of male and female cyclists commemorates, both cycling and riding horses, for example, were activities often framed as masculine. Women's riding outfits (usually labeled *amazonas* or Amazons), for example, were frequently included in men's tailoring journals, as the cuts and fabrics hewed to those more typical of menswear. Painter and playwright Santiago Rusiñol's portrait of his closest friend, Ramon Casas, offers a particularly generative example of the various contexts in which men embraced new middle-class cultures of consumption, at the same time as it shows how the subject was worthy of representation in the realm of high (visual) culture. Taking a break from a trip between Vic and Barcelona, recorded for posterity in the pair's articles and sketches for *La Vanguardia*, Casas is shown in repose as he takes a break from riding.[73] In a nineteenth-century description of the painting, the author writes that one might be surprised to see "the knight/gentleman without his horse [*caballero sin caballo*], dressed in a grey/green jacket, blue pants and wool socks. Seated on a bench, he puffs and takes a breath while his indefatigable iron mount rests beside him. For the journey he has undertaken, he doubtless has earned the rolled cigar he smokes."[74] Of course, absent in such depictions of the modern gentleman-knight are the consumerist activities behind them: such evocations of middle-class men and manliness relied on the availability and consumption of relevant merchandise, as is evident in department store catalogs advertising cycling apparel and its concomitant accessories (see fig. 0.12). To borrow Gabriel Pinós Guirao's summary, "every good bourgeois man had to be an authentic sportsman and dress the part."[75] As Chapters 3 and 4 will show, men's protagonism in other sports, including horse racing and hunting, offered similarly masculine contexts in which to showcase one's ability to afford a life of adventure and leisure.

Men from across socioeconomic classes, including ambitious students and cosmopolitan financiers, accepted the symbolic value of clothing, etiquette, posture, taste, and work because these were considered valuable

. clase fina, con
bres. y de mu- 5
, á Ptas. 7, 6, y

o, á Ptas. 9 y 8

CHALECOS de lana, punto ingiés, con pe
cho y solapas labradas, 10
género de mucho abrigo; uno, á Ptas. 14, 12 y

LOS MISMOS, clase superior;
uno, á Ptas. 18, 16 y 18

MEDIAS CICLISTA = el par, á Ptas. 5

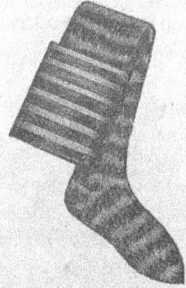

MEDIAS
de lana en bonitas combinacio-
nes de colores, para ciclistas, el par, á Ptas. 5

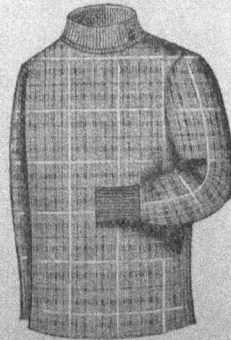

CAMISETAS
sedalina, dibujos escoceses, alta novedad, propias para
ciclistas; una, á Ptas. 10 y 12

Para las medidas véase la última página

FIGURE 0.12. Detail of a page from an undated issue of the El Globo
department store catalog from the turn of the century. Image courtesy of
the Arxiu Històric de la Ciutat de Barcelona, Barcelona, Spain.

currency in one's quest for productive and comfortable lifestyles. Beyond
their effect on individual self-improvement, these discursive fields and the
values they manufactured were also among the most visible tokens used by
the successful man "to make himself pleasant to his fellow men in order to

be respected and triumph socially."[76] Despite the prevalence of the myth of the self-made man, a trope that will appear in one way or another in realist novels representing such upwardly mobile, masculine figures, middle-class men's pursuits of self-fashioning and professionalization—including those of the novelists studied in this book—heavily relied on the shared, affective bonds and benefits of male homosociality.[77]

Between Men: Male Homosociality

To be sure, the tropes and values associated with nineteenth-century masculinity were the byproduct of conduct manuals, commercial ephemera, and the commodities they represented and promoted. However, they were also manufactured and shared among and between men, and in artistic and literary representations of male homosociality. Although masculinity as a construction or production within culture is inconceivable outside of its relationship to femininity, not least of all within a gendered cosmovision organized around the notion of separate spheres, it was also galvanized by male friendships sustained via epistolary correspondence, as well as socialization in bourgeois institutions and spaces including the university, the Church (sacristy and the ecclesiastical hierarchy), the atheneum, the casino, the office, the smoking parlor, the hunting grounds, the tailoring shop, and department stores. In Mercer's view, an examination of such spaces reveals that "the [masculine-]coded behaviors that make up ideal practices within these contexts often depend for their effectiveness on emotional operations," a reality that challenges facile dichotomies according to which modern masculinity is believed to be synonymous with a lack of emotionality.[78] Masculine-coded habitats such as the stock market or the casino were hotbeds of male homosocial networks that corroborate Eve Kosofsky Sedgwick's thesis, that "in any male-dominated society, there is a special relationship between male homosocial [. . .] desire and the structures for maintaining and transmitting patriarchal power: a relationship founded on an inherent and potentially active structural congruence."[79] However, such spaces provided more than mere backdrops for the galvanization of middle-class masculinity through male homosocial interactions. As George Mosse argues, "male friendships [. . .] increasingly became a social and political force during the nineteenth and twentieth centuries," and the branding of a modern, national image, together with the nationalist sentiment it inspired, "had a special affinity for male society."[80]

While men bonded over common "interests" (in the sense of both fascination and financial stakes), their responses to others and the material objects they surrounded themselves with were not devoid of meaningful affective and emotional attachments. Representations of men's affective or emotional responses to external stimuli—whether flesh-and-blood peers or rivals, or inanimate objects, like books, clothes, or hunting gear—help to better visualize seemingly concealed or unavailable expressions of masculinity from the past. Affect can best be understood as the body's preconscious but active response to external stimuli, whereas emotion is the conscious response.[81] According to masculinities studies scholars Todd Reeser and Lucas Gottzén, "unexpected male tenderness could be seen as expressing a form of laddish homosociality," that may result from a shared moment of "affective intensity."[82] Visual or textual descriptions of masculine affect maintain a capacity and potential for signification, particularly as they relate to otherwise concealed or overlooked expressions of masculinity.

An affective approach to masculinity is also useful in the analysis of artistic, commercial, and literary representations of men and manliness because it allows one to challenge imprecise stereotypes about men's displays of emotion as necessarily effeminate or emasculating. Paraphrasing Patricia Ticineto Clough in her introduction to the volume *The Affective Turn* (2007), Jo Labanyi writes that the bodily, precognitive nature of affective responses demonstrates "the impossibility of thinking of body and mind as separate," thus challenging the Cartesian trope that informs some assumptions about men's automatic disinterest in activities—including seemingly "mindless" ones like conspicuous consumption—that do not take into account the significance of context. It is worthwhile to insist on this point, because Western understandings of gender have historically associated the thinking mind exclusively with men and masculinity, and women and femininity with the feeling body.[83] To be sure, such misogynistic stereotypes pervade nineteenth-century discourses; Monlau's description of gender differences that, on the one hand, equates genius, meaningful mental activity, and inventiveness to men and, on the other, abnegation and passivity to women, immediately comes to mind.[84] However, men expressed emotions in many contexts without fear of censure or emasculation. Spaces designated for homosocial bonding, including the casino, the stock market, and the halls of congress, as Mercer has historicized, allowed men to frankly express affective and emotional responses with each other as a sign of frankness one might associate with camaraderie and friendship.

As Nils Hammarén and Thomas Johansson point out, male homosociality can be understood as either vertical (i.e., competitive and hierarchical) or horizontal (i.e., non-competitive and intimate).[85] Of course, in a patriarchal society like nineteenth-century Spain's, even male homosocial relationships informed primarily by camaraderie and intimacy stood to benefit or uplift men over their female counterparts. Emilia Pardo Bazán's status as a celebrity writer equaled or exceeded that of some of her male peers studied in this book, but her friendships and professional relationship with figures like Galdós were not enough to shield her from misogynistic institutions that barred her entry on the basis of her sex. On the other hand, a male author's sex was enough to grant him access to institutions like the university and literary academies. With celebrated academic Menéndez Pelayo's friendship and letters of support, both Galdós and Pereda were canonized within the homosocial institution of the Royal Spanish Academy in 1897.[86]

Novels and epistolary correspondence between men offer telling evidence of the potentially meaningful uses of affect in the literary and social sphere that informs this book's many analyses of interactions between men and the objects they produced and consumed. Galdós's *El Doctor Centeno* (1884), for example, depicts boyish students who buzz with pubescent joy over trysts, handouts from miserly aunts, and impromptu shopping sprees. In Narcís Oller's *La febre d'or* (Gold fever), bankers outwardly shed tears over failed stock market busts while delighting uproariously over the booms. When Marcelo encounters a bear in the Cantabrian mountainside in Pereda's novel *Peñas arriba* (The upper peaks), the character is terrified ("I shook in my skin"[87]) in spite of the advice given to him by his more experienced guide—the rugged but nonetheless idealized Chisco—to maintain "serenity and a steady hand."[88] As Mercer remarks in the case of more metropolitan spaces, "the Spanish novel's treatment of masculine performance in the public sphere problematizes the traditional associations between masculinity and reason on the one hand, and femininity and feeling on the other."[89] Both Marcelo's frightened initial reaction and the tempered reflection he later delivers bear Pereda's romantic imprimatur, given the author's desire to inculcate via episodic narration the merits of a rural (re)education on a bourgeois man previously interested exclusively in urbane models of manliness.

Though they were intimate keepsakes shared between and among young men and adults alike, portrait photographs and other ephemeral evidence like handwritten letters and unedited memoirs also emblematize

FIGURE 0.13. Portrait of Josep Yxart cataloged in the probate inventory of Narcís Oller (front). The photograph was produced by Alviach and Company, Puerta del Sol 14, Madrid. Image courtesy of the Arxiu Històric de la Ciutat de Barcelona, Barcelona, Spain.

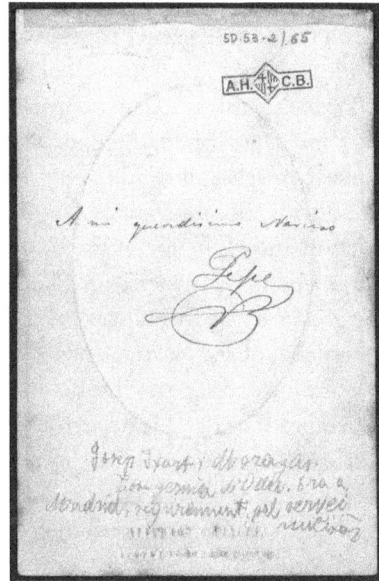

FIGURE 0.14. Portrait of Josep Yxart (back). The inscription in Castilian reads, "To my dearest Narciso. Pepe." Yxart's youthful countenance and the note penciled in Catalan help to date the portrait to Yxart's time in Madrid, where he completed military service between 1873 and 1874. Image courtesy of the Arxiu Històric de la Ciutat de Barcelona, Barcelona, Spain.

the centrality of masculine affect and male homosocial networks to configurations of manliness during the late nineteenth century in Spain, not least of all as they intersect with literary and novelistic discourse. In a portrait of Catalan intellectual and literary critic Josep Yxart (see fig. 0.13 and fig. 0.14), the youth's mustachioed countenance, bowtie, suit jacket, and three-quarter pose, together with the photograph's inscription, offer telltale signs of the subject's attention to self-fashioning, mainstream patterns of middle-class masculinity, and male homosociality during the nineteenth century. Bodily and sartorial signs like these reflect Yxart's adhesion to the trappings of manhood that were essential accessories to his bourgeois professional aspirations, not to mention his status as the heir to his affluent family's estate. When the portrait was produced around 1873–1874, Yxart—then in his early twenties—was completing military service in the Spanish capital, where he eventually hoped to pursue a doctorate in law.[90] Commissioned at a photography boutique in the central Puerta del Sol, the image memorializes Yxart's youthful mobility, even as his father's expectations would eventually see to his definitive return to Catalonia.[91] Addressed to Narcís Oller, Yxart's cousin and one of the forefathers of the modern Catalan novel, the portrait stands as a testament to the value the young Yxart afforded to bourgeois self-fashioning. The inscription on the reverse side—"To my dearest Narciso. Pepe"—also shows that masculine-coded signs of identity (e.g., men's fashion, hygiene, portrait photography) were also inextricably tied to ideas about male homosocial bonding and friendship.

Yxart's posthumously published memoirs originally composed between 1875 and 1876, for example, provide evidence of how at least one man saw himself in relation to his peers and vis-à-vis society's gendered behaviors and norms. In one episode that happened only a short time after the production and exchange of the photograph, Yxart records for posterity various elements of his close friend and cousin's (Oller's) wedding day: from the groom's stiff formalwear and the bride's nervous "I do" to an uncanny periphrasis of the marriage bed.[92] For Yxart, the occasion was cause for both celebration and sadness: his best friend since boyhood, Oller, was marrying Esperança Rabassa.[93] The nuptials marked the official end of Oller's bachelorhood and, together with his budding career as a lawyer, signaled his definitive progression from young man to adult. Yxart, who was six years younger than his cousin, often describes Oller in autobiographical writings as a brother, a fact that gives his affective recollection of the event undertones ranging from playful and possessive to melancholic and pensive:

In May of 1874 I returned to my cousin's side to usher him to the altar. It was difficult to look at him without having a few laughs, dressed as he was in a frockcoat with a white tie, standing there on the most solemn occasion of his life. After all, I knew him better and more intimately than she who uttered in that moment a tremulous "I do," thus uniting herself to him with a closer bond than that which had theretofore united the two of us. Up until the final and solemnest of instants preceding entry to that new life, my cousin had always been by my side. It was I who possessed the majority of his secrets and the key to his character. She, on the other hand, was marrying a man, a mystery. I could not stop myself from laughing, and he trembled and looked at me with compassion. I was his youth bidding him adieu with an ironic snicker; an echo of past loves, frivolity, happiness, and doubts.[94]

The would-be autobiographer acknowledges the bride without ever naming her, relegating her feminine presence to the margins because the almost sacred image he conjures is a fantasy of the transcendent character of male camaraderie. Read through Yxart's nostalgic lens, the homosocial altar scene not only symbolizes a manly rite of passage for the groom—betokened by Oller's formal frockcoat and tie and the betrothed's accessory presence—but it is also a testing ground for the strength of fraternal bonds between groom and groomsman, whose account virtually places him at the altar with the newlyweds. "My brother fled from me as if I were a prosecutor on behalf of his foolish youth," continues Yxart in his description of the honeymoon and its wake, during which the latter purports having spent an entire year "like the caterpillar in its cocoon," a zoological metaphor for masculine becoming.[95] Near the end of the passage, however, Yxart dispels any anxiety the moment may have initially stirred in him, reframing the events recounted as merely a chapter punctuating "the novel of [their] friendship."[96]

Yxart's use of the novel as a metaphor for his friendship with Oller is unsurprising since the two shared a passion for the production and consumption of theater and novels. In the exposition of his own memoirs, Oller draws attention to common literary obsessions, and especially novels, before highlighting the boyish phantasm that cohered for the cousins around a career devoted to reading and writing:[97]

> Naturally, that affinity brought us close together, and from then on, no one could separate us during the summer holidays. First he [Yxart] would come from Tarragona to Valls, and in Valls we would spend the entirety of our days holed up in the room set aside for us. We regarded it with grand illusions as the editorial office of a literary magazine, even though we had never actually seen one.[98]

The two were virtually brothers since the earliest days of their childhood. They spent summers together in Valls or Tarragona and lived together for long periods of time as adults in Barcelona (including after Oller's marriage to Rabassa). In the obituary Oller wrote for Yxart, which he reproduces in his own posthumously published memoirs, the novelist identifies his cousin as "a favorite brother" and "a master and the best guide in my

literary pursuits!"[99] Even as their careers would take them in slightly different directions—both studied law, but only Oller would continue to practice
even into the height of his novel-writing years—the two were inseparable
until Yxart died prematurely of tuberculosis.

Such correspondence was not at all extraordinary for the time. To be
sure, artists and novelists relied on constant collaboration and contact with
each other through epistolary correspondence and artistic and literary criticism. However, these brief anecdotes summarizing Yxart and Oller's bond
begins to shed light on many heretofore unexplored connections between
bourgeois self-fashioning, masculinity, and the production and consumption of literature, particularly as they relate to middle-class men who took
it upon themselves to revitalize the novel-writing profession during the
Bourbon Restoration after the sociopolitical turmoil of 1868.

Masculinity, Male Homosociality, and Novel Writers

After the revolution of 1868 and a failed experiment with liberalism during
the short-lived First Republic (1873–1874), the restoration of the Bourbon monarchy in the person of Alfonso XII between 1874 and 1875, as
alluded to earlier, brought some stability to a nation that had otherwise
been plagued by internal and external upheavals at least since the invasion
of Napoleon Bonaparte's troops in 1808.[100] Even if the political regime that
grew out of the turmoil of the Revolution of 1868 was plagued by caci-
quism, corruption, and stalemates between liberals and conservatives, the
revolutionary spirit galvanized a new generation of artists and novelists
hoping to modernize Spain on artistic and economic grounds in an effort
to restore prestige and international relevance to national art and literature.[101] After decades characterized by colonial loss, civil wars, and imperial decline, and amidst a kaleidoscopic panorama of visual and commercial media, "Realist and Naturalist authors such as Benito Pérez Galdós,
Leopoldo Alas, and Emilia Pardo Bazán redefined the novel as a work of
art—and, not coincidentally, the author as an artist."[102] This reframing of
the novelist as an artist is evident in the number of ways authors collaborated in the nineteenth century: from the highly aestheticized literary
magazines of which Galdós, Alas, Oller, and Yxart were contributing editors (e.g., *Arte y Letras* [Art and letters]), to editor Daniel Cortezo's related
enterprise *Biblioteca de Artes y Letras* (Library of art and letters), which produced luxuriously illustrated editions of novels like Alas's *La Regenta* and

FIGURE 0.15. 1885 translation to Castilian of Narcís Oller's most popular novel, *La Papallana*. Photograph courtesy of author.

Oller's *La mariposa*, the Spanish-language version of his bestseller originally published in Catalan, *La papallona* (see fig. 0.15), in the same series as reeditions and translations of pan-European literary greats both past and present (e.g., Cervantes, Shakespeare, Hugo, Núñez de Arce).

But even as these authors succeeded in their professionalization of novel-writing, which resulted in the conferral of prestige to their craft evidenced, for example, by their admission to gilded literary institutions (e.g., the atheneum, Royal Spanish Academy), their appointments as professors, lawyers, or politicians, and the translation of their work into French, they frequently bemoaned the lamentable state of novel-writing in Spain. Due to problems ranging from lower-than-average national literacy rates to arcane publishing practices, even successful novelists saw their attempts as comparable to those of middle-class, male social types whose realities provided fodder for self-deprecating or self-aggrandizing comparisons. In letters he wrote in response to encouragement to continue writing novels at the turn of the century, Narcís Oller, who once wrote that his production of novels was part of his maturation as a man ("jo em feia home" [I was becoming/making myself a man]), defeatedly looked back on his career as novelist and requested that a friend who encouraged him to write more books just let him be: "leave me alone to make and peddle my woodwork [i.e., literary translations]. After all, we are in a land [i.e., Catalonia] of merchants."[103] In his introduction to Clarín's second edition of *La Regenta*, as we will see later, Galdós historicizes the exchange of literary models (and Spain's role in exporting Cervantine realism to England and France) by using the language of international commerce, but immediately apologizes for the seemingly vulgar comparison according to which the novelist emerges as a businessman. In his acceptance speech to the Spanish Royal Academy, a sign of the rhetoric of humility he often donned, José María de Pereda envisioned himself as a mere heir to the greats of Spain's cultural and literary "Golden Age" of the sixteenth and seventeenth centuries. Such kinship was heightened by the fact that Pereda's friends saw in the hidalgo's own countenance and apparel (e.g., *chambergo* or slouch hat) "the memory of Cervantes," if not the "Castilian infantry soldier from the time of the Hapsburgs."[104]

Representations of masculine figures ranging from the businessman to the heir do not only invite readers to question wider cultural attitudes toward middle-class masculinity—reflected, as we saw earlier and, indeed, as we will see throughout this book, by autobiographical writings, epistolary correspondence, hygienic and behavioral discourses, visual cultural ephemera, and realist fiction. Such character types also aestheticize and help to reframe the trials and triumphs of the historical men who imagined them, not least of all because the latter group envisioned the vicissitudes of their literary careers as comparable to those of other middle-class men and aspirants to the bourgeoisie. The literary production of male novelists offers a rich discursive terrain upon which to survey middle-class masculinity in nineteenth-century Spain since its defenders operated within a capitalistic, patriarchal society where the artistic and intellectual labor associated with realist narrative—unlike other popular genres like theater and serialized fiction—was widely considered to be within the purview of men, as in other areas of social life, like artistic and literary academies, the university, the Church, and the stock exchange.

As was true elsewhere in England, France, Germany, and Portugal, realism's practitioners in Spain were primarily interested in the mimetic (but nonetheless aestheticized and critical) representation of contemporary social life in the form of the realist novel. To borrow Harriet Turner's phrasing, "they fused, in a single text, social critique, a theory of representation, and a reproduction, faithfully mirrored, of the mores, customs, objects, actions, beliefs, and rites of their times."[105] Of course, the Spanish realist novel's relatively late appearance in the nineteenth century—even though authors teleologically refer to a "centuries-old national literary tradition" tethered to the picaresque novel and the Cervantine irony of *Don Quijote*—also meant that it emerged from dialogue with or alongside complementary and competing aesthetic modes, such as naturalism.[106] As such, this book's use of the "novel" or "realist novel," as mentioned earlier, implies its coexistence with and representation of motifs and tropes that were also prevalent in the naturalist novels of Émile Zola, including the influence—if not entirely deterministic—of an individual's inherited traits and disposition, environment, and cultural/historical moment on their circumstances.

Even though the realist novel was sometimes viewed as intrinsically opposed (and superior to) the popular forms that preceded and co-existed with it (e.g., serial fiction, popular theater), this myth blurs a reality in which male writers capitalized upon popular forms, such as illustration and serialization, in their own professionalization and masculine self-fashioning. During the heyday of literary realism, the novel was increasingly viewed as a masculine genre because of the theses of authors like Galdós, who viewed the popular cultural genres that preceded and coincided with it as feminine (presumably because of its target readership) and, as a result, inferior.[107] Paraphrasing Alda Blanco, Lou Charnon-Deutsch writes that this kind of trajectory, from popular forms to realism, "is often narrated as a sexualized competition, in which 'feminine' forms, linked with mass culture, are despised or ignored, while more 'virile' forms are held up to compete with the work of celebrities such as Balzac or Zola."[108] However, as this book argues, even novels published in the bound form of a book (as opposed to serially) partook of the same strategies prevalent in popular cultural forms, which included, for example, illustrations by artists who were themselves constantly crossing the border thought to divide high culture from mass culture. Both Apel·les Mestres and Josep Lluís Pellicer, for example, frequently provided illustrations for the novels of Benito Pérez Galdós (e.g., *Episodios nacionales*), José María de Pereda (e.g., *El sabor de la tierruca*), popular newspapers like *La Vanguardia*, and even department store catalogs, as we saw earlier.[109]

Additionally, all the male novelists and visual artists studied in this book benefitted from the mediation of their likeness in the popular press, thus demonstrating the sometimes-underappreciated role of mass culture in the self-fashioning and professionalization of intellectual elites.[110] The portraits of an overwhelmingly male pantheon of authors were often represented or caricatured on the covers of nationally distributed magazines, thus giving visibility to aspiring literary celebrities eager to expand their readership. In a cover image from an 1883 issue of *Madrid Cómico* (Comic Madrid; see fig. 0.16), for example, Galdós emerges as a hero-author whose novels intermingle with laurels beneath a patently triumphant pose recalling French sculptor Auguste Rodin's similarly virile effigy of Balzac from the 1890s. Caricature-like portraits of Jacint Verdaguer and José María de Pereda, as we will see in later chapters, demonstrate that the printed press served not only to popularize well-known liberals, but also more conservative writers who were often critical of the circuits of modernity in which they were, nevertheless, active agents.

As the chapters in this book will show, all of these writers, along with their contemporaries working in the visual arts, commiserated in some way about circumstances that they thought most negatively impacted their careers as novelists, whether based on circumstances that were material or imagined. Census data demonstrate that in Spain around 1860, only 31.09 percent of men and 9.05 percent of women were literate, and by 1900, those percentages only rose to 42.15 percent and 25.14 percent, rates that pale in comparison to those of France and Britain around this time.[111] In a letter written by the artist Santiago Rusiñol to his friend Narcís Oller, the former addresses the disparity he perceived to exist between the propitious conditions available to the French and those working to the detriment of Catalan cultural producers:

> Take to Carme Street from end to end, together with Princess Street, the Rambles and all the others and then go around and ask [if you want to be statistical about it] if anyone knows what 'literature' is: they'll take you for a madman. The most anyone would be able to answer is that that which you name is not a recognized profession at all and any occupation without a guild cannot be respectable.[112]

Rusiñol goes on to cite the depression that supposedly plagued him after he witnessed an excellent theatrical production in Paris; he was envious of those artists and dramatists nourished from birth by French literature and customs which were, in his view, not only more fashionable, but also objective signs of a superior culture. As Casacuberta points out, the meager audience for novels written in Catalan reinforced the uncertain outcomes

FIGURE 0.16. Cover image of April 1883 issue of *Madrid Cómico* depicting Galdós standing triumphantly in front of laureled copies of his *Episodios nacionales*, *La familia de León Roch*, and *Gloria*. The caption reads, "Galdós, the glory of Spain, would be much more famous if his name were not Benito / and even more so if it were not Benito Pérez." Image courtesy of the Hemeroteca Digital of the Biblioteca Nacional de España, Madrid, Spain.

that awaited Oller and other writers publishing exclusively in the regional language: "the reading public for Catalan books during the final years of the nineteenth century is a minority relating in one way or another to the regionalist movement that found itself light years away from being able to confer to the writer the opportunity to professionalize as such."[113]

Other measurable factors contributing to the hurdles faced by the novelists whose lives and work form the basis of this book included the continued popularity of literary forms that were popularized earlier in the century (such as the local color sketch, the regional novel, and the historical novel), as well as the reading public's continued taste for French originals translated into Spanish.[114] Because correspondence between Spanish writers and their European contemporaries was infrequent, comparisons to circumstances in France, for example, were often superficial and relied on an imagined inferiority complex. Such comparisons and connections ignored or overlooked the fact that French and Russian authors, for example, faced their own hurdles that were not dissimilar to those faced by their peers living and working in Spain.[115]

Authors also faced anxieties about the meager income they were able to earn from writing and publishing their literary output, a major hurdle negatively affecting their understanding of literary success. Leopoldo Alas—one of the most (in)famous literary critics of the fin-de-siècle period in Spain—often complained to editors such as Manuel Fernández Lasanta and Sinesio Delgado about the insufficient compensation one could earn by writing novels in Spain. Summarizing Clarín's frequent grievances, Jean-François Botrel points out that in an era in which novelists sought the prestige of the bound volume, it was much more lucrative to publish journal articles, review essays, short stories, and novellas, not least of all because these genres could be published first entirely in serialized form, and then later reprinted as a collection in the format of a bound book.[116] Clarín justified these anxieties with recourse to his need to work to support his family: "I only write so that there's stew on the table"; "three children are a lot of children and they cost me three articles per month"; "I write to *regale* my offspring"; "I write a lot because life is expensive, not so that my children inherit an only slightly less paltry sum."[117]

Discourse surrounding the struggle of novelists to cohere either as individuals or as a community, of course, was not unique to Spain. In the late nineteenth century throughout Europe, as Pascale Casanova sustains, every member of what he calls the "world republic of letters," "struggle[d] to achieve recognition as a writer," particularly since the literary economy has, historically, been "based on a 'market' [. . .] which is to say a space in which the sole value recognized by all participants—literary value—circulates and is traded."[118] During the nineteenth century, the undisputed capital of this market was Paris, and Spanish novelists (like their contemporaries in the art and fashion worlds) frequently complained about the hegemony of French models and translations being a hurdle to the instantiation of a national cultural or literary industry. Aside from the novel's status as an artful and commodifiable cultural product capable of entertaining readers while also calling into question various elements of mainstream culture, including the patterns of gender over which authors obsessed and with which they gave shape to modern life, the novelists who matured in the wake of 1868 drew encouragement and inspiration from a predominantly male coterie of writers who devoted their careers to the restoration of prestige to national and regional Spanish literature, the so called Golden Age of which was thought to have already occurred between the fifteenth to seventeenth centuries.

The fact that only a small handful of female novelists achieved national recognition during this time is the exception that proves the rule about both nineteenth-century literary professionalization as a predominantly masculine affair and, of course, about the persistence of misogyny inherent in canon formation even through the twentieth century.[119] In reaction to the hand of misogyny they were dealt, female intellectuals and novelists like Gertrudis Gómez de Avellaneda, Fernán Caballero (the pseudonym of Cecilia Böhl von Faber), Emilia Pardo Bazán, and Víctor Català (the pseudonym of Caterina Albert i Paradís) sometimes avowed themselves of masculine tropes (or masculinized themselves) as a way to legitimize or frame their literary activity as ironic, and references to their "manliness" were employed in backhanded compliments or critiques of their literary output. For example, conservative author Böhl von Faber was and still is best known under her highly symbolic male penname, Fernán Caballero (Ferdinand Gentleman/Knight), which she adopted at least in part because she did not believe that women should publicly showcase their erudition, and because she was convinced that writing was "a man's profession."[120]

However, there is perhaps no female author besides Emilia Pardo Bazán who would come close to eclipsing the celebrity status of contemporaries like José María de Pereda, and yet even her expertise as a narrator of contemporary social life was not enough to break through the iron ceiling imposed upon her by a cultural industry that afforded most of its favors and privilege to men. As is evident throughout her career, Pardo Bazán sometimes reacted to these circumstances by taking on masculine tropes in her own self-fashioning. In a series of lectures she gave at the atheneum in Madrid on the subject of the modern Russian novel, which she was largely responsible for popularizing in Spain, the Galician novelist shrouded herself with the imagery of the soldier (masculine *soldado*, not the feminine variant *soldadera*), presumably as a rhetorical strategy to shield herself from the "bullets" she awaited from her predominantly male audience: "How could I not feel now the fear that grips the heart of the neophyte soldier upon hearing the whirring of the first bullet?"[121] Pardo Bazán was also known to elevate certain women writers above others with recourse to masculinizing them. According to Denise DuPont, for example, Pardo Bazán used masculine forms of nouns in order to canonize Romantic writer Madame de Staël as an equal to her male contemporaries such as François-René de Chateaubriand.[122] While Pardo Bazán's male friends, including Josep Yxart and Narcís Oller, benefited much from her elite status and social capital—as is evident in her introduction of the Catalan cousins to Parisian literary circles—her gender prevented her from fully capitalizing on the same benefits. Although this book focuses on the men whose self-fashioned personas and lives had much in common with the masculine types they represented, it does show how female novelists—especially Pardo Bazán, but also Víctor Català—served as meaningful interlocutors and peers whose professional trajectories and interactions with their male contemporaries were not irrelevant to abiding and evolving discourses of middle-class masculinity.

Epistolary correspondence and literary criticism (e.g., prologues and acceptance speeches prepared for induction into national academies) from the final decades of the nineteenth-century corroborate the notion that the literary profession was viewed as predominantly masculine in nature.[123] Writers not only confided in each other about personal and professional challenges, as was the case when José María de Pereda shared heart-wrenching letters expressing his grief about his son's premature death with friends like Narcís Oller, but they also challenged and held each other accountable. In letters to Galdós, Leopoldo Alas offered his Canarian friend frank critiques of his work, but also suggested in highly subjective terms that this was natural, given Galdós's status as the true analogue of the French trinity represented by Balzac, Flaubert, and Zola: "The only two living novelists that I like are you and Zola. What are you missing? Many things that Zola has. And Zola? Many things that you have. And the two of you? Some things that Flaubert had. And the three of you? Some things that Balzac had. And Balzac? Others that the three of you have."[124] As Laureano Bonet has argued, such correspondence between Galdós and Alas, Pereda, and Oller—who, together, sent some 380 letters to Galdós throughout their lifetime—can be read as attempts to ennoble the Canarian novelist, while fashioning themselves as the primary disciples in his entourage.[125] Such artistic camaraderie was another kind of "gentleman's paradise" or "boy's club" sustained by the homosocial interactions between men that extended beyond national borders. For example, Isaac Pavlovsky—a Russian journalist exiled in Paris, where he and Oller became friends—writes to Oller in a letter in which he distinguishes the Catalan novelist from Zola in an effort to uplift his own oeuvre as well as Oller's: "I do not share in naturalist theories when they seek to find the beast within the beast called man. Rather, should we not try to find the man within the beast? Every human being, however low he has fallen, maintains some degree of nobility and sympathy. Anyway, it is not you to whom I should say it, to you, the author of 'The Slap.'"[126] Since letters are themselves performative outlets in that they do not represent an author as he was, but rather as he imagined himself to be in relation to his audience, they do have much to tell us about the ways writers wished to frame themselves and their work, an integral part of self-fashioning, or what Stephen Greenblatt defines as "the fashioning of human identity as a manipulable, artful process."[127]

Yet another reflection of the literary industry's unabashedly male homosocial nature, admiration among male friends and writers extended to the acquisition and exchange of photographic portraits and other collectibles, which became talismans used to decorate personal studies and offices. Artists and novelists collected photographic likenesses of their peers, enshrining them alongside similar portraits they would purchase in department stores or shops abroad of pan-European names like Hugo, Balzac, and Tolstoy. In one of his many letters to Galdós, Alas reflects on his own likeness—in response to Galdós's request for a portrait—before asking his friend for a portrait to accompany that of Victor Hugo, and Polín, the nickname he gave to his first-born, Leopoldo Alas Argüelles:

> It is just that my portraits of yesteryear are now too legendary, and in order to have a new one taken I need to first look less like the Marquis of Molins, which is to say, I need to cut my hair and beard. But within a few days you can count on the portrait. [. . .] On the subject of portraits, I do not have one of you, either, and even though I do not have a designated place to store engravings and photographs, I do have in my office my favorite poet, Victor Hugo, and my most prized work, my firstborn *Polín*; I am just missing my favorite novelist.[128]

Similar interactions occurred between Narcís Oller and Santiago Rusiñol and show the bonding between male cultural producers over popular visual culture. In letters dating to the final decades of the nineteenth century, Rusiñol, writing to Oller from Paris, asks the Catalan novelist if he wished for him to acquire a poster advertising Zola's latest novel designed by famed lithographer Jules Chéret. Rusiñol also used the opportunity to goad Oller into writing his own novel about the booms of the Barcelona stock market during the 1880s, since Zola was in the process of writing his own stock-market novel or *roman de bourse* titled *L'Argent* (Money).

The masculine coding and male homosocial nature of artistic and literary camaraderie among writers within a male-dominated literary canon culminated in their embrace of what was and still is considered to be the first modern novel, *Don Quijote de la Mancha*, and the figure of its author, Miguel de Cervantes. During Realism's heyday in Spain, which began around 1880 and continued well into the 1890s, novel-writing had become a masculine enterprise whose constitutive representatives were the beneficiaries of the male homosocial networks they cultivated, as well as the self-proclaimed students and heirs of Cervantes. As acclaimed nineteenth-century literary critic Menéndez y Pelayo articulates in his response to the speech Galdós gave upon his admission to the Spanish Royal Academy, Cervantes belonged to a superior category of genius for intellectuals, not least of all because his work supposedly embodied the national spirit, but was also of universal relevance which, for the critic, was measurable in the influence it had on French and English writers like Balzac and Dickens.[129] The sense of a shared literary kinship with canonical forefathers extended to gilded icons including playwrights such as Lope de Vega (1562–1635) and Pedro Calderón de la Barca (1600–1681), who were themselves the originators of abiding tropes of Spanish masculinity founded upon honor and valor from and against which nineteenth-century novelists derived and branded their own patterns.[130] Leopoldo Alas's *La Regenta*, to cite only one notable example, frequently glosses the obsessions of his characters with classic Spanish plays like Calderón's *El médico de su honra* (*The Surgeon of His Honor*) and Tirso's *El burlador de Sevilla* (*The Trickster of Seville*), as well as nineteenth-century, romantic adaptations of them, thus submitting contemporary masculine figures like the retired, geriatric magistrate and the local casino's lothario to irony, as well as the measure of archetypes like the cuckolded husband and the Don Juan. Such juxtapositions shed light on the affinities between Cervantine methods of characterization and those of the realist novel, thus corroborating Harriet Turner's conclusion that "we find, particularly in the novels of Galdós and Clarín, a reinvented notion of the Quixotic: people inevitably become, in part, the images they make for themselves. It is this perception about human behavior that each writer captures as they mirror the uncertainties of the economic, political, and social life of their times."[131]

Intentional intertextuality with the Golden Age could be interpreted as male authors' recognition of a crisis or "deficit" in late nineteenth-century masculinity—where ironic depictions would appear to suggest that nineteenth-century copies of gilded originals were atavistic and inferior by comparison.[132] Constant evocations of Golden Age archetypes also signal the anxieties of authors not only hoping to live up to national and international models (ranging from Cervantes, Lope, and Calderón to Balzac, Flaubert, and Tolstoy), but who also strove to make their livings as bourgeois professionals at a time when Spanish empire was approaching its twilight hour. To be sure, authors like Galdós, Leopoldo Alas "Clarín", Narcís Oller, and José María de Pereda were regularly rewarded for their novelistic output in the form of national recognition (e.g., awards, admission to national academies and professorships, translations into other languages), whereas their female counterparts only experienced such acclaim as an exception. Additionally, critics regularly recognized their parentage in the male paragons of the national literary canon, evident in the speeches given by Galdós, Pereda, and Menéndez y Pelayo on the occasion of the former two authors' entry to the Spanish Royal Academy. However, the ambitious road they laid out for themselves was still paved with anxieties and discontents related to their place within Spanish literary history and pan-European literary markets, a reality that comes to light upon an analysis of the male social types that constitute their fiction. The affinities that weave through the self-fashioned personas of male novelists and the male social types they imagined are, of course, abundant, since Galdós and his contemporaries were not only writers, but they also envisioned themselves—either literally or metaphorically—as students, priests, businessmen, and heirs.

Through stock characters culled from national and pan-European sources, novelists identified fictional masculinity as essential to representing the challenges affecting bourgeois self-fashioning and modern nation-building projects, both of which they had a hand in shaping. While wealthy bankers and businessmen flaunt their bourgeois trappings as signs of their consolidated (but fragile) cultural and economic capital in Narcís Oller's masterpiece *La febre d'or* (Gold fever, 1890–92), students are forced to pawn and ragpick in secondhand markets and in their navigation of the slums of pre-revolutionary Madrid memorialized in Benito Pérez Galdós's *El Doctor Centeno*. When untangled vis-à-vis their various representations, such contradictions facing modern men and the gender codes to which they subscribed display an increasingly commodified, middle-class world at odds with the lofty ideals, values, and virtues inherited from an apparently more glorious, imperial past, and those that were being imported from elsewhere in Europe. This reality runs parallel to that of novelists, caught as they were between the novel-as-art and the novel-as-merchandise, which justifies, perhaps, the sometimes-defeated admissions of Oller, who referred to his output as comparable to that of a carpenter, and Alas, whose evocations of the chrematistic circumstances surrounding his publishing practices brought him to compare his career contradictorily, at times, to that of an errant priest preaching in the desert or a humble merchant.

As a necessity of nineteenth-century Spain's incipient capitalist economy, novelists came to see themselves as businessmen, since publishing practices in editorial centers (i.e., primarily Barcelona, but also Madrid) were still viewed as inferior to those of London and Paris, and thus required novelists themselves to do much of their negotiations on their own. Thus, even successful writers like Galdós and Pereda often worked as their own agents and editors. Critics and novelists also compared themselves to businessmen and their output as merchandise. Around 1891, Clarín—who, as we saw earlier, often spoke openly while ironizing the commercial demands of his literary profession—critiqued supposedly "protectionist and isolationist" stances on the construction of the Spanish literary canon by "those partisans of a literary trade balance [. . .] that want to turn the customs houses of letters into inexpugnable fortresses."[133] In his prologue to the second edition of *La Regenta* published in 1901, Galdós similarly uses the language of commerce, and, in particular, importing and exporting, as a way to comment ambivalently upon the way the exchange of literary ideas ran parallel to that of imports and exports:

> So it was that we received with deductions and additions the merchandise that we had exported (let us not be afraid of the commercial comparison), and we almost disregarded our own blood and the Spanish vitality that that literary entity preserved even after the alterations incurred by its travels. On balance: France, with its incomparable power, imposed upon us an alteration of our own construction (*obra*), without us realizing that it was ours; we accepted it by restoring its humourism and employing it in the narrative and descriptive forms in keeping with the Cervantine tradition.[134]

Pursuant to illuminating the intersections of the nineteenth-century Spanish literary industry with middle-class manhood, this book focuses on the recurring fictional social types that figure contradictions and fantasies of nineteenth-century masculinity at the same time that it centers their relevance to the male artists and writers responsible for engendering them in popular visual culture (e.g., advertisements, illustrations, paintings, photographs) and novels.

Masculine Figures

Masculine Figures tells the story about how images and novels, along with those who produced and consumed them, articulated modern ideals of masculinity or manliness in late nineteenth-century Spain. Because this book is concerned with recovering how both historical men and their representations in visual culture and the novel figure a variety of anxieties and ideals about Spanish manhood, its methodological approach to reading calls for what François Proulx—drawing on Margaret Cohen—has labeled "dynamic reading," a hermeneutical strategy that can be adjusted to different types of evidence without flattening or losing sight of conventions associated with specific media and genres.[135] In this book, evidence ranges from fashion advertisements and caricatures to portraits and realist-naturalist novels. Aside from calling for a resituating of the novel within such a range of other artistic, cultural, and economic discourses, following Jo Labanyi's foundational *Gender and Modernization in the Spanish Realist Novel*, Lou Charnon-Deutsch goes as far as calling for a rebranding of the novel as a "historical document" in and of itself.[136] Of course, nineteenth-century intellectuals themselves were not ignorant of the historical quality of novels written in the realist mode, as is evident in Menéndez y Pelayo's description of the "highly sociological value, which should be appreciated undeviatingly by future historians," and of Galdós himself, "without being a professional historian, has amassed the most extensive archive of documents about the nineteenth-century Spanish ethos."[137] While this book follows Charnon-Deutsch's imperative to read the novel as a historical document, it does so via close reading of passages in an attempt to search for patterns while also demonstrating why the conventions of realist fiction—with its ambivalence, criticism, and irony—offers an especially rich source with which to rethink historical configurations of masculinity.

By bringing to the fore a largely unstudied corpus of archival materials that gives visibility to anxieties and ideals related to manliness and masculine self-fashioning, this book unveils another facet of what Maite Zubiaurre has coined "a 'ghastly' mass-cultural Spain" that has not typically been considered in scholarly debates about issues as interconnected as class and gender.[138] While this book does not deal explicitly with the erotic—the cultural field plotted by Zubiaurre—it does point to a wealth of popular cultural evidence that sheds light on previously hidden or overlooked affective attachments between men and the objects they produced and consumed.

Masculine Figures comprises four chapters, each of which focuses on a male social type that was key to how men, and especially artists and novelists, imagined themselves, their peers, and their work during a historical period characterized, on the one hand, by artistic and literary rejuvenation, and, on the other, political stagnation and imperial loss. Given that it was in the purview of realist novelists to observe and interrogate their surroundings amid sweeping cultural and social transformations, each chapter also focuses on how representations of tailors, dandies, students, priests, businessmen, and heirs in novels not only index broader cultural anxieties and ideals, but rather how they figure specific concerns related to the homosocial networks and novel-writing enterprises of male writers. These are not only recurring types in realist novels, but they are also types whose defining habits, images, and traits were often appropriated by male novelists in their epistolary correspondence and other writings to articulate their ambitions and struggles as literary professionals. The first half of the Bourbon Restoration (1875–1931) provides the chronological backdrop for this study because it was during this time that a predominantly homosocial coterie of writers—whose most representative figureheads were Benito Pérez Galdós, Leopoldo Alas ("Clarín"), Narcís Oller, and José María de Pereda—unanimously chose the realist novel as the genre par excellence through which to observe and comment upon the changing faces of Spain's countryside and urbanizing cityscapes. In summary, this book's chapters emphasize the affiliative connection between certain masculine figures and the novelists who engendered them. In so doing, each chapter that follows highlights the ways male novelists articulated their own anxieties, discontents, and ideals related to their personal and professional successes, struggles, and shortcomings.

Roughly the first half of each chapter centers on cultural, historical, and visual contexts associated with a given masculine type (e.g., the student, the priest, the businessman, and the heir) while the second half focuses on how novelists and their peers imagined them in the pages of the realist novel and in their literary criticism. Chapter 1 uses visual evidence from the illustrated press and department store catalogs, together with close readings of novels by Benito Pérez Galdós and the Canarian novelist's own years as a student, to recover the ways rag-picking students struggled to pursue middle-class, masculine ideals like hard work and material comfort in pre-revolutionary Madrid. This chapter ultimately argues that Galdós's emphasis on the consumption and trade of borrowed or used accessories, clothing, and books in the characterization of impoverished student protagonists runs parallel to discourses that spotlight the imagined precarity of the Spanish novelist, whose ambitious project relied on studying and "rummaging" through national and international literary canons to engender a modern novel in the style of pan-European authors like Balzac, Flaubert, and Tolstoy, while also demonstrating Cervantes's—and, by extension, Spain's—primordial (or precocious) role in fashioning the novel.

Demonstrating one of the avenues for social advancement available to precarious young boys, Chapter 2 examines popular cultural and literary representations of the virile priest and his philandering rivals. With an eye to the role of celibacy and periodic abstinence from sex in such representations, this chapter explores the contradictory embodiment of nineteenth-century configurations of masculinity by Fermín de Pas, the psychologically tormented but strapping clerical protagonist of Leopoldo Alas's masterpiece, *La Regenta* (1884–85). Challenging arguments that frame the Roman Catholic priest as a cypher for emasculation, this chapter examines depictions of priestly materiality (e.g., clerical dress, liturgical ornaments) and, in so doing, contends that Clarín's novel casts the priesthood as a dynamic metaphor for struggles facing middle-class men more broadly, shedding light on the paradoxes undergirding mainstream patterns of masculinity manufactured throughout the nineteenth century in conduct and hygiene manuals. A reconsideration of the role of the priest in Alas's novel is particularly warranted given that Clarín and some of his peers often deployed in their literary criticism clerical and ecclesiastical imagery to allegorize (and ironize) their own authority and literary vocations, which they exercised from the pulpits of the university, the atheneum, and important culture and lifestyle magazines.

Chapter 3 turns its attention to Barcelona, which was the center of Spanish industry and the resurgence of Catalan art and literature during the turn of the century. This chapter historicizes visual and literary representations of businessmen that give contour to the myths of bourgeois masculinity capitalized upon by Narcís Oller in his most ambitious novel, *La febre d'or*. By relating his *indiano* protagonist's stock-market activities to the material worlds of figures like the businessman and the priest—each of which is also shown to embody anxieties and fantasies related to Spain's waning colonial empire—*La febre d'or*'s narrator identifies both the advantages and perils underlying male homosocial bonds within a capitalistic cosmovision. The anecdotes and images Oller uses to describe his own novel-writing enterprise in his literary memoirs, from his confraternal bonds to the "feverish" pace of his writing schedule and concomitant risks, reveal the ways the speculative affairs of the businessman influenced the author's own professionalization and masculine self-fashioning as a novelist.

Chapter 4 examines the contradictions in portrayals of male heirs and what masculinities studies scholars have called rural masculinity in representations of José María de Pereda's persona as celebrity author and genteel bourgeois in the illustrated press, as well as in his novels *Pedro Sánchez* (1883) and *Peñas arriba* (The upper peaks; 1895). It finds that fictional male heirs in the aforementioned contexts not only figure (and complicate) classic tensions between rural and urban people and settings in nineteenth-century Spain, but also those affecting Spanish novelists and discourses of masculinity writ large. This analysis sheds light on Pereda's own contradictory brand of novel-writing, which included the sale of highland fantasies to enthusiastic audiences in Madrid and Barcelona at the same time that it was made possible by the Cantabrian writer's bourgeois celebrity status and entrepreneurial activities. In an attempt to collapse the walls that have historically separated notions of urban/urbane and rural masculinity, this chapter concludes by suggesting that Pereda's writings (along with his persona as literary celebrity) illustrate the adaptability of bourgeois norms across evolving urban and rural contexts.

Looking beyond Galdós's and his contemporaries' role in manufacturing Spanish masculinity and modernity, a brief coda will discuss some of the ways in which nineteenth-century patterns and tropes of masculinity and middle-class culture continue to map themselves onto the contemporary imaginations of social media influencers and couture designers. After addressing how twentieth-century voices played a role in reducing nineteenth-century masculinity to a monolithic trope of the "man in black", this concluding section will show how some twenty-first-century cultural producers coincide with or take inspiration from nineteenth-century contexts, thus inviting new readings of historical texts while evoking directions for future inquiries into abiding and evolving patterns of bourgeois masculinity.

CHAPTER I

THE STUDENT

The cover image of the September 1883 issue of political and literary journal *El Globo* features a young student who, according to the print's corresponding prose description, has stopped listening to the lesson delivered by his droning teacher (see fig. 1.1). Often resorting to violence to reprimand daydreamers like "Perico," the teacher mentally and physically suppresses his students' creativity and imagination while giving apparently meaningless lectures about knowledge's ability to "carry men of the humblest means to the most lofty positions."[1] Perico's eye contact with the reader, together with the caption ("La pereza"; boredom or ennui), adds to the boy's picaresque character, particularly given the candid disinterest he displays in the teacher's lessons and his full awareness of imminent punishment. According to the columnist, the print is a mere reflection of what most of *El Globo*'s readers likely experienced as stifled schoolboys living in Spain:

> By dint of reprimands and punishments our natural laziness receded, and—
> though some more than others—we all learned something in primary
> school. If, instead of landing a severe instructor, we had been graced with
> a good man who told us: "go bird-nesting outside and don't torment your
> minds," we would have become men, just like general Martínez Campos
> became president of the Council of Ministers.[2]

La pereza.

FIGURE 1.1. "La pereza" (boredom or ennui) from the September
13, 1883, issue of *El Globo*. Image courtesy of the Hemeroteca Digital
of the Biblioteca Nacional de España, Madrid, Spain.

Presumably far from realizing an ideal as distant as that of Restoration-
era general Arsenio Martínez Campos (1831–1900), the young student in
the image bears a sleepy, wistful stare as he slumps alongside vain objects
like the textbook, quill, and inkwell.[3] The child's potential to mature as a
man in such an atmosphere is reflected in his dispirited countenance and is,
like the ephemeral fantasy folded into the paper crane, fleeting and fragile.[4]

   Writing from diverse backgrounds and across geopolitical contexts,
nineteenth-century novelists from Balzac (*Le Père Goriot* [1835; Old Goriot]),
Dickens (*Oliver Twist* [1839]; *David Copperfield* [1850]), and Flaubert (*L'Éd-
ucation sentimentale* [1869; Sentimental education]) to Eça de Queirós (*Os
Maias* [1888, The Maias]) and Galdós (*El Doctor Centeno* [1883]; *Miau* [1888])
often figured the challenges associated with maturation and upward mobility in modern European cities through the schoolboy or university student.

Categorically a male character type in the Spanish literary imagination until well into the twentieth century, the precarious but streetwise student also played a central role in the literature of the Spanish Golden Age. In his sketch in the 1843–44 edition of *Los españoles pintados por sí mismos* (Spaniards painted by themselves), Vicente de la Fuente (1817–1889) laments the disappearance of the defining attributes of the national student and, while regretting the loss of the figure's traditional physiognomy, fondly remembers its ubiquity in classic Spanish literature: "for writers of that time, a student was as essential to their novels as the Tarasca [giant dragon-like sculpture] is to the Corpus Christi procession."[5] From street urchins like Lazarillo de Tormes and Mateo Alemán's Guzmán de Alfarache to Alain René-Lesage's tremendously popular adaptation of the Spanish picaro in pan-European bestseller *Gil Blas* (1715–1735), however, young learners during the so-called Golden Age were more often than not representations of individualistic cunning and grit rather than indicators of any real possibilities available to young students during the Ancien Régime.

While by the nineteenth century the student had become a staple of the European bildungsroman for his seeming embodiment of upwardly mobile masculine ability or potential, Spanish novelists continued to deploy the figure as an indictment of the backwardness they considered endemic to the state of public (and, relatedly, religious) education in Spain, reflecting a similar spirit to that of *El Globo*'s "Perico." According to cultural historians, the panorama of primary and secondary education in the Spanish context was subject to political instability and, therefore, bleak for boys and, once they were allowed to attend, for girls alike.[6] This was perhaps especially true for children from the provinces, where the creation of educational centers and institutes lagged behind similar efforts in metropolitan locales like Madrid and Barcelona.[7] Even though the diffusion of Krausism during the 1860s and 1870s and the coetaneous establishment of the Institución de Libre Enseñanza (Free Institution of Education) in 1876 would provide idealistic panaceas for an intellectual minority, legislation like the 1851 Orovio decree (not to mention the contemporaneous concordat with the Vatican) had all but formalized the Church's monopoly over primary and secondary education in Spain during the second half of the nineteenth century.[8]

It is against this dismal backdrop from which the student-protagonists of *El Doctor Centeno* (1883), Galdós's most explicit foray into the theme of pedagogy, emerge.[9] To be sure, the Madrilenian "sentimental education" of Felipe Centeno and Alejandro Miquis—Galdós's two student protagonists—spans formal and informal contexts, and only one of the two succeeds in any meaningful way.[10] However, it is in the streets where their promise for advancement is truly put to the test.[11] Eventually exiled from the classroom, the two boys plunge into an urban underbelly that forces them to abandon the minimal creature comforts afforded to them by crowded pensions and frugal relatives in order to pawn, ragpick, and beg for survival. As this chapter will show, Galdós's complex narrative treatment of abject and impoverished boyhood as represented by his eponymous student, along with the latter's ambitious voyages around the Spanish capital with Miquis, take on a variety of ironic, metaliterary meanings when situated alongside nineteenth-century discourses and visual culture related to student life, secondhand consumerism, and Galdós's own vicissitudinous trajectory as a novelist.[12]

This chapter argues that Galdós's emphasis on the consumption and trade of borrowed or otherwise used clothing in the characterization of *El Doctor Centeno*'s impoverished students runs parallel to a discourse that spotlights the imagined precarity of Spanish novelists, who often expressed feeling dwarfed by the shadows cast by modern European paragons like Balzac, Dickens, Hugo, Flaubert, Zola, and Tolstoy. As we will see later and throughout this book, Galdós and his peers often used the rhetoric of struggle and perseverance to articulate the challenges they faced, imagined, and overcame as writers striving to restore prestige to the national literary canon. These discursive threads (studenthood, but especially ragpicking and novelwriting) converge in Felipe's surname, which evokes the Spanish word *centón*: on the one hand, a quilt or patchwork of heterogeneous fabrics or remnants, and on the other hand, a literary work composed of fragments and intertexts of disparate origins.[13] In the novel, Centeno's efforts to stitch together a presentable masculine identity in his frequently thwarted quest to assimilate the model of the nineteenth-century student and gentleman mirrors Galdós's own progression as a novelist, not only during the 1860s timeframe of the novel's plot, but also in the context of his transition from his earlier novels to the so-called *segunda manera* (second way) during the early 1880s.[14] Through the pervasive use of secondhand sartorial motifs and related concepts of provenance, wear, and resale in the characterization and development of the youthful Felipe Centeno, and later Alejandro Miquis, Galdós presents a critical portrayal of the conditions stunting bourgeois self-formation in Madrid, while simultaneously mythologizing the precarious but persistent state of the modern Spanish novel vis-à-vis its place in European literary history.

After providing an overview of the bildungsroman and student, we will see how the buying and selling of used commodities like clothing and books in secondhand ecosystems like Madrid's Rastro market may be read as an allegory for novel-writing in nineteenth-century Spain. I then analyze the "secondhand" narrative characterization of Felipe Centeno and his masters—particularly the doomed romantic Alejandro Miquis—as they appear in *El Doctor Centeno*, as well as in *Marianela* (1878) and *Tormento* (1884), each of which is linked by the common thread of Centeno.[15] Related visual evidence taken from the illustrated press and department store catalogs will help to point out how popular cultural ephemera participated in similar borrowings or ragpicking of classical, Spanish images and those imported from European neighbors. By figuring the difficulty of creating a modern, realist novel in a country that supposedly lacked obvious or immediate novelistic predecessors through two young students, Galdós—who was himself immortalized by peer Armando Palacio Valdés (1853–1938) as "Un estudiante de Canarias" (a student from Canarias)—draws attention to his own studies and mastery of the Spanish and European literary canons that preceded him. The Canarian author projects a self-reflexive awareness of the secondhand quality of his *centón*, while he simultaneously frames the production of all novelists as always and already the result of cross-pollination and intertextuality.

The Bildungsroman, Students, and Masculinity

Of all of Galdós's novels published during the 1880s and 1890s, *El Doctor Centeno* is perhaps the clearest example of the author's awareness and mastery of the conventions associated with the European bildungsroman, the subjects of which were often the development and education of young boys as students. As Francisco Caudet points out, the development of *El Doctor Centeno*'s student protagonists throughout the realist novel is "the result of a process of apprenticeship that inexorably leads to the negation of the idealized-romantic perception of reality. In other words: disappointment and disillusionment. It is precisely this that constitutes the education [or *Bildung*, apprenticeship] that Centeno will receive in the great theater of the world and not in university halls."[16] Since the guiding principle of the bildungsroman is the narration of becoming for aspiring bourgeois subjects, it is also the ideal genre through which to consider the co-existence of multiple and competing models of masculinity from which youthful students are able to choose. Through his apprenticeships, for example, Centeno has the ability to study and "ragpick" a variety models of masculinity that he then considers trying on for size: student, priest, teacher, literato, and *indiano* businessman. By situating his own bildungsroman in the years leading up to the September revolution of 1868, Galdós also gestures back to his own past as a student living in Madrid during this time. Centeno's and Miquis's characterization as precarious or struggling boys parallels some accounts of the Canarian novelist's own authorial self-fashioning and, thus, contributes to *El Doctor Centeno*'s engagement with motifs related to bad education, ragpicking, and novel-writing in the Spanish context.

Since the nineteenth-century bildungsroman often narrativizes the struggles of young male social climbers aiming to realize their ambitions in pursuit of bourgeois manhood, the genre is particularly well suited for inquiries into the dialogue between competing masculine ideals and the novel's own status as a talisman of writerly manhood at the turn of the century. As we will see throughout this book, male authors considered the production of a proper realist novel—as opposed to local-color sketches and serial fiction, for example—as a testament to their development as bourgeois professionals and peers who had already "made it" onto the pan-European literary scene. Defining the bildungsroman as the "novel of education," Mikhail Bakhtin highlights the interwovenness of the male hero with plot, according to which the developing young man and the stages of narration that tell the story of his development are inextricably interwoven: "Changes in the hero himself acquire *plot* significance, and thus the entire plot of the novel is reinterpreted and reconstructed. Time is introduced into man, enters into his very image, changing in a fundamental way the significance of all aspects of his destiny and life."[17] Building upon Bakhtin's formulation, Franco Moretti identifies masculine youth, in particular (such as that figured in European bildungsromans like Goethe's Wilhelm Meister and Balzac's *Le Père Goriot*) as "modernity's 'essence,' the sign of a world that seeks its meaning in the future rather than the past."[18] With narrative plotting and material advancement going hand in hand, the novel of education intuitively imagines and gives shape to boys' progression from childhood into manhood as an allegory for narratives of bourgeois modernization. Through the process of narration, then, the nineteenth-century bildungsroman is necessarily tied up in figuring fictional masculinities, the men who engender them and, by extension, patterns of masculine behavior that reflect both national and borrowed values and virtues, such as those summarized in this book's introductory chapter.

Nineteenth-century Spanish boys and men had access to various models for growth. As we saw before, conduct manuals and tailors encouraged men's attention to hygiene and meticulous sartorial self-presentation—particularly for those seeking entry into any number of bourgeois professions or vocations like business or the priesthood—while other texts including novels and portraiture offered retrograde fantasies of what Collin McKinney has termed "rough masculinity," which idolized rural environs and erstwhile models like the conquistador or the warrior.[19] Thus, the cultural mainstream was a constantly shifting arena for the articulation of competing configurations of masculine behavior, and the Bildungsroman's fictionalization of boys' development as bourgeois subjects also tracked their maturation as men.

Corroborating this fact in the British context, John Tosh argues that "manliness expresses perfectly the important truth that boys do not become men just by growing up, but by acquiring a variety of manly qualities and manly competencies as part of a conscious process."[20] In Doña Victoria's pension, for example, Felipe's perusal of the students' rooms and books provides a scene (analyzed later) in which the young boy has access to a variety of models to evade or follow. Similarly, when Centeno ultimately opts to work for the wealthy *indiano* businessman Agustín Caballero, whose surname simultaneously evokes the Golden-Age knight and the nineteenth-century gentleman, he chooses only one of a number of co-existing ideals. As we will see in Chapter 3, the *indiano* or colonial returnee was uniquely suited to give shape to fantasies of masculine development and ascendancy, given the number of men in Spain who emigrated to the Americas from around the Peninsula and the diffusion of tales of affluence and sociopolitical ascendancy undergirding mythical success narratives of men like Joan Güell i Ferrer and Antonio López y López.

The interplay between *Bildung* and inchoate or developing, plural masculinities with Galdós's education and self-fashioning as a writer (and the way others fashioned him in their own writings) takes on added significance when one considers the various accounts of his student years in Madrid.[21] In his own retrospections and those of colleagues like Armando Palacio Valdés, the author is often styled as the rebellious *flâneur* who preferred the freedom of the street to being fenced in by the walls of a classroom. In 1862, Galdós moved to Madrid to pursue a career in law which, as the narrator of his *Memorias de un desmemoriado* (1915–1916; Memoirs of a forgetful old man) recollects somewhat imprecisely, was short-lived due to his youthful vigor:

In 1863 or 1864 my parents sent me to Madrid to study law. I came to this court and entered university, where I distinguished myself by playing hooky. Escaping the university halls I wandered through the streets, plazas, and alleyways delighting in my observations of the bustling life of this enormous and motley capital. My literary vocation started with an itch for the dramatic arts, and I spent my days as a *flâneur* and my nights scribbling down dramas and comedies. I frequented the Royal Theater and a café in the Puerta del Sol, where a good number of my Canarian compatriots met.[22]

The author's septuagenarian reflections style a youthful Galdós whose rampant energy was untamed by the formal classroom. As we will see in the following section, Galdós's conflation of his literary professionalization and vocation with bohemian wanderings about Madrid echo Walter Benjamin's later articulation of the Baudelairean *flâneur* as a kind of ragpicking aesthete of modernity.

In an article titled "Un estudiante de Canarias" (1883; A Student from the Canary Islands), published in *Arte y Letras* (Art and letters) around the same time *El Doctor Centeno* appeared in print, literary critic and novelist Armando Palacio Valdés (1853–1938) not only describes a much more focused, hard-working, and melancholic youth than the one later memorialized by Galdós himself, but he also fashions the writer as a sort of romantic genius in line with his own bohemian notions of the modern artist.[23] The image of the writer that emerges in Palacio Valdés's article is a far cry from the polished bourgeois image projected by one of Galdós's earliest and now very iconic portraits, in which the fashionable talismans associated with an aspiring young gentleman are on display: three-piece suit, chain and pocket watch, mustache, and, of course, the photograph itself.

According to Palacio Valdés's account, Galdós became reclusive during his first several years in Madrid. He began to ignore some of the social conventions associated with young social climbers, adopting instead what Palacio Valdés labels an unhygienic, sedimentary routine that undoubtedly conjures the image of the quixotic literato that Galdós uses to characterize Alejandro Miquis:

> Little by little he started to spend more time at home and less in the café, and with such a sedentary and unhygienic life he soon became as thin as an asparagus. 'What could be wrong with that fellow?' people in the café asked. One of his close friends reported to our regular gathering that the student was spending all his time reading; that he spent all the money his

family sent him on books, and that all his clothes were falling apart and that it did not even occur to him to replace them.[24]

Spending the money his parents sent him on books rather than clothes (echoing more or less Miquis's expenditures in *El Doctor Centeno*), the Galdós immortalized here purportedly preferred a sui generis literary education represented by the acquisition of books to sartorial conventions which, as we saw in the introduction, encouraged young and mature men alike to update their wardrobe from season to season. Indeed, a substantial part of Palacio Valdés's mythologizing of Galdós rests on romantic stereotypes of the starving student, tropes that thread through the development of both Felipe Centeno and Alejandro Miquis as both streetwise students and ragpickers. Yet another apparent sign of Galdós's favoring of literary signs of bourgeois identity over his self-presentation as a polished dandy, Palacio Valdés writes that Galdós had prepared for a visit to Paris with his brother in what one might refer to as a Spartan wardrobe: "The luggage that our student tried to bring to Paris consisted of one shirt, some underwear, and a few socks."[25]

The fraternal voyage to Paris not only represents the start of Galdós's education as a novelist and bourgeois subject through homosocial trips both at home and abroad—a pattern that will repeat itself in the figures of Leopoldo Alas, Narcís Oller, and José María de Pereda—but his first exposure to the "City of Lights" also appears to have jumpstarted the work ethic that would fuel the composition of his first several novels:

> When he returned, he came back more alive and ready to enter into the commerce of life: his friends found him to have improved on all counts. As proof of it, the student continued to attend to his scholarly obligations and began to write literary articles, some of which were published in the capital's newspapers: his style was overwrought and stilted, but in those articles there was an uncommon boldness and color, and his friends encouraged him to keep writing.[26]

Inspired by both the literary models to which he was exposed in Paris and the encouragement of his peers upon his return, Galdós sought to produce a novel that would, unlike his earlier failures as a dramatist, bring him some professional acclaim and financial stability.

Though the article is tempting to take at face value, Dendle clarifies that Palacio Valdés's account must be tempered by the fact that it was likely Galdós himself who was the Asturian literary critic's source of such intimate details: "The interest of 'Un estudiante de Canarias' [. . .] lies not only in the narration of anecdotal information about Galdós's early years but also in the view of himself that Galdós, through the journalist Palacio Valdés, has chosen to proffer: that of the writer totally devoted to his art, heedless of health and social convention."[27] Both Galdós and his colleagues often use the rhetorical drapery of precarious boyhood and studenthood to reflect back on the Madrid of the 1860s. However, they do so with some irony, since the novelist had already made a splash on the Spanish literary scene: both by the 1880s, when Palacio Valdés framed Galdós as a humble transplant from the provinces, and in the 1910s, when Galdós was composing his memoirs. By *El Doctor Centeno*'s 1883 publication date, Galdós had published then critically acclaimed novels including *Gloria* (1877) and *La desheredada* (1881; The disinherited woman) and was well on his way to literary fame with the subsequent publications of *Tormento* (1884), *La de Bringas* (1884; That Bringas woman), *Lo prohibido* (1885; Forbidden fruit), and *Fortunata y Jacinta* (1886–1887).

Likely recalling his own years as a student, Galdós figures his protagonists' vicissitudes through images associated with the picaro and the ambitious social-climbing student after both Spanish and other European models. In so doing, the author criticizes Spain's backwardness in relation to what he saw as European neighbors' more visibly modern literary models at the same time that he is able to ironize and highlight Spanish realism's contributions to the pan-European literary canon and to the novel-writing profession more generally. As we will see later in this chapter, the reliance of Galdós's precarious but streetwise students on secondhand ecosystems to survive shows bourgeois self-fashioning and masculinity in the Spanish context to be in a perpetual state of becoming. Of all of the so-called "novels of modernity," to borrow Jo Labanyi's well-known phrasing, *El Doctor Centeno* reflects most clearly Galdós's desire to repackage the Spanish realist novel with the nineteenth-century Bildungsroman in mind. By doing so, however, he also highlights the role that paradigmatically Spanish genres like the picaresque novel had to play in paving the way for the modern European Bildungsroman. In the following section of this chapter, it will become apparent that Galdós was well aware of the secondhand market's role in playing host to nineteenth-century Spain's aspiring or already defined bourgeois subjectivities. The following historical overview of the secondhand trade will shed light on Galdós's authorial persona as both a student and ragpicker of European modernity who, in spite of a deficient education system and concomitant material hardships, is able to draw from and recycle heterogeneous sources in the *bricolage*-like creation of the Spanish realist novel.

The Secondhand Trade in Nineteenth-Century Madrid

Given the range of financial straits they found themselves in, students (like the young Galdós), bourgeois consumers, and the working poor alike had a number of reasons to participate in Madrid's used clothing trade during the nineteenth century. Whether to occupy leisure time, hunt for antiquities, bargain shop, or make ends meet by pawning and bartering, the stalls of popular locations like the Rastro market—also referred to as "Las Américas" (The Americas)—were also a site for the construction of modern consumer identities and tropes about Spanish national identity, reliant as it was on providing a counternarrative to the crumbling myth of empire. As the author of the *costumbrista* sketch "El estudiante" implies, students had particular cause to return to secondhand ecosystems, given their sometimes-necessary penchant for placing bets with the clothes on their back and their books due to a lack of any other currency:

> lacking money one bets with capes and pants, and books before anything else. Comparing the characters of nations, one writer says that the last thing a Frenchman will sell is his shirt and the Spaniard, his cape. For our student, everything comes down to returning to university [in winter] dressed in clothes meant for August, downplaying the frost as dewfall.[28]

Felipe Centeno and Alejandro Miquis's constant exchanges of used garments signal their changes in fortune and, thus, their struggle to succeed in their role as bourgeois social climbers. Through an overview of the abundance of literary and visual representations of the used clothing trade in the illustrated press, this section demonstrates the wealth of representations of secondhand ecosystems in nineteenth-century Spain while providing context for Galdós's metaliterary commentaries on the novelist as ragpicker in *El Doctor Centeno*. As we will see later, the presence of items of used clothing and correlated notions of provenance, consumption, wear, and resale in the novel signify beyond the characterization of *El Doctor Centeno*'s titular pauper; they also have implications for the novel's engagement with precarious boyhood and student life. While often inspiring well-established bourgeois socialites to craft popular and quickly consumable narratives about shopping and slumming, Madrid's Rastro also serves as an alternative site for the working poor and social climbers in search of cultural and economic capital amid the inept or remedial quality of education and the material hardships associated with struggling students in a country that also struggled to modernize.

A center for Spanish tailoring in the nineteenth century, Madrid was a known point of reference for consumers of fashion. The names of the capital's historic central streets enshrine the protagonism once enjoyed by sartorial craftsmen and women: c/Botoneras (Button makers), c/Bordadores (Embroiderers), c/Curtidores (Tanners), c/Hilanderas (Weavers), c/Tintoreros (Dyers). Madrid also played host to a sizable secondhand clothing trade, as the historical record and realist novels of the period attest. In Leopoldo Alas's *La Regenta* (1884–85), the widow Obdulia Fandiño is said to acquire the used dresses she shows off on Vetusta's Espolón from a cousin who lives in Madrid.[29] Galdós evokes the multifaceted uses of the secondhand market and its wares in a number of his modern novels, and often cites the Rastro market by name. In *La desheredada*, for example, the impoverished Angustias dresses her son, *el Majito*, in "rags from the Rastro," and Isidora Rufete dreads having to live near the flea market at the end of the novel.[30] In *Tormento* and *La de Bringas* (1884), Francisco Bringas's thriftiness is often exaggerated through descriptions of his excessively worn clothing, and in one case his trappings are even deemed unworthy of the Rastro's stalls: "enveloped in his robe from 1840, which could not even have been given away for free in the Rastro."[31]

The sordidly portrayed street children of *La desheredada* also arm themselves in the mismatched remnants of clothing to perform an inchoate, militaristic masculinity in their mock civil war in the southern neighborhoods of the capital.[32] As part of a misguided attempt to enact an altruistic and morally superior persona, the eponymous usurer of *Torquemada en la hoguera* (1889; Torquemada at the stake) donates his shoddy cape to a beggar to avoid having to part with the new one he had only recently purchased.[33] *Misericordia*'s (1897; Mercy) Benina and Almudena take advantage of their proximity to Madrid's Rastro market to trade in secondhand articles of clothing in their struggle to survive in the Spanish capital during the *fin de siècle*.[34] Whether the consumption of used clothing in the nineteenth-century novel signals pretentious imitation (*cursilería*), play, stinginess, charity, democracy, capitalism, or survival, its narrative frequency reflects the important role played by motifs of new and used clothing in the external characterization of Spanish realism's motley cast of socialites and social climbers.

Nineteenth-century Madrid's secondhand ecosystem remains a significant, if overlooked, site for interrogating the manner in which fictional men interface with an emerging marketplace in order to test agency and upward mobility in the narrative panoramas of the realist novel. Narrative descriptions of the used clothing trade and its agents reflect the existence of intricate commercial habitats in which consumers of all socioeconomic stripes participated. In Rebecca Haidt's estimation, "the work of ragpickers," for example, "extended the value and material applications of used clothing, lending complexity to the circulation of fashionable goods through the urban core."[35] The circulation of commodities like novels or clothes, whether used or new, was part and parcel of the rise of bourgeois identities and cultures of consumption during the nineteenth century. Printing technologies, along with textile production and its afterlife in secondhand circuits permitted the flourishing of outlets for self-identification and self-presentation by a heterogeneous group of middle-class consumers: from the lower-middle-class seamstresses and merchants to the upper middle-class bankers, bureaucrats, and entrepreneurs who policed and regulated the means of production.

Costume historians' and other scholars' tendency to overlook the secondhand status of clothing—both as it relates to objects in costume museums or to cultural studies of fashion—should perhaps not come as a surprise, given that used garments were by definition kept in constant circulation. Only the rare item was preserved for posterity, as most were repaired or refurbished until they were reduced to rags.[36] New apparel was exorbitantly expensive for most consumers, especially prior to the arrival of ready-to-wear fashion in the early twentieth century, and so alterations and repairs ensured continued use.[37] Furthermore, as fashion historians and restorers alike note, articles of clothing are notoriously difficult to exhibit and maintain, given their constant contact with the human body and the many alterations they experienced due to constantly evolving fashion paradigms.[38] Garments exhibited in the well-curated sartorial displays in venues such as the Museo del Traje (Costume Museum) in Madrid or the Museu del Disseny (Design Museum) in Barcelona were either particularly well-cared for by their original, undeniably aristocratic or middle-class owners, or are the byproduct of professional restoration.

Beyond the fact that they shared the same physical spaces in advertisements, shops, and secondhand stalls, books and clothes (whether used or new) also coincide in their function as sites for the development of fictions of identity. According to McNeil, Karaminas, and Cole, dressing is itself

an act of fictionalizing or textualizing, "since [it] functions as narration
and expression of self."[39] Used clothing is an especially meaningful locus
of study in this regard given the nineteenth-century practice whereby remnants of clothing and old rags were collected on the streets by ragpickers and
resold to paper manufacturers to be purified and transformed into the very
substance on which novelists from Dickens to Galdós commented on and
aesthetically transformed contemporary social reality.[40] Walter Benjamin
describes the ragpicker as one "who is obliged to come to a halt every few
moments to gather up the refuse he encounters."[41] Taking part in his own
ragpicking and aestheticizing of the type, Benjamin uses the metaphor to
characterize artists—like French poet Charles Baudelaire—as urban glean-
ers who scan the streets for the materials that ultimately constitute their art
and literature.[42] As Muñoz-Muriana notes in her recent analysis of marginalized subjectivities, ragpicking was a quintessentially modern enterprise:
"what starts as clothing ends in rags, which are then transformed into other
garments or into paper after passing through the urban stage. As such, the
ragpicker personifies the ephemeral and volatile nature of a modern, urban
life."[43] Galdós appears to recognize the discursive and thematic value of
such social realities in his novels in his intersection with the streetwise student and ragpicking novelist.

The trade of secondhand clothing and other valuable commodities like
antiques and books in nineteenth-century Madrid is well documented, particularly where it coincides with the Rastro market, described by *costumbrista* writer Ramón de Mesonero Romanos as "that extraordinarily famous
plaza, the central market where all utensils, furniture, clothing and knick-
knacks worn down by time, punished by fortune, or ingeniously stolen
from their legitimate owners end up."[44] In Mesonero's sketch, the market
comes into view as a dumpsite for objects that have shed any apparent use-
value or propriety. The used clothing trade has persisted for centuries in
various spaces of the Spanish capital: in the form of guilds of *ropavejeros*, or
secondhand clothing sellers regulated by the municipal government; in the
shops of *prenderos*, who would repair or transform old garments for resale;
and in unsurveilled ragpicking.[45] The galvanization of the Rastro market
during the nineteenth century cemented its permanence as a cultural institution for the buying and selling of secondhand commodities in the Spanish
capital, and one that would even inspire a homonymous novel by Ramón
Gómez de la Serna in 1910. Despite the fact that the Rastro currently plays
host to a wide variety of new and used clothing and accessories, appealing to locals and tourists alike, throughout the nineteenth century its stalls

specialized in the secondhand trade and were regularly policed and regulated by municipal employees.[46] At the Rastro market, consumers were able to buy and sell used garments either to earn a living, to ornament themselves according to their socioeconomic vicissitudes, or merely to browse and pore through the cultural bazaar's "Américas."

Narratives about the Rastro market abounded in newspapers and confirm its cultural place as a bazaar and narrative gold mine for the bourgeois imagination and, most significantly for this story, the ragpicking writer. The most common tales about forays into the Rastro's stalls come from newspaper columnists and bourgeois writers. Their ranks range from lesser-known journalists to literary celebrities like Emilia Pardo Bazán, all of whose consumerist interests differentiate them from the working-class or impoverished inhabitants of southern Madrid forced to pawn and ragpick as a survival mechanism. The second half of this chapter shows how Galdós's students meet at the intersection of middle and lower classes, consumers and producers. Felipe's upwardly mobile trajectory is represented through his various secondhand acquisitions, whereas Alejandro Miquis's downward trajectory is signaled by material losses. Additionally, imagery associated with secondhand markets inevitably glosses Galdós's own "secondhand acquisitions" of intertexts gleaned from his readings and studies of novels by Europe's premier novelists, calling to mind the character of *El Doctor Centeno* as an ironic *centón* or patchwork.

As is true of Galdós's novels, anecdotes and short fiction in which authors describe trips to bazaars, stores, and secondhand stalls tell the story of a mainstream masculinity that depended on men's open participation in consumerist ecosystems. Men's interest in the Rastro and the narratives that corroborate it demonstrate the market's potential as a gateway to the fulfilment of bourgeois fantasies of masculine identity and homosocial bonding. Journalists recognized Madrid's used clothing market (most clearly visualized by, but certainly not limited to, the Rastro) as a treasure trove for narratives ranging from the banal, post-Church shopping trip for bargain deals to fictions of self-fashioning and tales of survival. Writing for the literary journal *El Periódico para Todos* (1872–1883; The journal for everyone)—a Spanish analogue to the French *Le Journal pour Tous* (The journal for everyone)—M. F. "El Flaco" (The waif) introduces readers to "Las Américas," a common epithet used to describe the Rastro market in nineteenth-century Madrid's southernmost neighborhood. In its repetition of the phrase "En el Rastro" (In the Rastro), the 1875 article deploys anaphora to evoke the abundance of objects ready for the taking. By gesturing to the presence

EL AGUILA, Plaza Real, núm. 13.

GRAN BAZAR DE ROPAS HECHAS.

Este antiguo y acreditado Bazar há construido y bien confeccionado para la presente temporada de verano, un grandioso y variado surtido de prendas de todas clases y á precios, económicos, como puede verse en lo presenta nota:

		de	
Trajes completos en algodon, dril crudo y colores.		de	40 á 110 reales.
Dhos. id. en lanas novedad. vicuñas tricots y jergas.		de	80 á 380 »
Pantalones lanilla tricot, sa en y elasticotin		de	28 á 130 »
Dhos. algodon, dril crudo, blanco y colores.		de	4 á 50 »
Chalecos lanilla, tricot, cas mir y elasticotin.		de	16 á 60 »
Dhos. algodon, dril crudo blanco y colores.		de	10 á 30 »
Dhos. reps y piqués blancos y colores.		de	30 á 50 »
Chaqués. elasticotin, trico y jergas.		de	100 á 230 »
Leviñas cruzadas paño. elasticotin y casimir.		de	130 á 300 »
Sacos y sobretodos de entretiempo en vicuñas y diagonales.		de	80 á 300 »
Habaneras alpaca colores.		de	4 á 40 »
Americanas lanilla. jerga, tricot, paño y elasticotin.		de	44 á 170 »
Dhos. algodon, dril crudo, blanco y colores.		de	30 á 70 »
Chaqués y Americanas alpaca negra.		de	48 á 80 »
Guir a-polva dril hilo puro.		de	8 á 70 »
Fracks paño negro.		de	120 á 390 »
Togas pañete para abogados.		de	400 á 500 »

Hay además un grand oso surtido de géneros alta novedad para la medida, de la más rica y selecta que se fabrica y á precios sumamente módicos como podran ver los que se dignen visitar este grandioso establecimiento, tanto por su organizacion, como por la buena calidad de los géneros que se emplean en la confeccion de prendas, las que se construyen con prontitud y perfeccion.

OBRAS NUEVAS.

Perez Galdós.

EL DOCTOR CENTENO.

PENSAMIENTOS
DE SANTA TERESA DE JESUS

ESTRACTADOS DE SUS OBRAS

por la BARONESA DE CORTS.

Véndense en la LIBRERIA DE EUDALDO PUIG, Plaza Nueva numero 5, Barcelona.

FIGURE 1.2. 1883 advertisement in *El Eco de Barcelona* (The echo of Barcelona). Image courtesy of the Hemeroteca Digital of the Biblioteca Nacional de España, Madrid, Spain.

of cigar labels to broken-down parts of carriages once belonging to affluent bankers, "El Flaco" indirectly collapses class divisions, since ephemeral paper products and polished luxury goods are destined to meet the same end in the market's "mines."[47] The author's lexical choice while describing the so-called "Americas" simultaneously signifies a source of wealth and, more specifically, metaphorically alludes to Spain's colonial plundering, which included its own ongoing war with Cuba during the 1860s and 1870s.

By way of intertextual references to the Spanish Golden Age and the nineteenth-century book market, "El Flaco" also points to the various ways men engaged in consumerism in the Rastro. A sign of the commodification of literature and literary icons in commercial contexts during the nineteenth century, as well as shopping's relevance to amorous encounters and relationships, "El Flaco" references the enamored young men whose budgets make the Rastro market the ideal spot for them to realize their quixotic hopes with bourgeois Dulcineas: "the enamored squire may find in the Rastro, for little money, a pair of polished earrings with which he will satisfy the prosaic wishes of his beloved Dulcinea."[48] Baubles and books occupied similar space in Madrid's secondhand market, and those literatos in search of a bargain had plenty to choose from, so long as they had the patience to decipher the shoddy copies for sale: "Aficionados of bargain literature find in the Rastro a sea of books; some incomplete and others so manhandled that to pick them up one would need forceps, and to read them, a bath in lye."[49]

Because owning books (and possessing the scientific or literary knowledge they transmitted) represented a form of cultural capital related to bourgeois identity, such objects were, like clothing, valuable and necessary commodities for students eager to advance socially. As we see in this advertisement for *El Doctor Centeno* in an 1883 issue of *El Eco de Barcelona* (see Figure 1.2; The Barcelona echo), the announcement of Galdós's novel shares advertising space with a list of the sartorial novelties available at the El Águila (The Eagle) brand of department stores. El Águila was founded in 1850 and, by the 1880s, it had become a national chain with locations in Barcelona, Madrid, Cádiz, and Seville; according to Cruz, El Águila specialized in "the sale of ready-made clothes for men, women, and children."[50] All writers who narrativize their visits into the stalls of the Rastro market confirm that new clothing items and books alike shared similar fates as rags or riches for the would-be consumer, a reality that sheds light on the affinities weaving through clothing and novels during the nineteenth century.

A positive framing of men's shopping in the context of the Rastro market is apparent in Galician writer Antonio de San Martín's "La pantalla del velón" (The candle shade). In it, he tells the story of two men who enter the secondhand market's stalls in search of antiquities, books, and other difficult-to-find collectible items. He corroborates El Flaco's more general account while also gesturing to the inherent (if also ironic) narrative value of the Rastro and the consumption of forgotten but, nonetheless, still valuable commodities: "My friend turned over a large basket of old books, and in less time than it takes for a cock to crow, he bought three which, if I remember well, were: a copy of the second volume of *Don Quixote*, Ovid's *Ars Amatoria* [without a beginning or end], and *Ivanhoe* [all in quartos]."[51] Here, the market is not only a logical place for young men to search for gifts to buy their friendly or amorous companions, but also a locus for various types of men to bond in and around commercial spaces during weekend strolls. As such evidence demonstrates, secondhand markets had, like department stores, become "a way of pleasantly passing the time."[52] Furthermore, the collector's acquisition of these books, in particular, evokes the now familiar bricolage of literary works by Spanish (Cervantes) and pan-European (Ovid, Scott) writers that commingle across historical time-frames and whose works serve as intertexts in nineteenth-century Spanish novels. The illustration accompanying the story (see fig. 1.3) uses sartorial cues to characterize the bourgeois character of the male shopper, signaling once more the market's interest for working-class and bourgeois consumers alike. Armed with his top hat and frockcoat, the narrator's antiquing friend stands in stark contrast against the seller, who dons a less polished outfit in the form of a broad-brimmed hat and (probably secondhand) frockcoat.

Even though she focuses on women's acquisitive appetites, Emilia Pardo Bazán provides yet another bourgeois perspective that provides helpful con-text for the ways Galdós treats secondhand motifs as integral to the charac-terization of the ragpicking students in *El Doctor Centeno*. The journalistic interest she takes in the subject marks used clothing and its trade as literary motifs of undeniable narrative value; not to mention an integral aspect of "La vida contemporánea" (Modern life) which is the title of her ongoing column in the culture and lifestyle magazine *La Ilustración Artística* (The artistic illustrated). Pardo Bazán offers a frank, consumerist point of view that hovers between praise and dismissal of the kinds of shopping permitted by the market. Echoing the male authors discussed above, she writes that one must arrive early if one hopes to be "on time to skim the pot, for at nine or ten in the morning it has already been skimmed by countless pawnbro-kers, aficionados, prying eyes, collectors and freaks that hang out there to go fishing in the filthy and messy wave of shops, sheds, stalls, shacks, and stands that form the famous Americas of the Rastro."[53] Those who wait until after attending mass must settle for the "moths, dust, mold, impe-tigo, mildew, urine, rags and old metal pieces" that remain.[54] This sordid description recalls Anne McClintock's investigation of the Victorian obses-sion with cleanliness according to which "the iconography of dirt became deeply ingrained in the policing and transgression of social boundaries. Dirt is what is left over after exchange value has been extracted."[55] An epitome of the bourgeois consumer, Pardo Bazán frames the market as a marginalized site for the accumulation of social dirt, ragpicking, and leisurely slumming.

Another sign of her bourgeois purchasing power, the Galician author laments the absence of real treasures or *objets d'art* in the Rastro, as she com-ments on the "bachelorhood of the objects," from "pretty, nearly new theater binoculars" missing their case to bracelets robbed of their gems.[56] Despite her snobbery vis-à-vis the market's used commodities, the inter-est she takes in the subject appears to distance her from those "enemies of

FIGURE 1.3. Illustration published alongside San Martín's story "La pantalla de velón" in *El Periódico para Todos*. Image courtesy of the Hemeroteca Digital of the Biblioteca Nacional de España, Madrid, Spain.

secondhand shopping" that admonish spendthrifts who find everything in the stalls except what is actually needed.[57] Pardo Bazán's article ends with an anecdote meant to draw attention to the fact that rare, singular treasures—such as those sought after by El Flaco's enamored gift-seeker and San Martín's antiques aficionado—are often the product of disparate or peregrine origins:

> Would you believe what I saw dispatched just a few days ago? An elegant, woman's hat, one that no one would expect to see in such a place. I forged in my mind a story: the wife who buys that hat expensively; the husband who gets mad and censures; the woman who resells for two *duros* what had cost her fifteen or twenty, the pawnbroker who lets it go for five to the seamstress that hawks it to a *lionne*, who does not even suspect that the crown gracing her svelte silhouette was once in the Rastro in the company of a three-legged chair, a broken bread trough, and a sofa whose stuffing bursts from the seams.[58]

In this passage Pardo Bazán indirectly signals her socioeconomic status, which allows her to use the market for capricious or spur-of-the-moment shopping trips, and to publish the tales she has to tell about them for the enjoyment of her readers. Her reference to the grittiness inherent in the market—a perspective that is evoked by the male writers but emphasized by Pardo Bazán—echoes the views of nineteenth-century health officials, who identified the Rastro as potentially dangerous due to the unknown, insidious origins of objects for resale that threatened the spread of disease and infection: "confined spaces where piles of old clothing and bed linens enclose breeding grounds for pathogenic microbes which, by jumping from owner to owner, may serve as sources of transmission for many infectious diseases."[59] Pardo Bazán's narrative treatment of the Rastro—like Galdós's, as this chapter argues further—capitalizes on Madrid's complex, second-hand ecosystems in the nineteenth-century Spanish capital. Here, the Rastro emerges as a place where used garments, poverty, capitalistic circulation, dust, disease, and fiction intermingle and contaminate each other.

In stark contrast to Pardo Bazán's genteel perspective or the equally consumerist mentalities of "El Flaco" and San Martín—and more in line with the realities facing the struggling, working classes symbolized by precarious students Felipe Centeno and Alejandro Miquis—José Nieto Sánchez reminds readers of the abject living conditions of Madrid's impoverished southern neighborhoods flanking the Rastro. Commenting on a description of the "pack of beggars" described in an issue of *El Eco del Comercio* from the 1830s, Nieto Sánchez argues that the used clothing trade did provide a glimmer of financial stability to those most precarious members of the working poor who would have otherwise had to resort to begging.[60]

In *El Doctor Centeno*, the exchange of secondhand clothing and other objects in itself facilitates the modest social advancement of Felipe Centeno at the same time that it reflects the eventual downfall of his second master, the student and literato *manqué* Alejandro Miquis. Indeed, the romantic student's excessively worn, ragged clothing eventually impedes his ability to enter and thrive in urban spaces like the museum or the theater, where sartorial etiquette was expected, if not explicitly prescribed; his equally meaningful parting with his literature collection signals his loss of studenthood and the various intertexts constituting his own characterization as protagonist. Though Galdós's treatment of Centeno and Miquis's youthful potential was novel for its introduction of the conventions of the Bildungsroman to the Spanish context, his project also reflected earlier writings on the subject of the material conditions stunting students' success narratives.

Foreshadowing Galdós's ironic depiction, for example, Vicente de la Fuente's sketch of the nineteenth-century student also reports cheekily on the volatile relationship between the student and his sparse personal belongings, particularly when he finds himself in dire economic straits. As we saw in de la Fuente's account, by gambling for entertainment or to make ends meet, or some combination of the two, students often wagered their books and even the clothes off their back. The purchase and resale of items like used books and clothes is a motif that permeates *El Doctor Centeno*, a work that reflects the above realities throughout its pages. Perhaps most importantly for the argument of this chapter, Galdós's narrativization of young students' desires to emulate established bourgeois professionals like the playwright or the businessman by studying and ragpicking informs our reading of the Canarian novelist's self-framing as a struggling student and ragpicker of European realism as he developed as a professional writer.

Ragpicker as Student: Centeno

From his origins in *Marianela* (1878), before his enrollment in Pedro Polo's school or the informal classroom of the street in *El Doctor Centeno*, Felipe's narrative is studded with references to his precarious, threadbare existence, making his acquisition of "the paraphernalia of gentility" essential to his ambitious pursuit of bourgeois manhood.[61] A member of the numerous Centeno family in the fictional town of Socartes, Felipe distinguishes himself early in that novel for his thriftiness, thanks in part to the monetary donations of the benevolent Marianela, and to his motivation to shed his familial attachments and precarious material circumstances. Even in the abject environment symbolized by his family's household, "Doctor Centeno" occupies the most far-removed and marginalized spaces, all of which foregrounds this chapter's interpretation of his character—at least as he eventually appears in his eponymous novel—as a metaphor for the Spanish novelist's (real and imagined) marginalized status in the 1860s: "The runt of the family, Felipe was around twelve years old and had his bedroom in the kitchen, the most internal, remote, crepuscular, smoky, and uninhabitable of the three rooms composing the Centeno household."[62] Driven by his reasonable although nearly unattainable goal of bourgeois comfort that an education would supposedly guarantee him, Felipe dreams of modeling himself after the successful social climber and eye doctor Teodoro Golfín, who travels to Socartes in order to restore the vision of the local gentleman Pablo Penáguilas. To be sure, where Teodoro Golfín had succeeded in going to Madrid to become a renowned doctor, Felipe Centeno eventually falls short in spite of his picaresque savoir faire.

Throughout *Marianela*, Felipe's round characterization is energized by his repeatedly expressed machinations for socioeconomic advancement in the form of schooling and bourgeois attire. The semantic field that constellates around him in his ebullient projections to Marianela recall those of the fashionable gentleman epitomized by Teodoro and Pablo:

> You'll see just how fine and gallant I'll look once I put on my frockcoat and top hat. I'll also outfit myself with those things they call gloves, which I'll never remove except to check my pulse . . . I'll have a walking stick with a golden knob and I'll wear . . . Ah . . . Yes, only the finest fabrics for my skin . . . Golly! You'll laugh when you see me.[63]

It is perhaps because of, not despite, his extreme poverty, that Felipe recognizes these material objects as symbols that connote class identity, affluence and authority, labor, and power inherent to the ideals of masculinity manufactured by periodicals, popular literature, and conduct and hygiene manuals throughout the nineteenth century. Read through McClintock's theorization of social dirt in the Victorian era, Centeno's focus on gloves would appear to consecrate their role as a metonym of gentility, given their ability to retain the smoothness of the skin on one's hands and to sever contact between a clean body and the contaminating image of social dirt in a variety of contexts. Gloves, along with watches, cufflinks, cosmetics utensils, and toiletry bags are among the many objects counted by Cruz's survey of nineteenth-century probate inventories of bourgeois households that reflected "the increasing obsession of the middle classes with the care of the body."[64] While Felipe could never have read the kinds of conduct manuals available to middle-class gentlemen, he is able to read and study clothes' appearance and finery as visual markers of a better way of life. His related desire to become a doctor is inseparable from the commodified signs and symbols about which he fantasizes and quickly learns to decipher in his studies of Golfín and his brother's models.

After Golfín's arrival to Socartes, the eye doctor shares the success story of his and his brother Carlos's upward mobility. In *El Doctor Centeno* Felipe will attempt to study and replicate Golfín's "rags-to-riches" tale, which begins with references to self-fashioning and the homosocial transmission of knowledge between brothers:

I learned to read and then I taught my brother how to read. I served various masters who fed me and let me attend school. I saved up my tips and bought a money box . . . I saved up to buy books . . . I do not know how I entered the religious teaching order of the Piarists; but I entered, while my brother earned a living as a messenger in an import shop.[65]

The anaphora of the personal pronoun in Golfín's condensed autobiography underscores the myth of the self-made man, while evoking the kind of ego necessary to perform such a Herculean feat of mobility: a fantasy of mobility that fuels Felipe's own pipedreams of material advancement.

In one of Felipe's daydreams, Golfín's sartorial markers are conflated with mythical, regal symbols of power, and demonstrate the boy's childish ignorance of the social reality of which he hopes to form a part: "He saw himself covered in luxurious cloths, with his hands imprisoned in fragrant gloves and driving a coach pulled by swans (not horses) and beckoned by kings and queens, required by honest damsels, praised by magnates and brought to triumph over the people of the earth."[66] In the novel's denouement, Centeno is caricatured by the narrator as a vagabond who takes flight to Madrid, equipped only with the meager savings he has accumulated with Marianela's selfless donations.[67] Described in the epilogue as an imperceptible insect, Felipe's precariousness and dubious potential for success add to the challenges that await him upon his arrival in Madrid: "he is even smaller than the phylloxera pest that infests the great expanses of a vineyard. Buoyed by his own encouragement, he is sure to make it big."[68] The attention Felipe pays to sartorial markers, or to Golfín's example, will continue to motivate him, even as his idealism and optimism—often mocked or pitied by Galdós's ironic narrator—clash with the harshness of urban Madrid.

In the opening pages of *El Doctor Centeno*, the eponymous protagonist emerges as refuse from the Rastro market. A virtual pile of used and tattered clothing, Felipe "dons a torn and well ventilated jacket, sole-less boots, Burgundian pants full of slash marks and, atop his disheveled head, a shapeless military cap that is the most pitiful scrap the Rastro's stalls had ever seen."[69] A far cry from the respectable image of studenthood reflected in one of Galdós's most iconic portraits during his student years and that of boyhood marketed in contemporaneous department store catalogs (see fig. 1.4)—which promised bourgeois values like technical "perfection and solidity"—Felipe emerges from the page as the embodiment of the patchwork evoked by his surname.

FIGURE 1.4. Illustration of young boys' suits in the 1884 catalog of the El Siglo department store. Image courtesy of the Arxiu Històric de la Ciutat de Barcelona, Barcelona, Spain.

Sheltered exclusively by the Frankensteinian remnants of garments described in the cited passage, Centeno arrives to the hill upon which sits Madrid's Royal Observatory, where he prepares to "take over the capital."[70] Centeno's vantage point atop the Spanish capital recalls that of Eugène Rastignac, the iconic social climber and student who in the denouement of Balzac's *Le Père Goriot* (1835) directs his attention to Paris, from the heights of the Père Lachaise cemetery, and famously iterates: "Now it's just the two of us!—I'm ready!"[71]

Resembling one of Baroque painter Murillo's picaros—an image that returns later in the novel—Centeno and his burlesque external characterization distance him from the model of the bourgeois gentleman he attempts to study and emulate. The implicit reference to Balzac's novel further ironizes Galdós's depiction of the young boy from Socartes. Indeed, Centeno can only imperfectly perform the leisurely habitus parodically traced here, thus drawing attention to the self-reflexive, secondhand nature of Galdosian intertexts in the novel. This incongruity is heightened through the use of simile, indirect discourse, and epithet, culminating in an ironic mockery of the "manly" pride with which the boy admires the spiraling evanescence of cigar smoke: "after eating like a proper lord/mister, my old chap recalls that luxuriantly smoking a cigar is also something well-suited to the gentry. And with what virile pride the fearless lion heart contemplates the meandering trails of smoke that twist about in the clear air!"[72] This expository description is evidence of the "mock-epic" prose that characterizes the narrative voice of the novel in general, and draws attention to Felipe's threadbare beginnings.[73] It also displays to the reader that the young boy from the provinces will have to fight an uphill battle in his quest to navigate through and triumph over the city. Additionally, this consciousness of wanting to emulate what he perceives to be a more sophisticated way of life frames him as a student of bourgeois masculine identity well before he steps foot into the classroom, even if his potential is—like the fantasy of Perico's paper crane and the smoky, "virile" spirals—ephemeral.

If Centeno's lamentable wardrobe frames him immediately as a precarious or subaltern individual produced by the Rastro, his frequent comparison to animals—building off his earlier characterization as an insect—strategically summons around him an analogous, Darwinian discourse of adaptability ("struggle for existence" or "survival of the fittest") that undergirds his studies throughout the novel: snail, cat, tortoise, ass, bull.[74] The bestialization begins even earlier in *Marianela*, when Felipe laments to that novel's equally abject heroine: "We aren't people, we're animals. Sometimes the thought crosses my mind that we're even lesser than mules, and I wonder if I'm really any different than a donkey . . . Hauling baskets full of minerals and tossing them into a wagon, pushing the wagon up to the kilns, stirring about the minerals as they're washed."[75]

In his accumulation of this animal imagery, the Darwinian discourse it evokes, and an overabundance of artistic and literary referents—Murillo's beggars, *Lazarillo de Tormes*, Rastignac—Galdós's depiction of Felipe Centeno virtually bursts at the seams with intertextual references. These intertexts stitch together Centeno's persona and emphasize his own "secondhand" quality as literary character. The young boy's connection with other artistic and literary signs of dirt, poverty and social mobility also makes him a capacious symbol for the modern novelist as a kind of ragpicker of borrowed materials. In his discussion of the urban figure in Baudelaire's poetics, Benjamin remarks that "from the *littérateur* to the professional conspirator, everyone who belonged to the *bohème* could recognize a bit of himself in the ragpicker."[76] Recalling Muñoz's insight mentioned earlier, the ephemerality and transformational potential of the ragpicker's labor—collecting, recycling, renovating—made the figure an effective symbol for the tasks associated with literary production. As I show later, Galdós's metaphorical ragpicking culminates in Felipe's tutelage under Alejandro Miquis, and in Miquis's own decadence and failings as a student and writer, thus further pointing to the evocative resemblance of *El Doctor Centeno* and its titular hero to a *centón* in both its literary and material-sartorial dimensions.

Felipe slowly adjusts to his surroundings by accepting secondhand acquisitions from new friends, but the ironizing descriptions of the narrator frame him as an exotic and even racialized other. Following the burlesque exposition, the student and pensioner Alejandro Miquis and his friend, Juan Antonio de Cienfuegos, bump into Centeno after he faints from attempting to smoke a cigar on an empty stomach, a moment that parodies the fact that smoking tobacco was a proper habit for the fashionable male.[77] Miquis prods Centeno and offers him his coat: "Hey you, busybody, wake up, open your eyes. Would you put on my coat?"[78] To Centeno's delight, the material and the texture of the coat temporarily lent to him by Miquis affords him warmth, while also constituting a significant, if still only symbolic, material step forward. However, the narrator does not cease to remind the reader of Centeno's animalesque or even grotesque silhouette that he cuts in sharp relief against the polite society of Madrid. Newly fitted with his borrowed coat, the narrator casts Centeno in an esperpentic light as "such an outlandish figure, that one would have to look to Egyptian mummies or savage and hideous African idols for a similar likeness."[79] To be sure, Felipe's incongruous physical appearance distances him from that of the idealized student or aspirant to the bourgeoisie and is only describable in exotic terms that both draw attention to, and exaggerate, his marginalized or ridiculed otherness. However, despite such a defamiliarizing physical appearance, Centeno's study of the models projected by Miquis and Cienfuegos signals the commencement of the urban phase in the young boy's informal education that will eventually lead to his modest advancement up the social ladder.

Drawing dual inspiration from religious iconography in Golden Age paintings like El Greco's *Entierro del Conde de Orgaz* (1586; The burial of the Count of Orgaz) and nineteenth-century department store catalogs, Galdós's depiction of Felipe blends high and low cultural registers. On their way back to Doña Virginia's pension, the middle-class students discuss giving Centeno other used items of clothing (e.g., boots, shirts, ties), thus giving free rein to the provincial boy's imagination:

> Hearing such things, good old Felipe saw before him a world bursting with commodities, glories, grandeur, and bounty. The sky parted its blue

wardrobe curtains, showing one clothing item after the next: this one for winter, that one for summer, and behind the clothing, a thousand other luxury items like matchboxes, a little walking stick, a pocket watch with a dangling chain, rings, coin purse and notebook with a little pencil to take notes, umbrella, etc.[80]

The exaggerated character of this epiphanic mirage, provoked by Miquis and Cienfuegos's beneficent promises, reveals Centeno's naivety, and recalls the phantasmagorias of clothing and accessories he imagines while still in Socartes.[81]

Much like the heavenly host that parts the sky in El Greco's *Entierro del Conde de Orgaz* (see fig. 1.5), commodities associated with the gentleman emerge once more in Felipe's mindscape. However, unlike the kinds of instruments, toys, and other gadgets that populate the dreams of the bourgeois boy and girl represented on the cover of El Siglo's 1884 holiday department store catalog (see fig. 1.6)—a composition that illustrator Josep Lluís Pellicer accidentally or intentionally modeled after that of the iconic El Greco painting—the young ragpicker's dreams constellate around the "paraphernalia of gentility" recorded in the inventories studied by Cruz: matchboxes, walking sticks, pocket watches, rings, notebooks, umbrellas.

In its whimsical depiction of children's commodified dreams, the El Siglo cover appears to capitalize on, while rebranding, El Greco's fantasy of heavenly transcendence. Just as Galdós recycles Golden Age intertexts and iconography in the plotting of his student protagonists, department store catalogs similarly took inspiration from Spanish art and iconography for repackaging in the cultural mainstream.

When the newly formed trio arrives back at the pension, Alejandro asks if Felipe may stay in the attic. Doña Virginia, irritated, distances her locale from a "charity poorhouse," and she is critical of Miquis's donations to the boy: "There he goes giving away his clothing . . . He's given him the blue jacket that he hasn't worn more than three times . . ., and two shirts and a brand-new pair of boots . . . Good God!"[82] Knowing the cost of good clothing, and fully aware of Miquis's reliance on the capital of his father to pay his rent, Virginia is unable to fathom the idealistic student's excessive charity. Given Virginia's initial unwillingness to play host to Centeno, an arrangement is made to turn him over to the Polo family, where he is treated as the classroom dunce by the hands of the sadistic priest Pedro Polo, who unabashedly sends him to the shadowy attic in the exclusive company of clutter and unused Church decorations.

FIGURE 1.5. El Greco's 1586 masterpiece *El entierro del Conde
de Orgaz*. Image courtesy of Wikimedia Commons.

Galdós's narrator characterizes Polo almost immediately as a ruthless disciplinarian and, while some early critics of the novel, like Clarín, took pity
on the priest's clear lack of vocation, he is the analogue to Perico's violent
instructor described in the introduction to this chapter. Delivering more
than the kinds of slaps expected by Perico and his peers, Polo emerges in
the classroom as an overseer of galley slaves: "His maxim was: 'Sew beat-
ings and you will reap wisemen.'"[83] Metaphorically cast as a cruel overseer
of enslaved rowers, in a classroom that takes the shape of a battered galley,
Polo embodies the type of reprehensible education that Galdós fervently
opposed. In spite of the apparent levity signaled by exclamation marks,

FIGURE 1.6. Detail of the cover image from the El Siglo department store's 1884 holiday catalog. Image courtesy of the Arxiu Històric de la Ciutat de Barcelona, Barcelona, Spain.

the narrator effectively uses a racialized metaphor of inhumane treatment to lampoon another example of Spanish modernity's shortcomings made evident by an atavistic educational system that evoked signs of pre-modern coloniality: slavery was not officially abolished in Cuba—one of Spain's last overseas territories—until 1886.

Felipe's first apprenticeship with Polo is short-lived, and the youth's characterization as a simulacrum of the middle-class student coalesces in this section around his contrast with Polo's own success story of social advancement, and his further relegation to the abject and highly symbolic storage space of the attic.[84] The slow pace of Felipe's advancement is thrown into relief initially by the narrator's temporally contracted summary of Polo's successful (if vocationally bankrupt) progress and its concomitant sartorial markers: "Regarding his cassock, Polo thought to himself: "A priest, you said? Well get to it. Professor, you said? Happily. This age we are in is a blissful one in that a man can receive his destiny made-to-measure just as he would take a suit from the hands of a tailor."[85] While Centeno enters the house sporting the clothing donated to him by Miquis and Cienfuegos, the narrator reminds readers of the boy's incomplete, imperfect, and transitory material improvements through the combined use of the adverb "almost" denoting incompleteness, and the diminutive for "gentleman": "and as he wore the good clothes that Miquis had given him, he almost, almost looked like a page, a little gentleman . . ."[86]

Felipe's stay in the attic metaphorically substantiates his abasement and bleak objectification as a "a little child meant to deliver messages, sweep the house and the school, and provide other services."[87] From the start of this section, ironically titled "Pedagogía" (Pedagogy), Polo cruelly obliges Felipe to live in the remotest part of the home ("in the uninhabited attic of the house, full of junk and dust and cobwebs").[88] Whereas Felipe views his new living quarters in a positive light—"they were for him better than any palaces fathomable"—the omniscient narrator clarifies the way readers are meant to view the space as a gloomy and drab repository for "useless objects, or others without a spot in the sacristy, and there were also a number of images, some broken, others stripped; funerary equipment, a variety of cardboard and wooden pieces for Holy Week."[89] Prohibited from lighting a candle, Felipe spends his nights in the dark among the dust-covered refuse stored there. The boy's symbolic placement in the attic, the most unkempt and farthest removed site in the house and a repository for all sorts of "useless objects," recalling Mesonero Romanos's earlier description of the Rastro, casts the far-removed space as a metaphor for stifled mobility. Affluent middle-class tenants tended to live in well-furnished, first- or second-floor apartments, making the remote attic space described here a negative image of bourgeois comfort. Galdós never ceases to remind readers of the precarious position of provincial social climbers (or students of bourgeois customs) like Felipe, and thus, by extension, of challenges broadly affecting the self-realization of a bourgeois class. As we will see, Galdós's narrator also spotlights the circumstances stymying struggling young artists through Alejandro Miquis's own material-sartorial decadence and Felipe's symbolic attachments to him.

While Felipe ultimately does receive an education through his apprenticeship with Alejandro Miquis, his activities and external characterization throughout the remainder of the novel are bolstered by motifs that emphasize his and his master's material precariousness and the novel's self-reflexive, secondhand quality. Immediately after Felipe's abrupt ejection from the Polo household, the narrator can speak only elliptically and in objectifying terms about the boy, reminding the reader that any apparent steps forward are fragile and easily reversible. Subject to volatility, Felipe reportedly spends two weeks on the streets—ironically described as the "starry inn"—after having fallen "like shorn hair tossed into the corner and dumps, like living garbage."[90] The narrator surmises the places Felipe must have traversed during this time, which include "the Southern round-abouts, inundated with dung, misery, and malice."[91] A far cry from the genteel points of view described above in columns by "El Flaco" and San Martín, and recalling instead the more sordid elements of Pardo Bazán's assessment, *El Doctor Centeno*'s allusions to the Rastro conjure the market's negative connotations as a potential site of contagion, filth, and poverty, while remaining a store of narrative value for Galdós, who thrives as a sort of ragpicking novelist.

In Felipe's attempts to find the students who were the first to lend him their time and resources, he also circles back regularly to the hill of the Observatory. This spatial return evokes Felipe's "perennial adolescence," and is a sign of the novel's circular temporal structure that constantly loops back on itself and is symbolic of Spain's slow modernization during the 1860s timeframe of the plot.[92] Luckily for Felipe, he eventually does reencounter Miquis who, surprised to see the boy, exaggeratedly exclaims: "You're all civilized! Well now, look how beautifully you've worn my clothing! It's true that it's been a while . . . and now you talk like a person!"[93] What Fredrick Jameson would perhaps call Felipe's already deteriorating "protagonicity" or viability as a protagonist sublimates as it conjoins with that of the romantic idealist, Alejandro Miquis.[94] This narrative confluence is first signaled—aptly for the argument of this chapter—by a sartorial metaphor that conjures once more the image of a pieced-together *centón*, and then as a more explicit intervention by the narrator at the end of the novel's first volume: "Felipe sewed himself to the coattails of the boy from La Mancha"; "Instead of one hero, we now have two."[95] Felipe's attachment to Miquis's coattails—and the fraternal or homosocial bond it symbolizes between the boys—symbolically figures Galdós's own studies of, and unabashed attachments to, domestic and international literary canons in his own formation as a novelist.

Even if Felipe receives much needed shelter in the form of lodging in Doña Virginia's pension, Galdós's narration constantly reminds readers of the titular protagonist's precarious existence, signaled by his objectification by the pensioners, his ironic, naive "reading" of Miquis's literature collection, and his need to beg and pawn clothing and books on behalf of his sickly master. During his time in the pension, itself an image replete with allusions to Madame Vauqueur's Parisian bungalow in *Le Père Goriot*, Felipe is passed around and used by the pensioners as a personal errand boy of sorts. Felipe earnestly and doggedly embraces his new charge and is thankful for the roof over his head, but the narrator's omniscient vantage point frequently submits the boy's perspective to the crude reality it sometimes obfuscates: "the worst thing was that two days after Felipe's admittance to the house, the lad turned out to be everyone's servant, and they were all his masters, because without pause they sent him to the street with one message after the other."[96] When his various masters are at the café or elsewhere, Felipe does take advantage of their absence to study their academic subjects as represented by the books and notes left behind in their rooms, providing a window onto what Galdós and his contemporaries were reading during their studies in the Spanish capital.[97]

A culminating moment in the narrative that most clearly weaves together Felipe's uneven development as a student of bourgeois customs and shoddy material acquisitions with the novel's self-reflexive acknowledgment of its own intertextual, secondhand or patchwork (*centón*) nature occurs when Felipe examines and attempts to make sense of the titles of European novels strewn across Miquis's desk. Through an especially adept use of indirect free style, the narrator ventriloquizes through Felipe as he struggles to pronounce the titles in syllabic swatches:

> His master's desk was strewn with a collection of different works; but there was an endless number of big old books written in French. Let's see . . . Balzac, Scribe . . . What might that be about? *Le pe . . . re Gori . . . Gori . . .*, *Memo . . . moires*, memoirs of *Deux jeunes*, of Diogenes it must have meant . . . He would be damned if he could make it out. Centeno could not understand why his master read such nonsense . . . *Don Víctor Hugo . . .*, *Ruy Blas . . .*, that one was clear. *Schiller . . .*, *Don Carlos . . .*, also crystal clear. My good doctor read the first few scenes; but then he grew tired because, as far as he could tell, they all said the same thing.[98]

Felipe, who by this point in the narration has ironically evoked Balzac's Rastignac, Hugo's Gavroche, and Dickens's Copperfield or Twist—besides Spanish Golden Age types like the picaro and Murillo's beggars—encounters a symbolic difficulty while trying to articulate the titles constituting the modern European literary canon, some of which composed Galdós's own library. The eponymous protagonist's subsequent "reading" of the Spanish dramatic texts is cut short by his boredom and the repetitiveness he detects in the first few scenes. As Centeno scans the European and Spanish texts that constitute the very warp and weft of his own characterization, Galdós draws his readers' attention to the secondhand nature of the novel itself, underlining, on the one hand, *El Doctor Centeno*'s debt to those literary predecessors and, on the other, the need to deviate from them in the creation of something altogether new and unique.[99] The passage functions as a lynchpin for the various prongs of this argument: with the novel itself as a *bricolage* of texts from European neighbors and the Spanish Golden Age, Galdós becomes a metaliterary double for Centeno, who—even if partially—engages with iconic titles of the European literary historical canon.

Cognizant of this position in his own literary criticism, Galdós corroborates the dilemma of the aspiring Spanish novelist in his "Observaciones sobre la novela contemporánea en España" (1870, Observations on the modern novel in Spain), in which he rather bluntly states:

> We do not have a "novel"; the greater part of the works that have such pretensions feed the insatiable curiosity of an overly frivolous public. They have an ephemeral life determined solely by the first reading of a thousand or so people, who only seek out books for a fleeting distraction or a passing delight.[100]

In this early statement, Galdós pinpoints the stagnant market forces that determine and hinder the Spanish novelist's ability to establish his or her literary craft. Still cognizant of these realities in *El Doctor Centeno*—which takes place in the years leading up to the 1868 revolution—the narrator allegorizes the position of the Spanish novelist in the precarious social climber Felipe Centeno: just as the boy strives to piece together an education and identity as a bourgeois man, with the secondhand materials available to him in his often-thwarted quest for self-fashioning, Galdós and Spanish novelists in general must simultaneously draw inspiration and refurbish material from among the masters of European realism (Balzac, Dickens, Flaubert, Hugo), serial fiction (like *Los españoles pintados por sí mismos*), and the Spanish Golden Age (Cervantes, Murillo, *Lazarillo*).

However, the novel's secondhand character should not be viewed through a negative lens. As Jameson summarizes:

[Galdós] enjoyed the great good fortune of the historical conjuncture, not only arriving at the moment when everything remained to be said about the belatedly nascent bourgeois world of nineteenth-century Spain and of Madrid as the last great European metropolis; he also inherited fully developed all those novelistic innovations and instruments of representation which, since Balzac, a century of novelists had worked to perfection.[101]

While Galdós was late to the novelistic game, he constantly reminds his readers of Spain's rich tradition of realism that needed to be tapped into once more for the creation of a truly "Spanish" realist novel. In his 1901 prologue to Alas's *La Regenta*, for example, Galdós gestures toward the need to recognize the importance of Spain's Golden Age literary tradition in the realization of the modern Spanish novel.[102] Perhaps the ultimate irony in Galdós's narrative ragpicking is, of course, that the author was already a "full-fledged novelist" by the 1883 publication date of *El Doctor Centeno*.[103] Indeed, he had already succeeded in introducing realism to Spanish readers, at least as early as *La desheredada*, published in 1881, and he would continue to do so in short order with *Tormento* (1884), *La de Bringas* (1884), and *Fortunata y Jacinta* (1886–87). The deployment of images of precarious boyhood allows Galdós to gloss the challenges he faced in the creation of the nineteenth-century realist novel in Spain, and yet, given his use of these metaphors at this particular juncture in his career, some ambivalence remains. It is ironic that where Centeno, the earnest social climber, fails, Galdós, the novelist, had already succeeded in bringing attention to his realist agenda. By including such a passage in *El Doctor Centeno*, Galdós might have recognized his own success as a student of the Spanish masters and pan-European celebrity authors, though not without some insecurities about his role on the pan-European literary stage, not to mention his place in Spanish literary history.

From Student to Ragpicker: Miquis

As mentioned earlier, scholars have pointed to the many similarities threading through both Miquis's experience as an aspiring literato and Galdós's own aspirations as a playwright during the 1860s. Like Miquis, Galdós wrote badly received dramatic works that clouded his initial development as a student and writer of Spanish and European literature. For this reason, José Pérez Vidal labels Miquis "the alter ego of Galdós's apprentice," and confirms that Galdós uses the character as a stand-in for his own early failures as a dramatist.[104] Whereas Centeno's studenthood begins symbolically with his close studies of the bourgeois models provided by Golfín and his brother in *Marianela*, Miquis's education suffers a perpetual decadence. Establishing a sharp relief, Galdós first frames Miquis's seemingly limitless—if hyperbolic—potential as a student:

> At four he knew how to read, at six he could write in prose, poetry at seven, at ten he understood Calderón, Balzac, Victor Hugo, Schiller, and he knew the names of an infinite number of celebrities. At twelve he had read more than many who at fifty pass for learned scholars. At fourteen, serious men from the countryside consulted him on matters of history, mythology, and language arts.[105]

While Miquis is temporarily saved by his fraternal relationship with Centeno, which evokes Galdós's own reliance on the encouragement of friends to continue to pursue his career as a professional writer, he eventually dies penniless and robbed even of the clothes from his back. Thus, the material hardship and subsequent death of Miquis (particularly when juxtaposed with Centeno's modest success as a streetwise student) may be read as an index for Galdós's early years in Madrid when he aspired to be a romantic playwright. The fictional playwright's fate in the novel's denouement, for its part, simultaneously memorializes Galdós's boyish idealism while perhaps symbolically representing the novelist's embrace of a realist agenda in his adulthood.

The secondhand nature of Centeno's studenthood and his embodiment of the novel's own borrowed characteristics, which both coalesce in the scenes discussed above, are further emphasized by Miquis in the final sections of the novel. Like Miquis's wardrobe, his collection of European novels finds a tragic fate in the stalls of Madrid's resellers after he and Centeno are ejected from Doña Virginia's boarding house due to an unforgivable altercation among the tenants. As a result, the motley pair end up in a downgraded, ramshackle garret for impoverished university students. Undoubtedly a downgrade from Virginia's pension, the new lodging is described sordidly as "cheap and abhorrent," where "the rooms were filthy dens and the food was a mess."[106] In desperate financial straits, the two are constantly forced to pawn or sell otherwise decent pieces of clothing when in need of quick cash:

> When his credit dried up he would pawn a piece of his good clothing. Felipe was charged with these commissions, and he took them on with

diligence and with an innocent cheerfulness. He came to know all of the moneylenders in Madrid, and he already knew where they gave the most.[107]

Once the clothing is depleted, Miquis is forced to part with his library of European classics:

> Once the clothing was depleted, he began to sell off all of his books. The great and the lesser literature: Victor Hugo and Paul de Kock, Balzac and Pigault Lebrun, Manzoni . . ., all of them dispatched in a lugubrious procession, marching to those ramshackle secondhand shops, where they only gave a third of what they had originally cost in exchange.[108]

Miquis's parting with his books symbolically represents his undoing in the moments leading up to the denouement, even if literature and education are, as we saw before, intangible forms of cultural capital. The pathos of the material departure is heightened by the personification of the tomes as part of a funerary procession, which foreshadows Miquis's own lugubrious end. Additionally, Felipe's frequent trips to the pawnshops on behalf of his master evidence the secondhand market's function as a survival mechanism for the poor and working classes, and even for those who actively resist identifying with the working classes, like Miquis, as we have seen with respect to the Rastro. Unfortunately, however, the young students are trapped in a cyclical pattern of consumption and resale without any substantive improvements: Alejandro Miquis eventually expires, and Felipe Centeno ends up as a page for yet another master, thus failing to realize his goal to become a doctor like Teodoro Golfín. In *El Doctor Centeno*, Centeno and Miquis are able to continue to support themselves by their donations and sales in the short-term, but do not benefit greatly from them in the long-term. Providing a realistic alternative to the jocular tone of Vicente de la Fuente's sketch of the gambling student, Galdós insists on the real consequences that bad education and material hardship bestow in the context of nineteenth-century Spain. Just as the acquisition of books and clothing signaled a man's acquisition of cultural capital, representations of their loss undoubtedly foreshadow material and or cultural bankruptcy.

The sales of Miquis's higher-quality articles of clothing leave the two with only their heavily worn clothes that prevent their entry into bourgeois spaces like the museum or the theater; while used clothing permits survival in the Spanish capital, it does not necessarily expedite social advancement or access to bourgeois spheres. As a consequence, Miquis eventually starts to avoid his friends due to the deplorable state of his wardrobe: "He refused to present himself in the company of his friends as he was ashamed at the thought of them seeing him in such pitiful apparel and with boots that were falling apart at the seams."[109] In another allusion to the Rastro, Miquis's clothing not only prevents his entrance into the Prado museum, but it also recalls the initial portrait of a shoddily dressed Centeno on the hill of the Observatory: "One Sunday, enthusiastically standing by the museum's entrance, they were not allowed to enter for their odious silhouettes. A deeply embarrassed Alejandro was silent the whole day, only able to pay attention to his worn-out boots and his threadbare jacket and hat, all of which looked like it had been purchased in the stalls of the Rastro."[110] Unlike the case of the miraculously impeccable hat described above in Pardo Bazán's flea-market anecdote, Galdós's narrator juxtaposes the Rastro alongside Miquis and Centeno to call to mind the former's connotations as a site of abjection, particularly within the realm of the realist novel. Felipe's shoddy wardrobe matches that of his downtrodden master, and reads as an unidealized textual description of one of Murillo's paintings of young beggars, such as the iconic *Joven mendigo* (1645–1650; Young beggar):

> For footwear he donned a pair of busted old sandals begotten from who knows where and comprised more of mud than leather. The jacket covering his body was an unrecognizable color and begged to be tossed into a vat of used clothing to be transformed into paper. His pants similarly yearned to be paper, even if it was for scrap. One did not know how to distinguish between the head of the distinguished doctor and his ingrown beret, which bore a hole through which the boy's cowlicks protruded.[111]

In another connection between text and textile, the narrator alludes to Felipe's personified clothing's desire to transform itself into paper: the very material upon which the textual Centeno resides and which, during the nineteenth century was made with the purified tatters collected by ragpickers on the streets of Madrid and Barcelona.[112] While Felipe is enchanted by the idealized perfection of the boyish angels of Murillo's religious paintings he had seen in the Prado on one occasion, the narrator's description of the protagonists' distorted and patchy wardrobe more accurately glosses Murillo's paintings of starving youngsters. In keeping with a picaresque reading of this novel, the connection with Murillo represents a circular, temporal leap, with the effect of threading together the abject conditions facing poor beggars during the Golden Age with those still afflicting youths like Centeno and Miquis in Madrid over two hundred years later.[113]

Even in death, Miquis—who had failed both as a student and as an aspiring dramatist—is not spared a patchwork treatment. While Felipe begs on the streets in an attempt to save his ailing master, the romantic student dies of tuberculosis. In order to give him a proper burial, his friends are forced to

dress him in whatever spare garments are available to them. Felipe summarizes in his conversation with José Ido del Sagrario at the end of the novel:
"You know we had to clothe him with Cienfuegos's black pants, Arias's
vest and Cienfuegos's jacket. This was the only decent piece of clothing
on him; the rest were worthless."[114] But Felipe discovers that this already
Frankensteinian death shroud was in turn torn, as one of Miquis's dubious
love interests had stolen Cienfuegos's jacket from the cadaver. In an attempt
to soothe the incensed Felipe, Ido asks him, rhetorically: "why would he
need the aid of a tailor? Cirila could not possibly strip your master's glorious suit of immortality."[115] Like his own unfinished, monstrous drama *El
Grande Osuna*—itself a *centón*, even if unintentionally so—Miquis's failed
romantic quest for literary success is symbolized by the motley donations
of his friends. Where Felipe is at least on a path to success by the end of
the novel—when he joins his new master, the *indiano* Agustín Caballero—
Miquis fails to embody successful models of masculinity represented by the
student and the writer. Thus, he parodically represents Galdós's memorialization and farewell to the romantic ideals of his youth.

Conclusion

In the exposition of *El Doctor Centeno*'s sequel *Tormento*, Ido del Sagrario—
Pedro Polo's pedagogical assistant—finds himself once more with Felipe
Centeno in a tavern in Madrid. After a brief reintroduction, Ido quickly
realizes Felipe's newly polished veneer and the change in social status it
denotes: "I see that you have a nice cape . . . and a tie with a clip like that
of a gentleman . . . and decent clothing . . . My boy, you must have inherited from someone. Who are you going around with these days? Have
you spawned a rich uncle from the Indies [i.e., *indiano*]?"[116] The association between a young man's inheritance of wealth from an avuncular
source will be explored in depth in Chapters 3 and 4 in both national and
regional contexts. Here, Felipe corroborates his old teacher's observation
by identifying his new master—the *indiano* businessman Agustín Caballero—as "the best master in the world," and a "Capitalist!"[117] Felipe adores
the symbolically named Caballero as if he were a saint, an image that is
heightened when thrown into relief against those of his previous wardens.
Even though Felipe has discovered a way to maneuver his surroundings
to survive while educating himself, his original project to convert himself
into a doctor—an object of ironic mockery in the second part of *El Doctor*

Centeno when the youth performs an operation on the cadaver of a cat—or into an affluent gentleman, dissolves.

Pardo Bazán praises the novelty of *El Doctor Centeno* in her letters to Galdós, commending his ability to narrativize the life of "a boy like any other."[118] For his part, Clarín does not elide a frank critique of his friend's novelistic labor when he admits that the 1883 book was "not Galdós's best novel."[119] However, the Asturian literary critic concludes his article by applauding the labor and scope of Galdós's project. Clarín deems particularly noteworthy *El Doctor Centeno*'s significance in the larger corpus of works written and to be written by Galdós, in spite of the challenge presented by such a project as ambitious as the creation of the modern Spanish realist novel: "Galdós is crafting a bespoke style for the modern Spanish novel; toward this end he struggles against great obstacles that he never ceases to overcome."[120] In this way, readers may regard *El Doctor Centeno* much like we have regarded the patched-together, secondhand outfits of Felipe Centeno and Miquis described throughout the novel. But if the novelist experiments with and fine-tunes what Stephen Gilman has called "the ever-changing rules of the novelistic game," Galdós's novelistic production should be viewed as representative of a national literature that was, like the inchoate masculinity of *El Doctor Centeno*'s student protagonists, in formulation.[121] Foregrounding its own creation and status as a heterogeneous *centón* of a sort, *El Doctor Centeno* is a formidable vignette in the larger quilt of Galdós's panoramic fictions of Spanish modernity. Through an aesthetic of impoverished boyhood draped in heterogeneous secondhand clothing, Galdós ironically parallels his endeavors as a modern Spanish novelist during the 1860s, while simultaneously accentuating the many affinities weaving together text and textile (and Galdós's identity as a student of European realism) in nineteenth-century Spain. Even as he lampoons the material conditions stunting the proper development or *Bildung* of young Spanish boys like Perico, Centeno, and Miquis, whose lofty imaginations and youthful potential are stymied by an abysmal educational system, Galdós's narrativization of their examples functions as an efficacious vehicle for nineteenth-century aesthetics of and attitudes toward novel-writing.

When he leaves for France with Agustín Caballero and the eponymous heroine of *Tormento* at the end of that novel, Felipe's trajectory is left open-ended. In the chapters that follow, we will see many of the possible outcomes available to boys and young men who wish to fashion themselves into bourgeois gentlemen or professionals at the turn of the century in Spain: from the priest and businessman to the industrious heir. The various models embodied and resisted by these masculine figures bear striking family resemblances to the male novelists who engendered them in their own pursuit of recognition as middle-class men and professionals against the backdrop of a nation that struggled to modernize according to the patterns established by other industrializing Western nations.

CHAPTER 2

THE PRIEST

As we started to see in the previous chapter in the example of Galdós's Pedro Polo (*El Doctor Centeno* and *Tormento*), the gender expression of Roman Catholic priests was undeniably entangled in larger debates about bourgeois manhood during the fin de siècle in Spain. To be sure, "priestly masculinity" was especially called into question or targeted by those who resented or ideologically opposed the Catholic Church and its agents, or by those who saw a perpetual vow of celibacy as a threat to the reproduction of the "forces of the State."[1] Additionally, the Church itself embraced the feminization of certain elements of religious life in order to appeal to (and instrumentalize) its female parishioners and growing female religious communities in an era of waxing liberalism. The rhetorical feminization of Catholicism in nineteenth-century Spain was bolstered by events such as Pius IX's 1854 articulation of the Virgin Mary's immaculate conception as dogma, which, according to Raúl Mínguez-Blasco, coincided with an uptick in miraculous, Marian sightings, all of which helped to shed light on the role to be played by women in educating their families in Christian virtues of piety. However, the cult of the Virgin Mary also aided in the masculinization of the priest within Catholic configurations of masculinity. Priests like Isabel II's confessor Antonio María Claret y Clará, for example, cited devotion to the Virgin as a way to overcome or steel oneself against the temptations of the flesh in a masculinized rhetoric of self-control and restraint.[2] Given the priest's position at the intersection of discourses of femininity and masculinity during this time, he became for artists and writers a "bodily site for exploring anxieties about gender and social change, [. . .] or as a means of testing out new ways of writing gender identities."[3] While scholars have long pointed out how priests' gender expression was somehow contrary to the social expectations of other Spanish men—at least a partial result of some priests' own vision of themselves as categorically different from their lay counterparts—much less attention has been devoted to the ways representations of priests figure a variety of patterns of bourgeois manliness.[4] The kinship between priests and bourgeois masculinity is unsurprising when one considers that only men could receive the sacrament of holy orders within Roman Catholicism, and the priesthood was viewed as a way for young men to advance socially.

Perhaps few priests from the Restoration period are quite as emblematic for their embodiment of masculine tropes as the poet and priest Jacint Verdaguer (1845–1902), particularly given his widely recognized position as one of the patriarchs of the so-called Renaixença or rebirth of Catalan culture and language that took place from the mid- to late nineteenth century.[5] Especially after the 1877 publication of his epic poem *L'Atlàntida*, "mossèn" Verdaguer became a locally and nationally recognized poet laureate.[6] The 1887 cover image of *Madrid Cómico* depicts Verdaguer in his clerical streetwear (see fig. 2.1), including his cassock and outer cloak, which were mainstays and also signifiers of masculinity in a Catholic priest's wardrobe during the final decades of the nineteenth century. The cassock was seen by Church leaders as "a continuous exhortation to live according to the Church discipline" and failing or refusing to wear it was viewed as a sign of effeminacy, as writings by Isabel II's confessor Claret y Clará attest.[7] Undoubtedly a nod to the poet's revival of the classical epic tradition, illustrator Cilla's caricature of the priest deploys these items to fashion the Catalan priest as an orator or a Roman emperor, whose representations in ancient statuary were often similarly shown wrapped underneath the dramatic pleats of a *toga virilis* (see fig. 2.2). Standing in contrapposto, Verdaguer folds his arms into his cloak in clear imitation of Roman men donning the floor-length robe, a garment to which the priest's cassock traces its earliest origins. Verdaguer's presence in nineteenth-century print culture provides only one illustrative example of the ways priests were viewed as part and parcel of (rather than separate from or irrelevant to) nineteenth-century discourses of masculinity.

FIGURE 2.1. Cover image of 1887 issue of *Madrid Cómico* featuring a caricature of Jacint Verdaguer by Cilla. Image courtesy of the Hemeroteca Digital of the Biblioteca Nacional de España, Madrid, Spain.

FIGURE 2.2. Statue of Augustus dressed in a *toga virilis*. Image courtesy of Wikimedia Commons.

As this chapter will show, priests were also expected to abide by many of the behavioral and cultural expectations directed at laymen within the bourgeois mainstream, making them masculine figures whose signs, symbols, and struggles were not unanimously seen as separate from those of other bourgeois men, including novelists and literary critics. For his part, Verdaguer was also a chaplain for the Transatlantic Company founded by *indiano* businessman Antonio López y López—the entrepreneur to whom he dedicated his epic poem—thus illustrating his tacit participation in the mercantile ventures associated with the exigencies of an "imperial nation."[8] Additionally, the priesthood was embraced in the Iberian Peninsula as a way for men from rural and urban environs alike to acquire economic and cultural capital, a circumstance aestheticized in novels by José Maria Eça de Queiroz (e.g., *O Crime do Padre Amaro* [The crime of Father Amaro]), Emilia Pardo Bazán (e.g., *Los pazos de Ulloa* [The manner of Ulloa]), Benito Pérez Galdós (e.g., *El Doctor Centeno, Tormento, Nazarín*), and Leopoldo Alas (e.g., *La Regenta* [The judge's wife]).

Still, anticlerical and radical republican magazines like *El Motín* (1881–1923), along with decadent, naturalist novels by Eduardo López Bago and Alejandro Sawa, never ceased to caricature priests for their supposedly unmasculine behaviors, which presumably included an "unnatural" or unhealthy vow of celibacy, clerical dress (e.g., "dress-like" cassocks and liturgical ornaments), and a host of unmentionable vices like gluttony, lasciviousness, and greed, all of which threatened to undermine manly virtues of self-control.[9] In Clarín's *La Regenta*, for example, the atheist president of the local casino, Álvaro Mesía, imagines invisible threads connecting priests' cassocks to the skirts of women's dresses, a conflation that was also made in some of the large centerfold illustrations of *El Motín*.[10] In a miniature comic (see fig. 2.3), included as the centerfold for issue 53 of that year, a man in a bowler cap pursues what he believes to be a woman shielding herself from a torrential downpour with a large red umbrella. When the man approaches the figure, whose robe or skirt is held up presumably to avoid being splashed by a puddle—although clearly meant to resemble the bustle of a woman's dress—it is revealed to be a priest.

The abundance of stereotypical representations in the press notwithstanding, an equal if not greater number of nineteenth-century voices spanning the ideological spectrum recognized priests as complicated social types whose authoritative role in society—particularly in a traditionally Catholic country—figured many of the anxieties facing the male laity. Though this was especially true for Carlist, moderate, and other conservative writers and thinkers, we shall see that even more liberal-minded Spaniards did not constitute a unanimous bloc that viewed the Roman Catholic priest as a cipher for deviancy or effeminacy heightened by reference to other issues like political corruption, moral bankruptcy, and psychosexual perversion. As alluded to earlier, priests themselves occupied many roles in society, ranging from student (seminarian), spiritual father or guide to literato and businessman, a reality that helps to reposition the priest as central to configurations of nineteenth-century Spanish bourgeois culture, and, as this chapter will show, one of its most paradigmatic figures.

With an eye to justifying the priest's place within nineteenth-century Spain's gallery of masculine figures, this chapter argues that the Catholic priest and his world are symbolically rich loci for exploring compelling though heretofore overlooked patterns of masculinity and power during the Bourbon Restoration. It will also show that the priesthood functioned as an apt metaphor for male novelists and literary critics who sought to articulate their professional ambitions and struggles. Indeed, visual and

FIGURE 2.3. Detail of centerfold of October 3, 1891, issue of *El Motín* (The mutiny). Image courtesy of the Hemeroteca Digital of the Biblioteca Nacional de España, Madrid, Spain.

literary representations of clerical masculinity within nineteenth-century popular culture challenge received ideas about the priest's assumed effeminacy during the increasingly visible ascent of liberalism and secular nationalism. Texts ranging from hygiene manuals, autobiographical accounts, and academic genre painting to department store catalogs and novels not only visualize various masculine elements associated with the material world of the priest, but they also solidify the priest's identification as a social type who shared many characteristics with lay counterparts.

The second half of this chapter will then focus on how such cultural products help to reframe the characterization of Fermín de Pas, the priestly protagonist of *La Regenta* by Leopoldo Alas "Clarín", as well as nineteenth-century novelists' and literary critics' own appropriation of ecclesiastical signs and symbols. Indeed, the priesthood as figured through *La Regenta*'s protagonist functions as a pliant—not static or anachronistic—and imaginatively generative metaphor for bourgeois masculinity writ large in the nineteenth century. In Clarín's masterpiece, narrative descriptions of the Asturian priest's body function as effective discursive sites that signal broader anxieties and tensions related to notions of class and power. At times, clerical behavior and dress enable fanciful and performative fictions of an ostentatious configuration of masculinity based on "old regime values" that dwell nostalgically on a noble, powerful, and externally legible habitus.[11] In other moments, however, the cassock is rendered as an ascetic garment that binds, contains, and restricts, thus buttressing the "titanic efforts" (*esfuerzos de titán*) Fermín de Pas must summon to combat temptation and keep his desires in check.[12]

These paradoxical modes of comportment interwoven together in one fictional clergyman illustrate the internal contradictions in constructions of the nineteenth-century priesthood and discourses of masculinity writ large, particularly at a time during which bourgeois laymen were also contradictorily expected to enact masculine-coded ideals of strategic self-fashioning, self-control and restraint in matters related to the body (e.g., consumerism, sexual activity, etc.). Fermín's struggles to maintain his power over the cathedral and his parishioners, and his control over his own self-presentation, evidence Collin McKinney's assertion that bourgeois ideals—though increasingly mainstreamed and normalized in commercial arenas—at times relied on a man's contradictory "show of renouncing ostentation" also on display in some portraits of the bourgeois "man in black."[13] Because realist novelists and literary critics—including even self-professed liberals like Clarín and Galdós—interacted with, observed, and wrote about priests in particularly complex ways in their realist novels and criticism, their meaningful articulation of their own ambitions and struggles as bourgeois professionals naturally overlapped with those of their religious male counterparts. Furthermore, given the origins of literary hermeneutics in biblical exegesis, the literary critic's "vocation," parlance used frequently by critics like Josep Yxart, was similarly shaped by male homosocial networks and their (sometimes contested) authority and visibility as arbiters, readers, and producers of Spanish and international literary canons.

Clerical Masculinity: Bourgeois Priests and the Priestly Bourgeois

Priestly masculinity comes into particularly clear focus when viewed as one pattern within a wider array of complementary and competing nineteenth-century masculinities. As the introduction to this book historicizes, scholars including George Mosse, R. W. Connell, and John Tosh have demonstrated that masculinity is a multiple, shifting, and socially constructed category. Such work points to the interplay and dynamic oppositions between dominant or idealized practices of masculinity and those considered alternative or marginalizing, along with the ways discourses of power affect patterns of gender. While these theoretical frameworks have been applied successfully to laymen, priests are often absent from such discussion even though sacerdotal behavioral models have been constitutive of historical configurations of virility writ large. For example, even though "marital heterosexuality displaced monastic denial as the most honored form of sexuality" well before the Enlightenment, ascetic values still clung to idealized paradigms of secular masculinity later canonized in conduct literature.[14] Marital heterosexuality, though important, was not the *sine qua non* of behavioral patterns for all nineteenth-century men. Prolonged periods of celibacy, or careful regimens of self-discipline and restraint from sexual activity, industriousness, and productivity, along with tidy but inconspicuous self-presentation are among those virtues codified and praised in conduct and hygiene manuals as distinctively masculine during the nineteenth century and helped to forge what Zachary Erwin refers to as the "modern masculine ideal."[15]

Discursive terrains ranging from pseudoscientific hygiene manuals to Catholic propaganda aimed at defending a priestly virility corroborate the notion that there were many family resemblances connecting the masculine gender expressions of priests and laymen. Jesús Cruz and Collin McKinney, for example, have shown that these pan-European values were celebrated in Restoration Spain through the proliferation of conduct literature and novels, all of which undergirded the fantasy of a polite society. Drawing a sharp contrast to "today's celebration of sexuality," McKinney sustains that "middle-class men in the second half of the nineteenth century were encouraged to exercise extreme moderation" in questions of sexuality.[16] During the nineteenth century, prominent clerics like Claret—Isabel II's confessor and a particularly outspoken defender of Catholic values—viewed celibacy not as an automatic sign of effeminacy in men, but instead used language that mirrors that deployed by hygienists like

Monlau and Peratoner to encourage self-control. To borrow Mínguez-Blasco's words: "Although it is evident that priestly masculinity was not hegemonic since a priest's way of life was not common among the laity, some of their characteristics, such as the self-control of passions and temperance, contributed to shaping other models of masculinity which were an alternative to the figure of Don Juan."[17]

Examples of such discourses abound in *La Regenta*. The novel's representation of the paradigmatic dandy Álvaro Mesía particularly evidences the fragile and precarious balance required for maintaining modern ideals of restraint, according to which the body was an "economy whose resources must be properly managed."[18] As he prepares himself for Ana Ozores's eventual downfall, Mesía deliberately avoids less meaningful sexual encounters in order to preserve his vital energies: "And Mesía prepared himself. He read books about hygiene, he did physical exercises, he went for frequent rides. And he refused to accompany (his friend) Paco on his cheap adventures, paid for on the spot. 'The devil sick of flesh would be a monk,' Paco said."[19] When Vetusta's aging Mesía is unable to keep up with his trysts with multiple women, his embodiment of the Don Juan stereotype begins to wane: "He himself noticed that his face was losing the youthful look which it had recovered during those months of healthy living, exercise and abstinence—his prudent preparation for the decisive attack on the fortress of Ana's honor."[20] Too much sex was thought to sap men's virility, and yet too little, as Labanyi points out, could lead to feminized notions of blockage.[21] In the earlier quote from *La Regenta*, even the layman Mesía struggles to maintain the right balance. Though it is at best difficult to determine the extent of how nineteenth-century men pursued these mainstream norms, or "how people actually lived within the rules," they do represent culturally enshrined ideals and fantasies made widely available to the upwardly mobile male subject.[22] Most significantly for this chapter, decentering hyperactive sexuality as the model for ideal behavior among men sheds light on the masculinity of clerical figures who struggle with their compulsory celibacy.

During the nineteenth century, the primary reasons for ordaining priests included the need to recruit men for the care and cure of the faithful, as well as for the perpetuation of Catholic culture and values amid a surge in anticlerical nationalism. Entry into the priesthood was also viewed as a way for men from both rural and urban environments to achieve some level of socioeconomic prestige and power in a society increasingly steered by an affluent and politically empowered bourgeoisie. Although clerical and monastic life had been parodied and satirized since the Middle Ages, as has been well-documented in studies by Stephen Haliczer and Julio Caro Baroja, Catholic priests remained influential and powerful figures in nineteenth-century Spain; this was especially true during periods of state-sponsored renewal in religious piety, such as that attempted by the Bourbon Restoration. Both the Vatican and national representatives like Claret took advantage of the same technological advances as liberals did in order to produce a counter discourse to revolution and progressive reforms, as is evidenced in the mass production of texts like Pius IX's *The Syllabus of Errors* (1864) and manuals for seminarians and priests. As Frances Lannon importantly observes, even in a society that witnessed an uptick in violent, anticlerical outbursts against the Church, a priest's social distinction could be one of "disparagement" *or* "prestige."[23] Even for liberal-leaning intellectuals like Galdós and Clarín, priests more often than not occupied a point somewhere in the middle of these two extremes.

In F. Benoît Valuy's *Le Directoire du prêtre dans sa vie privée et dans sa vie publique* (Directory for the priest in his private and public life), a popular nineteenth-century conduct manual for male religious figures translated into its many Spanish editions as *Directorio del sacerdote en su vida privada y pública*, the appropriate comportment of priests was deemed necessary given their close contact with and influence over all social classes in Catholic communities.[24] The manual prescribes various behaviors, especially for those just beginning in their ministry. "Have in your library one or two books which treat of the rules of manners," Valuy urges, "and look through them occasionally; above all, notice attentively the language and manners of those priests who pass for models of politeness and good breeding."[25] Furthermore, the priest, "should be a person welcome to all good society; but to be faultlessly correct in matters of politeness before the public, he must put constraint upon himself to be so when not in company."[26] Catholic ministers were expected to follow rubrics of hygiene and comportment if they were to be taken seriously by society's most affluent members. Even though clerical masculinity may not appear initially to abide by the gendered language used to depict laymen, as Neal points out, clerics throughout history "were not sheltered from contemporary gender roles and expectations. It could hardly be otherwise when their status as clerics depended on their being male."[27]

A number of other texts instructed seminarians and priests not only on matters related to behavior, dress, and hygiene, but also on their presence in public. These included Claret y Clará's *El colegial o seminarista* (1860; The student or seminarian) and Jesuit José Mach's *El tesoro del sacerdote* (1861; The priest's treasury), both of which were republished throughout the second half of the nineteenth century. As Mínguez-Blasco summarizes, such texts reminded readers that "priests had to avoid going to the theatre, the café or the tavern and participating in activities like hunting, drinking, smoking or gambling. However, Claret agreed that priests should not have to live in isolation, so he included a section dedicated to urbanity in order to regulate priests' behavior at the table, when making visits or walking with others."[28] In other words, priests, quite like their lay counterparts, were not only expected to enact such recommendations in their public and private lives, but they were also encouraged to consume literature that was part of a wider cultural industry involved in policing men's behavior for personal and societal benefit. Driven at times by ceremonial or liturgical magnificence, and at others by asceticism and humility, a cleric's gender showcases analogous paradoxes in displays of masculinity by the "ascendant middle class" more broadly.[29] The clerical masculinity studied in this chapter oscillates between two modes—ostentation and ascetic self-control—both of which required strategic self-display and are inflected by the same gendered and sexualized language used to characterize bourgeois laymen.

Visualizing the Priest in the Nineteenth Century

Whether for their compulsory maleness, navigation of celibacy, or attention to matters related to hygiene, priests were viewed as men whose lives as spiritual fathers and guides, businessmen, and socialites served as inspiration for artists and novelists who recognized in them figures who were also central to bourgeois modernization and masculinity during the Restoration period in Spain. The frequent juxtaposition between the worlds of laymen and priests in nineteenth-century literature and visual culture— ranging from memoirs and academic paintings to novels, satirical caricatures, and commercial ephemera—offer further evidence of the ways the Roman Catholic priesthood functioned as a veritable treasure trove of metaphors with which Spanish artists and novelists could figure the ambitions, desires, and struggles that were also relevant to bourgeois masculinity writ large. It is difficult to imagine the reality otherwise, since, as we saw earlier, priests were instructed and trained to cater to affluent parishioners and were themselves viewed as bourgeois men. The prevalence of ecclesiastical imagery in the artistic and literary output of known liberals adds further credence to Valis's argument that even those who were critical of the Church's all-male personnel—including realist authors like Clarín and Galdós—intensely felt "the influence of religion on structures of the imagination."[30] Indeed, priests were not merely fodder for the anticlerical imagination during a time of struggles between secularization and religious revival. A survey of ecclesiastical tropes circulating in the cultural mainstream will later help to shed light on Clarín's complex representation of Fermín de Pas's clerical masculinity, as well as on nineteenth-century critics' and novelists' own styling as "high priests" of the Spanish literary canon. By foregrounding the many ways that the contours giving shape to representations of laymen and priests in autobiographical writings and commercial ephemera, this section will show that even the imaginations of cultural producers who championed liberal agendas capitalized on clerical aesthetics in their styling as modern men.

Autobiographical accounts and novelistic representations of boyhood offer telling evidence of the priest's effect on the imagination of upwardly mobile boys. In the third chapter of his memoirs, Spanish writer and literary critic Antonio Alcalá Galiano (1789–1865) recounts several moments that stand out to him from his youth in Cádiz, including a game of "liturgical dress-up" he would play with his childhood friends. The game, according to which the affluent boy would play the role of the Catholic priest, constitutes a detailed look at the generative effects of Catholic aesthetics and objects on young male Spaniards in the early nineteenth century:

> In Cádiz there was a guild of boys prone to saying mass, having altars, toy versions of sacred ornaments and objects, and singing solemn masses, acts that were sponsored by some clerics who did not see in such things an indecorous or sacrilegious imitation, but rather an equivocal effect of pious and even devout inclinations. I had my altar, my chalice and my paten [small silver plate to hold Eucharistic bread], my complete array of ornaments, more than one chasuble, and an embroidered pluvial cope with which I sang mass or other parts of the divine offices, sometimes alone, other times accompanied, having learned very well the divine psalms and no paltry number of the Church's prayers.[31]

Alcalá Galiano later describes his preference for guns and the uniforms of soldiers over the toy altars, sacred objects, and vestments of priests. Soon after this passage, the Andalusian goes on to write that he soon found there to be "other pulpits than those of the church."[32] However, the vivid reminiscence of the liturgical games of his youth, projected onto the autobiographical page by the perspective of a man already hardened and matured by decades of experiences with civil wars between conservative and liberal factions, demonstrates the author's tacit acknowledgment of the power and pull of religious aesthetics on his early formation as a boy. As this example illustrates, priestly models of masculinity were also formative in building one's masculine identity even at a young age.

Alcalá Galiano's account predates fictional scenes of a similar nature in novels by Galdós from the 1880s, in which the material world of priests is viewed as especially appealing to the puerile imagination of boys, perhaps for its potential to offer a life of authority, comfort, leisure, and bourgeois respectability. Toward the end of Galdós's novel *La desheredada*, for example, protagonist Isidora Rufete finds her son playing "Church" with the other boys in the home of Emilia and Juan José Castaño:

> the door opened and a bishop appeared . . . it was Riquín, who wore on his head a grand miter made of paper, and, delivering a blessing with his right hand, sang in the most hopeless Latin ever heard. [. . .] In the kitchen [the boys] had their magnificent altar, and every day they would place some new object atop it, whether a lamp or a chalice or a toy cross. In different areas of the house one would find tiny retables, shrines, and improvised pulpits with chairs. Last, they had made chasubles out of paper and said mass like cathedral canons, delivering every fear-inducing phrase in Latin and observing all the rules of that act religiously.[33]

Of course, such scenes are never devoid of irony. In this example, Isidora's macrocephalic son adorned in episcopal symbols may have even recalled for readers what Valeriano Bozal has called the "puppet-like" caricatures of prelates in the pages of *El Motín*, a venue in which it was common for illustrators to exaggerate the proportions of the clerics and politicians they skewered. However, the narrator's tone (more playful than anticlerical) and the jest with which the narrator treats the scene—not dissimilar from the jocular tone used in more neutral *costumbrista* sketches—point to it as merely a slice of life among nineteenth-century youths. Its juxtaposition against similar episodes where young boys pretend to be soldiers in mock battles in Madrid's southern neighborhoods, also recalls the dual pattern of social advancement common in autobiographical accounts (e.g., Alcalá Galiano) and pan-European novels dating back to Stendhal's *Le Rouge et le Noir*, in which the protagonist struggles to choose between clerical and military vocations.

Scenes like these are illustrative of the fact that such imagined ecclesiastical worlds are not merely by-products of a learned anticlerical ideology, but stem from much more elastic and whimsical sources. In *El Doctor Centeno*, young boys similarly idealize the ecclesiastical materiality of the Catholic priest and envision the figure as an apparatus of monarchy and empire. For example, as we saw earlier, Pedro Polo's masculine authority as a priest is enhanced and enriched in the novel by the aesthetic experiences of social climber Felipe Centeno. In another moment in that novel, Centeno and his friend Juanito del Socorro (a gilder's apprentice) stop to contemplate the royal palace and fantasize over comparisons between its decorative elements and the splendor of chasubles embroidered with gold. They also imagine the palace altar as if it were equipped with a priest saying mass and that could be accessed by activating an automatic lever; here, the Church and its male agents are reimagined as automatized or mechanistic technologies of the throne.[34] As will also be clear in *La Regenta*, a similar boyish fascination with priestly authority and materiality endows Fermín de Pas with a kind of virile authority, even if it is also ironized by Clarín's narrator. The classic binaries established by Alcalá Galiano, between the religious and the secular, the liturgical and the military, also echo prominent nineteenth-century fictions of masculine advancement in the style of Stendhal's aforementioned novel and Juan Valera's 1874 *Pepita Jiménez*.

Nineteenth century visual culture—ranging from academic painting to satirical and commercial ephemera—illustrates the blending of ecclesiastical and secular registers and further bolsters the priest's status as one of bourgeois masculinity's central figures. In Vicente Palmaroli's painting *La confesión* (1883, The confession) (see fig. 2.4), the Rome-based artist paints his young subject as an innocent neophyte, while it is the sophisticated young woman whose pastel-colored apparel more clearly imitates the liturgical ornaments of a priest hearing confession. Though writing within the context of erotic but lighthearted or playful representations of (male) confessors and (female) confessants, Noël Valis shows that sexual expression—such as that depicted in the flirtatious encounter between youths in Palmaroli's painting—were "dependent upon other cultural frameworks," including the Roman Catholic sacrament of confession.[35] Here, a sentimental avowal between young lovers lightheartedly reframes the confession of sins between a parishioner and priest. Palmaroli's depiction of womanly authority and maturity—particularly in comparison to the boy's overly earnest posture and seeming naivete—depends on her masculinization as a priestly figure.

FIGURE 2.4. *La confesión* (1883, The confession) by Vicente Palmaroli. Image courtesy of Wikimedia Commons.

Similar clerical patterns of masculinity give shape to the characterization of the secular protagonists of novels published around the same time as Palmaroli's painting, thus further demonstrating the importance of multivalent ecclesiastical motifs within the realm of bourgeois flirtation and romantic conquest. Agustín Caballero, Galdós's most well-rounded *indiano* and protagonist of *Tormento*, for example, enacts a similarly clerical habitus in the denouement of that novel, when he symbolically replaces the priest, Pedro Polo, in competition for the hand of Amparo, the novel's titular heroine. Once Caballero and Amparo have resolved their prior disagreements, the two are framed as (enamored) priest and female parishioner: "Doña Nicanora says that upon opening the door she saw the two seated, the one next to the other, with their faces close together: her, whispering, and him, listening with all five of his senses, like priests in the confessional."[36] The Galdosian narrator then foregrounds Caballero's deportment as similar to that of a virtue-signaling priest in a theatrical work: "Having closed the soliloquy with a grand sigh, Agustín approached the young woman, placing his hand over her head like the priests in a melodrama when they feign to bestow heavenly blessings upon some virtuous character, martyr or neophyte."[37]

Even anticlerical nationalists, whose heavily biased representations of priests in satirical magazines tended toward dehumanization and emasculation, often relied on the more complex depiction of the material world of the priest as an ornamental counterpoint to their own styling as secular radicals. Indeed, while priests were sometimes envisioned in the pages of satirical magazines like José Nakens' *El Motín* as Carlist guerrilleros or lascivious friars, they were also imagined as bourgeois foils to the magazine's artistic and editorial team, whose manliness, as Chapter 4 shows, relied on

FIGURE 2.5. Centerfold caricature of Emilio Castelar (flanked by kneeling effigies of Nicolás Salmerón and Francesc Pi i Margall as deacons) from the October 9, 1887, issue of *El Motín*. Image courtesy of the Hemeroteca Digital of the Biblioteca Nacional de España, Madrid, Spain.

a rhetoric of humility and rusticity. In a centerfold illustration published in an October 9, 1887 issue of the magazine run by Nakens (see fig. 2.5), the illustrator visualizes politician Emilio Castelar—once president of the short-lived First Republic (1873) and also one of Alas's university professors and collaborators—alongside kneeling effigies of fellow politicians Nicolás Salmerón and Francesc Pi i Margall. Preaching from a church altar's centerstage, Castelar is represented as a religious elite or pontiff in his embroidered, red and gold pluvial cope and white surplice. Even as the political figureheads are ironically fashioned as men of the cloth—where liturgical opulence and splendor signal corruption and political impotency—the politicians retain their whiskered visages, a sign of their status as laymen since priests were usually expected to keep cleanshaven faces.[38] In another

FIGURE 2.6. Centerfold illustration included in the May 17, 1885, issue of *El Motín*. The caption reads "*El Motín* excommunicating those who would excommunicate them." Image courtesy of the Hemeroteca Digital of the Biblioteca Nacional de España, Madrid, Spain.

image (see fig. 2.6), a rusticized allegory of *El Motín*, flanked by femininized virtues of liberty, work, and science triumph over a fleeing phalanx of priests and bishops armored in their ceremonial garb: crosiers, miters, and chasubles. These images corroborate the idea that even anticlerical nationalists defined their own rusticized, secular masculinity with the aid of the signs and symbols of the men of the cloth, perfect attributes for the villains within their ideological imagination.

Even though clerical dress was sometimes seen as a sign of difference or as a way to undermine the masculine gender expression of clerics in satirical caricatures, commercial ephemera including tailoring journals and department store catalogs show that the sartorial symbols of the priesthood coexisted with those of bourgeois laymen within the popular cultural imagination. In a March 1888 issue of a professional journal published for tailors, the included fashion plate displays five models with familiar silhouettes: one pharmacist, one legal professional, one cathedral canon, and two secular priests (see fig. 2.7). Though such journals only occasionally included a model for a priest's cassock, this issue demonstrates that the toga-like garment was part of the structure of other outfits relevant to the lives and

FIGURE 2.7. Fashion plate from March 1888 issue of *El Genio y El Arte* (Genius and Art). Image courtesy of the Hemeroteca Digital of the Biblioteca Nacional de España, Madrid, Spain.

work of other male professionals like doctors and lawyers. In a section of an El Globo department store catalog advertising men's hats, for example, the *sombrero de teja* or *tejo* is included alongside the bowler and the more formal top hat, indicating that the priest's headwear was categorically masculine (see fig. 2.8). This juxtaposition is unsurprising, since priests were discouraged but not prohibited from wearing hats or other clothing normally donned by middle-class men in general, particularly when not celebrating mass. As the above evidence would appear to suggest, and as we shall see in Alas's *La Regenta* and literary critics' employment of clerical metaphors in their own self-fashioning as literatos, the priest was central to the nineteenth-century Spanish cultural and literary imagination and, more specifically, to the way a variety of men articulated their own gendered identities.

Redressing Clerical Masculinity in La Regenta

Aside from its scathing portrayal of provincial life and its overarching focus on the spiritual and sentimental crises of Ana Ozores—the titular protagonist trapped in a loveless marriage plot not unlike that of *Madame Bovary* or *Anna Karenina*—*La Regenta* is also a story about the men who compete for her affection and, perhaps more accurately, for control over her body and soul. The novel is therefore an ideal text for the study of multiple patterns of masculinity, since it pits representatives of seemingly opposite ends of nineteenth-century ideological and political spectrums against one another in a competition for masculine hegemony over each other, their shared love interests, and the fictional town of Vetusta itself. As alluded to earlier, the atheist casino president, Álvaro Mesía, and the reactionary Church official with delusions of grandeur, Fermín de Pas, both try to leverage their cultural and political capital in their self-interested attempts to jockey for position. Since one of the main characters in the triangle is a man of the cloth, Clarín's realist novel is particularly effective in its demonstration of the priest's relevance to wider discourses of bourgeois masculinity that circulated in the fin-de-siècle cultural mainstream. In light of the previous overview of priests and laymen as adjacent and sometimes overlapping figures in the bourgeois mainstream, this section will reframe Fermín de Pas's embodiment of nineteenth-century discourses of masculinity by focusing on detailed descriptions of his rural origins, bodily comportment, and wardrobe, the meanings of which demonstrate that Roman

FIGURE 2.8. Detail of a page from a 1898 issue of the El Globo department store catalog. The store's offering for priest's headwear is included below the top hat in the center. Image courtesy of the Arxiu Històric de la Ciutat de Barcelona, Barcelona, Spain.

Catholic priests were widely viewed within bourgeois culture as masculine figures. A reconsideration of Fermín's nuanced embodiment of a clerical pattern of bourgeois masculinity based on the pursuit of authority, capital, and visibility will later help to shed light on the many ways literary critics and novelists articulated their own vicissitudinous professional trajectories with recourse to signs and symbols of the priesthood.

In its portrayal of Fermín de Pas's rural upbringing, *La Regenta* frames the priesthood as a modestly lucrative profession attracting young men from the provinces desiring to withdraw themselves from marginalizing socio-economic conditions. De Pas is spurred on by his mother, Paula Raíces, to study Latin and theology so that they might steer him away from the undesirable examples set forth by the brutishly depicted "cave bears" working in the coal mines of Matalerejo. Fermín and his mother come to regard entry to the Catholic ministry as a potential deliverance from abjection and a pipeline into a socially prestigious and respectable position within polite society. An education in the seminary, and a subsequent donning of the cassock, "the robe of the free man," would presumably "tear him away from the slavery to which he would be condemned together with all the wretches around him, if his efforts did not carry him to another, better life, a life worthy of his soaring ambition and of the instincts which were awaking in his spirit."[39] Doña Paula does not, however, want her son to end up like the ignorant, uneducated, and vulgar preachers of the provinces—"not just a run-of-the-mill parish priest" ("nada de misa y olla")—so often caricatured in illustrated satirical journals like José Nakens's *El Motín*.[40] While this idealistic fashioning of the cassock as a liberating talisman is not without some degree of irony—in Fermín's moments of self-deprecation and psychological torment, the narrator later likens the garment to chains—it is illustrative of the dynamic attitudes toward and values associated with the priesthood, both parochial and capitular. In Callahan's words: "The opportunity to secure an education in a world lacking decent rural schools and to enter an occupation endowed with modest social prestige made a clerical career seem attractive to a conservative peasantry."[41] For men from the working classes and their families, pastoral labor could signify augmented authority, social prestige, intellectual capital, financial comfort, and vocational stability.

Even before Fermín faces challenges stemming from his eventual infatuation with his confessant, the virtuous but vulnerable Ana Ozores, his dreams of advancement within the ecclesiastical hierarchy and his obsession with the concomitant symbols of power are metaphorically cast as masculine endeavors and feats. As a precocious youth, Fermín fantasizes about climbing the pyramidal hierarchy of the Church:

> Brilliant scenes, which ambition had painted in his imagination, were stored in his memory like recollections of some heroic poem read with enthusiasm as a youth. He had seen himself officiating in pontificals in Toledo, and at a conclave of cardinals in Rome: even the tiara itself had not seemed excessive.[42]

Young de Pas's masculine fantasy or "heroic poem" fashions him in the eyes of the reader as a religious warrior or spiritual conquistador of Vetusta's affluent neighborhoods, and an aspirant to the same in the newer and expanding districts: "he devoured his prey, churchly Vetusta, as a lion in a cage devours the miserable scraps of meat tossed to it by its keeper"; "La Encimada was Don Fermín's natural empire, the metropolis of the spiritual power which he exercised"; "a miniature Peru, of which he intends to be the spiritual Pizarro."[43] Though in Fermín's desire to "jockey for position within the local hierarchy," to borrow Valis's phrasing, he is hemmed in by his provincial surroundings, and the language through which his arduous pursuit is conveyed echoes earlier nineteenth-century tropes of the bellicose priest thought to participate in the Carlist Wars.[44]

The masculine coding of Fermín de Pas's clerical labor also bears a kindred resemblance to that of Pedro Polo in Galdós's *El Doctor Centeno* and *Tormento*. Even though his path to the priesthood is often thwarted by challenges and vocational indifference, it is the only logical option that will allow him and his family to escape a life of indebtedness and poverty in rural Extremadura. After finally being ordained with the help of his uncle and through his own ingenuity, Polo's newly acquired social and financial capital grants him purchasing power that facilitates his self-fashioning as a polished bourgeois subject and echoes the ambitions of other social climbers in nineteenth-century literature, such as Julien Sorel, the protagonist of Stendhal's *Le Rouge et le Noir*: "With regards to his cassock, Polo thought the following: 'A priest, you said? Well, go and get it. A professor, you said? Likewise. What a splendid age in which man receives his destiny premade and fitted as he would take the suit from the tailor's hands.'"[45] A native of Medellín, a rural town situated in the province of Badajoz, Pedro Polo y Cortés is drawn from the same stock as some conquistadors of the New World who also hailed from Extremadura, such as Hernán Cortés (Medellín) or Francisco Pizarro (Trujillo): "Don Pedro Polo y Cortés was from Medellín; as such, he had with the conquistador of Mexico the double connection of having the same last name and birthplace. Might they share some kinship?"[46] Indeed, this early connection with a belligerent temperament and physical violence, interwoven tightly with the image of the masculine conquistadors of Extremadura, is later echoed in his role as an aggressive disciplinarian and educator of children. Even though the priesthood is often chronicled as a demanding and restrictive vocation, it is represented in *La Regenta*, *El Doctor Centeno*, and *Tormento* as one that also secures some prestige and purchasing power for men with the strength and wherewithal to bear the burdens of an ancient institution and its rules.

Beyond the material conditions surrounding his taking of the robe, Fermín de Pas's style of dress is arguably the most evocative symbol of clerical masculinity in *La Regenta*. The garment for which he is sometimes emasculated in the novel—the cassock or soutane—is simultaneously that which

best exhibits the paradoxes inherent in the distinct modes of a clerical morphology of masculinity that flickers between liturgical pomp and monastic
asceticism, a binary that is also present in wider masculine ideals among the
bourgeoisie, as we saw in the introduction to this book. Narrative depictions of the cassock bring into focus an ecclesiastical formation of masculinity inflected by, on the one hand, an aesthetic of sartorial splendor and
spectacular, aristocratic self-display, and, on the other, an aesthetic of austerity, bodily restraint, and rigorous self-discipline.

The cassock was not always de rigueur for Spanish priests, who prior to
the late nineteenth century tended to dress in a sober version of laymen's
apparel.[47] Still in use today, from Oviedo to Madrid, the robe-like uniform
derives from clothing worn by medieval academicians and shows its influence in ceremonial regalia worn by university professors, a fact that further
marks the overlap of religious and lay models of bourgeois masculinity.[48]
Despite the fact that the cassock was not compulsory in Clarín's Spain, it
did become fashionable during the latter part of the nineteenth century,
due in large part to a deliberate return to liturgical ceremony encouraged
by Pope Pius IX's conservative modus operandi, which was established to
mark the unique status of the priest amidst a perceived rise in liberalism.[49]

The robe's popularity during the Restoration is echoed in *La Regenta*
by Fermín's occasional sartorial conundrums when presenting himself in
public:

> what clothes would he wear? He was finding his soutane heavier every day
> and his cloak more and more of a burden. The long shovel hat was odious,
> yet an excessively short one was affected, ridiculous, the sort of thing Don
> Custodio wore. With the sides turned up the shovel hat was old-fashioned,
> but if they were not turned up it was unworthy of a vicar-general. Wear
> a frock-coat? *Vade retro!* No, a priest in a frock-coat must be either a vil-
> lage priest or a liberal priest. The canon theologian seldom had recourse
> to such attire.[50]

Fermín de Pas's clerical pattern of masculinity first coalesces around
that portion of the ecclesiastical semiotic repertoire which denotes ostentatious self-display.

The initial portrait of Fermín as Magistral represents the focal point of
the lush "sketch of clerical life" of the novel's opening pages.[51] In the oft-
cited initial description of de Pas, the gaze of two young boys—Bismarck,
the bell-ringer, and Celedonio, the acolyte—defamiliarizes his sensuously

cloaked body. The plush fabrics of Fermín's outer cloak contrast starkly with the threadbare garments worn by the youths and encode Fermín as an omnipotent member of polite society:

> Can't you hear his cloak?' Bismarck was right. There was a hiss-hiss of cloth brushing against stone, like a soft voice demanding silence. Then the cloak was before them. It belonged to Don Fermin de Pas, the canon theologian of that holy cathedral church and the bishop's vicar-general. The post-boy shuddered, thinking, 'Has he come to belt us?'[52]

Fermín's clerical attire announces masculine disciplinary power as it swishes back and forth against the pavement. Upon hearing Fermín approach, Bismarck's affective defenses activate and he shivers while contemplating whether or not the Magistral has come to punish him for some misdeed.

Shortly after the reader's introduction to Fermín, *La Regenta*'s narrator catalogs priests among other masculine authorities in Vetusta, identifying a common thread of virility shared by gentlemen, mayors, priests, and night watchmen, at least when observed from the distant vantage point of a young boy of low socioeconomic standing: "If he were someone important, like a gentleman, a mayor, a canon, a plumber, a keeper of the botanical gardens, a box-office clerk, or a night-watchman, he would do exactly the same—kick everyone around! But he was just Bismarck, a postilion, and he knew his role in life: keeping out of the way of the nobs of Vetusta."[53] Though Bismarck's definition of social grandeur is accompanied by a dose of irony—it conflates priests with plumbers—it clearly inserts men of the cloth into a social category of masculine authority and power coterminous with the status of being a man. As Todd Reeser asserts, masculinity and its values are relational and situational, and even in a society where anticlericalism was on the rise, in a novel in which clerical corruption is rampant, points of view vis-à-vis the priesthood could range from ambivalence to admiration to anathema: "[a] boy at church might perceive one construct [of masculinity] in his minister, another in the Old Testament, another in the figure of Christ, and yet others in the actual men of his congregation."[54] As Vetusta's preeminent cleric, Fermín represents one of many models of masculinity available to the young boys.

Thrown into relief by the inchoate masculine subjects in his presence, Fermín's magnificence and grandeur are amplified by the richly described garments that adorn his body. Through Celedonio's ebullient internal monologue, Fermín is charged with an almost supernatural aura when cloaked in his clerical everyday wear:

> Down in the Calle de la Rúa Don Fermín had looked like a beetle, but now how huge he appeared to the altar-boy's lowered eyes and to the terrified eyes of his companion! Celedonio was waist-high to the canon. He saw before him a spotless soutane, with true, symmetrical, sculptural creases— an autumn soutane, of the best fine flannel—and flowing over it a volu-minous silken cloak, with numerous folds and flares. Bismarck, behind Wamba, could see no more of the canon than his lower legs, and was admir-ing them. This was real class! Not one stain! The feet were like a lady's; the hose was purple, like a bishop's; and each shoe was a work of painstak-ing craftsmanship in the finest leather, displaying a simple yet elegant sil-ver buckle which looked very splendid against the color of the stocking.[55]

Through this "luxury of words," Fermín's power is invested in him by the signs of his office.[56] Fermín de Pas's sartorial physiognomy recalls Fran-cisco Navarro Villoslada's mid-century satirical sketch of the "canónigo" or cathedral canon.[57] A "mobile wardrobe," the canon is depicted as a clothed monolith whose gargantuan male body is enveloped in rich and endless lengths and types of fabric, effectively reifying him according to the heav-ily codified sartorial paradigms of the Catholic clergy. Navarro Villoslada echoes trends in modern fashion marketing that attempt to excite a consum-er's desire for a garment made of high quality fabrics of noble provenance: "a cloth jacket with lapels, lined with wool," "wool or silk stockings," "shoes lined with rabbit fur."[58] The corpulence of the priest and the associ-ation of his size with that of the biblical giant Goliath are all reinforced by the cartoon that accompanies the sketch, depicting a proud and smug man who joyfully advertises the power invested in him by the signs of his office.

While Clarín's version of the stylish canon contains superficial allusions to the stereotypical femininity thought to reside in clerical dress, it is just as communicative of a noble or otherworldly masculinity. Almost in the same breath, the Magistral's clerical persona is enhanced by aristocratic pol-ish, patrician femininity, and episcopal power and sartorial splendor. Fur-thermore, Fermín's donning of episcopal purple and silver shoe buckles— sartorial details officially controlled by and reserved for bishops—is illustra-tive of his dominion over Vetusta's humble and saintly prelate, Fortunato Camoirán.[59] Though at times marginalized or subordinated by men in other spheres, Fermín's expertise and hegemony in ecclesiastical matters should not be taken lightly, especially when thrown into relief by the provincial background from which he springs. Additionally, as Andrés Zamora has argued, it is in this passage that Fermín—perched atop the cathedral tower high above Vetusta with his spyglass—functions as a symbol of the virile authority of the novel's omniscient narrator.[60]

By bringing the priesthood out of its familiar context—one bedecked with masculine authority and social prestige—the text stages only a momentary challenge to the priest that in no way nullifies the masculine potential of clerical identity displayed elsewhere in the novel, here sustained by the boy's marveling. As we saw earlier, boyish admiration for the priesthood as a noble or powerful model of masculinity is a recurring topos in nineteenth-century Spain. In *El Doctor Centeno*, to provide yet another example, the social climber Felipe Centeno's profound enchantment with the wealth of the Church, of which Pedro Polo forms an integral part, shapes the way the priest is perceived and admired by the young page. Indeed, Felipe's innocent admiration for Polo foreshadows that of Bismarck and Celedonio for Fermín de Pas: "He looked at Polo like a chosen one or eminence, an instrument of Providence, grand and terrific like that Moses who had such an appealing role in the scripture."[61] While such attitudes toward the priesthood are never devoid of implicit or explicit critique they demonstrate, in a subtle manner, the appeal of and "numinous" aura surrounding Catholic priests and their sartorial world, particularly from the perspective of young boys not yet indoctrinated by anticlerical ideologies.[62] Furthermore, it is worth remembering that a priest could connote masculinity and be seen as ironic or worthy of parody for others at the same time. In the nineteenth-century Spanish cultural imagination, priesthood and priestly masculinity occupied a gray area—common to the realist novel in general—altogether distinct from more clear-cut depictions circulating within the realm of the anticlerical cultural industry symbolized by *El Motín* or decadent-naturalist novels like López Bago's *El cura* (The priest).

Fermín's aristocratic and showy habitus is made further apparent when he is seen flaunting his image amid the aisles and halls of the cathedral or commanding the attention of the congregation at the altar and pulpit. Later in the novel's first chapter, he is seen strutting through the cathedral like a peacock with the ample folds of his cassock billowing around him: "The canon's cloak swung to the rhythm of his smooth swaying gait, and as it floated over the floor its voluminous folds took on the iridescent hues of a pheasant's feathers, at times even looking like a peacock's tail."[63] Fermín's crisp cassock metamorphoses in this passage, allowing him to broadcast his presumable dominance over the other men in the cathedral, including Don Cayetano, for whom Fermín "is the only outstanding man in the cathedral," as well as "a scholar, an orator, a politician, a man of letters, and, most important of all, Ripamilán believed, a man of the world."[64]

Given his investiture as a high-ranking cleric within Vetusta's cathedral, Fermín de Pas is constantly scrutinized by the novel's voyeuristic narrator and other characters. A pompous dandy in public, Fermín maintains an impeccable sartorial veneer that not only conveys the power he portends to wield in the provincial capital, but also is evocative of the ancient institution of the Catholic Church, in which male religious dress originated and evolved. Historically, religious men have projected their power by wearing "expensive fabrics such as silk, furs such as ermine and, in some centuries, precious gems, all in stark contrast to Christianity's humble beginnings. Such wealth of garments, however, has graced the male body uniquely, articulating not only rank but also male focus and power."[65] What makes Fermín such a formidable and contentious character is the fact that, unlike *Notre-Dame de Paris*'s Claude Frollo, whose shadow looms large over Victor Hugo's fantasy of medieval Paris, "*Alas* adheres to the present. The past, however, consistently intrudes as a subtle and sometimes not so subtle reminder of what was once the splendor of imperial Spain. The cathedral tower functions in this manner, and yet at the same time it is not a dead vestige of another century; it is the symbol of a still potent force within Spanish society."[66]

Fermín cuts a sharp figure in Vetusta, and Ana Ozores's friend Obdulia Fandiño finds him attractive in his lacy surplice (*roquete* or *sobrepelliz*) and mozzetta (*muceta*), a short cape, medieval in origin, that covers the shoulders and is usually clasped over the chest. The narcissistic Fermín also fancies himself in the pageantry of these liturgical vestments while on display at the pulpit:

> How often, standing in the pulpit, wearing a lordly mozzetta and under it a crimped white rochet which followed the lines of his strong yet graceful body, and seeing admiration and delight on the faces of the faithful below him, had he been forced to still his soaring eloquence, choking and speechless from the sheer joy of it all! [. . .] And in that expectant, attentive, enraptured hush he had well understood the speechless admiration which he savored, as it rose to him, sure that the thoughts of the faithful were for the elegant, well-graced preacher, melodious of voice and distinguished in manner, not for the God about whom he was speaking.[67]

Fermín's liturgical vestments and his affective response or sensorial perception within his ecclesial surroundings condition his experience of the sermon and enhance how he envisions himself reflected in an apparently expectant and enchanted congregation. Overtaken by the voluptuous pleasure provoked by the image of his svelte figure clad in his impeccable surplice and seigniorial mozzetta, Fermín enacts the sartorial performativity and pleasure that persists in spite of the rigid confines of ecclesiastical dress. While Fermín's ecclesiastical garments are sometimes anathema to his transgressive desires, the priest's delight in the sartorial signs that project his power in Vetusta are illustrative of the fact that his clerical masculinity is in part tethered to Ancien Régime patterns of masculinity based on outwardly legible signs and symbols of nobility, social prestige, and wealth.[68]

All of these icons of power shimmer around Fermín and contribute to the foreboding character he wields over Ana and others in Vetusta. According to Patrizia Calefato, "The officiator of a cult who dons a religious vestment is at this boundary [between the human and the divine], and it is his/her clothed body that sanctions such a spatial-social collocation."[69] A kind of magical, religious allure is common in descriptions of the influence Fermín has over several Vetustans. In the home of the Carraspique family, he is virtually the embodiment of the ecclesiastical infallibility he so passionately defends in chapter eleven: "Doña Lucía [. . .] confessed with the canon theologian, who was the infallible pontiff in their honorable home."[70] Similarly, the ineffable or otherworldly aura emanating from his interactions with Ana Ozores risks dissolving should his bodily temptations overcome his masculine restraint and vigor: "He was certain that the slightest hint of the flesh, intrusive and fearsome, would anger and repel the judge's wife; and then he would lose the almost supernatural prestige which he enjoyed in her eyes."[71]

Fermín's attachments to a restored Church are also manifest in passages in which he is shown imagining himself in the sartorial finery of those of a higher rank. In the novel's first volume, he reports having seriously entertained the idea of pursuing a bishopric or the papacy. Once again, Fermín's relationship with his clerical robes and accouterments demonstrates his embrace of the power visibly invested in him and the importance of this sartorial maneuver for further advancement. In chapter eleven, he unconsciously doodles while reciting a passage concerning papal infallibility, which had been declared dogma by Pius IX in 1870: "'Would the conquest of this lady's soul not be of more value than the battle for a bishop's miter, a cardinal's hat, even the tiara itself?' The canon theologian found that he was drawing a tiara in the margin of the paper."[72] A very similar passage can be found in the pages of Eça de Queiroz's *O crime do padre amaro*. Here the emotionally charged titular protagonist of that novel, similarly provoked by jealousy for his secular rival, João Eduardo, imagines himself marching down the aisles of the church in the trappings of an ecclesiastical prelate of the Ancien Régime, thus further corroborating the slippage between priestliness and erstwhile grandeur in the late nineteenth-century Iberian cultural imagination: "He was a God inside the Cathedral, but he had only to go out into the square and he was a mere obscure plebeian. [. . .] He wanted clerks and Amélias to tremble at the mere shadow cast by his cassock. He would have liked to have been a priest in the old Church."[73]

If on the one hand Fermín's clerical dress is emblematic of an Old Regime "desire to be seen," elsewhere in the novel it glosses other masculine-coded values and virtues including austerity, self-control, and bodily restraint.[74] In nineteenth-century Europe, it was common for artists and novelists alike to use the celibate priest or monk to explore fantasies of "an ascetic regimen" of masculinity, or "an elaborately articulated program of self-discipline," illustrating time and again that there was more to masculinity than a frock coat or an active and overt sexuality.[75] Such regimes were altogether different from the way feminine self-abnegation tended to be depicted in nineteenth-century cultural products. On the one hand, "masculine self-discipline, [was] represented as an ongoing regimen of aggressive self-mastery," in contrast to the stereotype of "feminine self-denial, which [was] represented as a spontaneous and essentially static surrender of the will to external authority."[76] Descriptions of Fermín's cassock illustrate how clerical sartorial aesthetics have the potential to operate as a capacious metaphor for discourses of masculinity that encouraged self-restraint and careful self-display, for example.

While the earliest portrait of Fermín's clerical morphology of masculinity in *La Regenta* is mobilized by the aristocratic veneer he affects in public, his behavior in private veers toward simplicity, and thus evidences the showiness and spectacle inherent in the priest's supposed renunciation of ostentatious self-display:[77]

Don Fermín was writing by the thin white light of the dawn. It was a cool morning and from time to time he took a rest, blowing his fingers and thinking. His feet were wrapped in one of his mother's old shawls and on his head was a threadbare black velvet cap. His cassock, embroidered with darns, was going brown with age, and the sleeves of the jacket which he wore under it shone with the sad sheen of worn cloth. These squalid clothes, such a contrast to the neatness, elegance and splendor which the canon displayed to the world, disappeared as soon as his work was done and the hour approached when visits were likely.[78]

In clear imitation of a monastic cell and behavioral regimen, Clarín's narrator spins a web of stringent austerity around Fermín that stands in stark contrast to the seigniorial Church official who inspires awe and dread in those who dare rub elbows with him in the streets of Vetusta. In the privacy of his home, this ascetic image glosses medieval scribes adorned only with humility, and contrasts with the more polished version he shows off during official visits and while in the cathedral: "Then he would don a fine, flowing robe, comfortable, brand-new and well-cut, and hide his selvage carpet-slippers and his grimy cap in a corner of his bedroom; and the shoes so admired by Bismarck, the postilion, and a skull-cap which glowed like a black sun would cover either end of this important personage."[79] Of course, the image of the ascetic priest scrawling notes in his cell makes possible yet another comparison between the cleric and the professional literary critic/novelist, united as they were by the solitary act of writing to which representatives of both vocations subscribed. San Quintín, Galdós's summer home and retreat in Santander, was also seen by the Canarian novelist's peers or "disciples" as a pseudo-religious space where the novelist was known to have written many of his works.[80] Although it does not include a reference to the writer's apparel, an account by José María Quintanilla (penname "Pedro Sánchez") corroborates the private solemnity of the space when describing a visit to Galdós's palatial estate: "we entered a small salon that appears to satisfy the function of a sacristy in that temple."[81]

In chapter eleven of *La Regenta*, a narcissistic Fermín stares at the image he casts in the mirror of his toilette, which recalls for the reader his use of the sermon's audience as another kind of mirror for his own self-congratulatory voyeurism. Here, the narrator invites the reader to peek into the priest's private quarters. With his cassock lowered to his waist, de Pas's brawny musculature is on display as the reader imagines the physical results of the priest's provincial formation in the Asturian countryside:

He was naked from the waist up. His powerful neck seemed even more powerful now, because of the strain put upon it by his tensed position as he leaned over the white marble wash-basin. His arms, like his broad, powerful chest, were covered with fine black curly hair, they were the arms of an athlete. The canon looked sadly at his muscles of steel, charged with useless power. His complexion was pale and delicate, the slightest emotion tinging it rose-color. On the advice of Don Robustiano, the doctor, De Pas exercised with heavy weights; he was a Hercules. [. . .] As Don Fermín washed, he recalled his prowess at skittles, back in his home village, where he had always made the most of the opportunities offered by holidays from the seminary to go half savage, running through rocky scrub in the high hills. The brawny, hairy young fellow before him in the mirror somehow seemed like a lost *alter ego* which had stayed behind in those hills—naked, as hairy as the King of Babylon, yet free, happy. He was alarmed by this sight, which carried his thoughts far away, and he dressed hurriedly. As soon as the canon had buttoned up his collar he was once again the image of Christian meekness, strong yet spiritual and humble, still well-built, of course, but no longer formidable.[82]

This hyper-masculine physique—a "voluptuous subject" caught in a moment of tension between dress and undress—is made manifest in spite of itself.[83] A physically robust male body is presumably of little value to the administrative and ministerial life of the Roman Catholic priest. Whereas his cassock seemingly represents the power invested in him as an authority figure among polite society in Vetusta, his bodily attributes—a broad chest and muscular arms—make him a modern-day Hercules. But when he covers up the muscles cultivated by sport and heavy weightlifting, Fermín is satisfied with the way his body is stored and tucked away under the sculptural folds of his cassock: "It was good to know that there was a strong body hidden beneath his epicene cloak and his flowing, sculptural cassock."[84]

The trope of the priest as a site for testing the boundaries of masculine self-display and bodily control is a common one across nineteenth-century Europe. Scholars have identified a similar dynamic, for example, in Thomas Carlyle's Abbot Samson in the 1843 novel *Past and Present*. In that work, Herbert Sussman argues, "it is the very power of Samson's male desire that makes his celibacy heroic, that makes the achievement of control a noble struggle."[85] While Carlyle's cleric pertains to a distant medieval past, his "noble struggle," to borrow Sussman's phrasing, offers an efficacious point of comparison with Clarín's and Galdós's modern priests. While the cracks in Fermín's celibate armor are exposed in the novel through implied trysts with the maids in his household, Teresa and Petra, his clerical persona is surrounded by a masculine rhetoric of struggle and self-control. Such a notion is altogether different from dominant discourses of Victorian-era femininity (e.g., Coventry Patmore's "angel of the hearth"), which perpetuated passive fantasies of self-erasure and abnegation and stand in contrast to the active struggles supposedly faced by the Catholic ministers.

After learning about Ana's fainting spell into the open arms of Álvaro Mesía, Fermín's tightly harnessed strength explodes from beneath his cassock, unleashing a superhuman blow: "The canon shook inside his soutane, as if he were bound by chains, and struck the sofa a herculean blow with his fist."[86] Though the soutane weights on him like a prisoner's chains, the garment's binding quality fortifies the Magistral's virility; it symbolizes masculine potential kept in check. This controlling function of the cassock is yet again on display when Fermín trudges through the woods with Víctor Quintanar in an effort to catch Ana and Álvaro in flagrante delicto. Here, the garment's restrictive, disciplinary mode becomes immediately apparent:

What was holding him back? The whole world. Twenty centuries of religion, millions of blind, indolent spirits who, since it did not affect them, could not see the absurdity of it all—calling it grandeur, abnegation, virtue when it was torture, unjust, barbarous, foolish, and above all cruel, cruel. Hundreds of popes, dozens of councils, thousands of towns, millions of stones in cathedrals and crosses and convents—all history, all civilization, a world of lead, were pressing down on him, on his arms, on his legs, they were his shackles.[87]

His robes, aptly alluded to as shackles, symbolize centuries of Church history brought to bear on his body. This scene coalesces around Fermín's soutane as a potent metaphor for masculine hardship and struggles.

Around the novel's denouement, Fermín—promoting himself to the role of judge and juror—is momentarily seduced by the appeal of his old hunting uniform when he considers what he may do to punish Álvaro and Ana. According to Fermín's inner monologue, which harks back to his self-contemplation in front of the mirror in chapter eleven, he contrasts the "man" he sees before him with the priestly garb he has just removed. Staring at his reflection, Fermín is temporarily satisfied in his affirmation that "there stood a man."[88] However, deeming this sartorial option ridiculous— or "foolish notions from novels"—he returns those items to the closet and summons once more the solemn, black image of the Magistral: "Don Fermín took off his brown hunting-jacket, removed his broad-brimmed hat, unbuckled his black belt, put clothes and knife away in the wardrobe, and donned his soutane and his cloak, as if they were a suit of armor. 'Yes, that was his coat of mail—that was his fighting equipment."[89] Re-envisioned as chain mail, perhaps glossing the image of an armored knight, Fermín's cassock once more serves as a cipher for his clerical disciplinary code.

The Priestly Literary Critic

As this chapter has shown, *La Regenta*'s multilayered and at times contradictory representation of Fermín de Pas's clerical masculinity—frequently expressed through the fictional priest's bodily deportment, wardrobe, and interactions with other masculine figures in Vetusta—is illustrative of competing discourses of bourgeois manhood circulating in the cultural mainstream during the fin de siècle in Spain. A question that remains, however, is why the material realm of the priest continued to give shape to the ideas middle-class male writers, including liberal-minded individuals like Clarín, had about their role within Spanish and international literary ecosystems at a time when they themselves were increasingly critical of the Catholic Church's personnel. As this section will demonstrate, nineteenth-century critics and novelists avowed themselves of hieratic metaphors in ways that shed light on middle-class men's anxieties about their cultural capital, professionalization, and authority as arbiters of art and literature.

Literary critics and novelists like Clarín, along with some of his most respected contemporaries like Emilio Castelar, Benito Pérez Galdós, and Josep Yxart at times envisioned a writerly profession as a vocation akin to that of the priest in a variety of symbolic registers ranging from the classical (pagan) to the Roman Catholic. As Valis importantly reminds her readers, scholars must consider nineteenth-century liberal writers' engagement with Catholic aesthetics "not simply as disabling but also as enabling, historically and imaginatively."[90] Even though comparisons between literary critics and clerics sometimes contain a layer of irony, Spanish writers' use of priestly or liturgical metaphors to ideate and make sense of their own identities and situatedness as bourgeois men and professionals demonstrates the priest's place as one of Spanish modernity's enduring masculine figures. To further illuminate how nineteenth-century intellectuals relied on priestly aesthetics in generative ways, this concluding section will show that the priest was often imagined as a figure whose androcentric spaces and uneven power and prestige in an era of competing ideological visions made him an effective symbol for homosocial communities of male writers who struggled to convince even themselves of their authority as professional readers of (and contributors to) Spanish and pan-European literary canons, their marketability within national and international literary ecosystems, and their ability to capitalize on such pursuits as breadwinners for their families.

The literary critic and the priest shared many affinities during the late nineteenth century, since both took part in cultivating or influencing their readership by transmitting their own interpretations of culturally significant texts amidst shifting ideological currents. For staunchly antiliberal priests like Claret this did not only involve a robust publishing campaign that sought to combat the spread of liberalism while imparting biblical teachings in line with the Vatican, but it also involved, as we saw earlier, the education of seminarians and recently ordained priests, who would presumably extend the Church's pedagogical mission in their own writings and teachings.[91] Though the goal of cultural and literary criticism was not a perfect analogy for those underlying the propagandistic aims of Church leaders like Claret—since critics were only unified symbolically within the literary confraternity or "gentlemen's paradise" sustained by shared affective attachments, epistolary correspondence, editorial collaborations, and academic institutions—literary criticism similarly sought to educate the public while also shedding light on Spain's role in establishing nineteenth-century literary canons and markets. As Sergio Beser asserts, criticism was a "literary genre that, together with the novel, represents the contribution of greatest importance and quality [of the Restoration period] to national literature, and signals the replacement of a conceptualization of literary art as a distraction, entertainment or evasion by one of literary art as a way to enrich and shape man."[92] The rebranding of literary criticism coincided with the idea that the critic himself required a serious pedagogical formation, and figures like Yxart increasingly alluded to the need for "one [. . .] to prepare himself appropriately, since criticism required a solid education in the discipline of aesthetics, as well as theory and literary history."[93] In his acceptance speech to the Spanish Royal Academy in 1897, Galdós's own self-professed (if exaggerated) deficiencies in such principles led him to use liturgically inflected metaphors when stating that he dared not "place [his] profane hands upon the sacred treasury of erudition and critical and bibliographical knowledge" by elaborating on a theory of the novel.[94] Instead, as he articulates, he wished to defer to his respondent, Marcelino Menéndez y Pelayo, his friend and one of nineteenth-century Spain's most visible (and traditionalist) literary critics, in taking on that hieratic role.

The affinities allowing comparisons between the priest and the literary critic took on particular significance in the example of Leopoldo Alas

"Clarín." Autobiographical anecdotes compiled by one of Clarín's biographers demonstrate the author's attention to comparisons between his and his peers' professional lives and those of the priest, particularly as a mode of ironic self-fashioning. While reflecting on his years studying in Madrid, for example, he once wrote that "at the same time that the cathedral's canons were headed to the chancel to take their naps," he attended lectures in political philosophy.[95] As a student of philosophy, he later cites being a more devout Catholic than the Pope, despite his waxing Voltairianism, shorthand for disdain of corrupt priests and sacristans whose own religiosity was, for Alas, questionable. Clarín also used ecclesiastical imagery to poke fun at his conservative peers, such as Menéndez y Pelayo who, according to the Asturian, dressed like a clumsy seminarian with his undergarments untied and who was a "precocious Torquemada-type," or, in other words, an "incendiary inquisitor."[96] However, as both Lissorgues and Valis have historicized, Clarín's Catholicism was not reducible to the kind of anticlericalism found in other authors—like López Bago and Sawa—a fact that provides helpful context for this chapter's and, as we will see later, the author's own multifaceted use of ecclesiastical imagery as a way to figure the critic's professional discontents.

Alas's anxieties about his dual role as literary critic-novelist and university professor are reflective of wider tensions about the Church's controversial and vicissitudinous control of state-sponsored education in nineteenth-century Spain. At the same time that Clarín continued his studies to eventually achieve an academic role as a university professor, which involved researching, writing about, and teaching Roman and Canon law, he also became one of nineteenth-century Spain's sharpest and most vocal critics, a reality enshrined in his penname "Clarín" (the bugle or clarion). On one notable occasion, for example, Alas entered into a public-facing dispute—recorded for posterity in local Asturian newspaper *El Carbayón*—with Oviedo bishop Ramón Martínez Vigil. The prelate accused the author of *La Regenta* of corrupting his law students by regaling them with free copies of his then recently published novel. Even though Clarín made no such offer and cited the exorbitant expense such a gift would entail, the accusation was probably believed by reactionary readers who incorrectly imagined liberal professors to be rabid anticlericals. Despite the fact that *La Regenta* was controversial in some conservative circles for its scandalous depiction of corrupt clergymen, even Carlist professors at the university came to their liberal colleague's defense.[97] The conflict between a professor from the University of Oviedo and the bishop of Oviedo bore some unspoken irony, since the symbols of the ecclesiastical hierarchy mapped onto those of the university, where a professor's chair (i.e., professorship)—including Clarín's—used the same language originally designated for the diocesan seat of a bishop (*cátedra*), a concept tracing its origins to the Church's earliest days in Roman antiquity.

His well-known scorn for and disputes with some priests notwithstanding, Leopoldo Alas was also cognizant of the rich metaphorical potential of the priesthood, which he and his peers sometimes used as a metaphor for manhood and a career in literary criticism. In an article reviewing Galdós's 1884 novel *Tormento*—included as part of the 1885 compilation of previously published critical essays suggestively titled "Lost Sermon" (*Sermón perdido*)—Clarín recounts an anecdote in which a skeptical priest comments on unrealistic literary representations of clerical figures:

> Not long ago an illustrious priest told me the following: 'The priests written about by novelists are almost always fakes: nothing like what writers concoct really happens beneath the cassock: the Jocelins are as real as Eurico, Claude Frollo, father Manrique, the abbot Faujas, monsignor Bienvenido, and the Champfleur clerics, each one as false as the next: we priests, for better or worse, are of a different stock.'[98]

The anecdotal man of the cloth establishes an antithesis between literary representations of priests and their real-life counterparts, asserting that the behavior and instincts of priests categorically deviate from those of laymen and clerical figures depicted in novels. Dissenting from his rhetorical interlocutor, Clarín commends the realist brush with which the priest Pedro Polo y Cortés, a prominent character in Benito Pérez Galdós's *El Doctor Centeno* (1883) and *Tormento*, is characterized: "Dare I say that I see in *Tormento*'s Polo a very probable priest, sketched with great prudence and a vigor we have not come to expect of our authors . . . He is no more or less than a flesh-and-blood man of the few of which modern Spanish literature has to speak."[99] Of course, Clarín's own evaluation of the priesthood as aestheticized by his most esteemed peer takes on added significance in the context of a collection of essays titled "Lost Sermon," in which the Asturian writer imagines the Spanish literary critic's fraught existence as similar to that of a preacher in the desert: "I have come to understand that all advocacy for good taste and any other of art's precepts is something akin to preaching in the desert, and that is if one preaches such things in Spain at all."[100] Here as elsewhere, as we shall see, the struggles of male religious figures—whether parish priests or hermitic wanderers—are envisioned by the writer as symbolic of wider anxieties facing men in other professions, like literary criticism and novel-writing, in ways that far exceed the exigencies of an anticlerical ideologue with an axe to grind.

Aside from his prologue to *Sermón Perdido*, another example of Clarín's vision of the literary profession's adjacency to the priesthood, and its relationship to modern masculinity, comes in the form of a lengthy introduction he wrote for a Spanish translation of Scottish writer Thomas Carlyle's *On Heroes, Hero-Worship, and the Heroic in History*. The book was translated to Spanish by Julián G. Orbón as *Los héroes* in 1893 and includes Clarín's two-part introduction, which follows a preface by Emilio Castelar, the short-lived president of Spain during the six-year revolutionary period, and one of Clarín's favorite professors during his time as a student at the Central University of Madrid. In his preface, Castelar explicitly identifies in Carlyle's androcentric tribute to heroism in the West a kind of priesthood when he envisions the author's devotion to the realm of the ideal as that of a (pagan) priest "lifting the victim crowned in flowers atop the marble pedestal, beneath the vaulted temple full of incense and music," or that of the "austere puritan who has imbibed his ideas from the churches of Scotland and applied the Gospel as if it were a political code."[101] Aside from comparisons that juxtapose reading Carlyle's treatise on heroism to the exercise of biblical exegesis, Alas's conclusion ends with a direct comparison of the Scottish author to a Christ figure and founder of the Church.[102] For Clarín, the comparison is not meant as sacrilege, but rather as a kind of sacralization of the writer (Carlyle), and the many historical men he consecrates with heroic status.

For his part, Benito Pérez Galdós echoed his Asturian friend and peer when evaluating the manliness of the latter's response to Polo in the figure of *La Regenta*'s Fermín de Pas. In his prologue to the second edition of Clarín's aforementioned novel—widely considered his masterpiece—Galdós describes Fermín de Pas as "the culminating figure of his work," a "great, complex character, so human for his physical merits, as well as for his moral weaknesses, which are no triviality, a block torn from reality," and later recognizes in him an "an athlete struggling to bear upon his shoulders the exorbitant and overwhelming weight of the world."[103] Galdós reimagines Fermín as an athlete or titan (e.g., Atlas) struggling with the overwhelming weight of his vocation on his shoulders. As each author surveyed the physiognomy of the other's literary priest, both Clarín and Galdós artfully infused their readings with evocative images of a definitively masculine gender expression proceeding from the priesthood and its accompanying challenges. Clarín's and Galdós's analogies of the Catholic priesthood with wider or universal masculine struggles and symbols resist stereotypes that pigeonhole clergymen as the anachronistic stewards of an emasculated gender or as "actual or potential libertines," reflective only of deviance and authorial anticlericalism.[104]

Of course, Clarín, Castelar, and Galdós were not the only male, liberal writers whose musings about "clerical" careers (e.g., professor, literary critic, and novelist) incorporated metaphors and symbols of the priesthood in their styling as intellectuals. Catalan writer Josep Yxart, for example, was often quite explicit in fashioning the professional devotion to art and letters as priestly in his autobiographical writings, epistolary correspondence, and literary criticism. In his unpublished memoir discussed in the introduction to this book, Yxart frequently frames a literary career as a religious calling. For example, throughout his unfinished and posthumously published memoirs he refers to a literary career as a religious calling or vocation relying on the total absorption of aesthetic "doctrines."[105] Elsewhere, he compares the followers of literary schools—such as naturalism—to disciples within a sect, fashioning Émile Zola as that movement's high priest ("hierofante").[106] Yxart also alludes to the obsession with aesthetics itself as a "cult of art and letters" with its concomitant doctrines and dogmas.[107] Viewed in the aggregate, the deployment of such imagery further corroborates Toni Dorca's recent comparison of Yxart's view of a career in literature as a "sacerdoci" (priesthood), a term Yxart himself uses to characterize his cousin Narcís Oller's devotion to his law career.[108] Recalling the image of the austerely-dressed Fermín de Pas in the confines of his private study, Yxart also alludes to his own "exile" from his close friend Oller as resulting in a return to his "cell" (*celda*), a term that in the 1817 and 1884 dictionaries of the Spanish Royal Academy prioritized its meaning as the room in a monastery or convent for use by male or female religious members.

The metaphorical coding of the literary profession and its agents as clerical or liturgical is heightened by the fact that the professional and social circles within which these writers rubbed elbows—dependent as they were on male homosocial spaces from the atheneum, university, and Spanish Royal Academy to more informal social venues like casinos, meeting halls, and taverns—were homosocial by design, not unlike the confraternities, sacristies, and seminaries attended by men of the cloth. Narcís Oller's *La febre d'or* emphasizes this connection when he compares the architecture and activity of the Barcelona stock exchange, which had become a veritable temple for the agents of an increasingly capitalistic and speculative economy, to Protestant and Catholic churches. Clarín's own *La Regenta* draws similar comparisons: aside from obvious parallels between Fermín and casino president Álvaro Mesía, the casino is located within close proximity to the cathedral, and the novel's narrator describes the youths who entered into some areas of that homosocial space as "young priests of some strange cult."

On the one hand, male critics' expertise on and fluency in cultural and literary matters gave them a great deal of visibility from important, predominantly homosocial pulpits like the atheneum and literary magazines like *Arte y Letras* (Art and letters). On the other, and given nineteenth-century Spain's low literacy rates relative to those of neighboring European nations, they were constantly under the impression that they were fighting an unwinnable, uphill battle in their attempts to rejuvenate, professionalize, and preach on behalf of the Spanish literary industry. Even as the beliefs of liberals like Clarín and Yxart straddled anticlerical and skeptical attitudes vis-à-vis Roman Catholic doctrine and the personnel who created and disseminated it, as this section has shown, they often professed their own devotion to aesthetics and serious literary criticism via clerical and liturgical semantic fields, thus revealing the many meaningful parallels between priestly figures and the professional writer.

Conclusion

As this chapter has shown, literary and visual signage related to the Roman Catholic priesthood was multifaceted and evocative of (sometimes contradictory) patterns of bourgeois masculinity during the fin de siècle. While casting the cassock or other priestly apparel in a patently negative light was commonplace as an anticlerical rhetorical maneuver, it simultaneously encodes the priesthood not only as a force that emasculates or feminizes, but one that glosses and tests the limits of nineteenth-century discourses and ideals of masculinity emphasizing bodily control and restraint. Furthermore, readings of the cassock as an exclusive symbol of emasculating oppression overlook its register of other masculine paradigms: disciplinarian, nobleman, consumer, socialite. Though Fermín's uniform is often characterized as chains that weigh him down, particularly in the novel's second volume, his clerical masculinity is at least partially, if not predominantly, constituted by his resistance against temptation or, to again echo Sussman, by his "noble struggle." The policing force of the cassock works toward subduing unrestrained male vital energies and, stretched to a breaking point, maintaining and repressing them in what amounts to a volatile bodily economy of constant battles or struggles with historical and sociocultural pressures.

A celibate priest may deviate from the hegemonic middle-class standard of masculinity crystallized in the pages of conduct literature and nineteenth-century novels. However, this should not disqualify him from conversations about masculinity, particularly since nineteenth-century perceptions of masculine ideals diverge from our own. Despite a pervasive rhetoric of anticlericalism in Restoration Spain, there exists an emphatically masculine coding in some cultural representations of clerical figures. Frequent references to clerical bodies and ecclesiastical modes of dress made throughout *La Regenta* and other novels clearly position "men of the cloth" as archetypal tropes governing modern fictions of masculinity writ large. Especially for Spanish authors like Clarín and Galdós, the Catholic priest had an essential and ongoing role to play in lending contour to the shapes of middle-class masculinity and manliness. As the following chapter will show, the symbolic weight of the Catholic priest was also relevant to the world of finance, perhaps unsurprisingly given the fact that economic speculation—part of a capitalistic cosmovision or belief system increasingly separated from the material realm—relied on a different kind of brahmin capable of navigating the booms and busts of the market.

CHAPTER 3

THE BUSINESSMAN

As Narcís Oller's monumental novel *La febre d'or* (Gold fever) attests, the Spanish economy experienced a boom in speculative financial activity between 1876 and 1886. With the backing of foreign and domestic investors, new companies sought to modernize urban centers from Madrid and Bilbao to Valencia and Barcelona in the style of cosmopolitan capitals like London and Paris. In Barcelona as elsewhere in Europe's expanding metropolitan areas, the buying and selling of stocks and bonds had become common ways for Spanish and Catalan businessmen and foreign and domestic investors alike to capitalize on "the thrust of newly founded companies [which] was measured in the stock trade," both to enrich themselves and in an effort to grow national and regional economies.[1]

Then, as now, the purchase of stock denoted an investor's faith in a company's ability or potential to multiply the wealth of shareholders. Bonds, another common form of investment, are debts that government entities or corporations took on in order to raise money during times of war or to fund ambitious domestic projects; the loan of capital, once matured, yielded returns for bondholders in the form of interest payments. Amid fluctuations in gains and losses, nineteenth-century investors bought stock as a vote of confidence in the futures of companies like La Compañía de Ferrocarriles de Madrid (1855; Madrid Railway Company), and municipal bonds were sold to bankroll events such as the Universal Exposition of

1888, a culminating moment for the rebirth or Renaixença of Catalan culture, language, and regional identity that symbolically catapulted Barcelona from provincial capital to European metropolis.² Since new railway companies and municipal expansion projects were often backed without guaranteed returns—imprudent or overly optimistic investment in underutilized rail lines, for example, was a common cause for bankruptcy in nineteenth-century Spain—they were, by nature, speculative enterprises.³ Slight differences between stocks and bonds notwithstanding, stockholders and bond investors share in common their belief and trust in a market economy, a system of representation and values in which infusions of capital will lead to increases in profit or a rise in socioeconomic status for the individual, the family, the community, and the nation.⁴ Turn-of-the-century Spanish financiers used these and other investment strategies to fill their coffers while attending to collective interests as they fantasized about their nation's ability to compete in and with global markets headquartered in cities from London, Paris, and New York to Berlin and Saint Petersburg.⁵ Inspiring novels like Galdós's *Lo prohibido* (1885; Forbidden fruit) and a craze for collectible photographs, figures like the Marquis of Salamanca, who invested in rail projects in Spain (e.g., Madrid-Aranjuez) and abroad, reflect the celebrity status of men whose risky business in European stock exchanges firmly situated them in the nineteenth-century Spanish popular imagination.

The Madrid Stock Exchange or Bolsa de Madrid was housed in a variety of buildings throughout the capital until its installment in its current location in the Plaza de la Lealtad; it was nineteenth-century Spain's official, state-sponsored investment center as early as its opening in 1831. However, smaller commerce halls or *bolsines* sprouted up elsewhere in the Peninsula, usually in locales where commercial or industrial optimism attracted investors hoping to capitalize on fledgling but promising networks of production and distribution via rail.⁶ Coinciding with the funding of railway companies to establish reliable, speedier trade routes across regions, particularly lucrative banks and local exchanges were founded in the Basque Country, where railway companies and shipbuilding yards were important motors for growth, and Catalonia, where the widescale manufacture and circulation of textiles in Barcelona and Llobregat river basin factories buoyed the region's commercial and industrial hegemony within Spain.

After the expropriation of Church properties in the 1830s and 1840s, together with the demolition of its medieval city wall and subsequent municipal expansion in the 1850s and beyond, nineteenth-century Barcelona had become the most important center for commerce and industry in the Iberian Peninsula.[7] As Mercer points out, masculine-coded spaces like the *casino* (men's club), local stock exchanges or the larger, public stock market had become "playground[s]" for middle-class men and aspirants to the bourgeoisie to test their financial acumen and luck in the city's bullish market.[8] A natural result of the newly acquired cultural visibility and social capital of businessmen in cities across Spain, Europe, and beyond, the men who operated in these spaces also served as inspiration for novelists who, in one way or another, integrate stock market activity and speculation into their novels published in English, French, Spanish, and Catalan: William Dean Howell's *The Rise of Silas Lapham* (1885), Émile Zola's *L'Argent* (1891, Money), Galdós's *Lo prohibido* (1885), and Oller's *La febre d'or* are perhaps the most noteworthy examples.[9]

While focusing on the lucrative but risky and, ultimately, doomed financial exploits of *La febre d'or*'s protagonist—Gil Foix—this chapter catalogs and analyzes the masculine imagery used by Narcís Oller to fashion new, capitalistic configurations of middle-class masculinity, whose representative agents made and were made possible by fin-de-siècle Barcelona's "speculative adventures."[10] In order to highlight the constructedness and internal contradictions ingrained in the plural patterns of middle-class masculinity represented in the novel, I first underline comparisons between the Restoration novelist and the businessman. As we shall see, a common denominator underlying the successful efforts of capitalists and writers—both bourgeois professionals—was their reliance on male homosocial networks driven by collaboration and competition. In the remaining sections of the chapter, a survey of the similarities between novelist and businessman will help to shed light on the competing patterns Oller deploys to engender Foix's upwardly mobile masculinity—along with the generative and destructive relationships that produce it—as it manifests in *La febre d'or*.

The masculine-coded imagery utilized by Oller to track Foix's meteoric rise and precipitous decline—a plot that maps neatly onto the novel's two parts (*La pujada* or "the rise" and *L'estimbada* or "the fall")—are drawn from a number of contexts in which male homosociality played a decisive role in middle-class configurations of masculinity. By invoking through direct and indirect characterization the material worlds of the Roman Catholic priest, the *indiano* (colonial returnee), the sportsman (gambler and horse jockey), and the artisan, *La febre d'or*'s narrator identifies the various patterns of masculinity informing the self-fashioning of the upwardly mobile businessman, while also hinting at the advantages and perils underlying male homosocial bonds within the capitalistic cosmovision to which he subscribes. Since the nineteenth-century Catalan bourgeoisie was a newly formed social class without deeply rooted symbols or traditions, as his- toricized convincingly by Jutglar, its representatives needed to absorb the signs available to them as they struggled to define themselves as modern, Spanish and Catalan men. By exposing the various threads constituting Gil Foix's heterogeneous embodiment of nineteenth-century patterns of middle-class masculinity—at times signaling values of social prestige and paternal authority, while at others exposing the pros and cons of risky financial activity—we will arrive at a new understanding of how *La febre d'or* reflects Narcís Oller's own place within a nascent Catalan literary mar- ket, as well as his relationship to his peers writing in Spanish.

Building upon scholarship focused on analyses of *La febre d'or* and Oller's other literary productions, this chapter asserts that a dual focus on gender and genre (namely, on masculinity and the realist novel) provides a genera- tive point of departure for restating the Catalan novelist's centrality to the regencration of Spanish literature in which his peers writing in Castilian were also engaged. Indeed, as we will see throughout this chapter, the para- textual anecdotes and language Oller uses to describe his own novel-writing enterprise in his literary memoirs (from his confraternal bonds with fellow writers to the "feverish" pace of his writing program and concomitant risks alluded to above) echoes the ways homosocial contexts shaped the author's own professionalization as a novelist. When read alongside his illuminating observations in his *Memòries: Història de mos llibres i relacions literàries* (Mem- oirs: History of my books and literary relationships; composed between 1913 and 1916, published in 1962), Oller's sometimes ambivalent investment in literary recognition was, like his protagonist's faith in the market econ- omy, boosted by male homosocial bonds but fraught with insecurities and uncertain returns amid Catalonia's cultural and literary booms and busts at the turn of the century.

La febre d'or, *the Businessman-Novelist, and Speculative Masculinities*

While Oller produced six novels and dozens of short stories and transla- tions, his longest and most ambitious work, *La febre d'or*, provides the clear- est and most convincing storehouse of competing models of masculinity, together with the collaborative and competitive spirit informing them and his own career as a lawyer and novelist.[11] Given Oller's memorialization of the challenges he faced in writing and publishing the novel, which he recounts in detail in his *Memòries*, it is also the novel in which paratextual evidence provides the most elucidating testimony of the nineteenth-century Spanish novelist's vicissitudinous professionalization and its relevance to his processes of masculine self-formation. Here, I first provide a brief summary of *La febre d'or* before contextualizing the affinities that exist between the masculine personas of the Restoration novelist and the businessman. Oller's concerns as a novelist overlapped with those of his fictional capitalists and illustrate the fact that aspiring Spanish writers relied on sought-after networks of male homosociality similar to those of the businessmen whose travails they fictionalize. The narrative ambivalence with which Oller treats Foix and his brethren, reflected in the shifting metaphorical registers he uses to portray them—from those of the priest to the *indiano*, sportsman, and artisan—is reflective of the Catalan author's professional uncertainties vis-à-vis his own speculative, literary gambits.

The two parts of *La febre d'or* narrate the acquisition and subsequent loss of wealth by the banker and broker, Gil Foix, and his immediate family, composed of his wife, Catarina, his daughter, Delfina, and his young son, Eudaldet. Motivated by a desire to establish a railway between Barcelona and Vilaniu—the fictionalized version of Oller's native Valls (Tarragona) and site of the novel's homonymous predecessor—the provincial social climber Josep Rodon sets the novel's plot in motion when he seeks out Foix's financial expertise in the grandiose halls of the Llotja (Barcelona's main commerce hall that also housed the Reial Acadèmia de Belles Arts de Sant Jordi [The Royal Academy of Fine Arts of Saint Jordi]). Gil is eager to lend whatever support he can, not least of all because his own success was only made possible by the investments of men like mossèn Pere, the priest who took him under his wing after a failed adventure in colonial Cuba.

As enthusiasm, investments, and trust in the quickly expanding company grow, and abetted by its enthusiastic agents, including Foix's pragmatic brother, Bernat, and cousins Jordi and Eladi Balenyà, Gil's own blind faith in the promising but volatile financial system represented by speculative trading in the stock market puts him at great odds with his wife's nearest of kin: primarily, his mother-in-law, the frugal matriarch Donya Mònica, and brother-in-law, the bohemian-bourgeois artist Francesc. In spite of the latter two characters' perennial admonitions, Gil moves the family from a modest home to a luxurious townhouse, takes high-profile business trips throughout Spain and elsewhere in Europe, sponsors fashionable visits to the Liceu theater and the newly inaugurated Hippodrome, and attends the celebration of political meetings in Madrid and Vilaniu.

Though Gil's successes in the first part of the novel are built atop the foundational investment of mossèn Pere, Gil's similar support of the opportunistic Balenyà family ultimately spells disaster for the Foix family's finances and reputation in the second part of the novel, the title of which (*L'estimbada* or "the fall") foreshadows a climactic crash. Toward the end of the novel, and under the pretext of celebrating Eladi's birthday, for example, the Balenyàs take advantage of Gil's magnanimity toward their son by cornering him into granting the young broker a more robust share of the business in order to increase his worth in the eyes of Rachel Llòpis, his soon-to-be bride. When Gil objects, citing that such patronage was only valid in the event of a union between Eladi and Delfina, the former protests, exploiting Gil's generosity by citing what he views as the supposed insolvency of avuncular ties, even those that are based on friendship and trust rather than bloodlines or contracts: "The uncle's word is worth more than all of the notary's papers."[12] Blinded by his vanity and ignorant of Eladi's deceit, Gil acquiesces, much to his disgrace.

However, any lasting peace between the Foix and Balenyà men evanesces when a Senyora Solervall—one of Eladi's clients and lovers—demands that her investment in "Almansa" stocks be returned. Unable to reproduce the stock—Eladi had sold them all, investing them instead in Vilaniu railway shares—Gil's anger erupts over such mercantile sacrilege when he cries: "Don't you know that a deposit is the most sacred thing in the world?"[13] Though Gil's indignation was in part righteous, his own failure to oversee his affairs is also to blame, since it was he who placed undue trust in undeserving men while he focused his attention on politics and personal ennoblement. Eladi's misstep with Solervall foreshadows larger issues for the near future. Having lost the management of the Vilaniu railway to Rodon and Balenyà and nervous about murmurs of an imminent crash, Foix lets himself be duped by the duplicitously shrewd Llassada and Girò (all but sealing his fate in the moments leading up to the 1882 stock market crash). Gil's failure is, therefore, the combined result of personal shortcomings and market circumstances.

After the betrayal by his closest business partners, and the resulting bankruptcy of the company, it becomes apparent that relationships between men are precarious, especially when based on speculative self-interest instead of altruism and (familial/fraternal) love. Having discovered the cause and agents of his ruin, Gil regrets his mistakes and the family-like treatment he afforded to his homosocial network of peers:

> Eladis, Jordis, Rodons: those hypocrites and wretches forming my entourage, being my men of confidence, making me fight with you, Catarina,

with my brother, with all of those who love me, so that they may pros-
per, so that they may take over my will, to make for themselves a position
at the cost of my own, to dishonor me with their theft, to then rob and
betray me.[14]

Gil's exclamatory identification of the men in the plural form ("Eladis,
Jordis, Rodons"), together with their collective identification as "hypo-
crites and wretches," betrays their prior singularity as trustworthy "men
of confidence" in the disgraced businessman's eyes. As we observed in the
introduction, the notion of trust was part and parcel of the associative language middle-class men such as tailors used to bolster and support homosocial ecosystems of production, distribution, and consumption during the
nineteenth century. The fragility or precariousness of the system, as Oller
imagines it in his conclusion, is exposed when constituent actors work in
bad faith.

As scholars have noted, Oller's narrator remains ambivalent about the
protagonist's speculative enterprises: while characters like Mònica condemn
her son-in-law's spinning of the roulette wheel with the family's finances,
other characters like Bernat, Gil's pragmatic older brother, frequently point
out that grandiose, meaningful, socioeconomic change can only issue from
the kinds of risks attempted by the Catalan banker who, in the denouement,
makes a symbolic return to his humble origins. Having ceded his shiny
top hat for the shirtsleeves of a carpenter, Gil devotes his time to cobbling
together wooden frames for Francesc, Foix's new son-in-law after his fore-
shadowed but unnarrated marriage to Delfina.[15] This final scene represents
the inversion of paterno-filial hierarchy that Foix sought but ultimately
failed to establish, and the stock market's failure to make him the kind of
father-in-law figure he wanted to be demonstrates the potentially devas-
tating consequences of risky financial behavior.

Perhaps because the first part of the novel appears so at odds with the
second, amounting to a dialectic that lacks a straightforward resolution, a
common thread connecting much criticism of *La febre d'or* is an interest in
diagnosing, explaining, or justifying Oller's ambivalent attitude toward
the risky business of his fictional stock-market speculators. Articulating
what he sees as "an insoluble contradiction in Oller's ideology," Toni
Dorca probes this question by juxtaposing the later novel against its predecessor, *Vilaniu*: "Oller seems to endorse the bourgeois ideal whereby the
individual is allowed to forge his or her own destiny. Yet at times he cannot conceal his nostalgia for the pre-capitalist era in which social mobility

was severely restricted by tradition."[16] While acknowledging that some ambivalence toward Foix's upwardly mobile trajectory is present in the novel, Kathleen Davis reminds readers that "at no point in [*La febre d'or*] is it ever suggested that consumerism is responsible for the Foix's eventual reversal of fortune, or that it has not indeed been necessary for the family to learn the tastes appropriate to their class and to consume goods according to their means."[17] Echoing Dorca and Davis, Leigh Mercer points out that the majority of *La febre d'or*'s pages are devoted to dramatizing the "financially productive and upwardly mobile social results reaped by the symbolic ties between family and business," and, thus, the novel registers a shift in values, enshrining those responsible for leading family and society toward the bourgeois customs necessary for access to European modernity.[18] Oller's insider perspective, as Joan Ramon Resina writes, gave him a unique vantage point from which to unpack the "inner contradictions of the feverish dynamism that carried the city forward."[19]

Building upon this and other scholarship of Oller's literary output, this chapter asserts that a dual focus on gender and genre (on masculinity and the realist-naturalist novel) provides a generative point of departure for reconciling the Catalan novelist with his peers writing in Castilian. *La febre d'or* (together with its paratexts in the author's literary memoirs) is the ideal text through which to read the questions that emerge, since it best reflects what Dorca articulates as Oller's "relentless pursuit of a Realist aesthetics against the most insurmountable difficulties," and, I would add, odds.[20] Read through a masculinities-studies lens, Oller's professional "limitations" are evidence of the multiple patterns of authorship available to the aspiring Spanish novelist.[21] Indeed, as this chapter illustrates, Oller himself viewed the unfolding of his literary program as a process that constituted his entrée into manhood as an aspiring middle-class professional in the Catalan capital. In his *Memòries*, Oller's nostalgic memorialization of the homosocial bonds that facilitated the realization of his projects demonstrate his own speculative investment in friendships and male homosociality. Through *La febre d'or*'s kaleidoscopic representation of the nineteenth-century businessman—whose image in the realist novelist's trick mirror shapeshifts from priest to *indiano*, sportsman, and artisan—Oller allegorizes the contradictions informing his self-formation as a middle-class man who simultaneously hoped to contribute to the modernization of Spanish literature by tapping into what his region and language had to offer.

If fin-de-siècle bankers and businessmen were the immediate or most obvious beneficiaries of successful business ventures, novelists, too, had vested interests in depicting the pros and cons of the new financial system as part of their realist project. Indeed, the novel functioned as both a ledger for their aestheticized observations of the new financial reality and as a commodity vouchsafing their tacit desire to participate in it. Oller's correspondence with Pereda and, as we will see later, Galdós, demonstrates that novelists did not feign ignorance about their place within capitalism. However, their surprise upon discovering the financial circumstances of their peers is a revelatory trope in their epistolary correspondences and memoirs, a fact that brings to light their awareness of how they perceived themselves and their place in national and international literary markets. Novelistic output, like that of stocks and bonds, was undoubtedly tethered to an awareness of and attention to a market that commodified both producer and product.

José María de Pereda surprised his friend Oller, who was flabbergasted to discover that the Cantabrian writer earned his living not from the sale of his novels, but as a consultant for the Bank of Santander and owner of La Rosario (the cosmetics factory he inherited from his older brother, the *indiano* Juan Agapito). Oller reports genuine shock that the preeminent novelist had a hand in the manufacture of soap and perfume: "Me, a lawyer, and him, a perfumer!"[22] For his part, Pereda was astounded to discover that Oller was a lawyer. The Cantabrian novelist was sure that Oller was a doctor or surgeon because of the precise skills of observation he detected in the Catalan's oeuvre. The shared assumption of a more lucrative profession in the case of both writers is evidence of the professional hurdles Spanish novelists had to overcome. Furthermore, nineteenth-century men's nonliterary vocations provided yet another discursive space for the cultivation of male homosocial bonds that was exclusive of women: while in exceptional circumstances a woman, like Emilia Pardo Bazán, could earn a living as a writer, clerkships, medicine, and entrepreneurial careers remained largely closed off to them. Besides their more lucrative professions, Spanish novelists were also critics, translators, and self-advocating literary agents; thus, novel-writing itself had much in common with the business world, not least of all because it existed within and as a result of it. The various patterns of masculinity represented by Spanish authors, who occupied a number of masculine-coded social roles throughout their careers, provides necessary context for the competing models of masculinity that take shape in the form of their fictional offspring.

Spanish- and Catalan-language novelists were particularly keen to the professional challenges they faced, and they often debated with each other about the market realities conditioning their work, as well as the implications of such decisions on matters related to literary aesthetics and national and regional identity. This was especially true for Narcís Oller, whose decision to publish his novels exclusively in Catalan—not without much encouragement from his cousin, Josep Yxart, and others like Albert Savine, Joan Sardà, and Pereda—put him at odds with Benito Pérez Galdós, whose friendship with Oller is recorded for posterity in their decades-long epistolary correspondence. For example, after commending Oller for his abilities as a narrator in his debut novel, *La papallona*, Galdós calls into question the use of Catalan in the format of the realist novel. According to one of Galdós's letters to Oller, novels should be written in a language legible to the widest number of readers, implicitly confirming the role of such a text as not only a product for self-identification and a commodity to be consumed by a bourgeois class, but also for a culturally and linguistically united nation:

> it is ridiculous that you write in Catalan. Sometime soon you will all cure yourselves of your mania for Catalanism and the rebirth. And if it is necessary for reasons I fail to comprehend that Catalan live as a literary language, leave it to the poets. The novel should be written in the language that can be understood by the widest number of people.[23]

Perhaps unsurprisingly given his commercial success as a novelist writing in Spanish and his ties to the Spanish capital, Galdós encourages his friend to prioritize paying audiences when considering the language in which to publish his novels.

In reply to Galdós's having engaged such difficult notions, Oller frankly defends his decision to write his novels exclusively in Catalan: "No, Galdós my friend. It is not exclusivism nor provincialism, nor is it separatism, nor any other bogeyman ending in ism. I write the novel in Catalan because I live in Catalonia, I copy from Catalan customs and landscapes, the types I depict are Catalan, and it is in Catalan that I hear them express themselves during all hours of the day."[24] Distilling Galdós's critique into a rhetorically potent gradation—exclusivism, provincialism, separatism, and other atrocious or ogre-like "-isms"—Oller volleys with a friendly if still sharp-edged rejoinder meant to bring the interlocutors toward some sense of closure. Oller's insistence on "copying" the Catalan customs, landscapes, and types he observes and aestheticizes not only reflects the affinity between his particular brand of realism and earlier *costumbrista* writing, but it also leverages markers of regional identity to justify the place of the novel written in Catalan within the national literary canon and market. Regardless of the writers' preferred language, Oller's deferral to realist aesthetics in his dialogue with Spain's preeminent realist novelist was undoubtedly a potent rhetorical weapon to wield in this debate.

Even if Oller privileges a response to Galdós based on aesthetic and philosophical (not financial or political) concerns for his writing in Catalan, his attention to regional audiences undoubtedly signals his recognition of the literate Catalan publics that would, at least eventually, be galvanized in their consumption and reading of his novels and the literary output of his like-minded peers, including Víctor Català, Josep Yxart, Joan Sardà, and Santiago Rusiñol. Drawing on Oller's *Memòries*, Mercedes Vidal Tibbits confirms that Oller's career was tied up in affective attachments to Catalonia from the very beginning of his career, and that his posterity was more dependent on his status as a representative of Catalan cultural production.[25] While such was the case earlier in his career, it should be noted that Oller's memoirs also confirm the author's withdrawal from literature and public life after the deaths of his closest friends and critics, most notably among them Yxart and Sardà, and then Pereda. Despite the minority status of Catalan language publications, Oller evidently privileges pride in regional identity over marketability, speculating instead in favor of the Catalan futures that might benefit from (while identifying with) his artistic labor. Indeed, Oller's investment in writing the novel of his class was destined to attract contemporary and future readers, reflecting the economic climate from which he and his work sprung: "The gold fever was a euphoric dance of money released from its metal prison into an open-ended speculation with *future* value."[26]

Though he was not an industrial oligarch like Pereda or popular enough as a stand-alone novelist, like Galdós, Narcís Oller—whose career as a lawyer kept him busy when he was not writing—was also an enthusiastic witness to and champion of the stock market's siren song. His capitalization on the auspicious moment for widely felt enthusiasm for Catalan regional identity reflects an affinity he shared with the men whose activities he chronicled during visits to Barcelona's hall of commerce. Even if he dissents with Galdós in the exchange cited earlier, throughout his writings, Oller displays an acute awareness of the ironies connecting the activities of speculative stock-market agents and the novelist. In his *Memòries*, for example, the Catalan comments on his aesthetic and commercial modus operandi while nostalgically memorializing his relationships with a predominantly male coterie of peers, highlighting commercial as well as aesthetic elements of his literary output.

Representing risky speculative enterprises in fiction necessitated visits to commercial spaces, and Oller's comments about the men who worked there in his literary memoirs, together with the mythological register with which he describes them, draws attention to the kaleidoscopic way realist novelists viewed evolving icons of middle-class masculinity. In the opening section of a chapter describing the composition and publication of *La febre d'or*, Oller makes a compelling reference to Greek mythology to lionize the brokers and capitalists whose lives and labor inspired his most ambitious work:

> The immense stock market fever, like a plague carried down by the northern winds, to borrow my good friend Sardà's language, had invaded Barcelona with such intensity and force that it eventually came over everyone. During that ardent fever of 1880 and 1881, even I—who in my life had only crossed the threshold of the grand entry of the Hall of Commerce during the celebration of the Floral Games—could not resist entering to see how all of those new argonauts combined their efforts to repeat with confidence, in the present day, the perilous expedition to Colchis without the favors of another Medea and ignoring who among them would be the new, gold-fleeced Jason.[27]

Here, the juxtaposition of the Jocs Florals (Floral Games; the resurrected literary competition associated with the Renaixença) with the Llotja, together with the legend of Jason and the argonauts, confirms the merger of stock market speculation, Catalan artistic and literary production, and myths of masculine adventures in the author's nostalgic imagination.

Relevant to his own enterprises, Oller uses a similar language of fever elsewhere in his memoirs to describe his frenzied pace of writing around this time, drawing frequent connections between the activities of his fictional businessmen and the way he framed his own ardent bursts of creativity. Citing his writing fever ("febre d'escriure") during the moments leading up to the 1888 exposition, Oller gives equal importance to creativity for creativity's sake, and his ability to capitalize on it in the form of manuscript pages: "such was my writing fever then, that despite the time taken up working as a lawyer and attending to an ever growing stack of correspondence to reply to, the day when I did not fill up multiple blank pages was a rare occasion"; "an ambition for rightful glory had entered me. But I was young and, with the ardor that rash behavior and enthusiasm gave to me during this time, I did not stop to consider the risk to which I had exposed myself: that of losing what I had gained."[28] The nature of the risk to which Oller thought he had exposed himself is unclear: was he referring to the fact that a lawyer's business depended on his reputation? Was he concerned that potential literary failure would spill out and threaten his career as a liberal professional? At the very least, he risked tarnishing the reputation afforded to him by the laurels he had earned in the Floral Games and, perhaps, the personal and professional connections that continued to assist him in his endeavors.

Oller uses the language of feverish activity yet again to evoke the vertiginous pace of construction of the pavilions of the Universal Exposition: "All that hustle and bustle, all that fever of labor never before seen here, all that tyrannical force that gave such courageous proof of our hidden energies and our thirst for progress, ignited my imagination, my Catalanism and the faith placed in this people, the hope of better days; what I saw had intoxicated me to such a degree that I did not even remember to read or write."[29] Using an effective contrast between first-person plural and singular possessives, Oller positions his own project alongside those of the men responsible for the physical construction of the exposition's pavilions, as well as those who funded the project and those who, like himself, wrote about it all (even if excitement sometimes prevented him from doing his share of the work). Thus, within the patriotic and potent "poble" (people or *pueblo*) signifier, he blends together the interests of compatriots across the working and middle classes. His idealistic conflation of class interests notwithstanding, the fact that Oller reports having forgotten to read and write in the midst of the feverish days leading up to the Universal Exposition draws a sharp distinction between himself and the laboring men he describes. In *La febre d'or*, Oller's description of Foix's origins as a carpenter, and his symbolic return to that profession following the risk to which he exposes himself as a broker, is only one among a number of instances in which attention is drawn to the various masculine types and labor patterns that the middle-class businessman capitalizes upon in his own strategies of self-fashioning (and which allegorically evoke Oller's own straddling of *costumbrista* origins and realist novel-writing).

Obviously enthralled by the spectacle presented to him by the Barcelona stock exchange's intrepid band of heroes—whose names were not Jason and Heracles but rather Evarist, Joan, Antoni, and Josep—Oller's reference to the mythical venture of the argonauts also sheds light on the male homosocial environment in which the adventures of these men— both businessmen and novelists—took place.[30] Masculine-coded habitats such as the stock market or the casino were hotbeds of male homosociality that corroborate Sedgwick's thesis, that "in any male-dominated society, there is a special relationship between male homosocial [. . .] desire and the structures for maintaining and transmitting patriarchal power: a relationship founded on an inherent and potentially active structural congruence."[31] However, such spaces provided more than mere backdrops for the galvanization of middle-class masculinity through male homosocial interactions. Providing evidence for George Mosse's argument about the relationship between male friendship as a national or political force, the potential of *La febre d'or*'s male protagonists to climb from carpenter to banker to politician demonstrates the codependence of patriarchal institutions like the government and the stock market, a place where public and private interests commingled.[32] Though Foix fails in his campaign to become a parliamentary representative of Vilaniu, his reputation and connections make the glimmer a possibility. Oller's representation of this reality in the context of the novel, furthermore, substantiates the novelist's role in producing and participating in the articulation of new patterns of middle-class masculinity. Evident in Oller's interactions with Pereda and Galdós, male homosocial bonds were just as integral to the professionalization of novelists as the middle-class professionals whose lives they fictionalize in their novels. Indeed, Foix's induction into the world of commerce—like Oller's own entrée into his careers as lawyer and novelist by his uncle and cousin, respectively—were built atop similar connections.

In the context of what Émile Zola labeled a "roman de bourse" (stock market novel), gender, like the realist enterprise itself, emerges as a speculative system of representation reliant on the legibility and exchangeability of masculine-coded values and virtues. Indeed, novelists like Oller, writes Mercer, "portray middle-class masculinity to be in a transitional, unstable, and yet promising position, much like the state of financial investment in the market economy in the latter half of the nineteenth century."[33] Given the stock-market setting, and his broader preoccupation "with the question of the sources of value," the Oller of *La febre d'or* foregrounds manliness itself as reliant on a set of abiding and evolving values and virtues.[34] As we saw in this book's introduction, masculinity is a constructed social category that draws meaning from a number of cultural and social cues. Demonstrating his awareness or belief in the affinities between financial, narrative, and gendered affairs in the professional novelist and businessman, Oller writes of his decision to participate in the Jocs Florals—the literary competition that would launch his literary program—as a kind of masculine rite of passage: "I was becoming [or, literally, 'making myself'] a man" ("Jo em feia

home").[35] Indeed, the Catalan novelist's narrative of stock market speculation and homosocial bonding between men was itself a speculative enterprise that he identified as integral to his development as a man and as a
bourgeois professional: speculative because it was based on the conjecture
that a market existed for the consumption of Catalan novels. Even if Oller
demonstrates how men's success in such arenas depends on the guidance and
support of capable and interested male mentors and peers, as is the case in
his association of Foix with the homosocial worlds of the Church and the
indiano, he also exposes the fault lines in capitalistic patterns of masculinity, particularly when collaboration among men is foiled by the solipsistic
interests of bad-faith agents.

Consecrating the Stock Market Priest

In *La febre d'or*, the ecclesiastical imagery used to characterize Gil (directly
or indirectly), and the subsequent references to his relationship with the
priest mossèn Pere (evident in the narrator's descriptions of his interactions
with a youthful Gil), rhetorically sacralize Gil's initial pursuit of fame and
fortune, reflecting Josep Domingo's assertion that the novel's exposition
dramatizes the fact that "money has now taken the place of the sacred."[36]
Mossèn Pere, whose name bears the imprimatur of the father—*pare* in Catalan and *père* in French—draws attention to his legibility as a kind of surrogate father figure for Gil, and, thus, to the patriarchal valences underlying
mentor-mentee relationships between older and younger men. Additionally, the name further centers homosocial valences, since "Pere" (Peter in
Catalan) also brings to mind St. Peter, the man through whom Jesus, who,
according to biblical accounts, did not have biological offspring, transmits
his legacy. Thus, the investment in younger men by surrogate fathers is an
important pattern throughout the novel. By tapping into readers' recognition of the signs and symbols of the Restoration Church through Gil's
early pipedreams of liturgical opulence as a seminarian, *La febre d'or*'s narrator consecrates the novel's protagonist as a high priest of nineteenth-
century Barcelona's speculative economy.

   While nodding to Foix's humble origins and the privilege afforded to
him by male homosocial bonds and kinship ties, Oller offers a convincing
portrayal of the newfound social prestige that nineteenth-century businessmen working in the Catalan capital enjoyed and capitalized upon in
their pursuit of wealth. The channeling of the middle-class businessman's

foundational narrative through imagery related to the figure of the priest also signals the coexistence of (and collaboration between) various masculine types during the Restoration period. Oller's deployment of clerical-liturgical metaphors of masculinity and metaphors of artisanal or manual labor are evocative of the author's ultimate uncertainty about the relative merits and alienating, capitalist excesses embodied by Gilet Foix. By foregrounding the extreme wealth of the self-made man with icons of humility and liturgical opulence, middle-class authors like Oller are able to gloss the anxieties and fantasies of men contradictorily encouraged to achieve extravagant wealth while displaying it in a way that was controlled and measured with an eye to pursuing the *juste milieu* enshrined in conduct literature, or the Catalan cultural ideal of *seny* or self-restraint.

Analogies or juxtapositions between careers in business and the priesthood in the imagination of cultural producers were to be expected in Spain, a traditionally Catholic country, since, then as now, Catholicism and capitalism did not exist in isolation. Amid surges in anticlerical nationalist and secularist propaganda, the Church's official responses relied on similar marketing strategies and techniques, making the agents of such programs both ideologues and savvy businessmen. Antonio María Claret, a Catholic bishop and confessor to Isabel II, was equal parts influential politico and businessman whose commercial savoir faire is reflected in his authorship and supervision of a wildly effective publishing program: his book *Camino recto y seguro para llegar al cielo* (1850, The straight and certain path to arrive at Heaven's doorstep) was a tremendously popular best seller with 185 editions. Additionally, the publication of behavioral manuals for a range of bourgeois men illustrates how men from across the middling classes were united under the umbrella of polite society. Even as historical priests publicly decried excessive consumerism in their sermons and columns written for reactionary newspapers, conduct manuals for priests—as we saw earlier in Chapter 2—enjoined them to cultivate a carefully disciplined gentility that depended on the consumption and use of hygiene products and tidy apparel. A minister's ability to successfully guide the members of a growing middle class depended at least in part on his mastery of its codes and cues that also conditioned his own behavior and respectability in the public sphere.

Evidence of the intermingling of religious and capitalistic registers among Catalonia's bourgeoisie and intellectual elites during the late nineteenth century culminate most clearly in the figure of Jacint Verdaguer

FIGURE 3.1. Charcoal portrait of Narcís Oller by Ramon Casas, c. 1897–1898. Image courtesy of Wikimedia Commons.

(1845–1902), the Catholic priest and patriarch of the Catalan Renaixença that we opened with in Chapter 2. A prominent minister in Barcelona, Verdaguer was also a chaplain who worked in the employ of the controversial *indiano* Antonio López y López's Transatlantic Company.[37] Proof of his role in generating the Catalan rebirth, Verdaguer was one of a number of Catalan artistic, cultural, and industrial figures immortalized in Ramon Casas's series of charcoal portraits created at the turn of the century; both Verdaguer and Oller (see fig. 3.1) formed a part of Casas' cast of influential Catalans. Similarities in color, shape, and value in both portraits reproduce the shared sartorial grammar threading through formal menswear for both laymen and priests. Verdaguer's avuncular presence within the institution of the Catalan rebirth was universally recognized by intellectual circles, and Oller's most devoted readers might have made this connection when reading about the patronage of Foix's mentor, mossèn Pere.

Early evidence of *La febre d'or*'s own confusion of signifiers relating to both religious men and laymen emerges in Josep Rodon's recognition of a priestly acquaintance of his toward the end of the novel's opening chapter, which takes place within the walls of the bourgeois institution of the stock exchange. Inside the crowded edifice, men from across the lower- and upper-middle classes rub elbows. Here, a reference to their babel of dialogues—reflective of the bourgeoisie's heterogeneity as a social group—also provides potent evidence of the narrative heteroglossia (as in Bakhtin) characterizing the realist novel in general, and Oller's Catalan-language novel in particular:

> Rodon began to hear dialogues as if expressly made to prove to him that not only were all the classes blended there, but also all professions and hierarchies: lawyers that talked about tomorrow's forecast, doctors who entrusted their friends with the diagnoses of some sick patient, judges, generals, and senators. In one moment, turning his head, he even recognized under a top hat the shaved face of a priest, an old acquaintance of his. It was clear: the stock market had conquered the world.[38]

Since money had become a universal sign of power and prestige for bourgeois agents, the interests of all men—from lawyers and doctors to senators and priests—were represented in the masculine habitat of the stock market. The fact that it is to their friends that the doctors reveal diagnoses shows how information flows through friendship, a network that runs parallel to (and apparently supersedes) professional confidentiality (in this case, that of the doctor and his patient). Additionally, the presence of lawyers who rub elbows with court officials and clerics is undoubtedly a self-referential nod to Oller himself, since the author visited the stock market on more than one occasion to observe and take notes for *La febre d'or*.

Foix's characterization as a priest is thrown into relief first by the description of Rodon's pilgrimage to Barcelona and subsequently by the stock exchange's Church-like edifice. Focalized through Rodon's point of view, the commerce hall's descriptors take on mystical qualities that resemble the affective ambience of a Catholic mass: "The four gothic columns whose rounded and extremely tall arches divided it into three naves, which gave it the airs of a Catholic church; but letting the eyes focus on the stone walls with Renaissance molding, the church adopted a Protestant mien."[39] Whereas the hall's cathedral-like architecture evokes Catholic opulence and wealth, the description's slippage into austerity recalls the Protestant work ethic and Dutch origins of stock exchanges in Europe.[40] Though the narrator's religious metaphors give way to others, an affectively charged Rodon, through whom this first chapter is focalized, continues to conjure the image of a church during a ritual: from the incense-like columns of smoke emanating from the brokers' cigars to the bell-like onomatopoeias ("In that moment, the invisible bell . . . brrring! brrring!") that mark the change of sessions.[41] Regarding the construction of the Madrid commerce hall in its final site at the Plaza de la Lealtad, Enrique María Repullés y Vargas cites the desire to make the building a "temple to the economy" thus justifying the basilica-like nave of the trading floor.[42] Comparisons between stock market architecture and that of religious buildings may have also simply been a reflection of the historical reality. Before it found a permanent home in the Plaza de la Lealtad, the Madrid exchange, for example, took place in dilapidated or disentailed religious properties like the Claustro del Convento de San Martín, the Monasterio de las Monjas Bernardas, and the Convento de los Basilios.

While the resemblance between the stock market and a religious temple is sustained here by allegory, such slippage also reflects the fact that convents and monasteries were literally replaced by commercial entities throughout the nineteenth century (particularly in densely populated cities like Barcelona). To be sure, the liberal expropriation of Church properties during the 1830s and 1840s affected the entirety of the Spanish urban and provincial landscape—Fernán Caballero's 1849 *costumbrista* novel *La gaviota* (The seagull) evokes the architectural losses in the Andalusian countryside in a nostalgic, Romantic key—but the metamorphosis was especially suggestive in large cities, where disentailments generated large amounts of wealth while also creating real estate in desirable downtown locations. In Barcelona, some convents and monasteries along the Rambla de Santa Mònica, for example, were eventually replaced by the banks, bazaars, and brokerage firms that would in due course become potent symbols of cultural embourgeoisement and financial enterprises in the Catalan capital. In 1884, the renaming of Saint Sebastian's square as the Plaça d'Antonio López, together with the installation of a statue in the capitalist's honor, was one such sign of the commonplace exchange between religious and financial registers in the modern Spanish cityscape.[43]

If the Borsa is a temple, then the lead bankers and stockbrokers who emerge from the commerce hall's inner sancta are the brahmins of its corporate liturgy. The disparity between the middle-aged Rodon and his superiors is first made clear to the outsider by sartorial differences that costume the latter in a clerical silhouette, which recalls the resemblance between Casas' portraits of Verdaguer and Oller:

> Looking at himself up and down, he felt out of place. 'Those gentlemen's clothes were brand new and cut by different scissors; the top hat, a different shape, was glossy like satin.' However, what shocked him most were the lacquered and stiff white collars that forced them to keep their heads erect, all in spite of the age he detected in their bald and wrinkled heads, when dentures and hair dyes did not hide it.[44]

Though the vain men described here are aging and alienating in their stiff, black and white clothing, they evoke the image of a Catholic priest in his black cassock and white collar, calling to mind the severe silhouette cut by figures like Fermín de Pas. As we saw in Chapter 2, Catholic priests could be viewed contradictorily as prestigious members of society or pariahs.[45]

The liturgical grain in Gil Foix's character is further drawn out in the following chapter, when the narrator summarizes the young Foix's humble origins in Vilaniu. Here, the self-made man's debts to interested male mentors become apparent, and another explicit connection is made between the material wealth of the Church—represented here by an abridged catalog of flashy episcopal ornaments—and the luxurious commodities for which Gil eventually opts. The list of liturgical commodities resembles, as we saw in Chapters 1 and 2, respectively, that of Felipe Centeno in *Marianela* and *El Doctor Centeno*, as well as that of Fermín de Pas during his own ambitious daydreams in *La Regenta*:

> The son of a carpenter from the neighboring parish of Sant Cugat who got by making altars and Church pews, Gilet served as his father's apprentice and an altar boy at Sant Just. One day, he felt a calling to the tonsure, to one day wield the bishop's ring, the golden crosier, the broad, golden pluvial cope and the bejeweled miter worn by so many saints and venerable prelates he had seen in the flesh from up close. Father Pere, an ecclesiastical beneficiary of Sant Just and a kindhearted friend of old man Foix, took the acolyte under his wing, prepared him duly, and found a place for him in the seminary.[46]

On the one hand, the list of episcopal ornaments corresponds to the (material) signs and symbols of upward mobility within the ecclesiastical hierarchy, as we saw to be the case in Fermín de Pas's similar chimaeras. As elsewhere in the novel, a sharp disparity emerges between material and immaterial or speculative enterprises: here, this dichotomy is signaled by the juxtaposition of mundane Church pews and the yet-to-be-attained episcopal ornaments. The second list, signaled by a suite of verbs conjugated in the preterit tense, contracts the time it took for Gil to achieve his first steps toward advancement within the Church. The swiftness, coupled with Gil's grammatical objectification and Pere's agency—also indicates the fast track to material advancement facilitated by male homosocial ties between the affluent priest and the business novice.

Alongside an emphasis on the material opulence associated with the Roman Catholic liturgy, Pere emerges as a surrogate father figure able to induct Foix into bourgeois subjectivity via the priesthood. Having lost his father at an early age, like Oller, Foix benefits from the material and emotional support of an interested male mentor. This surrogate father figure's omnipresence is referenced throughout the novel in his portrait that looms panoptically throughout *La febre d'or* as a reminder of Gil's debts and moral obligations. In moments of uncertainty or psychological torment, Gil beseeches his mentor—figured through the portrait—to aid him in his pursuits:

> A cold sweat erupted from his pores and his frightened eyes looked interrogatingly at the portrait of Father Pere. Yes, the portrait was moving, as if animated. Yes: Father Pere, that holy man to whom he owed everything, was listening to him, with that beneficent look; he had moved his head, and, in his hairless chin, that eternal smile stood out even more than before, that stamp of blessing possessed by those already called to heaven. All the fervor of the young, erstwhile seminarian erupted in the heart of the frightened banker.[47]

Ever since the construction of the new firm, Kathleen Davis points out, "[a] portrait of Mosén [*sic*] Pere, Gilet's spiritual advisor, hangs in the new brokerage house, and the priest is revered as the firm's nominal founder and heavenly overseer."[48] But the priest was also Foix's earthly benefactor, having acted as a surrogate father figure who not only provided him with his first substantial investment, but also introduced him to his future wife, Pere's niece Catarina.

If the narrator directly summons registers of a clerical masculinity in describing Gil's boyhood pipedreams and connections to his priestly father figure, he also indirectly portrays the businessman as a priest through his homosocial interactions with other characters. In a passage from the same chapter, Foix approaches his *caixa* (safe) to remove some bills to give to Jordi Balenyà, hesitantly replicating for his cousin and Eladi, his cousin once removed, what Pere did for the young Gilet: "The orator stood tall as he was, his eyes red from the zeal of improvisation, his hair stirred by the movements of his head, with hands that trembled, he opened the iron safe, took out two thousand in bills, and added: '. . . here you have it.'"[49] Gil's virtue-signaling maneuver is hardly altruistic: at this point in the novel, it is implied that Jordi's son, Eladi, will marry Delfina, Foix's daughter. Thus, this union would eventually funnel capital back into the family's coffers. The ceremonious extraction of money from the tabernacle-like safe box evokes Christ's partition of bread and wine in Matthew 26:26 ("Take and eat; this is my body") and takes on an ecclesiastical overtone here, particularly in light of the more explicitly liturgical descriptions of the stock market and its agents in the preceding pages. Furthermore, in Gil's attempt to replicate the foundational investment of mossèn Pere, the Catalan banker hopes to continue the chain of wealth—both for his own benefit and for that of his commercial pursuits. These investments attempt to recreate the perceived security in a biological relation between men via transmission of the surname, a public sign confirming bona fide heredity that ends up being impossible. It is as if these characters are trying to outdo nature and institute, through investments, ways for their identity and creeds to reproduce in other men. It makes sense that the ecclesiastical would be a sought-after model of masculinity, then. The clerical allegory comes full circle when Jordi, overcome with emotion and homosocial reverence, attempts to kiss Gil's hand as if he were in the company of a prelate.[50] The "sacralization" of the businessman as a priest recalls this book's earlier analysis of a similar scene from Galdós's *Tormento* in which Agustín Caballero and Amparo are represented as a confessor and confessant: a common metaphor for erotic and lighthearted depictions of amorous or flirtatious encounters between bourgeois men and women during the nineteenth century.[51]

If mossèn Pere's pastoral support and Gil's opulent dreams of advancement are illustrative of a kind of rhetorical sacralization of the businessman, not to mention the conflation of religious and economic registers that would emerge organically in the imagination of a Catholic novelist, they also illustrate the financial interests that have always been a part of Catholicism's civilizing mission at least since Columbus set sail for the "New World." As the following section will demonstrate, Gil's direct characterization as an *indiano* along with his indirect characterization as a priest coincide with other signs constituting bourgeois patterns of masculinity during the fin de siècle.

The Indiano: *His Myths and His Accessories*

By also patterning his protagonist after the *indiano* type, Oller anchors Foix's narrative of middle-class self-fashioning in both cultural myth and historical reality, positioning the colonial returnee as equal parts precarious adventurer, local oligarch, conspicuous consumer, and, eventually, bankrupt businessman. The atavistic kin of Golden Age explorers, conquistadors, and colonizers that came before him, the nineteenth-century *indiano* was a man who left Spain for the Americas—often Cuba or Puerto Rico—returning later to reestablish himself in Europe. The type exclusively referenced male emigrants and colonial returnees, reinforcing the masculine character of the *indiano* businessman.[52]

Indeed, writing about the British context, John Tosh points out that emigration during this time was considered a predominantly masculine enterprise: "the aspiration to emigrate and the experience of emigration were constructed in essentially masculine terms. Empire-building was man's work; the colonies were a man's world; and manhood might be secured or enhanced by becoming a colonist."[53] José Álvarez Junco corroborates the relevance of this decidedly masculine cosmovision in Spain via reference to observations made by Cánovas del Castillo, the architect of the Restoration regime: "colonizing savage populations was the 'new crusade' or 'divine mission' that 'civilized and progressive nations' had to realize 'in order for their culture to flourish, sewing progress everywhere while educating, elevating, and perfecting man.'"[54]

Meaningful references to Gil Foix's identity as an *indiano* manqué shed light on the gains and losses associated with the paternalistic, collaborative, and competitive nature of homosocial bonds shared between upwardly mobile, middle-class businessmen. A focus on the *indiano*'s accessories— where accessory may be understood as both a person who assists in carrying out an operation and as a thing or object that augments or embellishes— helps to reestablish both the homosocial network buoying the system as well as the culture of production and consumption in which such men

participated. Taking the form of explicit references to his past and to relevant secondary characters like his opportunistic cousin Jordi and the infantilized and reified black footman, Panxito—virtually a decorative accessory
to Foix's capitalistic masculinity—Oller's ambivalent narrative treatment of
his protagonist galvanizes both positive and negative stereotypes associated
with the exclusively male stock character. In having made the protagonist
of his "foundational fiction" (recalling Sommer) of regional embourgeoisement not only a capitalist, but, more specifically, an *indiano*, Oller draws
attention to the fact that the vanguards of the Catalan cultural and linguistic rebirth—Jacint Verdaguer chief among them—were the direct beneficiaries of Spain's continued, if waning, imperial projects. Furthermore, a
deliberate interrogation of Gil's embodiment of narrative tropes tied to the
manly *indiano* figure promotes what Lisa Surwillo calls an "awareness of
coloniality" in nineteenth-century Spanish and Catalan literature, in which
the dual pursuits of empire and bourgeois modernization go hand in hand.[55]
If ultimately ambivalent in his portrayal, Oller positions the *indiano* financier (like the priest, sportsman, and artisan) as a hallmark of contemporary
Catalan society.

    As with the other masculine archetypes analyzed in this book, the *indi-
ano* was a mythical personage and a contemporary social type. In Antonio Ferrer del Río's *costumbrista* sketch in *Los españoles pintados por sí mismos*
(1843–44, 1851), the author (an *indiano* himself) foregrounds the contemporary returnee as the descendent of Columbus and the conquistadors who
succeeded him: "Columbus, signaling to his travel companions unknown
regions from the deck of his caravels; Diego Velázquez, Hernán Cortés and
Francisco Pizarro, with the conquest and governance of the Americas, will
ready the stage for the *Indiano*'s glories."[56] Ferrer del Río's approximation
of the Americas to a theater for the *indiano*'s exploits—historically ranging
from the buying, selling, and trading of enslaved peoples to adjacent investment in the production and sale of commodities like sugar, leather, and real
estate—heighten the theatricality of the plot pattern associated with colonial returnees, thus establishing the failure-tragedy/success-comedy binaries present in many representations: *La febre d'or* straddles both ends of the
spectrum, narrativizing what Resina appropriately labels "effervescence
and abrupt decline."[57]

    Golden Age explorers and conquistadors are the *indiano*'s natural forefa-
thers, since the image of the transatlantic pioneer in search of gold and glory
had circulated among Spaniards, accumulating cultural capital and prestige,
at least as early as 1492. Such men provided apt raw material for writers like

Ferrer del Río and Oller to mine, since it was through the Spanish crown's speculative investment in their numerous expeditions to and from the so-called New World that the Americas and Spanish imperial hegemony were forged. Narratives of Columbus's maiden voyages, importantly, reignited the imaginations of turn-of-the-century cultural elites and producers wishing to commemorate and monumentalize the figure's fourth centennial as 1892 approached.

Columbus provided an apt symbol for Barcelona's industrial elites, particularly as his centennial nearly coincided with the 1888 Universal Exposition.[58] In a pamphlet titled *Monumento a Cristóbal Colón: Honrando a Colón, Cataluña honra a sus hijos predilectos* (Honoring Columbus, Catalonia honors its beloved sons), published in a decorative edition by the Renaixensa publishing house in 1882, architect C. Buigas Monrabá expounds on Columbus's relevance, conflating many of the variables present in Oller's own characterization of Gil Foix. In it, the author justifies the presence of a statue to Columbus in Barcelona, "Spain's second capital and its first in commerce," with recourse to the grandeur of the explorer as well as the historical significance of the fateful "discovery."[59]

Though Columbus and other conquistadors were virtually canonized in the national imagination and, thus, eclipse the majority of aspiring businessmen, some nineteenth-century *indianos* did achieve mythical status during their lifetime, and their success stories were likely present in the minds of Oller and his contemporaries. Indeed, the Catalan novelist's deployment of tropes related to the *indiano* in the characterization of Gil Foix's extravagant wealth enter him into a genealogy of nineteenth-century Catalonia's most famous cast of capitalists, whose names include Josep Xifré i Casas, Antonio López y López (First Marquis of Comillas), and Joan Güell.[60] The celebrity status of mythical *indianos* may have represented a cultural solution to anxieties among Spanish elites about imperial decline. At least on symbolic grounds, such men were likely viewed as potential agents of a restored imperial power, an aspiration that continued to manifest itself in Spain's colonial enterprises in Morocco and Equatorial Guinea.[61]

Front and center in the minds of the aristocrats, industrialists, and royals who bankrolled the 1888 statue to Columbus that towers over the Rambles, the distant memory of Columbus was perhaps less relevant to the masses of working-class emigrants who left Spain in search of more promising opportunities for socioeconomic advancement; few would achieve the mythical status of a López or Xifré.[62] To be sure, the *indiano* moniker applied to wealthy returnees, like those mentioned earlier, but it also may have been used in reference to the hundreds of thousands of soldiers sent to fight in the Cuban War, only to return in defeat, and, of course, to those other aspiring businessmen who returned as impoverished as they were upon departure.[63] During the nineteenth century, tens of millions of men like Foix departed from ports in Catalonia, Galicia, Cantabria, and Asturias to find work as clerks and merchants in young nations like Argentina, Chile, or Mexico, or Cuba and Puerto Rico, colonies that remained officially tethered to the Spanish imperial yoke until 1898.[64]

Reflecting *La febre d'or*'s dichotomous narrative structure, literary representations of the *indiano* almost exclusively hew to the failure-success binary. Perhaps establishing the literary model upon which later representations would draw inspiration, *Los españoles pintados por sí mismos*, for example, includes not one, but two versions of the type in Ferrer del Río's sketch "El indiano," ultimately showing how the *indiano* is bifurcated by the predictable patterns of defeat or triumph. Representations of the type also abound in the nineteenth-century novel, if perhaps most notably in Galdós's *novelas contemporáneas*, and short stories by Alas, Pereda, and Pardo Bazán.[65] Short stories and novels, like the *costumbrista* sketch that sets the pattern, also hew to either success stories or narratives of defeat. In *Tormento*, for example, Galdós idealizes Agustín Caballero, a colonial returnee whose rugged countenance, if still meeting the refined contours expected by polite society and evoked by his symbolically significant surname, is a constant reminder of the role played by fantasies of American expeditions in his self-fashioning and characterization. In one memorable passage from that novel, for example, a description of Caballero's beard and skin blends exoticizing and racializing allusions to Spanish empire: "In his black beard shone white specks like threads of silver, and his yellowish skin, bathed in bright light, took on the warm tone of terracotta, comparable to Indian, Egyptian, or Aztec artefacts."[66] Success stories like Caballero notwithstanding, writers tend to grant more visibility to those who fail: in Pereda's "A las Indias", for example, the short story is laced with foreboding predictions of the young, Cantabrian protagonist's inevitable downfall, an irony given Pereda's having benefited tremendously from the wealth accumulated by his *indiano* brother Juan Agapito. In Clarín's "Boroña" (Cornbread), the *indiano* protagonist returns only to be circled by his vulture-like relatives before a death foretold by descriptions of his melancholy and sickliness.

Demonstrating allegiance to both trends, Oller's *La febre d'or* roots Foix's success in the challenges he faced in his attempt to professionalize himself as a businessman in Cuba. Drawing on both historical and literary source material, Oller initially traces his own pattern for the *indiano* in the second chapter when he details the reasons for Foix's departure:

> In a long letter, he waxed eloquently about his motives and purpose before fleeing to Havana, praying that—during his absence—his generous uncle would shelter the splinters of his heart that he left behind. But then the Cuban war broke out, industries and businesses were devalued, and Gilet's stay on that island was nothing but a sterile, bitter, and woeful struggle lasting four years, until he was forced to return with some white hair, a beggar's bag full of regret around his neck, and an empty purse, even if he was dressed like a gentleman.[67]

Beyond a mere desire to plough quickly through relevant background details, Oller's contracted narration of Gil's time in Cuba betrays the precipitous nature of the trip and its equally abrupt end, all of which hewed to the reality experienced by most who left the provinces in search of a more sustainable way of life. Still, as Stacy Davis has convincingly argued, the notion, even if chimeric, of "making the Americas" was intricately interwoven with myths of masculine self-formation in the nineteenth-century Spanish imagination.[68]

Indeed, for some Catalans, Francesc Cabana writes, "a stay in Cuba represented what for many Englishmen was known as 'a trip to the colonies': a personal experience, the first building block of a fortune and an upwardly mobile promotion."[69] Here, in spite of his failure, Gil's trip to the Americas allowed him to cut his teeth in the global realm of finance and industry, thus preparing him for his efforts back at home; at least for the purposes of Oller's fiction, success itself was less important than fulfilling this masculine rite of passage, a point that emerges in cousin Jordi's flattery of Foix: "not without difficulties, it is true; but those same difficulties, once one has figured out a way to overcome them, are proof of one's worth."[70]

Alongside explicit references to Gil's time in Cuba, *La febre d'or*'s narrator also indirectly evokes ties to the *indiano* type through maritime metaphors that allegorize the signs and symbols of stockbrokers as those pertaining to transatlantic sailors or navigators. In the commerce hall, for example, the mass of male bodies in their black business suits takes the shape of waves, where sweaty handkerchiefs approximate breaks and seafoam: "The black waves rippled and handkerchiefs drenched with sweat sprayed like seafoam."[71] Rodon's uncertain future there is evoked by his feeling of being tossed about: "Blinded, stifled, and battered by the surge, he heard the waves roar through the air while he looked for his friend in vain."[72] After the shared excitement about propagandizing the railway line that will connect Gil's birthplace, Vilaniu, to Barcelona, Gil and his peers decide to celebrate, taking to the water—not far from the future location of the monument to Columbus—in a scene that symbolically represents an adventurous expedition at sea:

> Foix and his companions groped around for a place to situate themselves in the boat. Once accommodated, the boat began to gain access among the multitude of other little boats surrounding it, and it took off followed by a silvery wake, which bubbled up in some moments and in others extended smooth and tranquil over the still mass of water.[73]

The ambiguous description of the wake of the waves, which serves as a conclusion to the novel's second chapter, forecasts turbulence and tranquility for the seafarers. Thus, the narrator portends both good and bad moments for the men aboard the ship, which may have recalled for readers the enterprising caravels of Columbus, whose likeness newly towered over the end of the Rambles overlooking Barcelona's Old City and coastline.

As if expository discussion of Foix's Cuban adventure and the subsequent maritime metaphors were not enough to demonstrate the role of the colonies in conditioning imaginative configurations of modern, middle-class masculinity, the Catalan financier's employment of Panxito, described as a *negret* (little black boy), functions as an illustrative signpost of Gil's paternalistic and imperialist undertones.[74] Though there are few explicit references to Foix's American past, it materializes most clearly and problematically throughout the novel in the secondary figure of Panxo, a virtual fixture of the Foix household and an accessory to the *indiano* manhood of its namesake.

Panxito's adjacency to Gil's youngest son, Eudaldet, makes him an accessory of Foix's *indiano* masculinity which straddles both paternalistic and imperialist valences. Described as the family's bellhop ("botons"), the youth doubles as errand boy and chaperone to Eudaldet: the two are often mentioned together, thus conflating Gil's fatherly persona with that of the boss or patron. Upon entering his new, palatial estate, decorated extravagantly for Christmas festivities, Gil is "followed by a little black boy."[75] Elated, the young Eudaldet greets the pair in his characteristic childish register, which the narrator then imitates in his summary: "It is papa, and he brings bobons [infantilized pronunciation of *botons*] with him. Having said that, he had just enough time to take the basket over which the *neguito* [little black boy] competed with him, and entered with it in front of his satisfied father."[76]

Although his role in the novel is undoubtedly ornamental, his very objectified status, which has illustrative parallels in contemporaneous visual culture, functions as a figure of Gil's success story and, as Fradera remarks, a potential sign of the origins of the Foix family's wealth.[77] Through both direct and indirect characterization, the first description of Panxito hinges on his reification by both the narrator and Foix himself: "A little decorative figurine with his impossibly tight-fitting, olive-green suit, his chest adorned with three rows of brass buttons, straight as an Easter candle and spinning on one axis, it seemed like he was plucked from one of those traveling street organs."[78] Compared to the mechanical figure or organ-grinding puppet/ animal associated with busking, Panxito's presence throughout the novel would appear to corroborate Fradera's evaluation of nineteenth-century Catalan literature's *negrets* as having only a "a decorative or ornamental function."[79] However, as this chapter's analysis will continue to show, a close reading of Panxito's presence in the novel, situated within contemporaneous visual cultural evidence, provides further evidence for the interconnectivity between bourgeois masculinity and modernization, and regional and national identity formation, particularly as they play out in the Catalan context.

Shortly after the scene, which Catarina compares to a chromolithographic advertisement (*cromo*), Catarina's mother, Donya Mònica, arrives on scene, piercing the otherwise positive affective bubble with her whispers: "I fear you are doing too much with all of this: I do not think that God wants it this way . . . And why do you all have that little black boy? Has he been baptized? Are you sure of it?"[80] Mònica's recourse to the boy's baptism as a Christian underscores the role of religion in the civilizing missions of imperialist expansion projects, which nineteenth-century Catalan elites were sure to recognize: in the discourse surrounding the monument to Columbus, for example, the authors of the project cite the Catalan priests who accompanied the various colonizing missions during the Golden Age.[81]

Panxito's objectification in the novel contributes to Foix's embodiment of masculine patterns associated with the *indiano* and also coincides with racialized advertising strategies that were ubiquitous in imperialist and imperializing nations during the nineteenth century. *Cromos* and department store catalogs advertising luxury items from cigar paper to clocks and children's toys participated in the infantilization and commodification of black and indigenous bodies (see fig. 3.2 and fig. 3.3).[82] Oller may have had this kind of commercial ephemera in mind when writing Panxito, since *La febre d'or*'s characters allude to *cromos* on at least two occasions.[83]

Many advertisements for luxury goods such as tobacco, chocolate, clothing, jewelry, and children's toys—including examples like this *cromo* promoting pocket watches and clocks—relied on racialized (and racist) iconography and demonstrate the tendency for cultural producers to capitalize on exoticized and infantilized representations of non-Westerners. It is worth pointing out that the white consumers and clockmakers depicted in Figure 3.3 actively work and shop, while the young black boy, who passively frames and is framed by clockfaces, is mechanized and frozen in his commodification. Exhibiting what Anne McClintock refers to as an "imperial metamorphosis," the image eerily recalls Oller's description of Panxito's mechanized movements upon Gil's return home.[84] "Commodity racism," to borrow McClintock's words, "became distinct from scientific racism in its capacity to expand beyond the literate, propertied elite through the marketing of commodity as spectacle. [. . .] Imperial kitsch as consumer spectacle, by contrast, could package, market and distribute evolutionary racism on a hitherto unimagined scale."[85] Readers of *La febre d'or* would have likely had such ephemeral figures in mind (not least of all because affluent families like the Güells, who also owned black servants originally from the Antilles, were conspicuous about the origins of their wealth).[86]

While Oller appears to criticize the presence of the exoticized footman in the voice of Donya Mònica, Gil's frugal mother-in-law and one of the spokespersons of Catalan *seny* and traditional morality in the novel, the specificity of the critique is diluted by the fact that she is just as scandalized by the tacky foreignness she sees represented in Delfineta's French tutor, perhaps symbolically named Blanche.[87] Still, Panxito's blackness particularly grates on Mònica, who frames the boy as a "tacky" accoutrement of Gil's self-fashioning as an *indiano* or *americano*: "if you must have a little boy, why does he have to be black? To look nice? To appear rich? To play the part of the fashionable *American* [i.e., *indiano*]? Good gracious—what foolish pretensions!"[88] Interpretations of the exchange depend on the reader's reconciliation of different points of view. Catarina's muffled laughter that follows Mònica's diatribe reflects either her failure to sympathize with her mother's excessive but reasonable critiques or, alternatively, a facetious response to Mònica's exaggeratedly reactionary attitude toward the Foix household's—and, specifically, Gil's—superficiality. Such ambiguity within the *indiano* register also reinforces Oller's already ambivalent framing of the businessman which he initiates in his association with the priest.

FIGURE 3.2. Advertisement for cigar wraps. The caption reads, "ATTENTION SMOKERS! All booklets of VILLAREY PAPER have the quantity of sheets indicated by the cover." Image courtesy of the Arxiu Històric de la Ciutat de Barcelona, Barcelona, Spain.

FIGURE 3.3. Chromolithographic advertisement for "The Blackman's Clock and Watch Shop by Luis Molas." Image courtesy of the Arxiu Històric de la Ciutat de Barcelona, Barcelona, Spain.

On the one hand, Panxito serves as a constant reminder to the reader of the specter of colonial exploitation that would continue to haunt nineteenth-century ephemera, given the slave trade's late abolition in Cuba.[89] According to Simon Gikandi, such figures, in spite of their apparent marginalization in narratives of white self-fashioning, actually bring from the background forward the colonial experience they sometimes obfuscate, since the slave trade's "primary commodity was black bodies, sold and bought to provide free labor to the plantation complexes of the new world, whose primary products—coffee, sugar, tobacco—were needed to satiate the culture of taste and the civilizing process."[90] Panxo draws attention to possible sources of the Foix family income, even if Oller's *indiano* did not return from Cuba wealthy because of it. When considered alongside nineteenth-century advertisements and Gil's general pursuit of the signposts of wealth and prosperity, the young boy serves metaphorically as an accessory that brands Foix's capitalistic manhood, which, as the introduction to this book demonstrates, relied just as much as femininity did on the acquisition and display of commodified signs and symbols.

The infantilization of the boy and his association with Gil's son, Eudaldet, also bolsters paternalistic valences in Foix which, in the context of the transatlantic slave trade allow us to read the character as one of imperialism's tokens. Indeed, Oller's discursive treatment of Panxito tethers his novel to the racialized strategies that readers would have been familiar with in consumer culture more broadly. Commenting on similar advertisements in the British imperial context, McClintock reasons that "in the iconography of Victorian racism, the condition of 'savagery' is identical to the condition of infancy. Like white women, Africans (both women and men) are figured not as historic agents but as frames for the commodity, valued for *exhibition* alone."[91] In the eye of the consumer, collector, or observer, the black body in Figure 3.3 is transformed into a fantasy of bourgeois production and consumption for the ultimate purpose of domestic decoration. Last, but perhaps not least of all, Panxito's presence in *La febre d'or*—evident, too, in Mònica's goading of her daughter and son-in-law—serves as a reminder of the human capital involved in the speculative adventures of the *indiano* businessman symbolized in the novel by Foix.

While Oller characterizes Foix directly as an *indiano* by foregrounding his tale of social mobility with his failed adventure in Cuba, his subsequent indirect characterization of *La febre d'or*'s protagonist as a sportsman (gambler and horse jockey) taps into the middle-class man's place within late nineteenth century Barcelona as both consumer and consummate risk-taker, while inviting obvious comparisons to be made between speculative stock-market transactions and the quainter but still potentially perilous gambling that took place in newly constructed *casinos* and horse-racing arenas.

Sportsmen: The Gambler and the Jockey

The juxtaposition of Foix and other businessmen with the competitive arena of sport and the gambling associated with it in chapter sixteen— where Foix and Rodon are indirectly characterized as gamblers and jockeys in a spectacular "rat race"—is yet another way in which Oller ambivalently frames the masculine gender expression of his fictional capitalists. The juxtaposition and emerging analogy signal the competitive nature of men who vied for stock shares and values, and, therefore, serve as an indication of the struggles for hegemony associated with certain brands of masculinity within capitalism.[92] The combination of gambling and horse racing in Oller's imagination, as this section will demonstrate, evokes both the Catalan novelist's effort to paint an accurate, if still aspirational portrait of Barcelona's ascendant middle class, while simultaneously underscoring everything it has to gain or lose with the speculative ventures of men like Foix. Indeed, as Franklin argues, "gambling threatened to reveal its analogical relationship to paper money and to the chancy flow of abstract value in the speculative channels of market capitalism."[93] Foix's and Rodon's celebratory gambling with their disposable income draws attention to the new leisure industry that encouraged their participation as well as to the gender expression inherent in the games men played at the turn of the century. Indeed, winning or losing mattered less than conspicuous display for the upwardly mobile businessman. Still, the decision to stage the chapter in the Hippodrome—not inaugurated until 1883, the year after the action of *La febre d'or* takes place—also throws into relief the animalistic drive mobilizing businessmen to compete (either disastrously or triumphantly) with their peers in an effort to advance in pecuniary rat races.

As we will see, by including a central, highly dramatized chapter that takes place in the horse racing arena, Oller also inserts himself and the Catalan novel into the pan-European literary canon. Leo Tolstoy's *Anna Karenina* (1878) and Émile Zola's *Nana* (1880), to name only two examples that Oller would have had at his disposal, both include similar scenes at horse racing tracks. Since Oller memorialized his personal ambitions and anxieties related to the pageantry and performance of the Jocs Florals in his posthumously published memoirs, we may also read the aforementioned narrativization of the new national pastime—of French and English extraction—as a metaliterary commentary on the novelist's own professional vicissitudes related to his experience writing *La febre d'or*: from his reticent submissions to the Floral Games and his performance as a literato in front of more established peers to his rush to publish *La febre d'or* once made aware of Zola's plans to launch his own novel about the Parisian stock exchange. Paratextual evidence also demonstrates the anxiety for Catalan artists and writers to "measure up" against English and, primarily, French models, thus highlighting additional metaliterary elements related to anxieties that emerge in Oller's depiction of the scene.

By the end of the nineteenth century, in Barcelona as elsewhere in metropolitan Europe, gambling and horseracing had become staples of a highly commercialized leisure industry. A sign of what Sara Muñoz-Muriana has cleverly coined "el negocio del ocio" (the leisure business), both activities—spectated by men and women but protagonized primarily by the former—are examples of the constellation of new, bourgeois lifestyles that came to be associated with modernizing nations.[94] Within the context of a novel about risky stock market speculation, gambling functions as a capacious metaphor for the men who played with the economy as they might place bets on horses. Instead of adopting a moralizing stance vis-à-vis the activity, however, and in keeping with the tenets of realism, Oller withholds judgment: he leaves it to his readers to make connections with the havoc the activity has the potential to wreak on the Foix family's (and, by extension, local and national) finances.

Although gambling was nothing new to nineteenth-century Spain, by that time, it had become one of the preferred hobbies of men with enough financial and social capital to rub elbows in the masculine-coded realms of the casino and the hippodrome. According to an article in the sports section in a June 1891 issue of *La Época*, the author compares casinos to English clubs, writing that "the Spaniard founded the 'Casino or Social Circle' to strike conversation with someone outside of a café, paying double the expenses of other mortals, and being able, without intervention by the police, to gamble and, if it's possible, to earn his daily bread."[95] As with other activities that took place in the casino, gambling was not just about low-stakes risk-taking or playing to win, it was also an important form of homosociality relevant to the articulation of "polite male society."[96] If money was at stake in such transactions, so too was a man's bourgeois identity, which was constructed not only against the grain of that of women, but also in relation to that of other men in the codified arenas of the casino and the hippodrome.

The casino was itself a heterogeneous space where men socialized, gambled, and made business deals.[97] Though the masculine gendering of the casino was bolstered by fictional representations, the exclusion of women was not imaginary. In his memoirs, Oller recalls an unfortunate occasion during a visit to the French capital when Emilia Pardo Bazán, who, hoping to introduce her compatriots into Parisian literary circles, was turned away at the door of a casino on account of her gender: "despite having been very well received by the folklorists at their monthly luncheons the previous year, [. . .] and now, hoping to introduce Yxart and me to them, they closed the doors to her, citing the casino's statutes which absolutely prohibited the entry of women to the luncheons now hosted there."[98] Even though Pardo Bazán's own pan-European social connections were responsible for inducting Oller, Yxart, and other Spanish male writers into French literary circles, their fragility was exposed when tested by the power structures of a patriarchal system that continued to work against the professionalization of women in male-dominated vocations.

Certainly not limited to the confines of casino spaces, which were misogynistic by design, gambling was a sanctioned practice in newly constructed horse-racing stadiums, thus demonstrating the game of risk's kinship with the sporting world and the symbiotic nature of some bourgeois cultural practices. In Modesto Lafuente's *Teatro social del siglo XIX* (1846; Nineteenth-century social theater), the publication date of which coincides with the inauguration of Madrid's first hippodrome on the Castellana, the author historicizes the sport as it emerged in Europe and Spain, citing the younger, Spanish version as a copy of a French copy of an English original:

> Does one even need to ask about the origination of this [horse-riding] society? Does one need to ask, perchance, from where we in Spain gather all of our fashions and all of our societies? It is one of two possibilities: they are either native or originate in Paris, and from there we borrow them directly, or the original is to be found in London, the copy in Paris, with Madrid hosting the copy of the copy. It is this second option to which can be traced both the horse-riding society and their steeplechases.[99]

Not unlike his peers writing about business, fashion, and literature, Lafuente was well aware of Spain's late entrée to such leisure activities, even if such statements often distort or exaggerate the supremacy of English and French models.

Although horse racing had existed in the Hyde Park area of London since the seventeenth century, and it was the English who coined horse racing terminology, Englishmen and women did not actually have access to a proper hippodrome until one opened in London's Notting Hill in 1837. It closed shortly thereafter in 1841 due to what Hannah Velten calls the city's "faltering racing scene."[100] A more lasting stadium opened in 1868, twenty-two years after Madrid's first stadium—which, not unlike its English counterpart, lasted only two years—and the same year as the Jerez track. And so while it is true that Spain was sometimes a laggard when it came to access to new technologies or sports in the cultural sphere, the presumption of inferiority or belatedness made nineteenth-century Spaniards prone to fetishizing or extolling British or French cultural products when, in reality, family resemblances between Western industrialized nations outnumber the differences. Still, Spanish horse racing enthusiasts had to wait for hippodromes to be established in Madrid (1846, 1878), Jerez (1868, well before the start of the September Revolution), and Barcelona (1883, one to two years after the action of *La febre d'or* takes place).

The same inferiority complex underlying Spanish cultural producers and consumers' vague feelings of secondary status among peers in industrialized Western nations, as we discussed in the introduction, also pervaded the anxiety-ridden novel-writing enterprises of Spanish novelists. Oller was perhaps foremost in this group, since his persona was virtually a metonym of the regionalist high notes of the Renaixença, whose leaders had lauded Oller in the form of literary awards and recognition. After discovering that Zola had decided to write his own "stock-market novel" titled *L'Argent*, Oller became particularly nervous about the timeline for his own novel, the composition of which actually predated that of the French naturalist. In an epistolary exchange with artist and playwright Santiago Rusiñol—a confidant of Oller's and an intimate friend of Casas's—the burden on Oller to finish the novel promptly, as well as the peer pressure through which it was articulated, become evident.[101] Writing to Oller from Paris in a letter dated 10 December, 1890, Rusiñol mentions the buzz surrounding the publication of Zola's novel, as well as the money he had already earned for the project and the high-profile marketing campaign advertising its future publication, while nudging Oller to finally put an end to his drafting of *La febre d'or*:

> Zola has begun to publish his "money": his "moneymaker," which I say because they've paid him a pretty penny. I tell you this so that you don't

snooze on publishing your "febre," and so that you finally put an end to the task. [. . .] Well, now that I've nagged on you enough I'll tell you that they've announced Zola's novel around the quartiers with beautiful posters made by Chéret. Do you want me to send you one?[102]

Still, since Zola had already proven very capable of making a living off his writing and, thus, could produce manuscripts at a fast pace, and Oller's profession as a lawyer meant that he had to resort to spending his holidays writing, it was not long before the French celebrity writer outpaced the Catalan. Viewed through this context, Oller's highly dramatized depiction of the horse races—and the chancy games played by the men who attend and spectate them—may be read in a metaliterary key, since his own efforts to succeed as an aspiring novelist were driven by anxieties associated with competition, encouragement, and pressure from his (male) peers.

Chapter XVI of *La febre d'or* opens with a short, descriptive exposition before announcing the debut of the new Hippodrome of Can Tunis, a radiant beacon of "the affluent Barcelona undergoing modernization."[103] Not completed until 1883, one year after the action of *La febre d'or* takes place, the Hippodrome was built by a French company with the support of the Catalan Society for Horse Breeding, following a fashion set by the English. Thus, echoing Lafuente's historicization, the arena stood as yet another reminder of the many ways Catalans imagined themselves and their city's aspirational kinship to Paris and London. Oller reproduces the scene based on the synthesis of his own nostalgic recollection of the event, contemporaneous news reports, and his observations during the time of composition. For example, he describes "the stretch of lawn or *pelouse* was softened and made greener by the morning dew," which cushions any noise made by the horses' trot.[104] This description of a fictionalized 1881–1882 inauguration contradicts an article published after the historical opening, which makes a point to describe the lack of attractive vegetation visitors to the London and Paris Hippodromes had come to expect.[105]

Published in an 1883 issue of *La Ilustració Catalana*, a centerfold that includes a number of vignettes corroborating Oller's panoramic description of the sportsmen—both athletes and spectators—as well as the newly constructed racecourse of Can Tunis bespeaks public interest in the inauguration (see fig. 3.4). Multiangle representations of the stadium emphasize the novelty of the structure, while the image of jockeys on horseback "preparing themselves for the race" establish the dual protagonism of the male jockeys and their horses. The panoramic image occupying the bottom half of the centerfold perfectly aligns spectators with the jockeys that race across the track on horseback, with the symbolically significant Montjuïc featuring prominently in the background. The masculine apparel of spectators in the foreground—recognizable by their top hats and shorter bowler caps—together with that of the jockeys, heightens the masculine-coded nature of the space, at least in the eye of the artist charged with representing the event for *La Ilustració Catalana*.

Despite the exclusively masculine character of the centerfold image, both men and women pour onto the scene Oller describes. Dressed in apparel corresponding to their gender, the masses focalized by the narrator represent polite society, even though subsequent descriptions mention the dividing of spaces according to ticket price (and, thus, socioeconomic class). The metaphorical treatment of the spectators as hordes of teeming ants foreshadows the comparison this chapter makes between male gamblers and the horses driven by their jockeys:

> Women and young girls dressed opulently in light colors lowered themselves [from the carriages] with a jump, opening their resplendent parasols. Arm in arm with gentlemen disguised as sportsmen in their gray frocks and their similarly hued top hats, with the binoculars resting over their chests and entrance tickets dangling from their buttonholes, they all darted across the newly shorn course to arrive at the pedestrian enclosure to join up with the rest of the *beau monde* that teemed there like an anthill.[106]

Sportsman was a name used to describe both men who attended sporting events and the athletes who participated in them. Contrasting with the etiquette of black or dark clothing that men followed when attending formal gatherings or to sit for a portrait, leisurely activities required men, like their female counterparts, to sport the corresponding apparel. As we saw in this book's introduction, men's ability to show their mastery of new social cues was yet another way in which they were able to display their embodiment of the "modern masculine ideal."[107]

In *La febre d'or*, Gil's inclusion within the sportsmen group is corroborated by the narrator's point of view of the scene in the subsequent sections, where he and his family become the object of the expectant gaze of two spectators. The couple ogles both race attendees and racers from a comfortable distance, conflating them all within the scopic regime of their shared pair of binoculars. After the initial description of the radiant day and the filing in of carriages and elegantly bedecked spectators, Oller's

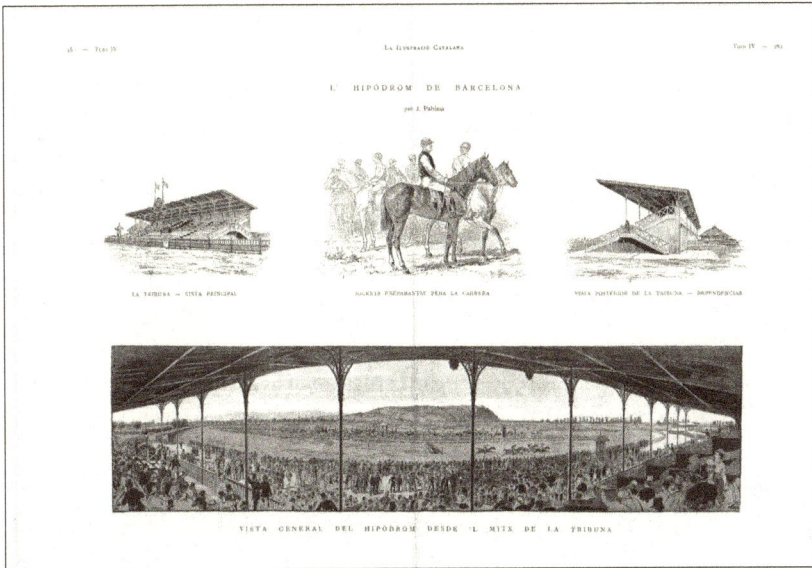

FIGURE 3.4. Centerfold image from an 1883 issue of *La Ilustració Catalana*. Image courtesy of the Hemeroteca Digital of the Biblioteca Nacional de España, Madrid, Spain.

chapter is filtered through a dialogue between an anonymous married couple, through whom the rest of the section is presumably focalized. While the pair watches everyone file in, they, too, compete for the focal vantage point made possible by their binoculars: "Could you pass the binoculars so that I can see who they are?"/ "Yes, my dear, yes: now I see them well. It's one of my clients . . . Gil Foix . . . one of those who has climbed to the top in short time. Why yes, dear! He's quite a character these days! He's the one who'll bring the railroad to Vilaniu, you know?"/ "Believe you me, Ramon: you must get yourself over to the stock exchange: it's the only place where money is made these days. Don't you see? Those who were unknown yesterday arrive today loftily atop such elegant coaches."[108] In passages narrating such high-profile outings, as is the case with theatrical moments in novels like *La Regenta*, *Nana*, and *Anna Karenina*, bourgeois spectators are as important actors as those performing on stage. As this scene illustrates perfectly, the same is true of the Hippodrome, where the lead actors in Barcelona's spectacular financial adventures are object to the gaze of others.

Despite the obvious intermingling of men and women occurring within the Hippodrome, certain activities and spaces divided along gendered lines:

for example, Foix's daughter, Delfineta, and her foil, Emília—whose rivalry over the hand of the Baron d'Esmalrich is also reinforced by the competitive setting—must eventually resort to another space in order to stage their heated discussion. While searching for an appropriate place to talk, for example, the narrator describes the impenetrable wall of men the two young women encounter: "Precisely there, in the French ring, the wall was impenetrable. A dense swarm of gamblers surrounded the foreign bookmakers, inscribing themselves at the stands, crying like they do in the commerce hall, the cigar in their lips, the top hat tilted to the napes of their neck."[109] Though the Catalan word for gamblers—*jugadors*—is inclusive of men and women, the subsequent description of the gamblers shouting as if they were in the commerce hall armed with cigars and top hats confirms the masculine coding of the space and its occupants.

The narrator's description of the high energy among both racers and spectators at the toss of the starter's pennant creates a parallel between both groups, drawing an inevitable comparison to the layered centerfold image described earlier:

> But the jockeys, following the orders of the restless racetrack starter, began to line up. The noise of the crowd died down, everyone distracted as they compared the number of registered animals with the fewer of those that were on the track. The bell sounded, the starter threw the pennant . . . and, at once, the horses took off. The crowd stood up at once, rousing the animals with their cries, bodies leaning forward, the neck elongated, following them anxiously with their eyes, breaking out in exclamations at every successive gain or loss. And the horses, moving farther out, diminishing in the distance, flew off vainly like hares, the jockey a handspan from the seat, bent down, their heads almost rubbing up against the horses' mane, left hand jostling the bridle, the right whipping the animal's pink hide.[110]

With the crowds standing up to cheer in the same moment that the horses take off, Oller's narrator confuses spectator and spectated and, thus, the different types of sportsmen vying for a win. Additionally, Príncipe, Rat Penat, and Pimpette, Broadside and Picador—names of horses mentioned by Oller—were the actual names of horses that raced in 1883, demonstrating Oller's attendance there or his close study of the outcomes published in culture and lifestyle magazines of the time. The conflation of spectator and horse continues in the subsequent section in which the high energy reaches its climax: "And the spectator, excited, heart racing furiously, their self-worth dependent upon their predictions, the greed of the gambler in peril, struggled internally, on the tips of their toes, their soul at their eyes, shouting, muffling, dependent upon the vicissitudes of chance, wishing to transmit all their strength and nervous fluids to their beast of choice."[111]

At the end of the race, the flippancy with which Foix and Rodon treat their losses signals the ability of homosocial bonding to alleviate the losses associated with risk: "Hem fet un pa com unes hòsties."[112] The literal translation of the phrase—"We have made a thin bread like the communion wafer"—reveals that "play served a connective or bridging function, tying the demonized issue of gambling, for instance, to the socially pivotal institution of the stock market, and linking both of these to two of the most important issues in Victorian thought: work and money."[113] The idea here is that of failing to make or cook something substantial and material, such as bread, and ending up instead with something thinner and more symbolic in nature. Present in this passage, then, is an opposition between the immaterial and the artisanal worlds, the latter of which the character returns to in a recuperation of a traditional Catalan ethos, and the kinds of fabrications on which modern bourgeois masculinity depends (engaging in stock trading, gambling as sportsmen, etc.). Modern men, who no longer separate work and play, risk losing the more modest but reliable power to generate the more material realities of pre-modern times, with modern masculinity amounting to little more than a matter of belief.

To be sure, horse races were a part of modernizing metropolitan spaces, and novelists inevitably identified them as appropriate events through which to focalize their bourgeois fictions. More than just a fashionable backdrop, however, the Hippodrome also represents a significant intertext that tethers Oller's novel to the pan-European literary canon after which he modeled his own novels. Similar scenes at the horse races occur in *Nana* and *Anna Karenina*, both of which were well known by nineteenth-century Spanish novelists and readers. In Zola's novel, the titular courtesan enters the racetrack at the Bois de Boulogne triumphantly in a horse-drawn carriage, not unlike Gil and his own retinue, and the novelist makes a similar juxtaposition between ambitious characters and racehorses by bestowing the name Nana to the horse who ends the race victorious. Tolstoy's version, which, like Oller's, insists upon the lens of the crowd ("All eyes, all binoculars were turned to the bright-coloured little group of riders as they lined up") also emphasizes the male homosocial character of the racers by giving readers direct access to Count Vronksy's desire to master his horse to crush his rival, the eventually triumphant Makhotin; Vronksy's attempts end tragically when a fatal accident forces him to mercy-kill his beloved horse Frou-Frou.[114] Both authors, like Oller, insist upon the pan-European character of such bourgeois events in which terminology and names blend English and French, thus drawing attention to the origins of the sport as well as the fashionability of British and French culture across Europe during the nineteenth century. Oller's inclusion of a similarly climactic scene in his foundational fiction of Catalan modernity communicates an awareness of and deliberate dialogue with the European literary canon that Zola and Tolstoy represented for the aspiring Spanish novelist. As we saw earlier in his conversations with Rusiñol, Oller participated in one way or another in his own anxiety-ridden "rat race" to produce *La febre d'or*, what is undoubtedly his most ambitious novel. Commenting on Oller's aspirational comparison of Barcelona to Paris, Joan Ramon Resina writes that "to be a *petit Paris* was to be a *Paris manqué*." Oller's aspirational representation of horse racing—again, somewhat *avant la lettre* in the context of the late nineteenth-century Barcelona he depicts—reflected the uneven modernization that was occurring in the city's urban panorama, and mirrors the discrepancies between his own professional aspirations (especially to succeed as a novelist writing in Catalan) and the material circumstances preventing them from being fully realized (e.g., the lack of a robust reading public, low literacy rates, his need to write while on vacation from his job as a lawyer, etc.).

Despite the fact that the Hippodrome did not officially open to the public until 1883, a year after the action of *La febre d'or* takes place, Oller's desire to contract time so as to make the structure's inauguration coincide with the 1882 stock market crash in Barcelona draws attention to his novel's own speculative enterprise. Like Gil, who hoped to connect his native Vilaniu to Barcelona via financial speculation in the railway industry, Oller took a risk—a speculative gambit—to write his "bourgeois epic" in Catalan in order to pull Catalan literature into pan-European literary markets and networks composed of established agents like Émile Zola, Leo Tolstoy, and Benito Pérez Galdós. Indeed, Oller wagered that his representation of the gambling of his businessmen at the steeplechase and their juxtaposition with the horses and jockeys on whom they place their bets would have been recognized as an intertext with novels like *Nana* and *Anna Karenina*. Although celebratory in tone, Gil's and Rodon's flippant spending of their time and money reflects the new lifestyles available to affluent businessmen with disposable income, as well as the various models of masculinity they identified in various outlets in the late nineteenth-century metropolis' leisure industry. Winning or losing was perhaps less significant than the conspicuous, masculine, display of risk-taking.

And yet within the scope of the rest of the novel, Oller's chapter is more ambivalent than it appears at first glance. While the married couple described in the chapter's exposition are overwhelmingly positive in their assessment of the Hippodrome's inaugural festivities, the husband cannot shake the distraction of the cemetery, which remained visible from the heights of the stadium seating. "Frankly, that is in poor taste: it is too front and center; it reminds us of our end and of the loved ones we've buried there."[115] Though the scene at the Hippodrome is firmly anchored in the novel's generally positive first part ("La pujada"), the memento mori foreshadows the fall that awaits Gil during the novel's denouement, a result of his "gambling" with the economy.[116] Though various elements of Gil's characterization in the second half of the novel point to the shift in the protagonist's fortune, the most telling image emerges in the novel's denouement, when Gil's upwardly mobile trajectory is brought full circle in the return to his humble origins as a carpenter, and in Oller's own return to narrative framing.

Conclusion: The Artisanal Laborer and a Return to Framing

Capitalizing on references to the interconnected, male homosocial worlds of the priesthood, colonial affairs, gambling, and horse racing, Oller demonstrates the various patterns of masculinity that brand the gender expression of late nineteenth-century Barcelona's businessmen and speculative adventurers. As we saw throughout this chapter, Oller's own vicissitudinous career relied on similar ecosystems of male homosociality. Encouraged to undertake his novel-writing career by peers like Yxart, Sardà, and Pereda, Oller persevered despite limitations and thanks to pressure from his peers—as evidenced by his epistolary exchanges with Galdós and Rusiñol. Of course, such pressure can also be read as a reflection of the substantial investments bestowed on him by interested mentors, colleagues, and competitors.

In a predictable coda (predictable because of the title of the novel's second part), Oller reframes Gil Foix as a carpenter, a career to which Foix's father dedicated himself in a pre-industrial suburb of Barcelona. Having failed to weather the stock-market bust of 1882, *La febre d'or*'s protagonist makes a symbolic return to carpentry and artisanal labor, marking a chute for his finances and a rise in his embodiment of traditional, moral values rooted in materiality versus ephemeral speculation. As virtually all critics of Oller's novel have noted, this return harks back to the productive grounds upon which the Catalan bourgeoisie was founded and to which some (especially those whose ideals are represented throughout the novel by Francesc and Donya Mònica) hoped it would return.[117] Newly installed in Francesc's home (a humble, domestic space, particularly when thrown into relief against the opulent mansion the family lived in earlier in the novel), Gil, emptied of his prior acumen and gregarious persona, is the virtual shell of the man he once was:

> in shirtsleeves and slackened pants, with one knee on the wood that he had extended atop a stool and the other planted on the ground, a gaunt Gilet put all his might into sawing wooden planks. Stupefied by what they saw, they continued watching him without comprehending the man's strange intentions. Once he had sawed a plank, Foix, without suspecting that anyone was watching, started to measure the edges of a picture frame that he had stacked against the wall.[118]

Foix's hubris resides in his earlier attempt to earn his bread without engaging in material/artisanal work. This narrative coda and return to framing may also be understood for its metaliterary connotations. In it, Oller draws attention to *La febre d'or* itself as a sort of frame for the market of ideas surrounding it.

In spite of Foix's tragicomic end, Oller ultimately remains ambivalent about the excesses of modern capitalism as they manifest in his sweeping portrayal of the booms and busts of Barcelona during the 1880s. *La febre d'or*'s coda—a return to the material and to framing, with Gil Foix's return to carpentry and, thus, the "precapitalistic habitat" he was originally destined to inhabit—would suggest a nostalgic narrative tactic on Oller's part.[119] However, as Toni Dorca has remarked, Foix's brother Bernat, in spite of the financially ruined state of his kin, makes a defense for the kinds of economic risks and ventures that were able to bring Vilaniu into a wider circuit of modernity: indeed, Bernat ultimately praises Gil for having put Vilaniu on the map. I would further argue that we might interpret Oller's narrative endeavor—here in *La febre d'or* as elsewhere in the novelist's oeuvre—as its own kind of speculative gambit. In other words, *La febre d'or* is the response of an individual author's personal, literary ambitions to write a modern novel in the style of Tolstoy or Galdós—exhibiting his own "insatiable desire to write a vigorous work, worthy of my country and of our time"—but also a narrative investment in support of the rebirth of Catalan cultural and linguistic identity for which Oller and his peers stood to gain in cultural, economic, social, and symbolic capital.[120]

Oller's narrative ambivalence toward Foix and the values he represents emerges clearly in the way his direct and indirect characterization transitions between the masculine-coded registers of the priest, the *indiano*, the sportsman, and artisan types. Unlike the homogeneous type or ideal that emerges from nineteenth-century portraiture and prescriptive conduct literature, the businessman is a heterogeneous type whose figuration within narrative necessarily draws on various masculine ideals and intertexts relevant to the Catalan and wider Spanish context.

Despite readers' enthusiasm for Oller's literary production, the novelist's own descriptions and recollection of his career accidentally or intentionally evokes Gil's anticlimactic end. In letters he wrote around the time of the composition of the *Memòries*, Oller expresses a great degree of trepidation about the idea of writing another novel, using the imperative in the negative to a friend who asked him to produce more: "never again advise me to produce more; leave me alone to make and peddle my woodwork. After all, we are in a country of merchants."[121] Oller's work as a novelist, as this chapter has shown, was very much subject to the pressures of the market, and he was well aware of what direct competitors like Zola were up to. As a novelist, he was not unlike a "mercader" (merchant), and he seems to strategize in ways similar to businessmen. Still, his oeuvre symbolizes a considerable literary achievement for a man whose struggles did not ultimately prevent him from taking risks. As we will see in the next chapter of this study, José María de Pereda—whose own identity as a businessman and bourgeois professional is often overshadowed by his almost mythical stature as a provincial patriarch—played a similarly generative role in fashioning modern patterns of middle-class masculinity he inherited, even as he sometimes wrote against them.

CHAPTER 4

THE HEIR

Illustrations of José María de Pereda (1833–1906) published during his life-time unanimously fashion his authorial persona in a provincial but refined and virile iconographic register. Offering a revelatory reflection of public perception, caricatures of Pereda help to shed light on his own embodi-ment of nineteenth-century masculinity and the masculine inheritances of his fictional mountain men—like the citybound social climber of *Pedro Sánchez* (1883) or the prodigal heir of *Peñas arriba* (1895; The upper peaks)—in more meaningful ways than have hitherto been recognized.[1] Figurations of the Cantabrian novelist as an unpretentious highlander and romantic painter of local color or rural life often drew upon stereotypical elements associated with his northern background and novels at the same time that they downplayed or ignored the trappings of his more overtly capitalistic career as a factory owner and board member of a bank. Situating Pereda's fiction somewhere between realism and regionalism, critics have recog-nized the author's definitive role in cultivating the regional novel, a subge-nre responsible for perpetuating "the myth of rural idyll" and the defense of "the restorative experience of direct contact with the natural world."[2] Despite their different uses, caricatures and portraits of Pereda also took part in legitimating the writer's professional identity as a regionalist writer via signs and symbols of rurality.[3] This was part of a process which helped to consolidate his celebrity status in a nation that continued to consume

FIGURE 4.1. Caricature of Pereda by Cilla for an 1883 cover of literary magazine *Madrid Cómico*. The caricature's caption reads, "A frank and modest Cantabrian highlander who constantly ricochets between Polanco and Santander. Cleverly he sketches from nature and has rightly acquired universal acclaim." Image courtesy of the Hemeroteca de la Biblioteca Nacional de España, Madrid, Spain.

costumbrista or "local-color" fiction voraciously amid the rise of realist or naturalist novels.[4]

In an iconic caricature and corresponding caption of an 1883 cover of *Madrid Cómico*, the artist Cilla and caption author (and Pereda's friend) Sinesio Delgado corroborate Pereda's early branding as a scion of literary regionalism around the time he was writing *Pedro Sánchez* (see fig. 4.1).[5] Unlike Cilla's caricatures of other writers from Spain's mountainous northern regions, this image lacks the more typically exaggerated attachments to rural symbols.[6] Instead, the artist's illustration of a bespectacled, mustachioed, and strapping Pereda depicts the austere but fashionably attired man from Polanco (Cantabria) as the embodiment of bourgeois self-control, seriousness, and provincial gentility underscored by the poetic caption's rhyming of Polanco and *franco* (frank).[7] In spite of the conspicuous absence of traditional icons of rurality, such as those that appear in Figure 4.2, the representation appears to match the myth of the sober "man of the north," which was mass-produced in photographs of the author.[8] As Raquel Gutiérrez Sebastián has remarked, the caricature's caption insists on Pereda's legibility as a representative of regionalist literature, where "the typically jocular verses that accompany the caricature, written by Sinesio Delgado, allude to the writer's places of residence and work, and to his affiliative *costumbrista*-realist ties and his literary reputation."[9] Pereda's friendship with *Madrid Cómico*'s then director Delgado was likely an influential factor in the positive depiction, which lacks the more humorous elements common to many of the magazine's other caricatures and captions. Pereda's probable hand in the composition of the favorable portrayal is evocative of his purchase in the enterprise of strategic self-fashioning one might expect of other bourgeois professionals during the late nineteenth century.

Printed in an issue of lifestyle magazine *Blanco y Negro* from March 1895, just a few months after the release of Pereda's penultimate and bestselling novel *Peñas arriba*, the full-page illustration by Mecachis for the "illustrious Spaniards" series brands Pereda's bourgeois literary celebrity by more playfully, if not parodically, cloaking him in the idealized or polished trappings of Cantabrian rusticity (see fig. 4.2).[10] Scaling a mountain range like the subject of Romantic painter Caspar David Friedrich's iconic *Wanderer above a Sea of Clouds* (1818), the author is shown hauling his novels to the "upper peaks" advertised on the side of his commercialized *cuévano*: a basket used by rural Cantabrians to harvest and transport crops, and to carry their children.[11] Outfitted with staples of the traditional Cantabrian man's costume, such as a peasant blouse, abdominal sash (*fajín*), clogs (*abarcas* or *almadreñas*), and harvesting basket (*cuévano*), the Peredan figure's display of an energized and even exaggeratedly youthful countenance appears to echo the trope of the health benefits of clean, mountain air commonly cited in the press, hygiene manuals, and travel literature as a panacea for the discontents and diseases associated with modern urban living.[12] Aside from projecting its own ambiguous fantasy of highlander rurality, this overt characterization of the author as a mountaineer coincides with the rhetoric of rusticity frequently employed in nineteenth-century reviews of Pereda's novels. In a representative example, one of his contemporaneous reviewers imagined him as a painter who, perched atop the highest crags, gathered onto his palette "traits, colors, and shades."[13] Insisting on the aromatic character of Pereda's words, Jerónimo Becker writes that in the chapters of his novels "one breathes the air of the countryside, laden with aromas and fragrances; air that expands the lungs and delivers oxygen to the blood, and with that

oxygenated blood, vital and fruitful tides to the heart and mind, respectively."[14] These images substantiate the mythical mountain man's embodiment of tropes related to the romanticized literato versus those of a bourgeois financial elite, even if the two identities, as this chapter contends, are
inextricably linked. In its arrangement of rural stereotypes that constellate
around Pereda, Mecachis's caricature would appear to foreground a reading
of the novelist's books as either a bountiful harvest uprooted from a fertile
landscape, or—given the Cantabrian basket's use in childrearing—as the
intellectual offspring of an invigorated author-father.

Less conspicuous in these illustrations was Pereda's more conventionally
bourgeois role as inheritor to a financial legacy founded by his brothers:
from the 1860s onward he was an owner of a soap, perfume, and chemicals
factory—La Rosario—and, between 1898 and his death in 1906, he was a
board member of the Bank of Santander.[15] His bona fide status as a literal
bourgeois heir and elite notwithstanding, it was the Cantabrian's metaphorical inheritance of his native *tierruca* (a Cantabrian word akin to native
homeland or birthplace), along with the means to represent its people, language, and customs via the local-color sketch and the realist-regionalist
novel, that factor most prominently in the ways Pereda's life and oeuvre
continue to be remembered. Despite their centrality to Pereda's livelihood,
these overtly capitalistic elements of his career have often been considered
at odds with the more prominent image he preferred to cast as the lofty
scion of provincial gentility or *hidalguía* (minor nobility).

While these more overtly commercial facets of Pereda's professional
identity have been used by scholars to reframe how one memorializes the
writer, the extent to which they bespeak the Cantabrian novelist's attachments to nineteenth-century masculinity has yet to be addressed.[16] The
fact that he and, perhaps to an even greater extent, his peers, reviewers,
and caricaturists, often chose to downplay or ignore those more stereotyp-
ically bourgeois identity markers (like owning a factory or having a hand in
finance) is indicative of Pereda's contradictory embodiment of modern masculinity which, to be sure, relied on archetypes of rurality like the country
bumpkin or the rugged mountain man as points of contrast or comparison
in routines of self-fashioning. As we will see, bourgeois men and the artists and authors who represented them relied on whitewashed rural signs
in an effort to bring "an air of the natural [. . .] to images of masculinity,
legitimating them as allegedly in touch with truths that are deeper than the
merely social."[17] Additionally, in Pereda's case, the motif of legacy and the
masculine transmission of inheritance between fathers and sons, uncles and

FIGURE 4.2. "Españoles ilustres" by Mecachis, *Blanco y Negro*
(March 16, 1895). Photo courtesy of the author.

nephews, and brothers—economic and otherwise—recurs in his representations of male heirs and simultaneously manifests in his own literal and
metaphorical inheritances as both a novelist and financial elite.

This chapter examines the contradictions and affinities in portrayals of
male heirs and what masculinities studies scholars have called rural masculinity in the illustrated press, as well as José María de Pereda's persona as
celebrity author and genteel bourgeois. A survey of evidence ranging from
visual cultural ephemera (e.g., magazine illustrations, advertisements, and
fashion plates) to Pereda's acceptance speech to the Spanish Royal Academy
will illustrate that tropes of male homosociality and masculine rusticity not
only figure classic tensions between rural and urban people and settings in
nineteenth-century Spain, but also within bourgeois modernity and manhood writ large. The chapter concludes with a section on how the Cantabrian novelist incorporates such tensions in novels from distinct moments
in his career: *Pedro Sánchez* (1883) and *Peñas arriba* (1895). On the one hand,
the protagonists in these novels, each of whom tends to complicate the
rural stereotypes proffered in the illustrated press, are expected to satisfy

the imperatives of patrilineal succession tying them to the land through the inheritance of motheaten pedigrees and provincial estates. On the other hand, they are drawn by the siren song of metropolitan Madrid, where they stand to capitalize on their youthful, masculine potential in the pursuit of desirable, "modern" careers as celebrated writers and politicians. In both cases, as was also true in the construction of Pereda's own public persona, "ruralized" patterns of bourgeois masculinity depended on strategic self-fashioning and male homosocial networks, whose agents capitalized on the signs and symbols of rural, working-class men but, in so doing, glossed over the harsher realities many were forced to inhabit.

Bridging older literary forms like the local-color sketch and the realist novel, and in light of the author's unequivocally regionalist political agenda, Pereda's novels—which straddle *costumbrista* regionalism, and realism, by design—constitute a compelling case study for tracing competing models of middle-class masculinity as they manifest against (and complicate) the familiar backdrops of the nineteenth-century city and country. After contextualizing and historicizing the figure of the male heir and visualizing the masculine inheritances of rural men in Restoration-era ephemera through the lens of rural masculinities, this chapter then turns its attention to how such conceits are emblematized and complicated by Pereda's highlander heirs in *Pedro Sánchez* and *Peñas arriba*. Through the urban and provincial development of their male protagonists and secondary characters, both novels imagine masculinity as a byproduct of male homosocial dialogues between the cosmopolitan and the rustic, even as the author ostensibly privileges attachments to the latter. Additionally, in an attempt to do away with the walls that tend to separate notions of urban and rural configurations of masculinity, this chapter concludes by suggesting that Pereda's multifaceted public persona and writings are illustrative of the colonizing and heterogeneous nature of bourgeois manliness, the constitutive representatives of which continue to reap the benefits of strategic affiliation with idols and idylls of rusticity like the farmer and the miner against the backdrop of an idealized hinterland.

Inheritance and Male Heirs During the Bourbon Restoration

Male heirs were common character types in nineteenth-century fictions that take place in urban and rural settings alike. Yet their omnipresence in Pereda's regional novels and their inheritance or embodiment of stereotypes and practices of rural masculinity reflects their meaningful place in the Cantabrian novelist's oeuvre as well as the role of masculinity in both his literary output and his own bourgeois self-fashioning. To be sure, nineteenth-century Spanish inheritance laws, which varied by region, allowed both women and men alike to inherit businesses, estates, titles, and thrones. But anxieties about patrilineal succession and paternal legacies in the context of familial inheritance practices, royal succession, and realist narrative reflect the wider cultural prioritization of and preference for male descendants, thus marking the heir (and related notions like authenticity and legitimacy) as central to the consideration of masculinity in the fin-de-siècle juridical, political, and literary imagination.[18] Additionally, as we will see, the male heir's proximity to (and ability to reproduce) patrimony through the father figure, a social type that scholars have recently begun to revisit in pan-European contexts, further demonstrates the affinities connecting the male inheritor with broader patterns of masculinity.[19] With an eye to illuminating Pereda's own literal inheritances from his parents and brothers, this section will conclude by highlighting the Cantabrian's metaphorical inheritance of rural paradigms across cultural and literary contexts before shifting attention to discussion of rural masculinity. This chapter's dual focus on the heir and rural masculinity will shed light on the masculine figures whose fictional development as regional inheritors provides a thematic key to *Pedro Sánchez* and *Peñas arriba* as relevant to Pereda's own gendered bourgeois identity as financial elite and novelist.

Daughters could and often did inherit in nineteenth-century Spain, not least of all in the northern regions of Galicia, Cantabria, and Catalonia, but the masculine transmission of patrimony between fathers and sons, or among brothers or uncles and nephews, was the default position—whether stated or unstated—in many modern inheritance practices.[20] As was the case in the numerous Pereda family, older brothers were especially common protagonists in the management and growth of family finances, particularly when parental legacies were non-existent or uncertain. Upon their mother's death in 1855, for example, José María de Pereda's older brothers Juan Agapito and Manuel took the reins of the family finances and were responsible for their younger brother's literary education and his eventual leadership role in the family business.[21] Given the mass migration of men from Spain's northernmost regions to the Americas—some of whom returned to the Peninsula as wealthier or at least more business savvy or connected *indianos* (colonial returnees), as was the case of Pereda's eldest brother—women could be named primary inheritors or operate as temporary executors of wills given the existence of more lucrative alternatives available to sons and brothers overseas and elsewhere in the metropole.[22] Still, according to Llorenç Ferrer-Alòs, the privileging of women over men only occurred "in exceptional circumstances [e.g., the long-term migration of males] ."[23] Martínez López confirms that this was the case because of the dependence of family finances on business networks for their growth: "The nineteenth-century consolidation of the ideal of the patriarchal bourgeois family favored paternal power but also that of older brothers."[24]

Pereda's interest in matters of inheritance was not limited to his own privileges as heir to a hidalgo namesake or the capital he acquired via the industrial pursuits of his older brothers. The Cantabrian novelist was, for example, a Carlist who did not hide his affiliation to the nineteenth-century political party borne of gendered disputes over the question of Isabel II's legitimacy as monarch, the origins of which date back to the misogyny of the Old Regime. Indeed, the prominent place of the male heir in the political imagination during the nineteenth century in Spain was perhaps clearest in the debates and wars fought over the question of royal succession which culminated—albeit anticlimactically for liberals like Galdós and Clarín—in the restoration of the Bourbon monarchy. Even before the death of Fernando VII (1784–1833), an absolutist despot who abolished the constitutional progress made by the Cádiz Courts (1812–1814) after his return from exile in France following the Peninsular War, the king's failure to produce a male heir set in motion a dynastic crisis that would incite or influence a series of conflicts that roiled metropole and colonial possessions alike: three civil wars (i.e., the Carlist Wars of 1833–1840, 1846–1849, and 1872–1876); the September revolution that would ultimately lead to the dethroning and exile of Isabel II (1868); and revolts in Cuba (1868–1878). While Isabel II reigned uninterrupted between 1840 and 1868, her regime and that of her mother, the queen regent María Cristina (1833–1840), were plagued by internal political strife. *Carlista* politicians and soldiers advocated for the candidacy of Don Carlos María Isidro Benito de Borbón (1788–1855), Fernando VII's younger brother, while even those liberals who supported or tolerated the reigns of Isabel and María Cristina placed constant pressure on them to accept more progressive policies. Although Prince Don Carlos died in between the first and second Carlist War, his descendants were subsequent claimants to the Spanish throne and their interests were defended in the second and third Carlist wars. If the failure of the September revolution of 1868 was a bane for more liberal-leaning novelists like Galdós and

Clarín for having compromised its integrity as a progressive movement in favor of a pact with moderates, some conservatives were at least placated by the restoration of the Bourbon monarchy in the person of Alfonso XII.

Pereda's advocacy for the androcentric Carlist cause, though sometimes exaggerated by critics, was made patently clear by his regionalist-traditionalist political modus operandi, as well as in his close friendships. Even though critics have identified Pereda's regionalism as more literary than political, the author ran for office as a deputy in the conservative party in 1871, although his campaign failed to bolster enough support to see him elected.[25] Far from an apologist of Pereda's Carlism, biographer Madariaga de la Campa clarifies that Pereda's participation within Carlism was uneven throughout his long career as a writer, and even those in whom he confided about his political beliefs via epistolary correspondence would characterize him as moderate.[26] In an 1877 letter to Galdós, Pereda defers more to the abstract values Carlists ostensibly defended rather than their overtly political elements: "I hold tradition in high esteem for its grand and patriarchal qualities, and I similarly regard the faith of my grandparents for its divine virtues, which is to say peace, charity, love, and hope."[27] Even if Pereda's own attachments to Carlism beyond his official support of the cause were uncertain, his appreciation for its advocacy of traditional Catholic values and his long-term friendships with major figures within the party, including one of its leaders, the Marquis of Cerralbo, made Pereda and his fiction at the very least guilty by association in the imaginations of more progressive realist novelists, like Galdós, and those of the younger generation of modernists, like Rubén Darío. Uncertainty about his bona fide attachments to the Carlist cause notwithstanding, Pereda's support of the pretender to the Spanish throne is but one example of the wider cultural anxieties about patriarchal legacy and masculine inheritance, motifs that also form the warp and weft of a number of canonical novels of the period.

The theme of familial succession is central to realist and naturalist novels during the Bourbon Restoration, and Pereda's fiction is no exception. Galdós's most direct engagement with the theme of inheritance is, without question, *La desheredada* (1881; The disinherited), the novel that initiated his so-called *segunda manera* (second way), or his series of novels that most effectively wed the Spanish realist tradition originated by Cervantes with nineteenth-century European models like Balzac, Flaubert, and Zola. In *La desheredada*, Isidora Rufete's father's insanity and her own obsession with quixotic fantasies of affluence cast doubt on her repeated claims as heiress to the Duchess of Aransis's fortune and namesake. In Galdós's novel *Fortunata y*

Jacinta, the familial desire for Juanito Santa Cruz to engender a male heir and the subsequent confusion over the legitimacy of his presumed son is central to the novel's plot, the focus of which is shared by the poor but fertile Fortunata and the bourgeois but barren Jacinta. For his part, Clarín's *Su único hijo* (1890) figures anxieties about birth and inheritance in Bonifacio Reyes, a melomaniac whose shortcomings as a husband and creator, as Cameron has argued, echo the author's own insecurities related to the engendering of a modern Spanish novel.[28] Motifs related to succession and uncertain paternity also emerge in fin-de-siècle French novels, like Émile Zola's Rougon-Macquart cycle (1871–1893) and Guy de Maupassant's *Pierre et Jean* (1888).[29]

As this chapter will show, Pereda's fiction is also entrenched in matters related to patriarchal succession and the male heir's place within it. In *Pedro Sánchez*, for example, the youngest son of a hidalgo family leaves his hometown to receive an education in politics and urbanity in revolutionary Madrid with the help of financial support from his brothers and questionably helpful male mentors functioning as surrogate father figures. *Peñas arriba* offers a culminating example of Pereda's engagement with questions of masculinity, paternity, and succession. In a pattern drawing inspiration from Galdós's *Doña Perfecta*, a young male heir born in the provinces but raised amid the creature comforts of Madrid is beckoned to the Cantabrian mountains to survey lands bequeathed to him, and to eventually claim his place as rightful heir to his uncle's (and, by extension, his father's) legacy. While this chapter focuses on *Pedro Sánchez* and *Peñas arriba*, nearly all of Pereda's major novels deal in one way or another with the masculine homosocial transmission of cultural and economic capital, which is perhaps unsurprising given the many ways his own life and literary output depended on such networks.

Despite the cosmopolitan character of his commercial and literary professionalization, the Cantabrian novelist tended to fashion himself—and was fashioned by others—as a benevolent, provincial patriarch.[30] Novelists' appropriation of paternalistic language and symbols is not limited to their desire to birth a modern novel or to their awareness of national anxieties regarding royal succession. Pereda's own complicated roles as heir and, later, father, underscore the many ways one may better understand the ties between his life and literary persona (and his representations of rural masculine heirs). Pereda was in many ways the literal legatee of a bourgeois namesake and fortune, not unlike the protagonists who populate his fiction. By the end of the nineteenth century, he was heir to a rural hidalgo namesake and a productive cosmetics factory in Santander, an enterprise into which he was initiated by his older brothers. He and his children also became the primary beneficiaries of his brothers' fortunes, making Pereda the paterfamilias par excellence.

Pereda was also a metaphorical heir in more ways than one. His acceptance of the "Silla k" (k Seat) upon his induction to the Spanish Royal Academy in 1897 (replacing *costumbrista* writer José de Castro y Serrano) made him the recipient of a coveted position in Spain's most prestigious literary institution, as we will see later. When Armando Palacio Valdés filled the vacant seat left by Pereda, he, too, referred to the impossibility of measuring up to such a "precious inheritance," in spite of the many affinities informing the authors' shared "spiritual kinship."[31] The mythification of Pereda as a paternalistic patriarch was under construction early in Pereda's career, but is perhaps most famously enshrined in Emilia Pardo Bazán's cheeky comment about the author's penchant for depicting country bumpkins and orchards in her then controversial treatise on naturalism in Spain. According to Pardo Bazán's pastoral analogy, Pereda was an adept novelist at least as long as he did not wander far from his native Cantabria: "a handsome orchard, well irrigated and taken care of, full of aromatic and healthy auras of rusticity."[32] Pardo Bazán's ironic evaluation notwithstanding, the Cantabrian novelist's embrace of the *costumbrista* tradition of painting local color using "autochthonous" pigments (e.g., backgrounds, language, character types) in the realist-regionalist novel—itself an inherited literary form— also made him and his fiction the metaphorical legatees of rural patterns of masculinity that aestheticize the rustic reality of nineteenth-century Spanish demographics at the same time that they betoken the relevance of rural paradigms of masculinity for an increasingly urbane populace.

Inheriting Rural Masculinity

The heir is, undoubtedly, a masculine figure that springs from urban and rural contexts alike. Until now, however, this book has been concerned primarily with complementary and competing configurations of middle-class masculinity as they take shape in the imagined urban spaces of texts that include nineteenth-century advertisements, fashion plates, and realist novels. With some notable exceptions, the masculine figures depicted in the cultural products examined throughout this book fit the mold of the "refined" city dweller: even the titular pauper of Galdós's *El Doctor Centeno*, as we saw in Chapter 1, aspires to this model. Fashionable representations of men like those examined in the introduction were most likely legible either as savvy urbanites or else as transplants who had begun to consume and assimilate (for labor or leisure) the models peddled in conduct manuals, professional guides, and visual culture. When fin-de-siècle illustrators took on the subject of the "rural man," they did so by drawing on earlier iconographies, such as those included in local-color sketches, which hewed more to romantic idealism rooted in nostalgia or stereotype than observable social reality.[33] Artists, illustrators, advertisers, and novelists alike inherited and capitalized on this earlier *costumbrista* iconography in their representations of men in rugged and cosmopolitan spaces. Nineteenth-century visual cultural artifacts tended to caricature rural or rustic men as humble workers, innocent bumpkins, bygone warriors, or ironic or potential urbanites, fancying them as a quarry from which to mine national pride. In what follows, I unpack clichés and tropes associated with rural men and the masculinity they ostensibly embody in print illustrations, historical painting, and fashion advertisements. Despite obvious differences in genre and medium, each tend toward idealization or "whitewashing" at the risk of obviating the grittier realities associated with the vast majority whose labor was responsible for farming the land, extracting ore from mines, and laying rail. In so doing, I will show how more complex representations of rural men provide us with a nuanced picture of bourgeois masculinity that breaks down artificial binaries like the rural and the urban and the country and the city. Despite the fact that Pereda and his critics regularly took part in the rhetorical ruralization of the former's public persona, as the latter part of this section emphasizes, a focus on what masculinities studies scholars have dubbed the "rural masculine" and the "masculine rural" will assist in this chapter's analysis of how Pereda himself achieved this aesthetic in two of his novels, while also allowing one to consider Spanish men's inheritance of and capitalization on tropes of rurality and rusticity in their self-fashioning.

The study of rural masculinity has hardly been broached in the context of nineteenth-century Spain, which is perhaps most surprising given the fact that migration from geographical peripheries—or rural areas—to urban centers marked a dramatic shift in Spanish demographics during the fin de siècle. An explosion in the national population could not be contained or sustained in the resource-poor countryside, leading many men (with or without their families) to either move to cities—like Seville, Bilbao, San Sebastian, Valencia, and especially Barcelona—or to the Americas in search of better conditions and more profitable opportunities.[34]

According to Adrian Shubert, Spain's population grew from 15,455,000 in 1857 to 18,109,000 by 1897, and "provincial capitals generally grew at a rate well above the national average and between 1843 and 1877 seventeen of them actually doubled in size."[35] Those who moved "between the rural and urban worlds but [were] not solidly integrated into either, frightened the respectable, many of whom were not too comfortable with the idea of a more urban Spain anyway, and prompted an intensive and wide-ranging debate about the problem of the poor."[36] It is impossible to make too many assumptions about the class of such populations, though, as the countryside was also inhabited by wealthy landowners who capitalized on cheap labor to maintain their estates.

While there can be no single or singular typology of rural masculinity, the gender expression of men in rural spaces, and men in urban spaces who identify with or appropriate rural signs and symbols, has special relevance for the study of masculinity writ large. Hugh Campbell and Michael Bell emphasize the idea that masculinity takes distinct shapes within what "rural social scientists would recognize as rural spaces and sites," and, on the other hand, that "notions of rurality help constitute notions of masculinity."[37] The authors summarize each of these possible patterns, respectively, as the "masculine rural" and the "rural masculine."[38] In this view, rural masculinity is not only a helpful framework for analyzing representations of men who inhabit rural spaces—such as Pereda's mountain heirs—but it is also revelatory of the many ways bourgeois men sometimes attempt to authenticate or legitimate their masculine identity via the appropriation of polished, sterilized signs and symbols of rurality. As we saw in Chapter 2, for example, Fermín de Pas nostalgically idealizes his rustic hunting outfit, which temporarily transforms the bourgeois priest from polished but dissatisfied cleric into a "svelte and well-built mountain man," which is noteworthy in a novel in which the narrator elsewhere pejoratively dismisses miners and other men who work in the mountains as "cave bears."[39]

Despite the variety of men who lived in rural areas, professional artists who worked as newspaper illustrators or academic painters romantically idealized male inhabitants of Spain's rural peripheries. In the late nineteenth-century illustrated press, working-class men from the provinces were for the most part depicted as farmers or day laborers subject to the whims of corrupt political elites who relied on them as expendable pawns in the civil wars roiling the Spanish countryside throughout the nineteenth century. In a centerfold image included in a March 1886 issue of republican satirical magazine *El Motín*, a soldier conscripts a young farm

FIGURE 4.3. Detail of a centerfold illustration from satirical republican
magazine *El Motín*, January 3, 1886, no. 1. Image courtesy of the Hemeroteca
Digital of the Biblioteca Nacional de España, Madrid, Spain.

laborer—attired in garments similar to those worn above by a caricatured
Pereda—taking him away from his distraught mother and work on the
farm (see fig. 4.3).

The image recalls Leopoldo Alas's canonical short story "¡Adiós, Cordera!" (Farewell, Cordera!)—published first in 1892 and later as part of a collection of short stories—in which the transportation via train of a beloved
family cow to a slaughterhouse parallels a young son's involuntary con-
scription into the army during the final Carlist War (1872–1876). Other
illustrations throughout *El Motín*'s long print run similarly figure the *pueblo*
through men in peasants' dress in an attempt to symbolically link the Spanish nation and masculinity with "authentic" or idealized portrayals of innocent young men from the provinces. Even though attention in examples like
this one is placed on the harsh realities faced by rural, working-class subjects, the appropriation of their symbols by urban elites (whether provincial
or cosmopolitan) was rhetorical. Such sterilized representations functioned
as a mask for the very real problem of mendicity, a result of migration of
rural folks to cities ill-equipped to offer adequate housing and jobs.

An 1888 illustration from the same magazine visualizes the Spanish *pueblo*
as another young man in rural attire and draws on biblical tropes in its

FIGURE 4.4. Detail of a centerfold illustration from satirical republican
magazine *El Motín*, April 22, 1888, no. 17. Image courtesy of the Hemeroteca
Digital of the Biblioteca Nacional de España, Madrid, Spain.

idealization of humble peasants and, perhaps ironically, its concomitant
villanization of the most "philistine" of politicians (see fig. 4.4). In the full-
page illustration, "El David popular" (A David for the people) successfully
takes down and brandishes an effigy of Emilio Castelar (1832–1899), a politician known for his intellect and oratorial eloquence and who, despite his
widespread popularity as a defender of liberalism in Spain, was later viewed
unfavorably by radicals and progressives. The mythification of the *pueblo*
by comparison to David, the masculine figure from the Bible responsible
for toppling the gargantuan Philistine, Goliath. Political illustrators did not
only imagine peasants as cyphers of victimhood, but they also identified
in them a potential victor capable of toppling ineffective political regimes
centered in Madrid. To a degree, the titular hero of *Pedro Sánchez* achieves
a similarly mythical status in his leadership of a barricaded street during the
1854 revolution in Madrid.

Young men in rustic environments were also idealized via the representation of biblical and mythological tales that was part and parcel of the late-
nineteenth-century vogue for historical painting; such iconography was
produced for consumption by a range of middle-class audiences. Old Testament figures like Adam, David, or Joseph gave painters an opportunity to

depict the heroic male body in dynamic poses and contexts that contrasted starkly with the high etiquette of fully outfitted bourgeois professionals commonly depicted in formal portraiture—such as that of the Madrazo brothers and Ramon Casas—and caricatures in the illustrated press. Visual cultural depictions of strapping farmhands and factory workers, as art historian Carlos Reyero has argued, reflect the late nineteenth-century interest in representing in a variety of media the new realities of the working classes at the same time that they aim to "convincingly characterize society's new heroes, who had become new masculine archetypes."[40] Muscular bodybuilders, sportsmen, and showmen were, naturally, the preferred models for representations of hard-bodied classical figures like Hercules and Apollo, whose representations in statuary and painting historically conformed to canons that valorized robust physiques.[41] In a particularly bucolic example, Salvador Viniegra's El primer beso (1891, The first kiss) depicts a herculean Adam seduced by an innocent-looking but cunning Eve. Adam's hirsute and brawny physique—which may recall for viewers Clarín's description of Fermín de Pas in La Regenta examined in Chapter 2—dwarfs the other figures represented on the canvas (perhaps ironically, given his imminent lapse in judgment and subsequent fall from the fatherly grace of God). His untamed hair, scruffy but classically rendered countenance, and rippling muscles coincide with what scholars have referred to as a hyper-masculine ideal that, while no less aestheticized or reliant on constructed codes, imagines masculinity to issue naturally from male bodies in rustic environs.[42] The primordial man of the Old Testament, Adam figured prominently in nineteenth-century cultural production as a figure of thwarted potential and antediluvian innocence or naïveté. Given his symbolic role as mankind's earthly father within the Judeo-Christian cosmovision, Adam also emerges as a protagonist in the nineteenth-century literary canon, as is exemplified by Espronceda's El diablo mundo (1840–41; The godforsaken world). As we will see later in this section, Pereda's 1897 acceptance speech to the Spanish Royal Academy refers to man's inheritance from Adam by tracing a direct line between the foundational archetype of masculinity and fatherhood and his program of literary regionalism, probably in a direct appeal to his androcentric audience.

The adoption or use of rural signs and symbols by bourgeois men is indicative of at least two truths about nineteenth-century masculinity. The first is the difficulty in separating gender into neatly prefabricated categories of rural/country and urban/city. The second is that any survey of masculinity must view it as relational and constantly under construction.

FIGURE 4.5. "Los forasteros" (Outsiders) by Mestres for one of El Siglo's 1884 catalogs. The caption reads, "One ticket for me and one for her. How much?" / "Nothing; the entry is free of charge" / "Maybe it's true that here they give away just about everything!" Image courtesy of the Arxiu Històric de la Ciutat de Barcelona, Barcelona, Spain.

It is for these and other reasons that Campbell and Bell remind readers of their crucial introduction to the study of rural masculinity that "[a] relational view of gender [must attempt] to render men's invisible normality a visible category (Kimmel 1990), but not a passive one. Rather, it seeks to understand the invisibility of masculine power as something that is actively constructed."[43] As middle-class men's work became more clerical and less manual in nature—a result of a variety of socioeconomic processes including women's increased presence in factories and offices, and a shift toward speculative financial markets over mercantile ones, as Chapter 3 demonstrated in the Catalan example—the strategic adoption of gender fantasies gave men a performative outlet.

Appropriations of rustic iconography were not limited to the performative and ideologically inspired maneuvers of political magazines or historical paintings rooted in Judeo-Christian mythology, and even creators of nineteenth-century commercial ephemera like those surveyed in Chapter 1 recorded the interconnectivity between the countryside and quickly urbanizing cityscapes. In the following illustration for the El Siglo department store in 1884, artist Apel·les Mestres depicts a couple wishing to enter one of Barcelona's preeminent shopping destinations (see fig. 4.5). Both are cast as rural outsiders by the image's caption and contrast starkly with the urbanites represented in Pellicer's illustration published on the opposite page (see fig. 0.10 in the introduction).

The male customer's wardrobe is analogous to that of the stereotypical caricature of Pereda which opens this chapter. Though the shirt and culottes are similar to other traditional, regional costumes, Mestres distinguishes the peasant man by his cap (*barretina*) and espadrilles (*espardenyes* in Catalan or *alpargatas* in Castilian), both iconic staple of Catalan regional dress for men. Despite the fact that department store catalogs may have advertised primarily to city dwellers, the existence of regional or provincial dispatch offices is evidence of the growing demand for fashionable commodities beyond urban centers (and of their tentacular reach into the provinces).[44] Even places as quintessentially urban in design and purpose as department stores were sites where the dividing line between urban and rural was blurry. The quantity of such images in texts ranging from *costumbrista* books, magazines, and department store catalogs works toward effacing the realities of rural men, particularly since stereotypes tend to figure traditionally dressed peasants as metonyms for the countryside. While working class farmers and miners were very much a part of the socioeconomic makeup of rural parts of Spanish provinces, so too were hidalgos and factory owners like Pereda.

Pereda in 1897: A Rural Male Heir in the Capital

Pereda and his peers relied on similar tropes in a variety of contexts. The Cantabrian novelist's 1897 speech commemorating his acceptance as a member of the Spanish Royal Academy, along with ephemeral evidence of the event, offers the most convincing testimony of the fusion of masculinity, the place of the male heir, and rurality in his authorial imagination and self-fashioned identity as a regionalist writer. Throughout the speech, Pereda appeals to the androcentric institution with recourse to his regionalist aesthetics of the novel as well as a rhetoric of patrilineal succession that undergirds many of his novels, including *Pedro Sánchez* and *Peñas arriba*. By hitching his novelistic regionalism to motifs of masculine transmission of cultural and literary capital, which he figures through a number of references to men's professions, Pereda appeals to the patriarchal consciousness of his male literary peers in attendance at the ceremony while also indexing the male homosocial character of the institution to which he has been admitted.[45] As a new inductee, Pereda naturally viewed himself as an heir to the masculine literary tradition enshrined in the halls of the Spanish Royal Academy.

After delivering a lengthy *captatio benevolentiae* summarizing the merits of José de Castro Serrano (the *costumbrista* writer whose vacant seat was assigned to the Cantabrian novelist), Pereda turns his attention to the regional novel. He positions the regional novel in stark contrast to the "urban novel" that Galdós defends in his own acceptance speech, itself modeled as a response to Pereda's. As a representative of Cantabria, Pereda mythologizes the Spanish regional novel by emphasizing its closer proximity to nature than civilization. But Pereda also masculinizes this mythos in his defense of regionalism as a literary aesthetic in the novel, thus fusing together tropes of rurality and masculine inheritance. The confluence of inheritance, rural masculinity, and the regional or "rustic" novel, as he also labels it, has the effect of conferring authenticity onto Pereda's literary output and his authorial persona while simultaneously offering a key to understanding the gendered characterization of his masculine protagonists.

Pereda's rhetorical appeal to his audience follows the pattern of the caption for Cilla's 1883 illustration (franco/Polanco; see fig. 4.1), whereby the author's humility and rustic geographical attachments form two sides of the same coin. Indeed, Pereda frames himself in the speech as a staunch defender and heir of regionalism and rurality by aesthetically linking himself to the mountainous and wooded regions of the north. Appealing like many other inductees to those who came before him, the writer humbly admits to those in attendance that his presence in the Spanish capital has made him feel quite like a fish out of water.[46] In the written version of the speech he cites a poem by Golden Age poet and playwright Lope de Vega—thus drawing an affiliative link between himself and a forefather of the Spanish Golden Age—before contrasting the climate and topography of Cantabria with those of Madrid to throw his feeling of inferiority in the company of esteemed literati in the palatial academy into sharp relief:

> if there is a man in this chamber who can truly be considered out of his proper element, then that man is me. For "from my solitude I come," a keen observer of the sun only through my homeland's dense foliage. Here and all of a sudden, I face the sun's beams without recourse to a single cloud

to soften their intensity in the beautiful sky from which they emanate and shimmer.[47]

The novelist's specific nod to Lope's ballad "A mis soledades voy" (Into my solitude I go) strengthens his link to canonical writers of the Spanish Golden Age, while also conveying the abiding myth of Pereda's embodiment of the secluded patriarch, a type he portrays in *Peñas arriba* in the personage of the protagonist's uncle Celso.

Whether the choice was intentional or not, Emilio Porset y Martínez's illustration of the acceptance speech—which appeared in a March issue of the literary magazine *El Nuevo Mundo* (The new world) shortly after Pereda's and Galdós's induction ceremony in 1897—taps into Pereda's reference to the verdure of his native Cantabria by framing the author with representations of foliage. Triangulated by the assembly hall's ornamental, architectural garlands in the background and a beribboned laurel branch or flower in the foreground, Pereda recites his speech in full etiquette to an audience of male peers. The image's display of ornamental greenery either signals the traditional award offered to winners of the medieval Floral Games or is meant to betoken the author's aforementioned ties to the flora of his native region.[48] Regardless of the interpretation, Porset's representation of the speech further partakes in the mythologization of Pereda as a laureled gentleman-writer who successfully availed himself of polished symbols of rurality and rusticity in the articulation of his literary regionalism.

Aside from fashioning himself as a humble transplant from the provinces, Pereda goes on in the speech to envision the content of his novels, and the novels themselves, as more indebted to "nature" than civilized society. The mixed metaphors he conjures help to bolster his brand as a scion of rurality and rusticity. Referring to the novel and its offshoots using a botanical lexicon, Pereda classifies the regional novel not as a genre or genus of its own, but rather as a distinct varietal or subspecies, an image that curiously blends the appreciation of the sublime in nature associated with Romanticism with the scientific interest of an ecologist or naturalist.[49] Bouncing between metaphors throughout the speech, Pereda continues to insist on the affiliation between regional novelistic production and the raw materials of nature by bringing them into close proximity. For example, he later alludes to local customs as the raw material to be mined by regionalist novelists, imagining them as an "an inexhaustible quarry from which the regional or rustic novel gathers its materials."[50] Contrasting the image of the more urbane novel's proximity to the artist's atelier, Pereda argues that the

FIGURE 4.6. Detail of an illustration by Porset of "Don José María Pereda [*sic*] in the Academy." Image courtesy of the Hemeroteca Digital of the Biblioteca Nacional de España, Madrid, Spain.

regional novel is more like the artwork of those painters who draw directly on (and within) the great outdoors: "the other sculpts its figures from the very rock of the mountainside, in the open air and lit by the sun's rays."[51]

While the novelist undoubtedly privileges the countryside as the ideal backdrop for the regionalist novel, as part of a nostalgic turn he leaves room in his aesthetic cosmovision for larger, provincial cities like his native Santander, which he views as responsible for cradling the memory of regional behaviors, customs, and dress. Even if it would seem that provincial cities like Santander would challenge the Cantabrian novelist's prioritizing of rural landscapes in his self-fashioning and fictional enterprise, it is really only Madrid (perhaps for political reasons) whose urbane pomp is undesirable in his view. Pereda first establishes a point of contrast by critiquing—perhaps ironically, given the high etiquette of the room to and from which he pontificates—urban (and urbane) experiences he views as artificial or superficial: "the pomp of the salons, the stench of big industry, businessmen, and hubbub of politics and all of its derivatives, congeners, kin, and participants."[52] To be sure, Pereda participated frequently in all of these activities (not least of all in 1897, a time by which he was already serving on the board of directors for the Bank of Santander). However unsurprisingly, he appears to make exceptions for provincial capitals that fall under regionalism's jurisdiction, "or to the parts in them where, the flame of that picturesque mass of primordial inhabitants, with their faith, signs, and ancestral laws, continues to flicker miraculously. Wherever some part of all of this remains, there is also the regionalism that I profess and extol."[53] The setting for a number of his earlier literary works including the collection of local-color sketches *Escenas montañesas* (Mountain scenes) and the novel *Sotileza* (Finespun), Santander is the paragon that Pereda has in mind here, even though he himself would regret the city's transformation due to industrialization, trade, and tourism in works like *Tipos trashumantes* (1888; Nomadic types). Pereda imagines even pockets of bustling and urbanizing Santander to be potential receptacles of regional-rural ancestry, culture, and heritage, perhaps especially when the pen and paper used to describe them belong to men with backgrounds and pedigrees like that of the Cantabrian novelist.

In yet another sign of Pereda's homosocial, paternalistic posturing that blends tropes of inheritance, masculinity, and rurality in the speech, the author justifies the existence of the regional or rustic novel (as separate from, for example, realism's focus on urban life) by comparing the novelistic genre's various manifestations to the plurality of coinage in a fortune, and then to the professions and vocations pursued by sons in a family. For his part, Pereda argues,

> a dose of aesthetics in the scientific realm of numbers or in the prose of domestic life is hardly unfavorable, and I cannot be convinced that a fortune is somehow worse for its heterogeneous composition, nor that the bonds between family members somehow loosen because the military son prides himself on his martial decorations, the priest on his black robes and pulpit, and the lawyer on his court dress and legal battles.[54]

Pereda's analogy of different types of novels to brothers in a family seeking to achieve different but equally legitimate occupations permits one to imagine novels as sons in a family while further reflecting the central place of male homosocial kinship within the Cantabrian novelist's imagination.

In another example toward the end of the speech, Pereda bolsters his earlier rendering of novels as a fraternal coterie by identifying a patrilineal genealogy between himself, the men in attendance at his induction ceremony, and some of Western European history's male agents. In so doing,

Pereda intentionally or unintentionally appeals to the homosocial community of writers and scholars constituting the Royal Spanish Academy and its audience. If all men are stripped of their clothing and accessories, Pereda pontificates,

> from the shepherd's crook and sheepskin of biblical times to the Caesars' rich purple cloaks, the crusaders' armor, or yesteryear's jerkin and breeches, or today's vest, coattails, or jacket. Beneath these volatile coverings, one will always find the same core, the same being, our fallen father, Adam, in the flesh, with his physical nature besieged by a whole pedigree of plagues.[55]

Pereda's gradation beginning with references to biblical shepherds and Caesars and ending with a clear reference to himself and his peers—all glossed metonymically by their sartorial trappings—creates an unbroken, homosocial lineage that unites masculine icons of Western civilization in a transhistorical kinship that culminates in the authorial bourgeois gentleman. The coda to Adam, mankind's shared fallen father in the Judeo-Christian cosmovision, illustrates a fantasy of patrilineal succession according to which all men share the primordial blemish, however different they appear to be on the surface. Not unlike that of the composition and antediluvian subject matter of Viniegra's "El primer beso," Pereda's paternalistic imagination leaves little to no room for Eve or, by extension, women and femininity. Here, the bourgeois novelist emerges as heir apparent to a manufactured, Western tradition tracing lineage back to Adam and biblical shepherds, with the regionalist novel itself being his privileged inheritance. As we will see in what remains of this chapter, the characterization and development of his fictional heirs—whether the humble, city-bound social climber or the prodigal lawyer—similarly rely on the interplay between rural and urbane tropes in the construction and fashioning of bourgeois masculinity.

Rural Origins and Returns (Pedro Sánchez)

Pereda's only novel that focuses on a young mountain heir's education and maturation in Madrid compellingly positions rural masculinity as central to the vicissitudes of bourgeois manhood. In its exposition, *Pedro Sánchez* characterizes the eponymous protagonist with recourse to rustic symbols

meant to underscore his humble beginnings and to throw into relief the
many hurdles he will face as he attempts to add a veneer of urbanity to
his rustic core while modeling himself after the patterns of masculinity
he observes in acquaintances, friends, and superiors in Madrid. Pedro's
eventual success in capitalizing on paternal and fraternal investments and
his youthful, masculine potential tracks Pereda's own attempt at a realist bildungsroman (a model which, as we will see later, Pereda inverts in
his bestseller *Peñas arriba*). Additionally, in its reliance on elements referring back to the author's own life experience and work, *Pedro Sánchez*
reflects the contradictions that inhere in Pereda's self-fashioning and the
public's perception of him as a scion of literary regionalism; his successful
embodiment or performance of rustic, patriarchal authority and nobility
depended on the commercial success and connections made by the author.
By highlighting the disparities between Pedro's unpolished silhouette and
the revolutionary backdrop of Isabelline Madrid, Pereda calls to mind the
incongruity he, too, felt when publicly presenting himself to peers and
colleagues, especially when he was far-removed from his native Polanco
and equally beloved Santander; this continued to be the case even later
in his career, as is evident in the rhetorical humility he affects in his 1897
acceptance speech to the Spanish Royal Academy in Madrid. After providing a brief summary of the two-part novel, this section will turn its attention to *Pedro Sánchez*'s representation of the male heir and rural masculinity through the novel's upwardly mobile protagonist.

Pedro Sánchez is a two-part novel centered on its titular heir's urban education in Madrid and bookended by a provincial beginning and return.
From the start of the novel, the first-person narrator—a man writing from
the comfortable position of bourgeois adulthood—describes himself as the
son of a humble hidalgo family with deep ties to the Cantabrian mountains.
While the young man's dreams are initially modest, limited as they are to
becoming a secretary for the local government, his sights are eventually set
much higher after becoming acquainted with Augusto Valenzuela, an influential Madrid politician on holiday in Cantabria with his daughter, Clara,
who is destined to be Pedro's first wife.[56] After several visits from Pedro,
Valenzuela proposes that the boy seek him out in Madrid so that he might
obtain a suitable position in what is revealed to be a corrupt political regime.
After collecting enough money from his brothers-in-law to subsidize his
stay in the capital, and despite his multiple thwarted attempts to make contact with the aloof Valenzuela, Pedro finds lodging and abiding friendships
in a student pension, lands a job as a cultural commentator and chronicler

for a republican journal, and takes part in the many recreational pleasures afforded by his new residency in the Spanish capital. Indeed, his idle time is spent reading novels, visiting the theater, attending literary gatherings, and partaking in urban strolls.

The majority of the novel's second volume is devoted to Pedro's maturation as a writer, which coincides with his transformation into an archetypal agent of the 1854 revolution.[57] Despite the revolution's failure to effect any meaningful change in liberal governance—a fact that is perhaps a sign of an older, more pragmatic Pereda, whose narrator here qualifies boyish optimism—Pedro eventually marries Clara Valenzuela and, pressured by her opportunism, prematurely accepts a civil governorship close to his Cantabrian homestead. His homecoming, however, is bittersweet, as he quickly realizes that his wife's materialism follows her from Madrid, and his naïveté and insufficient experience do not prepare him for the position. In the contracted final section of the novel, a cuckolded Pedro abandons Madrid for Andalucía before eventually returning, remarrying the daughter of one of his first acquaintances in the city, and fathers a son. After the premature deaths of his wife and son, Pedro spends the rest of his life in solitary exile before resettling in the paternal homestead without heirs but surrounded by the male homosocial company of friends, including a young village priest.

The eponymous protagonist's inheritance and embodiment of rural masculinity manifests itself throughout *Pedro Sánchez*; however, the symbolic communion of fatherly hope and youthful potential makes the novel's exposition particularly meaningful for this chapter's study of men's gendered ideals as they take shape in rural spaces. Indeed, the titular protagonist's desire to fulfill paternal expectations as both an employed, modern gentleman and inheritor of tradition emerges as a motif as early as the novel's opening passage. The first-person narrator begins by juxtaposing the literally crumbling façade (and dwindling coffers) of the family estate with the paternal fantasy of erstwhile grandeur:

> I never could make out for myself what those crumbling and dusty effigies were supposed to represent. However, my father, who claimed having seen them in their original splendor, assured me on many occasions that they were *abarcas* or clogs, such as those common to the region, and that the bust was that of a great man or lord with a full beard and hooded cape. Together it was like one of those Egyptian cartouches that in modern-day Castilian was a signpost equating to *Sancho Abarca*, a name from which we Sánchez in my family descended.[58]

The Sánchez Abarca surname—the anecdotal interpretation of which is enshrined in the tabernacle of fatherly memory—derives from the traditional Cantabrian footwear central to Mecachis's caricature of Pereda (see fig. 4.2). While many contemporaneous novels similarly gesture to the architectural decay of cathedrals and country estates of yesteryear—Hugo's *Notre Dâme de Paris* (1831), Dickens's *Great Expectations* (1861), or Pardo Bazán's *Los pazos de Ulloa* (1886) come to mind—Pereda deviates from these examples in his positive framing of the Sánchez estate's past glory and incorruptible patina betokening masculine honor and virtue. Indeed, instead of depicting urban and rural legacies as purely atavistic and worm-eaten, or as ideologically retrograde, as is the case in Pardo Bazán's aforementioned novel, Pereda emphasizes the potential for regeneration in the figure of Pedro, the Sánchez family's young trustee.

The story is more than just a parochial family legend but is also a part of competing paternal legacies. Indeed, beyond a mere show of respect for the paterfamilias, Juan, Pedro's embrace of these symbols and the mythos they betoken are a sign of a desire to cling to the tall-tales of a storied past in order to maintain appearances with the rival García clan, a group made up of "unextraordinary folks" who look down upon the Sánchez family, primarily because of their superior territorial holdings and, presumably, because of their virtual monopoly over the leadership of the local town hall (a thick hide Pedro wishes to one day pierce).[59] The García clan represents a competing view of masculinity based exclusively on bossism, pedigree, and inherited land holdings. Even though Pedro's father recognizes the need for his youngest son to cut his teeth in the city before returning to pursue local governance or an alternate career in politics, he still relies on narratives of past glories (and their potential rejuvenation in the rural heir-figure of Pedro) for his own self-fashioning as a man.

Indeed, Juan's faith in Pedro as an agent of familial regeneration (and his ability to compete with the García clan) corroborates the idea that the young male heir was best suited to carry on family legacies in Pereda's paternalistic imagination. Indeed, the notion of the young boy's promise or potential, gestured to in the novel's opening pages but later explicitly referred to in such terms by Valenzuela, is related to the language one might expect in the context of a financial investment. As the youngest child and only son in his family, Pedro seems to internalize paternal expectations, reporting an awareness of the fact that his father's full attention was on him. If at first only metaphorical, Valenzuela's dialogue (and Juan's eventual embrace of the decision resulting from it) makes the connection between youthful, masculine promise and the accrual of capital or equity patently clear. While Valenzuela envisions the spoiling of young rural men by imagining a future Pedro in obscure solitude, "like a tree in the mountains," the politician pivots back to the potential of the young sapling before him, contrasting the lack of opportunities available to the father and emphasizing those now ripe for the picking by the son: "today, doors that were previously sealed shut to the enterprise of men like you are now open, and young gentlemen like Pedro owe it [to themselves/this opportunity] to break a lance in that stockade where vigorous lads now seize honor and profit."[60] In the family meeting to discuss Valenzuela's proposal, described suggestively as "that patriarchal assembly," the viability of the proposal takes on the language of a cost-benefits analysis including the discussion of "advantages and disadvantages of the idea of Pedro's potential adventures" and "the indispensable resources and method to acquire them for expenses related to equipment, travel and housing, for whatever might occur."[61] While the young boy's lack of connections makes his attempts to immediately transcend Madrilenian high society impossible, the bellicose imagery used in Valenzuela's intervention, together with the financial language used to describe the family's discussion foreshadows Pedro's eventual participation in the construction and defense of the barricades that eventually occupy sections of the capital during the popular uprisings of 1854, and the financial difficulties he will encounter during the first half of his urban "education."

Let us return for a moment to the interaction between Pedro and Valenzuela, which not only further confirms the boy's characterization as a naïve but promising symbol of masculine rusticity, but also represents the hieratic character of male mentors and the almost magical balm of youthful potentiality common to the European bildungsroman. After hearing Valenzuela's lofty projections, a now-mature Pedro retrospectively sees himself as a country bumpkin witnessing his first magic show: "All of these reflections—expressed with such affection and fervor—were entirely new for me; I stood there in a daze, like a bumpkin seeing the curtain part to reveal a host of enchanting marvels. I could not even muster a word in reply."[62] While it is later revealed that Valenzuela barely recalls having made such an impression on or having given related promises to the boy, the interaction's effect in the moment coaxes an awakening in Pedro's worldly aspirations. The Sánchez-Valenzuela relationship depicted here recalls Felipe Centeno's respect for the eye doctor Teodoro Golfín (*Marianela, El Doctor Centeno*) and his awed admiration for Agustín Caballero, while foreshadowing Bismarck and Celedonio's astonishment before Fermín de Pas (*La Regenta*), all of which are examples that similarly depict young provincial boys mes-merized by the maturity, polish, and success of older, patently urbane men. Such examples lend credence to the notion that affluent, fatherly or avun-cular surrogates or patrons were central to bourgeois development accord-ing to the nineteenth-century Spanish imagination that takes shape in the realist novel surveyed in the chapters of this book.

The gendered accessories alluded to by Pereda's narrator to fashion the novel's male characters offer additional evidence of the confusion of rural and cosmopolitan patterns of masculinity that Pereda inherited and capi-talized upon in his own self-fashioning as an author. For example, while father and son take a walk, Juan taps the ground with his walking stick, "his old bamboo walking stick [from the Indies] with a silver handgrip and black silk tassels," as a way to punctuate his assessment of the nature of Valenzuela's visit to Pedro.[63] An extension of the masculine habitus, such accessories (see fig. 4.7, and fig. 0.1 in this book's introduction), though per-haps indicative of an *indiano* ancestor, were widely available for purchase in department stores and smaller boutiques, where similar items were sold to men, women, and children.

Whereas the outfit Pedro eventually wears as part of his leadership of urban barricades during the popular uprisings of 1854 is similarly punctu-ated by proud evocations of his northern heritage, dress is an early factor determining the rural transplant's affective responses to the urbane environ-ments to which he is exposed in the capital. On his first visit to the Valenzu-ela mansion, for example, Pedro's apparent lack of external polish leads him to question his place in the capital's urbane settings: "I was ashamed to step on the fine carpet with my calfskin boots, and I did not dare to take a seat atop the polished satin. The uncertain quality of my suit, regardless of its newness, heightened its vulgarity and coarseness among those bright and delicate shades. Even though my profile was not unattractive, my reflection in the mirrors gave off a feral and coarse *je ne sais quoi* that made me sweat with dismay."[64]

If the novel's exposition emphasizes the masculine potential of the young heir's development in the capital—an experience meant to allow him to capitalize upon resources otherwise unavailable to him—the denoue-ment frames a rural return as ultimately restorative of the rustic patterns of masculinity Pedro was encouraged to sublimate during his time in the capital. After a contracted melodramatic interlude in which the protago-nist finds himself cuckolded, dishonored in a duel, divorced, remarried, and widowed, the climactic turmoil of Pedro's life finds its resolution in his

FIGURE 4.7. Page depicting walking sticks and foldable fans from a catalog for the El Globo department store located in Barcelona. Image courtesy of the Arxiu Històric de la Ciutat de Barcelona, Barcelona, Spain.

acquired wealth, which allows him to reclaim his inheritance as the patriarch of his vacant family estate (an act that would not have been possible had he not left in the first place). Upon returning to Cantabria, Pedro's reclaimed agency is figured through a list of actions conjugated in the preterit tense: "I found the paternal household whole and shuttered up. I bought the shares of my remaining co-inheritors; I made repairs to it and now I live there. I also tended to the garden and fenced in a great stretch of land around the small hill rising over the sea. I subscribe to many newspapers and magazines of a variety of colors and creeds."[65] While his cousins visit him because he is "wealthy and without any heir-apparent"—echoing the downtrodden *indiano* protagonist of Clarín's short story "Boroña"—and at times feels "alone and foreign in his native place," his days are taken up with bucolic

and intellectual pursuits that he enjoys in the context of homosocial camaraderie with the local priest.[66] Despite the fact that the novel begins with
the story of Pedro's humble youth, which, as Dorca comments, "is very
different from the solitary and prematurely aged 50-year old who offers to
the reader the chronicle of his life," the end of the novel idealizes precisely
the kind of lifestyle Pereda himself was able to enjoy in his maturity.[67] Even
if Madrid sapped Pedro of much of his vitality, his ability to overcome the
challenges encountered there made his reclamation of his homestead possible in the first place. Despite a similar attempt to valorize the rural over the
urban, the fusion of rural and urban tropes in the masculine self-fashioning
of *Peñas arriba*'s protagonist takes on additional, capitalistic valences given
the fact that he must not only accept his rightful place as heir to the legacy
passed down to him by his uncle and father. He must also leverage his bourgeois experiences in the capital in order to triumph as a hero over the rustic
challenges awaiting him in the "upper peaks" of the Cantabrian mountains.

Peñas arriba *and the Peak of Pereda's Literary Celebrity*

Written more than a decade after the composition and publication of *Pedro
Sánchez*, and widely considered Pereda's masterpiece, *Peñas arriba* further
visualizes for readers the many ways in which tropes related to rural masculinity hold particular sway over the imagination of its protagonist—
the epicurean heir, Marcelo—and its hidalgo author. Having sold several
thousand copies within the first few weeks of its publication, Pereda dedicated *Peñas arriba* to his son, Juan Manuel, who died unexpectedly in 1893;
more than just a bestseller, then, it was also the memorial of a father to his
beloved son.[68] As we saw earlier in the favorable caricature of Pereda (see
fig. 4.2), *Peñas arriba*'s early success figured into the way the writer was subsequently mythologized by others as a scion of rurality, echoing Menéndez Pelayo, a friend and critic who wrote that Pereda was more a highland
hidalgo who wrote novels, rather than "a professional literato."[69] Pereda
perpetuated this myth on his own in private by suggesting to friends that
his novels earned him very little, and that the real source of his income was
output from the family factory, La Rosario; in other words, for Pereda, his
novels were a product of a man's leisure time spent in "solitary splendor"
(Valis), not the cultural products of a bourgeois manufacturer of perfume
and soap.

Through the return of its epicurean protagonist to the rural homestead of his forefathers in the fictional mountain town of Tablanca, *Peñas arriba* is animated by Pereda's literary and political vision according to which Spain's regions (along with their representation in art and literature) were not obstacles, but rather vehicles for Spanish cultural and literary regeneration. Deviating from while building upon the caricaturized or excessively idealized versions of rural men represented in the late-nineteenth-century visual culture examined earlier in this chapter, the image of masculinity that emerges in *Peñas arriba* depicts a range of rural men who stand to benefit from the urbane, if not "princely," model brought to them from Madrid by Marcelo.[70] For his part, Marcelo, accustomed to the seemingly emasculating creature comforts offered by life in the capital, stands to rusticize his habitus and external image, thus adding a veneer of authenticity and moral transcendency to his self-fashioning as a masculine subject. This combination is perhaps unsurprising since, as we saw earlier, tropes of rural idyll and urbane celebrity were part and parcel of Pereda's own public image as a nationally renowned novelist. Pereda's novel occupies a similarly privileged intersection, since it blends the local-color sketch (which often relied on Manichean depictions of regional customs via the transcription of local dialects, and physiognomy) with realist and naturalist trends that had taken firm root in the Spanish publishing industry during the 1880s and 1890s. Through close readings of a few scenes that characterize Marcelo as the rightful heir to his paternal or avuncular homestead (of course, with the constant encouragement of a male homosocial community comprised of Tablanca's rugged "mountain men"), this final section will show how Pereda's patriarchal, ruralizing vision of Spain, like bourgeois masculinity and Pereda's own self-fashioning, depended and capitalized upon the strategic reconciliation of both rural and urban signs and symbols.

Peñas arriba tells the story of Marcelo, the son of a Cantabrian father and an Andalusian mother, who is beckoned to the ancestral family homestead by his ailing paternal uncle Celso. Having failed to produce a worthy heir, Celso identifies his nephew Marcelo as the natural choice to not only continue the family name and estate, but also to protect and bring its interests to a place of renewed fruition. Along his journey to the "upper peaks" signaled by the novel's title, Marcelo faces a variety of episodic challenges. By surveying and studying the landscape, hunting bears, enduring the harshness of winter, absorbing the lessons of a homosocial coterie of peers, and, ultimately, accepting his uncle's offer to succeed him, Marcelo eventually fulfills his legacy as the local patriarch of the northern land he was destined to inhabit. Additionally, activities like hunting and surveying show how Marcelo seeks to dominate the natural world, and also how he considers adaptation to a naturally hostile environment. While scholars have identified in Marcelo's quest a number of narrative patterns, including the guidebook or enchiridion, this chapter's focus on Pereda's representation of nineteenth-century Spanish masculinity will help us to resituate his novel alongside those of Galdós and Alas at the same time that it will demonstrate how Pereda's masculine figures echo some of his own anxieties and ambitions as a bourgeois elite and novelist.[71]

The opening pages of the novel place the burden of paternal legacy onto the promising but flawed or inchoate young lawyer from Madrid, whose re-education must take place under the supervision of his father's brother, Celso: a surrogate bearer of fatherly expectation and masculine rusticity, tropes that first emerge in the uncle's repeated letters to his nephew. More than an expository maneuver meant to draw Marcelo (and, by extension, the urbane reader) into the Cantabrian countryside, the letters serve as an intertextual or metaliterary gambit by the Peredian narrator, who figures the rustic scrawling of a "quintessential Patriarch of the Mountains" through the typescript of a novel printed and sold in Madrid.[72] Celso's many epistles communicate his failing health and, more urgently, the need for Marcelo to return to take the reins of his ancestral home in the absence of an immediate male heir; Celso describes his family as conniving and greedy, and Marcelo's sister is similarly deemed unworthy for the task at hand, given her excessive materialism (recalling, perhaps, that of Pedro Sánchez's first wife Clara).

While Marcelo reads the letters, his uncle's penmanship stands out to the Madrilenian gentleman for its embodiment of the rustic environs from which the notes are dispatched: "The reasons upon which my uncle based his tenacious endeavor were thoughtful, and he started sending them to me regularly by mail. Scrawled on handmade paper purchased at the local store by his clumsy hand, the letters were written with a feather quill, ancient ink, bold lettering, and old-fashioned orthography."[73] Celso, like his compatriots who will eventually see to Marcelo's rural education in Tablanca, appears to embody naturally the rough environs that molded and produced him, down to the rural patriarch's atavistic but heartfelt scribbles. With this intertextual and metaliterary gambit meant to communicate Marcelo's obligation to not only cultivate the family tree but to also embrace the land from which he sprung, Pereda draws attention to his novel's own intention to direct his readership to the obligation to (and potential of) Spain's mountainous northern regions. Additionally, the expressions of masculinity contained within this relationship to the land is undergirded by a need to adapt and conquer or dominate it—evoking Sarah Sierra's similar observation in her rereading of Galdós's *Doña Perfecta*—which speaks to the capitalist bourgeois man who can instrumentalize the natural landscape, contradictorily seen as passive and hostile.[74]

Though it takes many letters for Marcelo to accept his uncle's offer to accept his rightful place as heir—indeed, only in the novel's denouement does he ever fully accept his destiny in that regard—his affective response to the epistolary correspondence leads ultimately to a volte-face on his original stance in one of the novel's most direct indictments of urbane models of masculinity based on consumer culture. In order to more fully embrace a transcendent manhood, Marcelo convinces himself that his uncle's request is just what he needs to help him to shed his seemingly emasculating attachments to his consumerist lifestyle in Madrid:

> One day, when I received the penultimate letter from my uncle—one that moved me deeply—I set out to discover within me why I was so insensitive to Nature's agreeable charms. Did my body lack the right cord, or perhaps I had it but had not yet given it the opportunity to vibrate? I had to find out one way or another, because the fear of lacking it started to afflict me. Besides, one either is or is not a man; he either has a core of humanity and the backbone to go where and do what others do; he either does or does not serve a purpose greater than treading carpeted salons, fattening the livers of Jewish innkeepers and fashionable tailors and shoemakers, attending shows, traveling incessantly while crammed into the railroad's cages like a sausage, and, in a nutshell, spending time and money on futilities typical of vain women. With this train of thought, I arrived at a feeling of spiritual vigor, a virility theretofore unknown to me. Having aroused in me the self-esteem of a lad cured of body and soul, but taking advantage of the rush for fear that it might be fleeting and could thus take with it my burning resolve, I wrote to my uncle to tell him that I was on my way, even going so far as to give him my departure date from Madrid.[75]

As we saw earlier, consumerist and urbane patterns of masculinity were not automatic causes for censure. After all, the modernizing vision of those who looked to England and France for models relied on the economic benefits of capitalistic networks of production and consumption by men and women alike. Here, however, consumption is merely one of modernity's flaws holding back the manly embrace of a life in nature—which was also, of course, a myth—beyond the boutiques, plush salons, and utilitarian trains that had become metonyms of bourgeois modernity by the late nineteenth century.

Tellingly, the highly symbolic first chapter ends with literary and historical references that heighten the stakes of Marcelo's individual trajectory and elevate his path of masculine becoming to the level of the pan-European literary canon and ancient history. While Marcelo, perhaps contradictorily after the previous passage, went about placing orders for "abundant provision of outerwear, resilient footwear, and offensive and defensive weapons" that his sojourn would require, he also brings along with him books by Romantic-era novelists and travel writers including Aimard, Töpffer, and Chateaubriand for the "pleasant stories [they have to tell] about the mountains, forests, and savages."[76] Echoing Suetonius's description of Julius Caesar's crossing of the Rubicon in 49 BC, Marcelo says aloud to himself, "Alea jacta est" (The die has been cast), "resolved to cross over [his] own Rubicon."[77] As we saw to be the case earlier in Pereda's speech to the Royal Spanish Academy, the masculinization of literature and history envisions the heir and inheritance as a homosocial enterprise between men. Of course, it is worth noting that the earlier inhabitants of the zone now called Cantabria met invaders with some of the fiercest resistance seen in the Iberian peninsula's response to Roman invasion. Pereda's passage, then, is not without some irony, as Marcelo will be met with the fierce resistance in the form of episodic encounters that test his virile resolve. The first-person narrator's manly disavowal of urbanity's potentially feminizing influence is somewhat betrayed by the preparatory provisions made for the trip, as well as his erudite literary and historical references, but then it is precisely Marcelo's intellect and urbanity that make him the candidate best suited to bring a crumbling Tablanca into the civilized circuit of modernity.

But Marcelo's initiation as a mountain man is less the result of a sort of passing on of the torch from his uncle, as it is much more the product of help from a homosocial cohort of experienced guides and peers that his bourgeois manliness will achieve a veneer of rustic authenticity. The manner by which Marcelo learns from surrogate father figures like his uncle Celso, Sabas the priest, and Chisco demonstrate that even rustic patterns of masculinity are not naturally begotten but are rather transmitted through homosocial communion between men. The other men with whom Marcelo quickly acquaints himself appear to confirm the appraisal of Hannah Lynch, a nineteenth-century critic of the novel according to whom "the 'life' of the landscape melts into the life of the mountaineers, and they become inextricably one."[78] The virile priest don Sabas clearly exemplifies this affirmation in representations of his hikes with Marcelo, during which the latter sees the former fused as one with the mountain:

> the way he came upon the mountain, like a masterful statue would upon its designated pedestal; that way in which he savored the nature surrounding him, filling himself up through his senses of smell and sight, and even through all the pores of his body; filled to the brim, he read aloud to me as he passed his eyes over the pages of that immense book that was sealed shut and practically Greek to me.[79]

While both of these examples appear to exhibit the novel's romantic and idealistic attachments, they also represent a modern rhetorical strategy that privileges the experiences of men as paragons of rural living. Pereda's patterns of masculinity in rural spaces are bolstered by the undeniably secondary and subordinate status of women in the novel, and the exclusively male coterie consisting primarily of Marcelo, the priest don Sabas, the doctor don Neluco, and the guide Chisco. Here, it is less important that Marcelo become one with the land, in the way that his guides and mentors do, but more significant that he be able to stand upon it as a bold heir and conquering male.

Through Marcelo's self-reflexive recognition of the modern image he cuts alongside his fellow mountaineers, Pereda openly dialogues with bourgeois textual and visual registers of the rural, thus exposing the way his own fantasies of rurality are not the natural products of the Cantabrian terroir, but rather issue from critiques of and cross-pollination with wider bourgeois discourses. During another outdoor excursion with Chisco, who will later become one of the focal points of the bear hunt, Marcelo compares himself to the figures included in fashion plates of hunters, an image that distances him from Chisco, who sports his rough, unpolished gear without effort:

> Chisco carried an enormous rifle with thick straps reinforced with waxed twine around the very long, rusty barrel, a horn for powder and a green chamois bag for pellets and other equipment. For my part, I had an elegant and fine, double-barreled Lefaucheux rifle accompanied by a utility belt, a mountain knife, rubber hiking boots with sturdily studded soles, English

leather gaiters, and all the equipment of a hunter in a fashion plate. Looking at me out of the corner of his eye, Chisco smirked, especially when
glancing at my footwear as I slipped in the soft clay soil or atop the slabs
along the intractable mountain paths. He finally disclosed to me that for a
firmer step, all I had to do was settle for a pair of hiking clogs like his, adding that my attire was *passable* and that, with regards to my armaments, *we
would just have to wait and see.*[80]

Fashion plates used by nineteenth-century tailors and department store
outfitters to advertise to their affluent clientele—like Marcelo—exhibit the
way bourgeois masculinity itself is authenticated or naturalized by its contact with symbols of rurality and rusticity. In a promotional card or *cromo*

FIGURE 4.8. Advertising card for Luis Vives & Company, a Barcelona-
based outfitter specializing in armory and related hardware. Image courtesy
of the Arxiu Històric de la Ciutat de Barcelona, Barcelona, Spain.

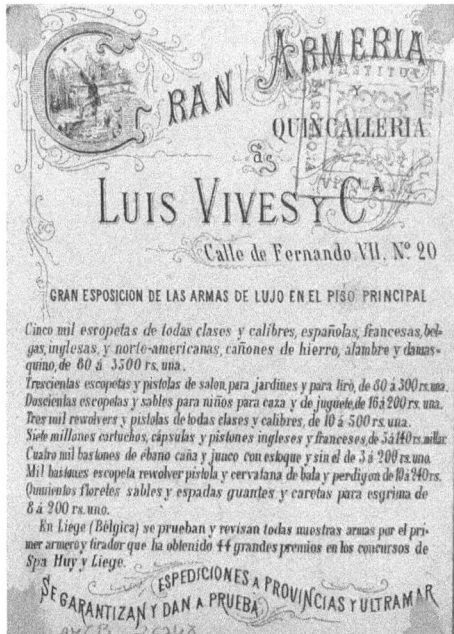

FIGURE 4.9. Reverse side of Figure 4.8. Image courtesy of the Arxiu
Històric de la Ciutat de Barcelona, Barcelona, Spain.

distributed by Luis Vives & Company to market hunting apparel and gear,
a hunter is frozen in place as he walks through the woods with his hound
(see fig. 4.8 and fig. 4.9). The homosocial world of hunting provided a relevant arena to be capitalized on by tailors in order to outfit their male clients
taken with the nineteenth-century's diversifying leisure industry.[81] Even
though hunting was historically considered a "paradigm of aristocratic leisure," it had also become an acceptable way for middle-class men to pass
their free time.[82] As Jo Labanyi reminds readers, even Pereda's preference
for rurality and rusticity in his characters' (and his own) styling as subjects
was part and parcel of the "project" of realism or modernity, because his
"rejection of modern exchange value for a pre-modern value system based
on inherent worth [. . .] derives its meaning from his urban readers' acceptance of modernity as the norm. [. . .] Even the most progressive writers
[like Galdós and Alas] construct modernity as a problem."[83]

Marcelo eventually learns to overcome any obstacles presented by his
urbane upbringing, thus authenticating his modern masculine persona by
reconciling a seemingly out-of-touch bourgeois urbanity with regional

FIGURE 4.10. Illustration by Porset of the "bear hunt" scene from *Peñas arriba*. Image courtesy of the Hemeroteca Digital of the Biblioteca Nacional de España, Madrid, Spain.

rusticity. The fusion of urbanity and rusticity culminates when Marcelo participates in a bear hunt, an event that recasts the protagonist as a heroic highlander and, thus, as an heir worthy of carrying on his uncle's and father's namesakes. After suffering a fever dream in which he prophetically envisions a cavern full of bears, Marcelo accepts an offer to accompany his homosocial entourage of mountain guides to go on a serious hunting expedition. Chisco, intellectually inferior but physically and culturally more in tune with nature, first proposes the trial to Marcelo with recourse to hunting as game: "Didn't you want to give big game a try? [. . .] The bear has been spotted."[84] Unbeknownst to his uncle, whose expectations of Marcelo's role as heir apparent would have likely led to his protestation of the outing, the protagonist consents to hiking to the bears' dwelling with Chisco, Pito Salces (Chorcos), and a hound named Canelo.

Despite Marcelo's continued feeling of inferiority—described by the narrator with recourse to his nerves ("My skin shook") and the bravery of his uneducated but brave guides ("two rough mountain men with more heart than wits")—the chapter's semantic field gradually masculinizes the protagonist with recourse to images and tropes of classical heroism, recalling the earlier reference to Julius Caesar.[85] The chapter is littered with allusions to Marcelo's gradual acquisition of heroic contours, demonstrating the conquering of his fears as well as foreshadowing his eventual apotheosis as the patriarch of Tablanca. Before the troupe leaves for their adventure, for example, Marcelo outfits himself "with the resolution of a hero."[86] Upon arriving at the mountain crags, the immensity of the snowscape is amplified by its comparison to a "titan's blanket," thus raising Marcelo and his men to the status of Olympians destined to challenge titanic rivals in ways not dissimilar to those employed by Oller in his description of the men responsible for erecting the pavilions of the 1888 Universal Exposition in Barcelona.[87] After defeating the adult bears and slaughtering their offspring with the help of their well-equipped outfit—represented in an illustration of the scene included in *La Lectura Dominical* (see fig. 4.10)—the distribution of winnings further frames Marcelo as a kind of bourgeois version of Hercules, a figure who after defeating the Nemean lion was often represented wearing the skins of his beastly foe.[88] After a squad of men reenter the mountain to bring down "the glorious trophies of [their] feat of beastliness," "they regaled [Marcelo] [. . .] with the bearskins, and [he] gave to Chisco and Pito Salces a handful of coins that pleased them immensely."[89] The exchange is a highly symbolic one: even as it was the guides who made his Herculean conquest possible, it is Marcelo's gift of coins (representative of the larger infusion of economic and cultural capital he brought with him) that demonstrate the benefits the region stands to reap with Marcelo's inevitable inheritance of his uncle's patrimony.

Marcelo's inevitable apotheosis as a hero, initiated in the previous scene, presages the similar conferral of success and recognition on Pereda, which reviewers of the novel deemed just compensation for the writer's heroic labor. As mentioned in the introduction to this chapter, cultural and literary gazettes of the caliber of *Blanco y Negro* were quick to recognize both the quality of his novel and the celebrity status of its author. Appearing once more on the cover of the popular *Madrid Cómico* in the summer of 1895, the Cantabrian novelist emerges again as the austere if still fashionably attired hidalgo from Polanco (see fig. 4.11). The caption included below the illustration, focalized through Pereda's voice, draws attention to the epiphanic character of regional discovery and novel-writing, styling the writer unironically as the one destined to describe the mountains of his birthplace and thus draws a parallel between Marcelo's own inheritance and that of Pereda: "I have discovered in *Peñas arriba* magnificent horizons . . . God put the mountains here for me to describe them!" One review of the novel published in the *Revista Contemporánea* (Contemporary review) further adds to the process of mythologization of Pereda as regional hero whose command over the nature he describes is semantically framed as heroic or even

FIGURE 4.11. Cover image of June 1895 issue of *Madrid Cómico*. Image courtesy of Hemeroteca Digital of the Biblioteca Nacional de España, Madrid, Spain.

godly. For example, after gesturing to Pereda's characters as if spontaneous creations springing from nature, Melchor de Palau frames Pereda himself as a master of nature capable of directing and transforming it via literary technique: "paraphrasing the rocks, personifying the summits, commanding nature's forces to sing in chorus."[90]

Conclusion

For Madariaga, *Pedro Sánchez* is a novel about a man's return to his rustic homeland in search of moral convalescence after being ruined by his adventures in the exciting but, nonetheless, corrupting influence of the capital.[91] This chapter's reading deviates slightly from Madariaga's, as it considers the unresolved tension in Pereda's own life, in which his celebrity status was the byproduct of his affinities to the moral comfort of rural settings and the celebrity and readership attained in cosmopolitan centers. Even as Pereda largely inverts the pattern of the promising heir who must first leave his homestead to cut his teeth in the city, the patterns of masculinity he articulates later in *Peñas arriba* similarly draw on the rural-urban divide for signification.

According to Michael Iarocci, "if one negates the key terms of Pereda's Utopian fiction, what emerges is an outline of the historical reality consistently repressed by that fiction: the history of the transformation of the landed *hidalgo* class into the industrialist, merchant class."[92] Despite Pereda's seemingly conscious retreat from the realities of the world he portends to represent—after all, it was the country hidalgo, too, who, like Pereda, came to form part of what Jesús Cruz labels the dominant groups—he inadvertently intervenes in discourses that call into question the modern role of Spanish men in his rural fantasies. Given Pereda's own participation in bourgeois economies, his provincial men and the rural masculinities to which they give contour may be read as attractive allegories for their unique ability to speak to the challenges and tensions facing bourgeois readers, and, by extension, the nation, during Spain's modernizing pursuits during the fin de siècle. Even if *Peñas arriba* peddles in seemingly retrograde regional identity politics, the novel's manners, themes, and tropes inadvertently pull it into a wider world of bourgeois economies of which Pereda, his mountain men, and his novels—if at times reluctantly or in reactionary ways— form inseparable parts.

CODA

Around the time I started writing *Masculine Figures*, I also started to catalog an ever-growing number of twenty-first century cultural products that continue to capitalize on the aesthetics and values of bourgeois manhood that coalesced during the nineteenth century and that form the basis of this book's chapters. As I wrote about some of Restoration-era Spain's iconic masculine figures—from fictionalized social types like the businessman and the priest to the artists and writers who engendered them—I noticed how content creators and designers, for example, reproduce certain tropes from the not-too-distant past, even as they appear to cleverly rethink or rewrite many of its traditional scripts. Popular social media accounts on platforms like Instagram plumb the visual cultural depths of Victorian-era portraiture at the same time that they pull it out of the familiar context of art museums and palaces and into a world where a portrait of Alfonso XII (1857–1885) by Federico de Madrazo can be reframed under the guise of "#hotvictorians," and a male nude by the painter Marià Fortuny (1838–1874) can rub elbows with representations of other hard-bodied men (past and present) tagged as "#muscleboys."[1] Their imaginative transformations of nineteenth-century sartorial mainstays like the cape and the three-piece suit notwithstanding, the directors of couture fashion labels like Oteyza and Palomo Spain, based out of Madrid and Posadas (Córdoba) respectively, continue to employ the signage of department-store dandyism and homosocial bonding common to many of the visual cultural objects and novels studied in the previous chapters, even as they chip away at the walls that previously excluded women and racialized others from homosocial boys' clubs like the tailoring emporium, the atheneum, the casino, and the university.[2]

In what ways do authors like Galdós, whose recent centennial in 2020 projected his mustachioed likeness across the internet, fit into this new media landscape? How does the proliferation of older forms, like novels and autobiographical narratives, and the popularization of new forms, like fashion campaigns on Instagram, bring nineteenth-century gender patterns into clearer focus? As we will see, contemporary cultural products exhibit Christopher Breward's argument that the suit and its accoutrements, for example, are "staple signifier[s] for myriad impulses, not just for writers and folklorists, but also for architects, artists, film-makers and designers."[3] With an eye to addressing the aforementioned questions, and in concluding, I would also like to signal how some of nineteenth-century masculinity's constitutive signs and symbols continue to shape how present-day cultural producers and consumers—from Instagram influencers to Spanish couture designers—imagine what it means to be and look like a man.

Of course, the aesthetic patterns associated with bourgeois masculinity during the nineteenth century have not always been framed positively or viewed as a source of inspiration for creative or whimsical cultural productions, and it is largely the mythical script of men's supposed irrelevance to fashion or consumerism that contemporary creators attempt to challenge or rewrite. Many widely accepted evaluations of middle-class men's constitutive signs during the nineteenth century can be summed up by the acceptance of the mythical figure of the serious and somber "man in black."[4] Such theories inevitably draw inspiration from other twentieth-century voices, such as the psychoanalyst J. C. Flügel. Flügel was one of the first critics to make the flawed but lasting generalization that Western men stopped taking interest in fashion after 1789, when, as his historicization goes, Frenchmen—as part of the French revolutionary distrust of and hatred for the aristocracy, and men's desire to remove themselves as objects of the gaze—abandoned their erstwhile desire for colorful and ornate brocades in favor of no-frills, three-piece suits in black.[5]

Coinciding with (if not a byproduct of) the assumed homogeneity of patterns of middle-class masculinity during the nineteenth century, the early legacies of figures like Pereda were heavily informed by the monolithic myth of the bourgeois "man in black" which both reductively imagined their identities as writers while flattening the context from which they emerged. The so called *modernistas* including Rubén Darío proffered some of the earliest and harshest critiques of the previous generation's literatos, a group that was emblematized for them by figures like Pereda and his peers. Although Pereda's regionalist aesthetics and masculine persona were generally viewed positively by contemporaries in the 1880s and 90s (surely a sign of the continued vogue for moralizing literature and regionalism), the novelist from Polanco had many critics who saw his literary and political attachments to his homeland as decadent and retrograde. In his 1900 book titled *España contemporánea* (Modern Spain), for example, Darío caricatures Pereda not only by taking aim at his penchant for rural environs, but he also does so by disparaging him for his business activity and traditionalist aesthetic, framing the Cantabrian novelist as equal parts bourgeois miser and motheaten throwback to the Spanish Golden Age. The Nicaraguan poet places particular emphasis on agist stereotypes when criticizing the Spaniard's "unflattering odor" and "dusty" wardrobe:

> Don José María de Pereda, owner of a soap factory, rests from his earlier conquests. A rabid regionalist, his world is based in the Sardinero [the name of a coastal neighborhood in Santander] or in Polanco; his aesthetic gives off a musty odor; his neck is held up and tightly squeezed into an ancient *golilla* collar. He is a fossil and hardly kind to anyone whose ideals do not include that which is antiquated and constrained.[6]

Darío needles Pereda again when he suggests that the latter's conformist and materialistic devotion to the industrial manufacture of soap was a result of not having been able to earn enough money from book sales.[7] Of course, contemporary cultural producers have long since abandoned such stereotypes, thus inviting new approaches to understanding how images of Victorian men and masculinity (in all of their patterns) are sources of inspiration and evidence for ideals that were not monolithic, but heterogeneous and plural.

The notion that even dominant, normative ideals of nineteenth-century Spanish masculinity (e.g., "man in black") were heterogeneous and plural, a central thesis of this book, is reflected in a number of popular Instagram accounts whose users editorialize painted and photographic portraits of men from the global fin de siècle under an all-encompassing, "Victorian" aegis.[8] With more than ten thousand followers each, @victorianboyfriend (14.5K followers) and @hotvictorians (32K followers) regularly cull from museum websites, Google, and their own studies in Western European art history to introduce twenty-first-century Instagram users to nineteenth-century iconographies of masculinity, while reframing them as contemporary objects of desire. In a post dedicated to King Alfonso XII (see fig. 5.1), who, as we saw earlier, unevenly embodied bourgeois masculine ideals during the Restoration, @hotvictorians juxtaposes a number of images of the "dashing king," unintentionally echoing the Restoration-era accounts describing him as a "particularly strapping lad," as this book's introduction discussed. By giving visibility to the king's official (and undoubtedly idealized) images, the Instagram account overtly broadcasts the desirability of the formal portrait while also shedding light on how we continue to inherit nineteenth-century visual cultural practices.

In their curation, the aforementioned Instagram influencers virtually digitize analogue forms like the album, scrapbook, or wall-hangings, genres of popular culture that similarly unify a plurality of images on a page or wall space (see fig. 5.2). Thus, they flatten the divide that once separated formal academic painting and popular cultural forms (e.g., advertisements, fashion plates, *cromos*). They also diversify the monolithic and sometimes mythical image of the affluent white man in a black suit by revealing a heterogeneous array of nineteenth-century masculinity's avatars, which ranged from working-class figure-drawing models to bourgeois artists who styled themselves as bohemians. All of the male authors studied in this book were also consumers and collectors of their peers' painted and photographed likenesses, as we saw reflected in the epistolary correspondence between Galdós, Clarín, Oller, and Pereda. Their own collection of the photographed countenances of their international peers like Hugo, Tolstoy, and Zola reveals that men were eager to acquire images of their friends and heroes, either to associate themselves as part of a homosocial brotherhood or kinship network, or to better visualize their models. When considered alongside the literary and visual evidence surveyed by this book, Instagram accounts and the micronarratives or fantasies they share further emphasize the kaleidoscopic image of bourgeois manhood that is sometimes paved over by the ubiquitous image of the man in a black suit and top hat. Of course, with their own distinct formal elements, social media profiles—like those made possible by Instagram, an application that effectively allows downloaders to create their own username and (strategically) curate their corresponding page with photographs of themselves, others, or objects—also function as vehicles for strategic self-fashioning. Not unlike nineteenth-century autobiographical accounts, epistolary correspondence or portraiture, they envision "human identity," and, I would add here, masculinity and gender expression more generally, "as a manipulable, artful process."[9]

FIGURE 5.1 SCREENSHOT OF THE INSTAGRAM FEED MAINTAINED BY @HOTVICTORIANS. Image courtesy of @hotvictorians, Instagram.

FIGURE 5.2 SCREENSHOT OF THE INSTAGRAM FEED MAINTAINED BY @VICTORIAN-BOYFRIEND. A thumbnail of Fortuny's drawing is the second from the last in the central column of images. Image courtesy of @victorianboyfriend, Instagram.

Often citing regional folklore and traditional Spanish garments like the cape as inspirations, designers at the helm of popular fashion label Oteyza—Paul García de Oteyza and Caterina Pañeda—intentionally rebrand classic images of "Spanishness" for consumers of high fashion on the catwalks of New York, London, Paris, and Madrid. Trained by La Confianza—a professional association for tailors that founded its school in Madrid in 1897—García and Pañeda take icons of bourgeois masculinity codified in fashion plates and department store catalogs during the nineteenth century, from the cape and the hat (see Cordovan hats, bowlers in fig. 2.8), rebranding them for fashion-forward consumers, and especially although not exclusively for men who identify as men. In their spring/summer 2018–19 collection,

Oteyza's directors outfitted their models in looks whose patterns were first published by Golden Age tailors like Juan de Alceaga, but later codified in nineteenth-century tailoring journals like *El Arte Español* (see fig. 5.3), at the same time that they reimagine classic Spanish garments through an array of brightly saturated hues ranging from orange and yellow to chartreuse. Emphasizing the craftsmanship and regional/rustic provenance of their garments during the 2018 show, García de Oteyza performed a live "cutting" of a traditional cape, surrounded by the aforementioned male models cloaked in rainbow hues, as well as a handful of merino sheep fenced in around the catwalk. Thus, the creative team of Oteyza fused together ideas about the durability of rustic (and traditional) models of masculinity with modern ones, echoing similar processes in which José María de Pereda (and his contemporaries) participated. Oteyza's citing of Golden Age precedents mirrors that of their counterparts in nineteenth-century visual culture and literature, who similarly drew upon the work of their forefathers from El Greco and Velázquez to Cervantes in their own attempts to modernize Spanish art and letters. Recalling again Pereda's own embrace of rurality and rusticity in the fictions he wrote and published for a largely urban readership, Oteyza's most recent collection titled "Arcadia" for fall/winter 2021–22 depicts men and women in outfits inspired by Spanish regional menswear, thus demonstrating how elite cultural producers continue to mine rural contexts and texts in their output destined for urban audiences in national and international contexts.

If Oteyza more overtly embraces the contours of nineteenth-century bourgeois manliness emblematized by traditional sartorial icons for men like the suit and the cape, Alejandro Gómez Palomo's menswear—also marketed and embraced by contemporary divas from Beyoncé to Rosalía—draws more on the longue durée. The Córdoba native's contemporary fashions, for example, excavate the iconography of the Ancien Régime, from the codpiece to the embroidery and laces of liturgical dress and Golden Age ruffles. But Gómez Palomo also relies on traditional narrative conceits and tropes in his artistic memoir, thus demonstrating the durability of strategies of self-fashioning capitalized upon earlier by fin de siècle writers from Galdós to Oller. Gómez Palomo's eponymous memoir—a book that he defines as a "testament of [his] project," much like Oller's own posthumously published literary memoirs—the designer narrativizes his life as it relates to his various collections, beginning with the Virginia Woolf-inspired "Orlando" and ending with "Wunderkammer."[10] Even though his collection titled "The Hunting" draws inspiration from the homosocial

FIGURE 5.3 FASHION PLATE FROM DECEMBER 1, 1877, ISSUE
OF *EL ARTE ESPAÑOL*. Image courtesy of the Biblioteca Nacional
de España (National Library of Spain), Madrid, Spain.

sport of the hunt, and his references are decidedly masculine (e.g., portraits of Golden Age kings by Baroque masters Velázquez, Titian, and Sánchez Cotán), Gómez Palomo invites and actively broadcasts his collaborations with women—including the many seamstresses making up his design team—thus doing away with or at least providing a corrective for the myth of all-male society perpetuated by nineteenth-century autobiographical accounts, commercial ephemera, and some of the novels analyzed in this book. Gómez Palomo's references to the movers and shakers of the fashion industry, who continue to reside in London and Paris, further substantiates the anxieties and desires of Spanish cultural producers to be seen by their peers working elsewhere in Europe, as we saw to be true of Spanish novelists who idolized figures like Balzac, Dickens, Flaubert, Tolstoy, and Zola.[11]

From Instagram influencers to two of the contemporary Spanish fashion world's rising stars, the cultural production of contemporary creators exhibits how nineteenth-century contexts, texts, and strategies continue to reproduce themselves in contemporary cultural products at the same time that they reveal the patterns from which they draw to have always been kaleidoscopic and plural. Illustrating the draw of nineteenth-century masculine aesthetics on the contemporary artistic and cultural imagination, Oteyza and Palomo Spain inventively rethink menswear by culling from historical models ranging from the European Renaissance (which occurred during Spain's Golden Age of empire) to the nineteenth century. Although some contemporary cultural creators like designers of menswear are perhaps less direct in their dialogue with nineteenth-century aesthetics of masculinity than the previously mentioned social media accounts—since the speed with which fashion trends change means that their sources of inspiration are constantly shifting—their whimsical refashioning of classic silhouettes, together with their similar reliance on narrative as a meaning-making strategy (whether in the captions of their posts to Instagram accounts or their artistic-autobiographical "testaments"), help to unveil the many ways themes and tropes related to Restoration-era images similarly weave through their artistic output. Whether on the runway, in fashion advertisements, or in their own literary self-fashioning, the modus operandi of both Oteyza and Palomo Spain goes beyond the mere appropriation of nineteenth-century Spanish men's classic symbols (e.g., hats, three-piece suits, capes). In their creative takes on contemporary menswear staples, the designers at the helms of Oteyza and Palomo Spain appropriate or reproduce many of the narrative tropes associated with nineteenth-century manhood as part of wider attempts to transgress while redefining the contours of modern masculinity. Although each does so differently, producing radically diverging aesthetics, both labels open dialogues with Victorian-era models and texts in their rebranding of the sartorial options available and desirable to all consumers regardless of their gender expression or identity. With their award-winning fashions, the Spanish designers rewrite historical patterns of fashionable masculinity—from visual icons like the black city suit to narrative tropes like male homosocial bonding—by making them fluid and inclusive with regards to gender, even if their bespoke and ready-made offerings are still only accessible to those able to afford them. They also blend rural and urban tropes in their styles and strategic self-fashioning, as we saw to be the case with figures like Pereda, while producing solutions to some of the problems nineteenth-century writers like Galdós identified in the menswear available to bourgeois "dandies" of his day, such as the supposed lack of fantasy and comfortability in items ranging from the top hat to the necktie.

Although the writers studied in this book did not always participate as overtly in discussions surrounding men's fashion as did their British analogues during the second half of the nineteenth century, all of them commented on menswear in one way or another, regardless of any personal hang-ups that sometimes led them to label it a feminine affair.[12] One noteworthy example is an essay from the 1890s titled "El elegante" (The dandy or The elegant man), in which Benito Pérez Galdós facetiously toys with the idea of rescuing the dandy—"el elegante," a term that alluded to any fashion-conscious gentleman during the fin de siècle—from sartorial ennui brought on by oppressive and uncomfortable formalwear: namely, the dark-colored, supposedly uncomfortable articles of clothing like the top hat and three-piece suit. As part of his historicization, Galdós privileges the menswear of prior centuries, as well as that of foreigners (e.g., Middle Eastern and Japanese men), whose traditional modes of dress were, at least for the Canarian novelist, characterized by facility of movement, freedom, and comfort. His preference for the exotic and the timeless takes a surprising turn: after praising the Roman toga (a sign of masculinity in the nineteenth century, too, as is apparent in fig. 2.1), he calls for modern men to don the robes of male religious orders in order to break free from the sartorial "chains" of the "odious" top hat. Whereas fashion for Galdós and other writers during this time was often predicated on a sense of a modernity in constant flux, monastic clothing was, for them, resistant to modernity's fickleness, since it had remained virtually unchanged since the Middle Ages. Clarín suggests as much, if ironically, in his short story titled "El sombrero del cura" (The priest's hat), a tale in which a country priest boasts about the timelessness of his dress, which, because of fashion's volubility, inevitably reenters the fashionable mainstream from time to time. In the view of the Galdosian narrator of "el elegante", men are encouraged to embrace the sartorial rubrics of their religious male counterparts, using colors according to their station in life: "Let us all be Dominicans, Franciscans, bearded capuchins or hairless Carmelites; let us change the color of the habits, wearing more eccentric and flashy ones through youth, greys or lighter tones when matured and brown or black in old age. [. . .] In other words: absolute unity in form, freedom of color and quality of the fabrics."[13]

Though he might still be disappointed if he were able to stroll down Madrid's Gran Vía or Barcelona's Passeig de Gràcia, the Galdós of "El elegante" would perhaps be delighted by the ways contemporary fashion brands like Oteyza and Palomo Spain have begun to reinvent the shapes and shades of bourgeois masculinity's mythical image, which was, like masculinity itself, a byproduct of active processes of self-fashioning. The fact that novelists like Galdós and his peers did, in fact, take on the subject of masculinity and its fashionable merchandise, a reality examined throughout this book, invites heretofore unanswered questions and avenues for future scholarship. For example, what is the relationship between masculine consumerism—shopping for oneself or others—and religious and political affiliation? How does men's positionality within circuits of production and consumption evolve across time, from young adulthood to old age, and what is its relevance to questions related to sexuality? How might other bourgeois social types traditionally unassociated with consumer culture—from the supposedly "self-made" man to the rational doctor or the more traditionally virile soldier—reflect or resist Spanish elites' embrace of capitalism? How do present-day memorials (e.g., centennial celebrations) of nineteenth-century men challenge or reproduce stereotypes about Victorian-era masculinity?

Before the novel coronavirus would send most of the world into a year of phased lockdowns and quarantines from which we are only now emerging, the centennial of Benito Pérez Galdós's death in January 2020 brought the Canarian novelist's name back to the Spanish Royal Academy in the form of a series of roundtable discussions about the legacies of the author and his work. The central elements of the banner designed specifically for the event include an offset photograph of Galdós cropped from one of the *cartes de visite* he shared with fans and friends alike, as well as a minimalist, iconographic representation of the author, reducing the Canarian novelist's persona to two symbols long associated with photographs and painted portraits of the author, which were also two common icons of middle-class manhood from the turn of the century: a bowler hat and mustache.

The use of symbols like the top hat, the bowler, the cape, and the necktie often oversimplify more complex patterns available to bourgeois men—from the student and the priest to the businessman and the heir—while obfuscating the masculine cultures of production and consumption in which they actively participated. It has resulted in the erasure of what Rita Felski has termed "the vulgar act of shopping" as one of masculinity's signs.[14] Indeed, the hyper visibility of bodily adornments like bowlers and mustaches, along with other accessories like top hats, gloves, walking sticks, and shoes—alongside the assumed absence or insignificance of a cultural industry for menswear and men's grooming—would appear to suggest that dandies (i.e., the fashion-conscious bourgeois man or aspirant) interested in self-fashioning for any number of reasons, simply sprung from the ground bedecked in three-piece suits, silk hats, gloves, and walking sticks. This process of naturalization whereby masculinity is viewed less as the result of an active process and more as a natural product issuing from a male body is, of course, central to one of the myths of mainstream masculinity that rural masculinities scholars like Campbell and Bell have begun to demystify, as Chapter 4 demonstrates. As we saw earlier, in his novels, Galdós shows that men's consumerism and self-fashioning are not reducible to censures of his characters' masculinity: from the upwardly mobile ambitions of students like Felipe Centeno and Alejandro Miquis to the acquisitions, gifts, and palatial estate of colonial returnees like Agustín Caballero.

The image of the fashionable bourgeois gentleman or dandy of the nineteenth century is also one that we may use to reconsider the legacies and personas of the writers whose work is analyzed by the chapters of *Masculine Figures*. If, as James Eli Adams writes, "the dandy's anxious desire for a literal visibility [. . .] figures an aspiration closely akin to [a] longing for literary authority," then dandyism itself—a notion born of the fusion of masculinity and fashion or self-fashioning—functions as a particularly efficacious conceit with which to better understand the personas fashioned by the nineteenth-century Spanish novelists studied in this book.[15] Emilia Pardo Bazán seems to have been especially cognizant of the affinity between dandyism and self-formation in *Memorias de un solterón* (Memoirs of a bachelor), a novel in which she disguises herself as the first-person narrator and sartorialist Mauro Pareja, thus evidencing what Beth Wietelmann Bauer calls "narrative cross-dressing."[16] The fashionable bourgeois gentleman and the various registers of his representations, along with those authors who aestheticized and ironized them in nineteenth-century visual culture and novels, were accessories to Spanish modernity that provided realist novelists like Galdós and his peers yet another opportunity to display Spanish culture's contributions to wider networks of consumer culture and, by extension, modernity, while also betokening their own literary artistry and originality. While some exceptional women artists and authors were able to achieve national and international recognition during the nineteenth century in Spain, literary critics' and novelists' masculine-coding of literary professionalization and self-fashioning led to the creation of a kind of "Gentlemen's Paradise," a homosocial fantasy in and of which male artists and authors saw themselves as the foremost progenitors and protagonists.

Notes

INTRODUCTION

1. During the final decades of the nineteenth century and the early twentieth century, advertising cards like these were distributed at the point of sale or mailed to clients to announce the arrival of new merchandise. They are known as *tarjetas comerciales* in Spanish and *targetes comercials* in Catalan and are also included under the umbrella term *cromos*, a word used to refer to any small, chromolithographic card or paper distributed as advertisements and invitations, or originally affixed to commodities like cigars, chocolate, and children's toys. Those cataloged by the Spanish National Library and the Historical Archive of Barcelona were often first collected and fixed to the pages of albums or scrapbooks. See Eliseo Trenc Ballester, *Las artes gráficas de la época modernista en Barcelona* (Barcelona: Gremio de Industrias Gráficas, 1977) and Rosario Ramos Pérez, *Ephemera: La vida sobre papel* (Madrid: Biblioteca Nacional/Ministerio de Educación, Cultura y Deporte, 2003).

2. All translations from Spanish and Catalan to English are my own unless otherwise noted. Jesús Cruz, *Gentlemen, Bourgeois, and Revolutionaries: Political Change and Cultural Persistence among the Spanish Dominant Groups 1750–1850* (Cambridge: Cambridge University Press, 1996), 3. Pointing to the heterogeneous constitution of the Spanish bourgeoisie, cultural historian Jesús Cruz argues elsewhere that "in the social context of nineteenth-century Spain, the 'bourgeoisie' or 'middle classes' was the diverse social conglomerate situated between the old nobility and the working classes. These individuals and families range from the wealthy capitalists to the modest middle class with limited income but pretentious lifestyles, and also include members of the bourgeoisie that attained aristocratic titles." This book follows Cruz in its utilization of the terms bourgeois/bourgeoisie and middle-class/middle classes synonymously, since they all refer to "the same social reality." Jesús Cruz, *The Rise of Middle-Class Culture in Nineteenth-Century Spain* (Baton Rouge: Louisiana University Press, 2011), 10.

3. Santiago Ramón y Cajal, *Recuerdos de mi vida*, ed. Juan Fernández Santarén (Barcelona: Editorial Crítica, 2006), 205–14.

4. Eusebio Güell y López, *Perspectivas de la vida* (Madrid: Compañía Ibero-americana de Publicaciones, 1930), 50.

5. Laura Casal-Valls, "La figura de la modista i els inicis de l'alta costura a Barcelona: Trajectòria professional i producció d'indumentària femenina (1880–1915)" (PhD diss., Universitat de Barcelona, 2013), 502.

6. José María de Pereda, "A las Indias," *Escenas montañesas*, 41, Biblioteca Virtual de Miguel de Cervantes, accessed December 15, 2021, https://www.cervantesvirtual.com/obra/escenas-montanesas-coleccion-de-bosquejos-de-costumbres-tomados-al-natural—o. Although the boy's pretensions described here only undermine the output of seamstresses in his family, and not seamstresses in general, his attitude encapsulates more widely held stereotypes

about the inferiority of women's sartorial labor. See Casal-Valls, "La figura" for a comprehensive overview of the subject.

7. Benito Pérez Galdós, *Mendizábal* (Madrid: Alianza Editorial, 2010), 37–38.

8. Yvan Lissorgues, *Leopoldo Alas, Clarín, en sus palabras (1852–1901)* (Oviedo: Ediciones Nobel, 2007), 393, 522.

9. Benito Pérez Galdós, "Discurso del Sr. D. Benito Pérez Galdós," in *Discursos leídos ante la Real Academia Española en la recepción pública del Sr. D. Benito Pérez Galdós, el domingo 7 de febrero de 1897* (Madrid: Impresor de Cámara de S. M., 1897), 8.

10. Pérez Galdós, "Discurso," 13.

11. Because the emergence of realism was coterminous with that of naturalism during the 1880s in Spain, references to the "realist novel" or the "novel" in this book refer to works that employ aesthetics and plot devices associated with both realism and naturalism (not to mention other trends such as *costumbrismo* and literary decadence) unless otherwise stated. I return to this idea later in this introduction. For the most recent survey of definitions and debates surrounding the heterogeneity of realism and naturalism in Spain, see Mary L. Coffey and Margot Versteeg, introduction to *Imagined Truths: Realism in Modern Spanish Literature and Culture*, ed. Mary L. Coffey and Margot Versteeg, 3–35 (Toronto: University of Toronto Press, 2019).

12. Leigh Mercer, *Urbanism and Urbanity: The Spanish Bourgeois Novel and Contemporary Customs (1845–1925)* (Lewisburg, PA: Bucknell University Press, 2013), 12.

13. Pierre Bourdieu, *The Field of Cultural Production*, edited by Randal Johnson (New York: Columbia University Press, 1993), 112

14. Drawing on Jo Labanyi's *Gender and Modernization*, Collin McKinney provides an overview of the hygienic discourses surrounding the treatment of men's sexuality as a kind of bodily economy. Collin McKinney, "Enemigos de la virilidad: Sex, Masturbation, and Celibacy in Nineteenth-Century Spain," *Prisma Social: Revista de Investigación Social* 13 (2014–2015): 74. Speaking elsewhere to the existence and dissemination of physiognomic discourses in Spain, McKinney concludes that "every element of an individual's appearance, from the angle of their nose to the shoes on their feet, was viewed as a virtual map of the soul." Collin McKinney, "Men in Black: Fashioning Masculinity in Nineteenth-Century Spain," *Letras Hispanas* 8, no. 2 (2012): 87.

15. Leo Braudy, *From Chivalry to Terrorism: War and the Changing Nature of Masculinity* (New York: Vintage, 2005), 9–10. George Mosse asserts that the imperative for men to embody certain attributes over others has a long history in industrialized Western cultures, in which "masculinity was regarded as one piece from its very beginning: body and soul, outward appearance and inward virtue were supposed to form one harmonious whole, a perfect construct where every part was in its place." George L. Mosse, *The Image of Man: The Creation of Modern Masculinity* (Oxford: Oxford University Press, 1996), 5.

16. Mosse, *The Image of Man*, 6.

17. Cruz points out that "care of the complexion was foremost, and individuals who did not have a fair and glowing facial complexion—considered not only a sign of beauty, but also of good health and character—were advised to recur to artificial treatment." Cruz, *The Rise*, 45. See Jennifer Smith's analysis of Pardo Bazán's representation of this reality in the Galician novelist's 1889 book *Insolación* (Sunstroke). Jennifer Smith, "Cultural Capital and Social Class in Emilia Pardo Bazán's 'La mujer española' and *Insolación*," *Anales de la Literatura Española Contemporánea* 41, no. 1 (2016): 148.

18. R W Connell, *Masculinities* (Berkeley: University of California Press, 1995, 77.

19. The king's failure to "measure up" to the standard is not especially surprising when one considers Connell's caveat that "individual holders of institutional power or great wealth may be far from the hegemonic pattern in their personal lives. [. . .] Nevertheless, hegemony is likely to be established only if there is some correspondence between cultural ideal and institutional power, collective if not individual." Connell, *Masculinities*, 77.

20. Quoted in Catherine Jagoe, Alda Blanco, and Cristina Enríquez de Salamanca, *La mujer en los discursos de género: Textos y contextos en el siglo XIX* (Barcelona: Icaria Editorial, 1998), 389.

21. The Spanish National Library catalogs editions of the *Higiene del matrimonio* from 1850, 1858, 1865, 1898, and 1928. The hygienist was also known for his advocation for the demolition of Barcelona's crumbling medieval walls in the interest of public hygiene and urban expansion. Monlau was also a member of the Spanish Royal Academy.

22. Connell, *Masculinities*, 70.

23. "Parte política," *La Época*, November 28, 1875, 2.

24. Mosse, *The Image*, 6.

25. Collin McKinney, "Pogonology, Physiognomy, and the Face of Spanish Masculinity," in *Modernity and Epistemology in Nineteenth-Century Spain: Fringe Discourses*, edited by Ryan A. Davis and Alicia Cerezo Paredes (Lanham, MD: Lexington Books, 2017), 66–67.

26. Carlos Dardé Moreno, *Alfonso XII* (Madrid: Arlanza, 2001), 75.

27. Dardé Moreno, *Alfonso XII*, 74.

28. Rafael Fernández Sirvent, "Biografía de Alfonso XII de Borbón (1875–1885)," Biblioteca Virtual de Miguel de Cervantes, accessed December 15, 2021. http://www.cervantesvirtual.com/portales/reyes_y_reinas_espana_contemporanea/alfonso_xii_biografia.

29. Quoted in Nicolás Fernández Medina, *Life Embodied: The Promise of Vital Force in Spanish Modernity* (Montreal: McGill-Queen's University Press, 2018), 243. Unamuno praises physical exercise, and its most significant advocates, like Felipe Serrate, and cites his own quest for self-improvement by way of physical education. I quote here from Nicolás Fernández Medina's translation to English of excerpts from Unamuno's writings on gymnastics, compiled in the so-called *Escritos bilbaínos* (Bilbao Writings).

30. *La descoberta de la gran ciutat: París, 1878*, ed. Rosa Cabré (Tarragona: Institut d'Estudis Tarraconenses Ramon Berenguer IV, 1995), 28, 30, 32, 36, 37, 40, 42, 43.

31. According to one report, "the products displayed in the Exposition [were] perfumes from Pereda and Company's factory *La Rosario*. To be sure, the aroma emanating from the products of that factory [was] a pleasant one indeed, but it could never compare to that of the alluring scents of the author's *Escenas montañesas* (Mountain scenes) or *El sabor de la tierruca* (The feel of the good earth)." Carlos Frontaura, *Barcelona en 1888 y París en 1889* (Madrid: P. Aguilar, 1899), 55–56.

32. Bueno de Guzmán describes having once seen "a wonderful photograph of Constantino, depicted in the style of those presuming to be athletes, who inspire laughter with their statuary frankness, gymnast's physique, girdle and weightlifting belt, arms crossed so as to show off their well-developed biceps and thorax, and arrogant packaging and mien." Benito Pérez Galdós, *Lo prohibido* (Madrid: Cátedra, 2001), 217. In Galdós's earlier novel *El Doctor Centeno*, a friendship with a local photographer leads to the virile priest Pedro Polo's possession and display of a number of photographic portraits of his likeness in a variety of guises: "the walls were studded with different images in as many forms as one can imagine: Don Pedro, in his clerical garb, seated; Don Pedro, dressed as a countryman, with a book in his hand; [. . .] Don Pedro and his mother in front of a backdrop depicting the

jungle and a waterfall, with the latter seated and looking puzzled, and the former standing and looking at his mother, and many others." Benito Pérez Galdós, *El Doctor Centeno*
(Madrid: Alianza Editorial, 2012), 69.

33. Leopoldo Alas, *His Only Son*, translated by Margaret Jull Costa (New York: New York
Review of Books, 2016), 77.

34. Due to an abundance of satirical and novelistic representations, coupled with the supposed silences of the archive (silences that Christopher Breward [1999] and Alison Matthews David [2003] have addressed in English and French studies, respectively), many
Hispanists who write about menswear and masculinity of the Spanish nineteenth century
reproduce the view that fashionable consumption and knowledge were universally coded
as feminine. According to this perspective, men's conspicuous interest in fashion was an
automatic and universal motive for censure. For a summary of the arguments made by
Pena González, McKinney ("Men in Black"), Heneghan, and Díaz-Marcos, see Nicholas
Wolters, "The Spanish Cut: Tailoring Men's Fashion and National Identity in Nineteenth-
Century Spain," *Journal of Spanish Cultural Studies* 21, no. 3 (2020): 3.

35. John B. Thompson, introduction to *Language and Symbolic Power*, by Pierre Bourdieu,
ed. John B. Thompson, trans. Gino Raymond and Matthew Adamson (London: Polity,
1991), 14.

36. Cruz, *The Rise*, 20–21.

37. Eric Zuelow, *A History of Modern Tourism* (New York: Palgrave Macmillan, 2016), 78.

38. Derek Neal, "What Can Historians Do with Clerical Masculinity?" In *Negotiating Clerical
Identities: Priests, Monks and Masculinity in the Middle Ages*, ed. Jennifer Thibodeaux (Basingstoke: Palgrave Macmillan, 2010), 30. Many bourgeois values were, of course, shared
by men and women alike. Comfort and elegance were embraced by the households of
affluent families wishing to enjoy their resources while broadcasting their social status
to others. For example, this phenomenon is made abundantly clear in Narcís Oller's *La
febre d'or* (Gold fever), a novel that visualizes both men and women's enjoyment of posh
lifestyles, whether in the form of real estate upgrades to home and office or extravagant
soirées in Parisian opera houses and dance halls. Ramon Casas's genre paintings similarly
depict consumerist men unabashedly and without censure to their manhood, especially
in the contexts of the bohemian art world and sport. For some of society's moralizers,
however, men's proximity to women within consumerist spheres was cause for censure,
as was evident in satirical cartoons and negative depictions in novels (see fig. 0.7). To
provide a counterpoint to *La febre d'or*, the narrators of Pereda's *Pedro Sánchez* and *Peñas
arriba* frequently frame consumption—although perhaps only when "excessive"—as feminine and feminizing. Overall, novelists were more discreet when it came to representing
male acquisitive appetites. Men who participated in consumer culture were less prone to
stigmatization by artists and novelists than their female counterparts, and men tended to
be lampooned only when their embrace of bourgeois consumer culture was found to be
exceptionally lacking—for example, due to a miserly obsession with saving, as is apparent in the case of Francisco de Bringas from Galdós's *La de Bringas*—or excessive—as we
see in characters like Frasquito Ponte from *Misericordia*.

39. Connell, *Masculinities*, 76–77.

40. This introduction builds on the work of several scholars who have insisted upon the value
of visual cultural ephemera in recovering bourgeois cultural practices writ large during
the nineteenth century. Mercedes Pasalodos Salgado's articles, for example, highlight the
role of tailors' manuals and department store catalogs in galvanizing modern practices

of production and consumption in Madrid. Trenc and Ramos Pérez have cataloged and described the hundreds of *cromos* (chromolithographic cards, paper, and other ephemera) contained in the Spanish National Library, arguing that such objects form a fragmentary but nonetheless meaningful corpus reflective of men's, women's, and children's participation in a burgeoning consumer culture. Though his focus is not framed by masculinities studies and relies primarily on probate inventories of bourgeois family archives (and not visual cultural ephemera), Jesús Cruz's *The Rise of Middle-Class Culture in Nineteenth-Century Spain* represents a major contribution to our understanding of men's place within nineteenth-century consumerism by suggesting that consumption was also a common activity among men. By shifting the focus to visual culture and novels, this section insists upon the generative relationship between cultures of capitalistic production and consumption and the multiple patterns of middle-class masculinity they engendered.

41. Cruz, *The Rise*, 106, 107, 129.
42. Though fashion advertisements are hardly unproblematic referents, visual cultural ephemera give visibility to the many consumable styles of masculinity, or accessible ideals of manliness to which boys and men had access or could aspire during the turn of the century in Spain. Marcia Pointon, "Enduring Characteristics and Unstable Hues: Men in Black in French Painting in the 1860s and 1870s," *Art History* 40, no. 4 (2017): 748.
43. Salvador Oropesa Márquez, *Literatura y comercio en España: Las tiendas (1868-1952)* (Málaga: Universidad de Málaga, 2014), 50.
44. Homi Bhabha, *Nation and Narration* (New York: Routledge, 1990), 3.
45. Jo Labanyi, *Gender and Modernization in the Spanish Realist Novel* (Oxford: Oxford University Press, 2000), 6.
46. Oropesa Márquez, *Literatura y comercio*, 52.
47. Nerea Aresti, "La hombría perdida en el tiempo: Masculinidad y nación española a finales del siglo XIX," in *Hombres en peligro: Género, nación e imperio en la España de cambio de siglo (XIX–XX)*, ed. Mauricio Zabalgoitia Herrera (Madrid: Iberoamericana, 2017), 27.
48. Shifra Armon, *Masculine Virtue in Early Modern Spain* (Farnham, UK: Ashgate Publishing, 2015), 8. Although French fashion was criticized by some for its supposedly effeminate qualities, and English fashion, on the contrary, was deemed appropriately masculine by other cultural commentators, the distinction was largely rhetorical, and rooted more in historical stereotype than observable reality. McKinney, "Men in Black" 87. Negative stereotypes about the feminizing potential of French fashion among Spanish men date back to at least the start of the Bourbon regime in the eighteenth century when terms like *petimetre* (from the French *petit-maître* or "little master") were used to skewer fashion-obsessed Francophiles at a time when many Spanish elites embraced the cosmopolitan values symbolized by French aesthetic and philosophical ideals. Anxieties about men's consumption of French fashion notwithstanding, nineteenth-century tailoring journals, department store catalogs, and more recent studies by Mercedes Pasalodos Salgado attest that both men and women's fashion was an international affair by the end of the nineteenth century. Wolters, "The Spanish Cut," 7. Presumably English cuts, colors, and styles were also widely visible in the promotional materials of French tailoring shops and department stores, and apparently "British" fashions (e.g., the black city suit, tartans) were produced and consumed around the world: from London, Edinburgh, and New York to Paris, Barcelona, and Tokyo (Edo). As Christopher Breward historicizes, the Englishness of the city suit is itself a cultural construct, given the ways "Britain's long colonial relationship with South Asia, for example, [. . .] had a significant influence on the traditions of suit

construction, accessorizing and wear." Christopher Breward, *The Suit: Form, Function, and Style* (London: Reaktion Books, 2016), 86–87.

49. Having lost control of the majority of its American colonial possessions earlier in the nineteenth century, Spain's overseas territories had dwindled to Cuba, Puerto Rico, and the Philippines by the start of the Bourbon Restoration. It also continued to hold some territories in Western Sahara and the Gulf of Guinea. Though it would not cede control of Cuba, Puerto Rico, and the Philippines until its cataclysmic failure to defeat the superior US American forces during the Spanish-American War of 1898, Spain experienced a variety of conflicts with its colonies, particularly after the dethroning of Isabel II during the September 1868 revolution. War in Morocco (1859–1860) and revolts in Cuba (1868–1878; 1895–1898), for example, put pressure on Spanish imperial hegemony during the second half of the nineteenth century. As recent studies by Chang, Coffey, Copeland, Murray, and Tsuchiya convincingly demonstrate, motifs of empire were especially relevant to the nineteenth-century cultural and literary imagination in Spain, even if they sometimes occupy the background.

50. "Nuestro Grabado," *El Globo*, April 2, 1878, 1.

51. "Nuestro Grabado," 1.

52. For the influence of *japonisme* in Spain, see David George, "'Playing Japanese' in *Fin-de-siècle* Zarzuela," in *Intersections of Race, Class, Gender, and Nation in* Fin-de-siècle *Spanish Literature and Culture*, eds. Jennifer Smith and Lisa Nalbone, 123–48 (New York: Routledge, 2017). I thank David George, too, for first drawing my attention to Figure 0.8.

53. Anne McClintock, *Imperial Leather: Race, Gender, and Sexuality in the Colonial Context* (New York: Routledge, 1995), 5.

54. Josep Fradera, *The Imperial Nation: Citizens and Subjects in the British, French, Spanish, and American Empires*, trans. Ruth MacKay (Princeton, NJ: Princeton University Press, 2018), 128.

55. José Álvarez Junco, *Mater dolorosa: La idea de España en el siglo XIX* (Madrid: Taurus, 2017), 504.

56. Álvarez Junco, *Mater dolorosa*, 510.

57. Mosse, *The Image of Man*, 4, 5, 7, 15, 23, 26. Mosse goes on to assert that such ideals were "not bound to any one of the powerful political ideologies of [the nineteenth or twentieth century]," and their universal appeal is demonstrated by their being co-opted by far-left and far-right ideologies alike (7). Once aristocratic values, such as "the idealized platonic love of a noble lady that was supposed to spiritualize knighthood," for example, were "made commonplace through the monopoly exercised by the institution of marriage" (19).

58. Franco Moretti, *The Bourgeois: Between History and Literature* (New York: Verso, 2014), 16.

59. Moretti, *The Bourgeois*, 35, 39, 44, 67, 120, 131.

60. Shifra Armon and Faith Harden historicize the myths of chivalric and military masculinity based on honor and martial valor forged during the early modern period. Scholars working on the Spanish Age of Enlightenment (1740–1808) have also begun to recontextualize the styles of masculinity represented in eighteenth-century literature in Spain. Rebecca Haidt and Mehl Penrose, for example, have traced anxieties and behavioral ideals inscribed on the male body through literary representations of the philosophe, the upper-class fop, and the working-class *majo*. Irene Gómez Castellano's work complicates the image of enlightened gentlemen guided exclusively by reason and sang-froid by analyzing the rhetoric of drunkenness and homoeroticism at play in their classically inspired poetry. Focusing on paintings and ephemeral visual cultures, Tara Zanardi updates our

understanding of the Enlightenment-era bullfighter as the figure relates to nascent ideas about celebrity status, national character, and manly braggadocio.

61. José Rementería y Fica, *El hombre fino al gusto del día, Manual completo de urbanidad, cortesía y buen tono, con las reglas, aplicaciones y ejemplos del Arte de presentarse y conducirse en toda clase de reuniones, visitas, etc.; en el que se enseña la etiqueta y ceremonial que la sensatez y la costumbre han establecido; con la Guía del tocador y un tratado del Arte cisoria* (Madrid: Imprenta del Colegio de Sordo-Mudos, 1837), 9.

62. Rementería y Fica, *El hombre fino*, 78. The slippage between classes was hardly viewed as utopian by tailors, whose merchandise in many ways stood to benefit from clear-cut class divisions, and nineteenth-century tailors often complained about diminishing attention to etiquette and the confusion of classes. In an article from 1885, for example, tailoring professional Juan López criticizes the generalized use of the bowler hat and the informal blazer: "It is an undisputed fact that both items of modern dress are agreeable and bestow comfort upon the individual who uses them; but their misuse has reached such heights that, it would seem, as one commonly says, that there are those who even wear them to bed." Juan López, "El hongo y la cazadora," *La Moda de Madrid*, no. 1, April 1884, 12. The writer continues by critiquing those couples whose fashionable appearance is characterized by incongruity. López cites being scandalized upon seeing an elegant woman in the finest French jewels and laces accompanied by a man who looked more like her butler rather than a husband or lover. Betraying a latent anxiety about confusion among socioeconomic groups, tailors believed that their fellow men should match the elegance of their wives or other female companions. The bowler hat and blazer, which became metonyms for the democratization of menswear during this period, were viewed as informal articles of clothing that threatened to encroach upon the traditional "paraphernalia of gentility." Cruz, *The Rise*, 91.

63. Jesús Cruz, "'El hombre fino': Courtesy Books and Male Bourgeois Conduct in Nineteenth-Century Spain," *Bulletin of Hispanic Studies* 89, no. 4 (2012): 174.

64. Rementería y Fica, *El hombre fino*, 77.

65. Men's fashion plates were considered a valuable commodity by tailors for both their artistry and attention to detail. Plates consisted of a large, richly illustrated centerfold image displaying developments in menswear from month to month. Even if, as Cruz observes, "the color, quality, and design of male attire became more uniform" in the *longue durée*, the creators of Spanish tailoring journals devoted much time and energy to advertising niches of choice to help shoppers achieve a "correct" manner of self-display. Cruz, *The Rise*, 101.

66. Michael Zakim, "Customizing the Industrial Revolution: The Reinvention of Tailoring in the Nineteenth Century," *Winterthur Portfolio* 33, no. 1 (1998): 42.

67. The professional literature's emphasis on specific fabrics and the morphology of the outfit is characteristic of all textual descriptions of fashion plates and signifies both a dedication to surface and structural details, along with the tacit acknowledgment of the tailor's expertise. Indeed, as Roland Barthes articulates in his iconic study, "the Fashion text represents . . . the authoritative voice of someone who knows all there is behind the jumbled or incomplete appearance of the visible forms." Roland Barthes, *The Fashion System*, translated by Matthew Ward and Richard Howard (Berkeley: University of California Press, 1990), 14.

68. Benito Pérez Galdós, *Las novelas de Torquemada*, 284.

69. Not all were convinced by the tailor's skill as a producer of comfort. At times, Emilia

Pardo Bazán and Galdós wrote ironically or sarcastically about the discomfort that, for them, characterized contemporary menswear. In his article "El elegante" (The Dandy), for example, Galdós calls for a champion to crusade against the tyranny of ill-fitting and uncomfortable clothing and accessories. For a summary of Pardo Bazán's critical remarks about men's suits, see Dorota Heneghan, *Striking Their Modern Pose: Fashion, Gender, and Modernity in Galdós, Pardo Bazán, and Picón* (West Lafayette, IN: Purdue University Press, 2015), 79.

70. Illustrations included on advertising cards did not necessarily depict perfectly contemporaneous fashions, thus pointing to the fictional quality of many of these kinds of commercial products. Additionally, advertising cards were mass-produced by lithographers or other printing shops, and the image contained on a given card was not necessarily unique to the emporium being advertised. The Historical Archive of Barcelona, for example, contains a handful of *cromos* that promote completely different shops—both French and Spanish—but bear nearly identical illustrations. It is worth noting that men's fashion during this time, as Mercedes Pasalodos-Salgado reminds her readers, was an international affair. Mercedes Pasalodos-Salgado, "Algunas consideraciones sobre la moda durante la *Belle Époque*," *Indumenta* 00 (2007): 107.

71. Nicholas Wolters, "The Spanish Cut," 4.

72. Anecdotes, short stories, and poems included in retail catalogs also framed the department store as a site for romantic entanglements. In one representative example from an El Siglo catalog from 1883, a woman writing to her friend says she met her soulmate while he was shopping for gloves.

73. Gabriel Pinós Guirao, "De *sportsman* a *motorman* (parte I): Descripción detallada de los vehículos de dos ruedas de Ramon Casas," in *Ramon Casas: Catálogo Completo, vol. I*, ed. Gabriel Pinós Guirao (Barcelona: Gothsland, 2018), 132.

74. Pinós Guirao, "De *sportsman*," 127–28.

75. Pinós Guirao, "De *sportsman*," 130.

76. Cruz, *The Rise*, 34.

77. As Geraldine Scanlon suggests, the myth of the self-made man was appealing to intellectuals like Galdós who were eager to embrace a Krausist worldview cohering around the "meritocratic ideals" of education, individuality, and progress. Such ideals were also distributed and consumed by men in conduct manuals, such as Samuel Smiles' bestseller, *Self Help* (1859), which was translated to Spanish in 1876. Geraldine Scanlon, "Problemas sociales y Krausismo en *Marianela*," in *Actas del Tercer Congreso Internacional de Estudios Galdosianos*, vol. 1 (Las Palmas: Cabildo Insular de Gran Canaria, 1990), 84–88.

78. Mercer, *Urbanism and Urbanity*, 10. Pursuant to challenging or complicating the relegation of emotions to "a feminine intimate sphere" in modern Spain, this book's view of masculine affect or emotion challenges a priori assertions of the manly ideal's assumed dependence on stoicism or unemotionality. Elena Delgado, Pura Fernández and Jo Labanyi, introduction to *Engaging the Emotions in Spanish Culture and History*, ed. Elena Delgado, Pura Fernández, and Jo Labanyi (Nashville, TN: Vanderbilt University Press, 2016), 2. To be sure, *excessive* displays of emotion or "overwrought emotionalism," as Gabrielle Miller has articulated, could have been interpreted as unbecoming of bourgeois men expected to exercise self-restraint in some domestic and public contexts. Gabrielle Miller, *"¡Mi hijo es mío, puñales!:* Excessive Paternal Devotion in Benito Pérez Galdós's *Torquemada* Novels," *Decimonónica* 17, no. 2 (2020): 66. However, just as attitudes toward male shoppers cannot be reduced to censure and stereotypes of effeminacy levied by moralists and

satirists, bourgeois men's affective and emotional lives were not limited to the apodictic proclamations of hygienists like Monlau. As Wadda Ríos-Font demonstrates, nineteenth-century expressions of "patriotic love," for example, coincided with men's emotive defense of equality, fraternity, and liberty, wherein "love, loyalty, *adoration*, and sacrifice as a means to shared glory" were extolled within the context of patriotism and nationalism. Wadda Ríos-Font, "'How Do I Love Thee': The Rhetoric of Patriotic Love in Early Puerto Rican Political Discourse," in *Engaging the Emotions in Spanish Culture and History*, ed. Luisa Elena Delgado, Pura Fernández, and Jo Labanyi (Nashville, TN: Vanderbilt University Press, 2016), 43. The complexity of masculine affect is especially apparent when one revisits epistolary correspondence between friends and the many facets of male bonding and friendship depicted in realist fiction.

79. Eve Kosofsky Sedgwick, *Between Men: English Literature and Male Homosocial Desire* (New York: Columbia University Press, 1985), 25.

80. George Mosse, *Nationalism and Sexuality: Middle-Class Morality and Sexual Norms in Modern Europe* (Madison: University of Wisconsin Press, 1985), 67.

81. Jo Labanyi, "Doing Things: Emotion, Affect, and Materiality," *Journal of Spanish Cultural Studies* 11, nos. 3–4 (2010): 224–25.

82. Todd Reeser and Lucas Gottzén, "Masculinity and Affect: New Possibilities, New Agendas," *NORMA: International Journal for Masculinity Studies* 13, no. 3–4 (2018): 146.

83. Labanyi, "Doing Things," 225.

84. Catherine Jagoe, et al., *La mujer en los discursos de género*, 389.

85. Nils Hammarén and Thomas Johansson, "Homosociality: In Between Power and Intimacy," *SAGE Open* 1, no. 11 (2014): 25–26.

86. Though Pardo Bazán was eventually granted access to the university after being named the first woman to be chaired professor of Romance Languages at the Universidad Central de Madrid (Central University of Madrid), despite having never been able to earn a degree, the accolade was undermined by both the Royal Spanish Academy and the university's philosophy and humanities department. According to Isabel Burdiel, protests stemmed from both her womanhood, as well as the fact that the focus of her professorship was contemporary literature. Isabel Burdiel, *Emilia Pardo Bazán* (Madrid: Taurus, 2019), 603–5.

87. José María de Pereda, *Peñas arriba*, ed. Antonio Rey (Madrid: Cátedra, 2011), 390.

88. Pereda, *Peñas arriba*, 386.

89. Mercer, *Urbanism and Urbanity*, 10.

90. During his time in the capital Yxart lived with his maternal cousin, Estanislau Figueras (i de Moragas). Figueras was a politician who was also one of the short-lived presidents of the First Spanish Republic after the abdication of King Amadeo I de Saboya between February and June of 1873. For details about Yxart's years in Madrid, see Rosa Cabré's edition of his posthumously published memoirs: Josep Yxart, *Escrits autobiogràfics, 1872–1889*, ed. Rosa Cabré (Lleida: Punctum & Grup d'Estudi de la Literatura del Vuit-cents, 2007).

91. Yxart's eventual departure from Madrid in 1874 was precipitated by a letter from his father, who reminded Josep of his future as heir and, thus, of the importance of proximity to the family estate in Tarragona that he was destined to inherit. Yxart, *Escrits autobiogràfics*, 21n3.

92. Before symbolically outstretching his hand to Yxart and producing a single tear, the groom abandons his cousin to join his betrothed "in the marriage bed, where the bride trembled and blushed in the presence of the most stirring of mysteries." *Escrits autobiogràfics*, 61. Both Yxart and Oller comment separately upon the former's early penchant for parody and

satire, and so one might categorize parts of this passage as cheeky or facetious.

93. Yxart and Oller were first cousins (*cosí germà*, or fraternal cousins, in Catalan). Oller's eventual reputation as the progenitor of the Catalan novel notwithstanding, his career as a novelist would not begin until the 1880s with the drafting and publication of his first and most well-received novel, *La papallona* (1882; The butterfly).

94. Yxart, *Escrits autobiogràfics*, 60–61.

95. Yxart, *Escrits autobiogràfics*, 61. Butterflies were also commonly used as symbols of the dandy. In Ramón de Navarrete's 1843–44 physiognomy "El elegante," for example, the titular social type's gallantry and social skills with women at a soiree are compared to those of a butterfly who dexterously flutters from flower to flower. Oller's novel *La papallona* evokes the protagonist's capricious courtship of women in similar terms.

96. Yxart, *Escrits autobiogràfics*, 61.

97. Titled *Memòries: Història de mos llibres i relacions literàries* (Memoirs: The story of my books and literary relationships), Oller's memoirs were composed between 1911 and 1916 but not published by his son until 1962, more than thirty years after the novelist's death.

98. Yxart, *Escrits autobiogràfics*, 32.

99. Narcís Oller, *Memòries: Història de mos llibres i relacions literàries*, ed. Arnau Soler Pejoan and Enric Cassany (Valls, Spain: Cossetània Edicions, 2014), 168.

100. Benito Pérez Galdós identified the Napoleonic wars and the more or less coetaneous independence wars in the Americas as turning points in the development of modern Spain, as is made clear in his decision to set his three-part series of *Episodios nacionales* (National episodes) during this period. Mary L. Coffey, *Ghosts of Colonies Past and Present: Spanish Imperialism in the Fiction of Benito Pérez Galdós* (Liverpool: Liverpool University Press, 2020), 17.

101. Lou Charnon-Deutsch, "Gender and Beyond: Nineteenth-Century Spanish Women Writers," in *The Cambridge Companion to the Spanish Novel From 1600 to the Present*, ed. Harriet Turner and Adelaida López de Martínez (Cambridge, UK: Cambridge University Press, 2003), 122.

102. Mercer, *Urbanism and Urbanity*, 12.

103. Margarida Casacuberta, "Dues novel·les per a dues burgesies: Notes per a una comparació entre *La febre d'or* i *L'Argent*," in *El segle romàntic: Actes de Col·loqui Narcís Oller* (Valls, Spain: Cossetània Edicions, 1999), 208. In his posthumously published memoirs composed during the early twentieth century, analyzed more fully in Chapter 3, Oller reports having told Émile Zola in their meeting in Paris that Catalans, in particular, "are only able to make literature as a pastime or a spiritual divertissement," before concluding that he makes his living off of lawsuits. Oller, *Memòries*, 100.

104. Oller, *Memòries*, 65.

105. Harriet Turner, "The Realist Novel," in *The Cambridge Companion to the Spanish Novel*, ed. Harriet Turner and Adelaida López de Martínez (Cambridge: Cambridge University Press, 2003), 100.

106. Labanyi, *Gender and Modernization*, 13–14.

107. Alda Blanco, Maryellen Bieder, and Carmen Pereira Muro have argued that Pardo Bazán's own desire to legitimize herself as a "manly" writer provides further evidence of the masculinization of literary realism during the final decades of the nineteenth century.

108. Charnon-Deutsch, "Gender and Beyond," 122.

109. For their part, prestigious artists like Ramon Casas and Santiago Rusiñol similarly relied on publications like *La Vanguardia* to narrativize their travels around Spain and France,

not to mention as venues for the publication of prints of their drawings. See Cueto-Asín's articles on Casas and Rusiñol's travels and travelogues. The sometimes-gendered divide between the masculine (high art) and the feminine (mass culture) was not clear-cut.

110. By contrast to her male counterparts, some caricatures of Emilia Pardo Bazán in the illustrated press were quite vicious. See Maryellen Bieder's articles and chapters on this subject.

111. See Antonio Viñao Frago, "The History of Literacy in Spain: Evolution, Traits, and Questions," *History of Education Quarterly* 30, no. 4 (1990): 574, and Narciso de Gabriel, "Alfabetización, semialfabetización y analfabetismo en España (1860–1991)," *Revista Complutense de Eduación* 8, no. 7 (1997): 203. Compare such statistics to those from France: shortly before 1789, 47 percent of the male population and 27 percent of the female population were literate, and by 1872–1876, the period corresponding to Zola's first naturalist novels, around 77 percent of French males and 67 percent of French females were literate. Martyn Lyons, *Readers and Society in Nineteenth-Century France: Workers, Women, Peasants* (London: Palgrave Macmillan, 2001). Michael J. Heffernan, "Literacy and the Life-Cycle in Nineteenth-Century Provincial France: Some Evidence from the *Département* of Ille-et-Vilaine," *Journal of the History of Education Society* 21, no. 2 (1992): 149. In England and Wales around 1870, literacy rates were even higher at 80 percent for males and 75 percent for females. Amy J. Lloyd, "Education, Literacy and the Reading Public," in *British Library Newspapers* (Detroit: Gale, 2007).

112. Núria Cabré and Enric Gallén, "Set cartes de Santiago Rusiñol a Narcís Oller," *Faig*, no. 11 (1980): 46.

113. Casacuberta, "Dues novel·les," 201.

114. Elisa Martí-López and Mario Santana, "Spain 1843–1900," in *The Novel*, vol. 3, ed. Franco Moretti (Princeton, NJ: Princeton University Press, 2007), 479–94.

115. European novelists like Gustave Flaubert, Émile Zola, and Leo Tolstoy, to name just a few examples, faced their own struggles when producing their most famous works. Even though he fared well in the end, Flaubert was put on trial in 1857 by Napoleon III's government for supposedly corrupting young readers with the questionable actions of the eponymous heroine of *Madame Bovary*. The poet Charles Baudelaire was put on trial the same year for his treatment of controversial themes in his infamous collection of poems *Les Fleurs du mal* (The flowers of evil). Although it was his defense of Alfred Dreyfuss in the pamphlet "J'accuse!"—and not his novels—that would force him into exile in England in 1898, it is well known that Émile Zola's Rougon-Macquart series depicting the more sordid elements of contemporary social life during the Second Empire was not universally embraced by critics and readers, even if Zola was able to make a living as a professional novelist. Bob Blaisdell points out that Tolstoy almost gave up writing *Anna Karenina* on several occasions for a variety of personal and external circumstances. Bob Blaisdell, *Creating Anna Karenina: Tolstoy and the Birth of Literature's Most Enigmatic Heroine* (Cambridge, UK: Pegasus Books, 2020), xv–xvi, 131–48. Additionally, Tolstoy's reading public was comparable to, if not smaller than, those of his Spanish contemporaries, and the success of his literary output outside of Russia is in large part due to his early reception by nineteenth-century France's reading public, virtually all of whom would have read his novel in French translation. Gregory Guroff, "A Note on Urban Literacy in Russia, 1890–1914," *Jahrbücher für Geschichte Osteuropas Neue Folge* 19, no. 4 (1971): 520–21.

116. Jean François Botrel, "Producción literaria y rentabilidad: El caso de 'Clarín,'" in *Hommage des hispanistes français à Noël Salomon* (Barcelona: Editorial Laia, 1979), 129.

117. Botrel, "Producción literaria," 123n1.
118. Pascale Casanova, *The World Republic of Letters*, trans. M. B. Debevoise (Cambridge, MA: Harvard University Press, 2004), 4, 13.
119. Wadda Ríos-Font, *The Canon and the Archive: Configuring Literature in Modern Spain* (Lewisburg, PA: Bucknell University Press, 2004), 40–41.
120. Leslie Kaiura, "Fernán Caballero's Lessons for Ladies: Female Agency and the Modeling of Proper Womanhood in *Clemencia*," *Decimonónica* 9, no. 1 (2012): 17; and Diana Arbaiza, "The Marketing of Cecilia Böhl von Faber: Gender, Economy, and the Professionalization of the Artist," *Revista Hispánica Moderna* 72, no. 1 (2019): 3.
121. Emilia Pardo Bazán, *La revolución y la novela en Rusia (Lecturas en el Ateneo de Madrid)* (Madrid: Imprenta y Fundición de M. Tello, 1887), 1.
122. Denise Dupont, "Masculinity, Femininity, Solidarity: Emilia Pardo Bazán's Construction of Madame de Staël and George Sand," *Comparative Literature Studies* 40, no. 4 (2003): 377.
123. Of course, nineteenth-century misogyny contributed to the masculine-coding of such circuits, too. Pardo Bazán, who also collaborated with male literary critics, was lampooned by erstwhile friends like Alas with vulgar terms like *jamona* (a sow or fat old woman) because of her supposedly frank or crude representation of female sexuality in novels like *Insolación*.
124. José-Carlos Mainer, introduction to *El Doctor Centeno*, ed. José-Carlos Mainer (Madrid: Editorial Biblioteca Nueva, 2002): 46. Such comparisons between Spanish authors and their European counterparts had become an obsession of writers like Clarín. As Alda Blanco posits, "the point of departure in their thinking and writing about the *Spanish* novel was the need to understand a felt difference with regard to the appearance and development of the novel in other European national literatures." Alda Blanco, "Gender and National Identity: The Novel in Nineteenth-Century Spanish Literary History," in *Culture and Gender in Nineteenth-Century Spain*, ed. Lou Charnon-Deutsch and Jo Labanyi, 123 (Oxford: Clarendon Press and Oxford University Press, 1995).
125. Laureano Bonet, "Galdós visto por Clarín, Narcís Oller y Pereda: Los mil matices de una conversación," in *La hora de Galdós: Actas*, ed. Yolanda Arencibia and Germán Gullón et al (Las Palmas: Cabildo Insular de Gran Canaria, 2018): 1016–17.
126. Oller, *Memòries*, 103.
127. Stephen Greenblatt, *Renaissance Self-Fashioning: From More to Shakespeare* (Chicago: University of Chicago Press, 2005), 2.
128. Yvan Lissorgues, *Leopoldo Alas, Clarín*, 510.
129. Marcelino Menéndez y Pelayo, "Contestación del Excmo. Señor D. Marcelino Menéndez y Pelayo," in *Discursos leídos ante la Real Academia Española en la recepción pública del Sr. D. Benito Pérez Galdós, el domingo 7 de febrero de 1897* (Madrid: Impresor de Cámara de S. M., 1897), 22, 26.
130. The literature on masculine types and values during the Spanish Golden Age is robust. See Armon for a comprehensive overview of masculinity as it relates to martial valor, Barlow for the multiple meanings of male-male friendship among Renaissance poets like Garcilaso de la Vega and Juan Boscán, and Harden for a novel approach to understanding Spanish martial masculinity via epistolary correspondence among soldiers during sixteenth- and seventeenth-century Spain's imperial campaigns.
131. Harriet Turner, "The Realist Novel," 100.
132. On the notion of a crisis or deficit, see Nerea Aresti, "La hombría perdida en el tiempo," 27.

133. I quote here from Blanco's translation of this passage to English in "Gender and National Identity," 125). Sergio Beser, *Leopoldo Alas: Teoría y crítica de la novela española* (Barcelona: Editorial Laia, 1972), 163.

134. Benito Pérez Galdós, "Prólogo," in Leopoldo Alas, *La Regenta*, ed. Gonzalo Sobejano, 2 vols. (Madrid: Clásicos Castalia, 1981), 84.

135. François Proulx, *Victims of the Book: Reading and Masculinity in Fin-de-Siècle France* (Toronto: University of Toronto Press, 2019), 13.

136. Lou Charnon-Deutsch, "Between Agency and Determinism: A Critical Review of Clarín Studies," *Hispanic Review* 76, no. 2 (2008): 150.

137. Marcelino Menéndez y Pelayo, "Contestación del Excmo. Señor D. Marcelino Menéndez y Pelayo," in *Discursos leídos ante la Real Academia Española en la recepción pública del Sr. D. Benito Pérez Galdós, el domingo 7 de febrero de 1897* (Madrid: Impresor de Cámara de S. M., 1897), 43, 47–48.

138. Maite Zubiaurre, *Cultures of the Erotic in Spain, 1898–1939* (Nashville, TN: Vanderbilt University Press, 2012), 1.

CHAPTER 1

1. "Nuestro Grabado," *El Globo*, September 13, 1883, 1. The author likely intended Perico to refer both to the *perico ligero*—a Spanish word for the sloth—and "Perico [el] de los palotes," an indeterminate name akin to "John Doe" or "Tom, Dick, or Harry" in English.

2. "Nuestro Grabado," 1883, 1.

3. Establishing a contrast with the male populace at large, the text identifies military general and politician Arsenio Martínez Campos as an unequivocal model of modern masculinity. Presumably having overcome any challenges impeding his own exceptional ascendance to manhood and political prominence, the general's uprising against the First Republic and his subsequent pronouncement of Alfonso XII as the restored king positioned Martínez Campos as a national ideal to which male readers of *El Globo* might have been able to aspire had their educational backgrounds been more conducive to learning.

4. Such scenes were common in the nostalgic imaginations of fin-de-siècle writers. Antonio Machado (1875–1939), for example, wrote a poem entitled "Recuerdo infantil" (1906, Memory from childhood), in which he describes a classroom full of weary schoolboys bored to death by their teacher. According to one of José María de Pereda's biographers he, like Perico, suffered the violent pedagogical model evoked in the maxim "a lesson learnt through blood is not one quickly forgotten." Madariaga de la Campa, *Pereda*, 61.

5. Vicente de la Fuente, "El estudiante," in *Los españoles pintados por sí mismos*, 2 vols. (Madrid: I. Boix, 1843–44), 225.

6. Catherine Jagoe, Alda Blanco, and Cristina Enríquez de Salamanca, *La mujer en los discursos de género: Textos y contextos en el siglo XIX* (Barcelona: Icaria Editorial, 1998), 106. Educational outreach in metropolitan centers also extended to working-class adults. Aurélie Vialette, *Intellectual Philanthropy: The Seduction of the Masses* (West Lafayette, IN: Purdue University Press, 2018), 4.

7. Jagoe et al., *La mujer*, 106.

8. Julián Sanz del Río (1814–1869) and Francisco Giner de los Ríos (1839–1915) introduced and defended the merits of Krausism in Spain. Paraphrasing Hans Jeschke, John Kronik

writes that "nothing less than the 'humanization' of Spain was the task to which Sanz del Río and Giner de los Ríos set themselves, with the former planting the ideological seed and the latter devoting himself to the concretization of this 'ideal de la humanidad' in the terrain of education." John W. Kronik, "Leopoldo Alas, Krausism, and the Plight of the Humanities in Spain," *Modern Language Studies* 11, no. 3 (1981): 4. Krausists supported academic freedom and a moral life inflected by both scientific inquiry and personal religiosity, among other values and virtues ("Harmonious spirit, defense of liberty, devotion to science, affirmation of reason, moralism, pedagogy and religiosity are considered the general characteristics that correspond to the intellectual attitude of Spanish Krausism." Quoted in José Luis Gómez-Martínez, "Galdós y el Krausismo español," *Nueva Revista de Filología Hispánica* 32, no. 1 (1983): 56. For José Luis Gómez-Martínez, the lasting appeal of Krausism was related to its opening of Spain to Europe; its followers worked toward achieving that goal by championing a liberal "attitude" toward the individual, women, family, society, and education (56). Many late-nineteenth-century figures like Emilio Castelar and Leopoldo Alas were among Krausism's greatest defenders. According to Gómez-Martínez, Galdós's fiction, too, demonstrates the effect the philosophical movement had on artistic and literary representations of modern individualism (79).

9. Though professional titles are not capitalized in Spanish, I capitalize *Doctor* since it is used in the novel as a nickname that signals a title that the protagonist seeks, but ultimately fails to acquire. Some early critics of the novel, including Pardo Bazán and Clarín, also capitalize the novel's title in their reviews and letters.

10. Francisco Caudet, "*El doctor Centeno*: La educación sentimental de Galdós," in *Zola, Galdós, Clarín: El naturalismo en Francia y España*, ed. Francisco Caudet (Madrid: Ediciones de la Universidad Autónoma de Madrid, 1995), 42.

11. In her recent book, Sara Muñoz-Muriana theorizes the street's role in the formation of modern subjectivities by unpacking the concept of marginality as reflective of both deviation from social norms and physical displacements through geospatial peripheries. Sara Muñoz-Muriana, "*Andando se hace el camino*": Calle y subjetividades marginales en la España del siglo XIX (Madrid: Iberoamericana, 2017), 15. El Doctor Centeno provides further evidence of this conceptualization of the street, since both Centeno and Miquis evade educational norms of the classroom through their wanderings around the Spanish capital's liminal spaces.

12. While scholarship of the novel to date has overlooked its depiction of used clothing and the relationship between its representations of used clothing and Galdós's own self-fashioning as a novelist, scholars have focused on a range of other interconnected themes: its apparently "disparate" or "disjointed" structure (Shoemaker, Montesinos); its categorization as a Bildungsroman (Gullón, Cardona, Caudet); its circular structure that critically but nostalgically reimagines the years leading up to the 1868 revolution (Gold); its realist semiotics (Tsuchiya, *Images*); its narrative points of view (Willem); and its damning portrayal of nineteenth-century education (Moreno Castillo, Scanlon, Varela). In contrast, this chapter draws attention to the novel's heterogeneous intertextuality as it relates to the titular protagonist's "secondhand" characterization and development from boy to young man. Instead of viewing *El Doctor Centeno* as somehow flawed for its heterogeneity, as Montesinos and Shoemaker do, this chapter follows Hoddie and Mainer in arguing that the novel's structural and thematic *bricolage* reflects Felipe Centeno's and Alejandro Miquis's inherent volatility as aspiring bourgeois subjects (not to mention the turbulent atmosphere of their pre-revolutionary surroundings). Indeed, Felipe's shoddily

cloaked entry into Madrid, as Hoddie remarks, "foreshadows the synthetic nature of the novel derived from tragedy, the picaresque, medieval and Renaissance lyric poetry" James H. Hoddie, "Reexamen de un enigmático texto galdosiano: *El doctor Centeno,*" *Cuadernos Hispanoamericanos,* no. 521 (1993): 52. For comprehensive bibliographies of the novel, see Hazel Gold, "Looking for the Doctor in the House: Critical Expectations and Novelistic Structure in Galdós's *El doctor Centeno.*" *Philological Quarterly,* no. 68 (1989): 220, and Akiko Tsuchiya, *Images of the Sign: Semiotic Consciousness in the Novels of Benito Pérez Galdós* (Columbia: University of Missouri Press, 1990), 36n2, 40n6.

13. The Spanish Royal Academy's 1884 dictionary entry defines *centón* as a "crude quilt used to cover military machines" and a "literary work, in verse or prose, composed entirely or primarily of extraneous statements and expressions." *Diccionario histórico de la lengua española,* "Centón," accessed 8 September 2022, https://www.rae.es/dhle.

14. As Hazel Gold has argued, the 1883 novel's retrospective portrayal of pre-1868 Spain is illustrative of a circular structure that constantly folds back on itself. This pattern, according to Gold, demonstrates Galdós's desire to show that little had changed between the 1860s timeframe of the plot and the novel's 1883 publication date ("Looking," 236). See Linda Willem for a critical summary of the elements characterizing Galdós's *segunda manera.* Linda Willem, *Galdós's Segunda Manera: Rhetorical Strategies and Affective Response* (Chapel Hill, NC: University of North Carolina Press, 1998), 12–13.

15. Centeno also makes an appearance in *La familia de León Roch* (1878; Leon Roch's family), in which he is introduced briefly as "a tightly-buttoned up footman with a happy and sprightly countenance, a shorn head, a quick gait and red-stained hands covered with warts" (Pérez Galdós, *La familia,* 191). He surfaces again in the Álvarez Quintero brothers' theatrical adaptation of *Marianela* in 1916. According to reports of the play's rehearsals, Galdós—by then fully blind—had an emotional reaction upon hearing the performance of the actor assigned the role of Felipe: "The first emotional crisis came with the appearance of Celipín. At the sound of the plucky ragamuffin, Galdós shivered with nervousness, stretched out his arms, and exclaimed 'Celipín!' 'Celipín!'" Chonon H. Berkowitz, *Pérez Galdós: Spanish Liberal Crusader* (Madison: University of Wisconsin Press, 1948), 441.

16. Caudet, "*El doctor Centeno,*" 43.

17. Mikhail Bakhtin, "The Bildungsroman and Its Significance in the History of Realism (Toward a Historical Typology of the Novel)," in *Speech Genres and Other Late Essays,* trans. Vera W. McGee, ed. Caryl Emerson and Michael Holquist (Austin: University of Texas Press, 1986), 21.

18. Franco Moretti, *The Way of the World: The Bildungsroman in European Culture,* trans. Albert Spragia (New York: Verso, 2000), 5.

19. Collin McKinney, "How to Be a Man," in *Spain in the Nineteenth Century: New Essays on Experiences of Culture and Society,* ed. Andrew Ginger and Geraldine Lawless (Manchester: Manchester University Press, 2018), 148.

20. John Tosh, "What Should Historians Do with Masculinity?," *History Workshop,* no. 38 (1994): 181.

21. Marco Ramírez López has made a number of connections between various plot elements related to Centeno and, in particular, Miquis. Galdós, for example, wrote *La expulsión de los moriscos* (The expulsion of the Moors) and *Un joven de provecho* (A promising young man), which the Canarian author likely had in mind while writing about Miquis's failed drama *El Grande Osuna.* Not unlike Miquis's failures, Ramírez López reminds us, Galdós's aforementioned theatrical works "ended up in the pile of unread and rejected works by

Manuel Catalina, director of the Teatro Español." Marco A. Ramírez López, "*El doctor Centeno* de Benito Pérez Galdós: Aspectos autobiográficos," *Fuentes Humanísticas* 28, no. 54 (2017): 165.

22. Ramírez López, "*El doctor Centeno*, 165.

23. Brian Dendle, "Palacio Valdés's 'Un estudiante de Canarias': A Forgotten Article of 1883," *Anales Galdosianos*, no. 24 (1986): 98

24. Dendle, "Palacio," 99.

25. Dendle, "Palacio," 99.

26. Dendle, "Palacio," 99.

27. Dendle, "Palacio," 98.

28. Fuente, "El estudiante," 101.

29. Leopoldo Alas, *La Regenta*, 2 vols., ed. Gonzalo Sobejano (Madrid: Clásicos Castalia, 1981), 2: 54.

30. Benito Pérez Galdós, *La desheredada*, ed. Germán Gullón (Madrid: Cátedra, 1999), 144, 373.

31. Benito Pérez Galdós, *Tormento* (Madrid: Alianza Editorial, 2012), 178.

32. Pérez Galdós, *La desheredada*, 143–69. For an analysis of representations of boyish and military masculinity in these scenes, see Collin McKinney, "'Jugamos a la guerra': Boys, Toys, and Military Masculinity in Galdós's *La desheredada*," *Revista Canadiense de Estudios Hispánicos* 44, no. 2 (2020): 415–36.

33. Benito Pérez Galdós, *Las novelas de Torquemada*, 44.

34. Benito Pérez Galdós, *Misericordia*, ed. Luciano García Lorenzo (Madrid: Cátedra, 2006), 36–39.

35. Rebecca Haidt, *Women, Work, and Clothing in Eighteenth-Century Spain* (Oxford: Voltaire Foundation / University of Oxford Press, 2011), 42.

36. Madeleine Ginsburg, "Rags to Riches: The Second-Hand Clothes Trade 1700–1978," *Costume* 14, no. 1 (1980): 121.

37. Haidt, *Women*, 13.

38. Carmen Pérez de Andrés, "Una visión global sobre aspectos de conservación, restauración y montaje," *Indumenta* 00 (2007): 24.

39. Peter McNeil, Vicki Karaminas, and Cathy Cole, introduction to *Fashion in Fiction: Text and Clothing in Literature, Film and Television*, ed. Peter McNeil, Vicki Karaminas, and Cathy Cole (Oxford: Berg, 2009), xv.

40. Madrid, Basque Country, and Catalonia hosted such factories until the end of the nineteenth century, when rags were replaced with less expensive raw materials like wood pulp and other vegetable fibers. Miquel Gutiérrez-Poch, "Is There a Southern European Model?: Development of the Pulp and Paper Industry in Italy, Spain, and Portugal (1800–2010)," in *The Evolution of Global Paper Industry 1800–2050: A Comparative Analysis*, ed. Juha-Antti Lamberg, Jari Ojala, Mirva Peltoniemi, and Timo Särkkä (London: Springer, 2012), 212–13. See Wynne for connections between paper-making and tabula rasa in Dickens's representations of boyish ragpickers in *Bleak House* (1852–1853) and *Oliver Twist*. Deborah Wynne, "Reading Victorian Rags: Recycling, Redemption, and Dickens's Ragged Children," *Journal of Victorian Culture* 20, no. 1 (2014): 34.

41. Walter Benjamin, "The Paris of the Second Empire in Baudelaire," in *The Writer of Modern Life: Essays on Charles Baudelaire*, trans. Howard Eiland, Edmund Jephcott, Rodney Livingston, and Harry Zohn, ed. Michael W. Jennings (Cambridge, MA: Belknap Press of Harvard University Press, 2006), 108–9.

42. Benjamin, "The Paris," 108–9.

43. Muñoz-Muriana, *"Andando,"* 239.

44. Ramón de Mesonero Romanos, *El antiguo Madrid: Paseos históricos-anecdóticos por las calles y casas de esta villa* (Madrid: Establecimiento Tipográfico de F. de Mellado, 1861), 180–81.

45. José A. Nieto Sánchez, *Historia del Rastro: Los orígenes del mercado popular de Madrid, 1740–1905* (Madrid: Editorial Visión Libros, 2004), 22–23, 49.

46. Nieto Sánchez, *Historia*, 103.

47. M. F. El Flaco, "Las Américas," *El Periódico para Todos*, January 5, 1875, 77.

48. El Flaco, "Las Américas," 77.

49. El Flaco, "Las Américas," 77.

50. Cruz, *The Rise*, 126.

51. Antonio de San Martín, "La pantalla de velón," *El Periódico para Todos*, January 16, 1875, 250.

52. Rachel Bowlby, *Just Looking: Consumer Culture in Dresier, Gissing and Zola* (Grantham, UK: Methuen, 1985), 4.

53. Emilia Pardo Bazán, "La vida contemporánea," *La Ilustración Artística*, no. 847, March 12, 1898, 186.

54. Pardo Bazán, "La vida contemporánea," 186.

55. Anne McClintock, *Imperial Leather,* 153.

56. Pardo Bazán, "La vida contemporánea," 186.

57. Pardo Bazán, "La vida contemporánea," 186.

58. Pardo Bazán, "La vida contemporánea," 186.

59. Philip Hauser, *Madrid bajo el punto de vista médico-social: Su policía sanitaria, su climatología, su suelo y sus aguas, sus condiciones sanitarias, su demografía, su morbicidad y su mortalidad* (Madrid: Est. Tipográfico "Sucesores de Rivadeneyra" / Impresores de la Real Casa, 1902), 286.

60. Nieto Sánchez, *Historia del Rastro*, 45.

61. Cruz, *The Rise*, 106.

62. Benito Pérez Galdós, *Marianela* (Madrid: Mestas Ediciones, 2001), 35.

63. Pérez Galdós, *Marianela*, 102–3.

64. Cruz, *The Rise*, 107.

65. Pérez Galdós, *Marianela*, 88–89.

66. Pérez Galdós, *Marianela*, 105.

67. Pérez Galdós, *Marianela*, 139.

68. Pérez Galdós, *Marianela*, 185–86. The phylloxera blight during the 1860s—the timeframe for *Marianela, El Doctor Centeno, Tormento,* and *La de Bringas*—was responsible for the decimation of French vineyards and the related boom in the consumption of Spanish and especially Catalan wines. Raymond Carr, *Spain 1808–1975* (Oxford: Oxford University Press, 1993), 18. As Chapter 3 will show, revenues generated by winegrowers thanks to the uptick in consumption and bullish optimism contributed to the "gold fever" that buoyed stock market speculation in Madrid and Barcelona during this time.

69. Benito Pérez Galdós, *El Doctor Centeno* (Madrid: Alianza Editorial, 2012), 12–13.

70. Rodolfo Cardona, "Nuevos enfoques críticos con referencia a la obra de Galdós," *Cuadernos Hispanoamericanos*, nos. 250–52 (1970–1971): 68.

71. Honoré de Balzac, *Père Goriot*, trans. Burton Raffel, ed. Peter Brooks (New York: Norton Critical Editions, 1994), 217.

72. Pérez Galdós, *El Doctor*, 15.

73. Hazel Gold, *The Reframing of Realism: Galdós and the Discourses of the Nineteenth-Century*

Spanish Novel (Durham, NC: Duke University Press, 1993), 168.

74. Pérez Galdós, *El Doctor*, 24, 33, 99, 74, 96.
75. Pérez Galdós, *Marianela*, 38.
76. Benjamin, "The Paris," 54.
77. Cruz, *The Rise*, 33. Caudet recognizes the scene as an intertextual reference to Cervantes's "El licenciado vidriera" (The lawyer of glass), in which two students stumble upon a young boy who becomes their page. "*El Doctor Centeno*," 41.
78. Pérez Galdós, *El Doctor*, 19.
79. Pérez Galdós, *El Doctor*, 23.
80. Pérez Galdós, *El Doctor*, 48–49.
81. The constant disparities between Felipe's pipe dreams of material comfort and his socioeconomic circumstances call to mind Akiko Tsuchiya's argument about Felipe's naïve faith in language's potential to accurately reflect or shape reality. Tsuchiya, *Images of the Sign*, 35.
82. Pérez Galdós, *El Doctor*, 51, 52.
83. Pérez Galdós, *El Doctor*, 57–58.
84. The attic has similar connotations in other nineteenth-century European novels. In *Le Père Goriot*, the eponymous character's altruistic donations to his daughters lead to his eventual relocation to a cramped, undesirable attic apartment; and in Charlotte Brontë's *Jane Eyre*, Rochester virtually imprisons his wife Bertha, forcing her to the confines of a far-removed attic apartment.
85. Pérez Galdós, *El Doctor*, 60–61.
86. Pérez Galdós, *El Doctor*, 72.
87. Pérez Galdós, *El Doctor*, 72.
88. Pérez Galdós, *El Doctor*, 72.
89. Pérez Galdós, *El Doctor*, 72.
90. Pérez Galdós, *El Doctor*, 151.
91. Pérez Galdós, *El Doctor*, 151.
92. Hazel Gold, "Looking," 227.
93. Pérez Galdós, *El Doctor*, 148.
94. Frederick Jameson, *The Antinomies of Realism* (London: Verso, 2013), 96.
95. Pérez Galdós, *El Doctor*, 183, 202.
96. Pérez Galdós, *El Doctor*, 223.
97. Cardona, "Nuevos enfoques críticos," 71.
98. Pérez Galdós, *El Doctor*, 227.
99. Harold Bloom coined this phenomenon the "anxiety of influence" in his eponymous volume on the subject.
100. Benito Pérez Galdós, "Observaciones sobre la novela contemporánea en España," in *Ensayos de crítica literaria*, ed. Laureano Bonet (Barcelona: Península, 1999), 115.
101. Jameson, *The Antinomies*, 95.
102. Benito Pérez Galdós, "Prólogo," 84–85. Emilia Pardo Bazán makes similar arguments in *La cuestión palpitante* (1883), arguing that realism was invented by the Spaniards (not the French) with Cervantes.
103. Cardona, "Nuevos enfoques críticos," 67.
104. José Pérez Vidal, "Las pensiones madrileñas del estudiante Benito Pérez Galdós (años de aprendizaje)," in *Philologica hispaniensia: In honorem Manuel Alvar* (Barcelona: Gredos, 1983), 325.

105. Pérez Galdós, *El Doctor*, 233.
106. Pérez Galdós, *El Doctor*, 276.
107. Pérez Galdós, *El Doctor*, 277.
108. Pérez Galdós, *El Doctor*, 277.
109. Pérez Galdós, *El Doctor*, 279.
110. Pérez Galdós, *El Doctor*, 282.
111. Pérez Galdós, *El Doctor*, 282.
112. Miquel Gutiérrez-Poch, "Is There a Southern European Model?" 212–13.
113. For a picaresque reading of the novel, see James H. Hoddie, "Reexamen de un enigmático texto galdosiano: *El doctor Centeno." Cuadernos Hispanoamericanos*, no. 521 (1993): 52.
114. Pérez Galdós, *El Doctor*, 426.
115. Pérez Galdós, *El Doctor*, 426.
116. Pérez Galdós, *Tormento*, 12.
117. Pérez Galdós, *Tormento*, 13.
118. Emilia Pardo Bazán, *"Miquiño mío": Cartas a Galdós*, ed. Isabel Parreño and Juan Manuel Hernández (Madrid: Turner, 2013), 48.
119. Leopoldo Alas, *"El Doctor Centeno." El Día* [Madrid], August 5, 1883, 3.
120. Alas, *"El Doctor Centeno,"* 3.
121. Stephen Gilman, *Galdós and the Art of the European Novel. 1867–1887* (Princeton, NJ: Princeton University Press, 1981), 361.

CHAPTER 2

1. Francisco Vázquez García, "La patologización del celibato en la medicina española (1820–1920)," *ASCLEPIO: Revista de Historia de la Medicina y de la Ciencia* 70, no. 2 (2018): 2.
2. Raúl Mínguez-Blasco, "Between Virgins and Priests: The Feminisation of Catholicism and Priestly Masculinity in Nineteenth-Century Spain," *Gender and History* 33, no. 1 (2021): 105–6. As Isabel II's confessor and a staunch voice of religious conservatism, Claret sought to counter the rise of liberalism and anticlerical nationalism in Spain by overseeing the publication of millions of books and pamphlets in defense of Pius IX's antiliberal stances, as well as the and its personnel more broadly. Enrique A. Sanabria, *Republicanism and Anticlerical Nationalism in Spain* (London: Palgrave Macmillan, 2009), 27.
3. Kirsty Hooper, "Reading Spain's 'African Vocation': The Figure of the Moorish Priest in Three *Fin de Siglo* Novels (1890–1907)," *Revista de Estudios Hispánicos* 40, no. 1 (2006): 174.
4. Scholars have analyzed the supposedly non-normative character of clerical behavior and dress, and compulsory abstinence from sex as signs of gender-deviancy or feminizing traits that would presumably exclude priests from bourgeois manhood. See Labanyi ("City, Country"), Ricardo Krauel, and Kathy Bacon for examples of this line of argumentation. Jo Labanyi, "City, Country and Adultery in *La Regenta," Bulletin of Hispanic Studies* 63, no. 1 (1986): 53–66.
5. Verdaguer later alienated himself from ecclesiastical authorities and the Marquises of Comillas for his volte-face on Barcelona polite society that steered him toward displays of charity that were viewed by cultural and ecclesiastical elites as excessive. Walter T. Pattison, "Verdaguer y Nazarín," *Cuadernos Hispanoamericanos*, nos. 250–252 (1970–71): 538–39. Pattison highlights the parallels between the circumstances of the Catalan priest's life and the fictional world of the protagonist of *Nazarín* (1895), Galdós's later novel about

a secular priest who undergoes a mystical transformation in his altruistic or "saintly" wanderings around the outskirts of Madrid. See Ismael Souto Rumbo's 2015 dissertation, and especially his chapter, "'¡Ay, si en vez de santo fuera hombre . . .!,'" which includes a reading of Galdós's *Nazarín* as a representative of what he calls "religious masculinity," which blends elements of masculinity and femininity. The pattern of clerical masculinity analyzed in this chapter deviates from that detected by Souto Rumbo in *Nazarín*, since *La Regenta*'s Fermín de Pas lacks the more androgynous or feminine-coded elements of spirituality present in Galdós's titular protagonist (and, for that matter, in other priests like Julián Álvarez in Pardo Bazán's *Los pazos de Ulloa*); furthermore, whereas *Nazarín* eschews bourgeois trappings, Fermín embraces them as a way to climb the social ladder and the local Church hierarchy.

6. The Catalan equivalent of the French and English Monseigneur, *mossèn* was originally a title bestowed upon princes, knights, bishops and other courtly or ecclesiastical dignitaries during the Middle Ages. By the nineteenth century, the term had evolved into a title used exclusively for men in the Church's hierarchy. Chapter 3 revisits Verdaguer's business and literary activity as it relates to the Catalan rebirth and Oller's literary representation of avuncular mentors and risk-taking stockbrokers.

7. Mínguez-Blasco, "Between Virgins," 103. When citing Claret's writings here, I use Mínguez-Blasco's translations from Spanish to English.

8. Fradera, *The Imperial Nation*, 34.

9. Despite its popularity and almost mythical status, *El Motín* was sometimes characterized elsewhere as a low-brow magazine catering to the lowest common denominator, a fact that should temper evaluations of its cachet within the cultural mainstream. Valeriano Bozal, *La ilustración gráfica del XIX en España* (Madrid: Comunicación, 1979), 187. As Gabrielle Miller has pointed out, Emilia Pardo Bazán's *La Madre Naturaleza* (1887) places the magazine in the hands of the liberal doctor Máximo Juncal, whose reading of the journal is viewed critically and problematically by the Galician novelist's narrator. Gabrielle Miller, "Disrupting Nineteenth-Century Dichotomies of Gender: Reading and Imagination in Emilia Pardo Bazán's *La Madre Naturaleza*," *Hispanic Review* 83, no. 3 (2015): 324–25.

10. Leopoldo Alas, *La Regenta*, trans. John Rutherford (Cambridge, UK: Penguin, 2005), 456.

11. Noël Valis, *Sacred Realism: Religion and the Imagination in Modern Spanish Narrative* (New Haven, CT: Yale University Press, 2010), 173.

12. Alas, *La Regenta*, ed. Gonzalo Sobejano, 2: 247.

13. Collin McKinney, "Men in Black," 89.

14. Connell, *Masculinities*, 186.

15. Zachary Erwin, "Fantasies of Masculinity in Emilia Pardo Bazán's *Memorias de un solterón*," *Revista de Estudios Hispánicos* 46, no. 3 (2012): 549.

16. Collin McKinney, "Enemigos de la virilidad," 74.

17. Mínguez-Blasco, "Between Virgins," 106.

18. Labanyi, *Gender*, 216.

19. Alas, *La Regenta*, trans. John Rutherford, 567. For close readings of *La Regenta*, this chapter relies on Sobejano's 1981 edition, but all translated material from the novel is taken entirely from Penguin's 2005 reprint of John Rutherford's 1984 translation to English.

20. Alas, *La Regenta*, 652.

21. Labanyi, *Gender*, 216.

22. Neal, "What Can Historians Do," 30.

23. Frances Lannon, *Privilege, Persecution, and Prophecy: The Catholic Church in Spain, 1875–1975* (Oxford: Clarendon Press, 1987), 97–98.

24. The National Library of Spain records Spanish-language editions of Valuy's manual from 1859, 1861, 1862, 1893, and 1899, including one Mexican edition. I quote from the 1898 English translation.

25. F. Benoît Valuy, *Directorum Sacerdotale: A Guide for Priests in Their Public and Private Life; with an Appendix for the Use of Seminarists* (Dublin: M. H. Gill, 1907), 78.

26. Valuy, *Directorum*, 78.

27. Neal, "What Can Historians Do," 16.

28. Mínguez-Blasco, "Between Virgins," 103.

29. McKinney, "Men in Black," 88–89.

30. Valis, *Sacred Realism*, 5.

31. Antonio Alcalá Galiano, *Memorias de D. Antonio Alcalá Galiano: Publicadas por su hijo* (Madrid: Imprenta de E. Rubiños, 1886), 46–47.

32. Alcalá Galiano, *Memorias*, 47.

33. Pérez Galdós, *La desheredada*, 482–83.

34. Pérez Galdós, *El Doctor Centeno*, 123.

35. Valis, *Sacred Realism*, 165.

36. Pérez Galdós, *Tormento*, 344.

37. Pérez Galdós, *Tormento*, 345.

38. McKinney, "Pogonology," 67.

39. Alas, *La Regenta*, 336.

40. Alas, *La Regenta*, 337.

41. William James Callahan, *Church, Politics, and Society in Spain, 1750–1874* (Cambridge, MA: Harvard University Press, 1984), 221.

42. Alas, *La Regenta*, 28.

43. Alas, *La Regenta*, 29, 33, 34.

44. Valis, *Sacred*, 13.

45. Pérez Galdós, *El Doctor*, 60–61.

46. Pérez Galdós, *El Doctor*, 58.

47. Soledad Miranda García, *Pluma y altar en el XIX: De Galdós al cura Sta. Cruz* (Madrid: Pegaso, 1983), 126.

48. Pauline Johnstone, *High Fashion in the Church* (Leeds: Maney Publishing, 2002), 8.

49. Sally Dwyer-McNulty, *Common Threads: A Cultural History of Clothing in American Catholicism* (Chapel Hill: University of North Carolina Press, 2014), 45.

50. Alas, *La Regenta*, 614.

51. Pérez Galdós, "Prólogo," 86.

52. Alas, *La Regenta*, 24.

53. Alas, *La Regenta*, 26.

54. Todd Reeser, *Masculinities in Theory*, 28–29.

55. Alas, *La Regenta*, 26.

56. Roland Barthes, *The Fashion System*, xi.

57. The unpolished country priest was a social type invested with much less cultural capital than the cathedral canon or capitular priest of the nineteenth-century city. In the 1843–44 multi-authored compilation *Los españoles pintados por sí mismos*, the "clérigo de misa y olla" (run-of-the-mill priest)" (73) and the "canónigo" are sketched respectively by Fermín Caballero and Francisco Navarro Villoslada. Therefore, it is worth remembering that

the plurality of positions available to men of the cloth also meant that they were not a homogenous bloc, even if they were in the distorting imagination of anticlerical nationalists like Nakens.

58. Francisco Navarro Villoslada, "El canónigo," in *Los españoles pintados por sí mismos*, (Madrid: Gaspar y Roig, 1851), 180.

59. Francisco Mundi Pedret, "Los estamentos eclesiásticos en tiempo de Clarín," in *Clarín y La Regenta en su tiempo: Actas del simposio internacional* (Oviedo: Universidad de Oviedo, Servicio de Publicaciones, 1987), 718.

60. Andrés Zamora, *El doble silencio del eunuco: Poéticas sexuales de la novela realista según Clarín* (Madrid: Fundamentos, 1999), 133.

61. Pérez Galdós, *El Doctor*, 84.

62. Valis, *Sacred Realism*, 16.

63. Alas, *La Regenta*, 36.

64. Alas, *La Regenta*, 54.

65. Lynne Hume, *The Religious Life of Dress* (London: Bloomsbury, 2013), 15.

66. Noël Valis, *The Decadent Vision in Leopoldo Alas: A Study of* La Regenta *and* Su único hijo (Baton Rouge: Louisiana State University Press, 1981), 28.

67. Alas, *La Regenta*, 30.

68. Erwin, "Fantasies," 550.

69. Patrizia Calefato, *Luxury: Fashion, Lifestyle and Excess*, trans. Lisa Adams (London: Bloomsbury, 2014), 19.

70. Alas, *La Regenta*, 244.

71. Alas, *La Regenta*, 498.

72. Alas, *La Regenta*, 227.

73. Jose María de Eça de Queirós, *The Crime of Father Amaro*, trans. Margaret Jull Costa (New York: New Directions, 2003), 123.

74. Collin McKinney, *Mapping the Social Body: Urbanization, the Gaze, and the Novels of Galdós* (Chapel Hill: University of North Carolina Press, 2010), 85.

75. James Eli Adams, *Dandies and Desert Saints: Styles of Victorian Masculinity* (Ithaca, NY: Cornell University Press, 1995), 2.

76. Adams, *Dandies*, 8–9.

77. McKinney, "Men in Black," 89.

78. Alas, *La Regenta*, 218–19.

79. Alas, *La Regenta*, 219.

80. Bonet, "Galdós visto por Clarín," 1017.

81. Oller, *Memòries*, 383n15.

82. Alas, *La Regenta*, 232–33.

83. James Mandrell, "Estudios gay y lesbianos: La revelación de un cuerpo masculino: Una mirada gay," in *El hispanismo en los Estados Unidos: Discursos críticos/prácticas textuales*, ed. José M. del Pino and Francisco LaRubia-Prado (Madrid: Visor, 1999), 217.

84. Alas, *La Regenta*, 233.

85. Herbert L. Sussman, *Victorian Masculinities: Manhood and Masculine Poetics in Early Victorian Literature and Art* (Cambridge: Cambridge University Press, 1995), 32.

86. Alas, *La Regenta*, 563.

87. Alas, *La Regenta*, 662.

88. Alas, *La Regenta*, 687.

89. Alas, *La Regenta*, 688.

90. Valis, *Sacred Realism*, 9.

91. Mínguez-Blasco, "Between Virgins," 103.

92. Sergio Beser, *Leopoldo Alas, crítico literario* (Madrid: Editorial Gredos, 1968), 10.

93. Toni Dorca, "Al llindar del comparatisme: El regionalisme literari i la teoria de la novel·la en la crítica de Josep Yxart," in *Comparatistes sense comparatisme: La literatura comparada a Catalunya*, ed. Teresa Rosell and Antoni Martí (Barcelona: Edicions de la Universitat de Barcelona, 2018), 2. The obituary Joan Sardà wrote in commemoration of Yxart's death similarly framed his late friend as someone who did not believe that the critic should merely serve as a passive spectator of art, but should rather *"profess* [. . .] laws and principles" (qtd. in Montoliu, *José Yxart*, 26).

94. Benito Pérez Galdós, "Discurso del Sr. D. Benito Pérez Galdós," in *Discursos leídos ante la Real Academia Española en la recepción pública del Sr. D. Benito Pérez Galdós, el domingo 7 de febrero de 1897* (Madrid: Impresor de Cámara de S. M., 1897), 7.

95. Lissorgues, *Leopoldo Alas*, 107.

96. Lissorgues, *Leopoldo Alas*, 305, 349.

97. Lissorgues, *Leopoldo Alas*, 435–38.

98. Leopoldo Alas, *Sermón perdido* (Madrid: Librería de Fernando Fé, 1885), 70. The article originally appeared in June 1884 in *El Día* (The daily), just a few months after the publication of *Tormento*. The other priests mentioned are characters in canonical nineteenth-century European novels. For example, Frollo and Bienvenido (Bienvenu) are characters in Victor Hugo's *Notre-Dame de Paris* and Faujas is the antagonist in Émile Zola's *La Conquête de Plassans*.

99. Alas, *Sermón perdido*, 70–72.

100. Alas, *Sermón perdido*, v.

101. Emilio Castelar, "Prólogo," in *Los héroes: El culto de los héroes y lo heroico en la historia*, by Thomas Carlyle, trans. Julián G. Orbón (Madrid: Manuel Fernández y Lasanta, 1893), vii.

102. Leopoldo Alas, "Introducción," in *Los heroes: El culto de los héroes y lo heroico en la historia*, 2 vols., by Thomas Carlyle, trans. Julián G. Orbón (Madrid: Manuel Fernández y Lasanta, 1893), 31.

103. Pérez Galdós, "Prólogo," 86, 90.

104. Stephen Haliczer, *Sexuality in the Confessional: A Sacrament Profaned* (Oxford: Oxford University Press, 1996), 192.

105. Yxart, *Escrits autobiogràfics*, 26, 29, 30.

106. Montoliu, *José Yxart*, 22.

107. Montoliu, *José Yxart*, 49.

108. Yxart, *Escrits autobiogràfics*, 104. Though I draw on Dorca's metaphor, his article on Yxart's criticism ("Al llindar") does not consider the religio-ecclesiastical imagery embedded in the semantic fields of the Tarragona native's autobiographical writings.

CHAPTER 3

1. Joan Ramon Resina, *Barcelona's Vocation of Modernity: Rise and Decline of an Urban Image* (Stanford, CA: Stanford University Press, 2008), 15.

2. Joan Ramon Resina clarifies that the "initial budget for the fair was 5.6 million pesetas, of which the government provided 2 million on credit. But the final cost rose to 11 million, and the balance had to be covered by municipal bonds. By the end of the exposition,

Barcelona was deeply in the red. But fair-related construction mitigated the crisis, employing thirty thousand workers during a recession." Resina, *Barcelona's Vocation*, 45.

3. Summarizing Joseph Harrison's work on the subject, Inma Ridao Carlini reminds us that "the inability on the part of the railway companies to match profit expectations was one of the main causes of the financial crash of 1866" (15). Inma Ridao Carlini, *Rich and Poor in Nineteenth-Century Spain: A Critique of Liberal Society in the Late Novels of Benito Pérez Galdós*, (Suffolk, UK: Boydell & Brewer, 2018), 15. This was ultimately a catalyst that sparked the 1868 Glorious Revolution. See Gabriel Tortella, *The Development of Modern Spain: An Economic History of the Nineteenth and Twentieth Century*, trans. Valerie J. Herr. (Cambridge, MA: Harvard University Press, 2000), 164, and Resina, *Barcelona's Vocation*, 15.

4. Labanyi stresses the interconnectedness of these entities especially where they intersect in and with the novel: "the construction of privacy through a series of discourses centering on the family was accompanied by the privileging of an economic discourse based on the 'free' market: twin forms of individualism that complement yet contradict each other." *Gender and Modernization*, 1.

5. Though Spain's ability to compete with superior English or French markets was a pipedream, self-help manuals and textbooks for aspiring and established businessmen alike included tables of stock exchanges relevant to traders whose work might bring them into contact with foreign markets. In Francisco Castaño's popular *Guía-Manual del comercio y de la banca* (1860, Commerce and banking manual), he includes brief histories and tables related to commerce halls in the cities mentioned earlier, as well as those in non-European countries from Egypt, Turkey, and Uruguay to the United States of America.

6. Bankers, industrialists, shipping magnates, and other businessmen established local stock exchanges elsewhere in Spain throughout the nineteenth century. They represent the collective interests of those seeking to introduce stock-market trade in growing cities like Bilbao, Santander, Seville, Valencia, and Zaragoza. Stefan O. Houpt and Juan Carlos Rojo Cagigal, "The Origins of the Bilbao Stock Exchange, 1891–1936," *Working Papers in Economic History* 10, no. 5 (2010): 2–3. The opening of an official exchange in Bilbao in 1890 (not operational until 1891)—the second after Madrid—reflected continued and widespread interest in trading in public debt, which was a strategy used to support large-scale infrastructure projects, Houpt and Rojo Cagigal, "The Origins," 4.

7. Tortella, *The Development*, 76.

8. Mercer, *Urbanism and Urbanity*, 107.

9. One scholar has compared *La febre d'or* and Howell's 1885 novel in a 1991 article, pointing out that both can be cataloged under a subgenre he labels as the "economic novel" or "business novel." See Pere Gifra i Adroher, "Gil Foix i Silas Lapham: El petitburgès vist per Narcís Oller i William Dean Howells," *Catalan Review* 5, no. 2 (1991): 55–63.

10. Resina, *Barcelona's Vocation*, 274.

11. Though *La papallona* (1882, The butterfly) was his first and most popular novel—a letter written by Zola was famously used as the prologue for Albert Savine's 1885 French translation—Oller was the author of two other novels during the 1880s: *L'Escanyapobres* (1884; The miser) and *Vilaniu* (1885). After finishing *La febre d'or* (1890–92), Oller wrote and published the novella *La bogeria* (1898; Madness), and *Pilar Prim* (1906), both of which further incorporated techniques associated with "psychological realism" and modernism. He also published several well-received collections of short stories, and translations to Spanish and Catalan of works by European authors, including Émile Zola and Leo Tolstoy. Alan Yates,

"The Creation of Narcís Oller's *La febre d'or*," *Bulletin of Hispanic Studies* 52, no. 1 (1975): 73.

12. Oller, *La febre*, 421.

13. Oller, *La febre*, 438.

14. Oller, *La febre*, 442–43.

15. Though Foix's enterprise does fail in the end, Oller's evenhanded treatment of his protagonist distances him from the tenants of French naturalism, a distance that Zola remarked on as early as 1885 in his prologue to the French translation of *La papallona* (The butterfly). Oller's ability to highlight the humanity of his protagonists—whether social climbers or usurers—is summarized by Lev Tikhomirov's often-cited dictum: "give a man to Zola and he will not stop until he finds the beast within; give a beast to Oller and he will not stop until he finds the soul within" (Oller, *Memòries*, 103). As we saw earlier, Oller's friend Isaac Pavlovsky makes a similar defense of the Catalan novelist's embrace of humanity in an 1885 letter cited in the introduction to this book (see Introduction, 42).

16. Toni Dorca, "The Town and the City in the Narrative of Narcís Oller," *Catalan Review* 15, no. 2 (2001): 61.

17. Kathleen Davis, "The 'Cosmorama' of Barcelona: Social Mobility in *La febre d'or*," *Catalan Review* 9, no. 1 (1995): 45.

18. Mercer, *Urbanism and Urbanity*, 119. Scholars have analyzed the Catalan novelist's professionalization and oeuvre, and this chapter's readings are enriched by these analyses. Laureano Bonet, for example, uses *La papallona* and *La febre d'or* to argue that Oller's literary attempts were always conditioned by the existence of middle-class patterns of consumption in which he himself formed a vector (*Literatura*, 67–68). My work further develops connections between Oller's novel-writing enterprise and the Catalan publics he mythologizes and to which he markets his novels, by showing how his heterogeneous representation of the middle-class businessman reflects his own multifaceted identity as a man and bourgeois professional. Joan J. Gilabert, "El mito burgués y la literatura catalana de fin de siglo," in *Mythopoesis, literatura, totalidad, ideología: Ofrecido a Joseph J. Duggan por su distinguida aportación a los estudios literarios*, ed. Joan Ramon Resina (Barcelona: Anthropos, 1992), 178.

19. Resina, *Barcelona's Vocation*, 62.

20. Dorca, "The Town," 76.

21. Sergi Beser ("Les limitacions," 336) and Enric Cassany ("Pròleg," 17) refer to Oller's limitations when describing personal and historical conditions affecting his failures and successes. Enric Cassany, "Pròleg," in *Memòries: Història de mos llibres i relacions literàries*, ed. Arnau Soler Pejoan and Enric Cassany, 9–26 (Valls, Spain: Cossetània Edicions, 2014), 17.

22. Oller, *Memòries*, 366n13.

23. William H. Shoemaker, "Una amistad literaria: La correspondencia epistolar entre Galdós y Narciso Oller," *Boletín de la Real Academia de Buenas Letras*, no. 30 (1963–1964): 267.

24. Shoemaker, "Una amistad," 268.

25. Mercedes Vidal Tibbits, "La 'memoria' como apología: *Memòries literàries*, de Narcís Oller," *Romance Notes* 39, no. 3 (1999): 238.

26. Resina, *Barcelona's Vocation*, 37.

27. Oller, *Memòries*, 117. Given its relevance to one of Barcelona's foundation myths, the story of Jason and the argonauts may have also recalled for inhabitants of Barcelona the indirect role of the heroes in the establishment of their city. According to the authors of the recent volume *La Barcelona d'Hermes*, Hermes and Heracles, stepbrothers and sons of Zeus, joined the company in their search for the golden fleece before eventually separating and

landing on the shores of what would come to be called "Barca nova" (10). According to some genealogies, Jason was also a descendant of Hermes. Caçadors d'Hermes, *La Barcelona d'Hermes* (Barcelona: Albertí Editor, 2016).

28. Oller, *Memòries*, 70.

29. Oller, *Memòries*, 107.

30. Even though Oller's epic "is not based on legends (as Jacint Verdaguer's *L'Atlàntida* was) but on contemporary events," his writings suggest that he was well aware of his project's roots in myth, and his own mythologization of those men most responsible for transforming the city they inhabited. Resina, *Barcelona's Vocation*, 34.

31. Kosofsky Sedgwick, *Between Men*, 25.

32. Mosse, *Nationalism*, 67.

33. Mercer, *Urbanism and Urbanity*, 108.

34. Resina, *Barcelona's Vocation*, 14.

35. Oller, *Memòries*, 36.

36. Josep Domingo, "Pròleg," in *La febre d'or*, ed. Roger Roig (Valls, Spain: Cossetània Edicions, 2013), 15.

37. Lisa Surwillo, *Monsters by Trade: Slave Traffickers in Modern Spanish Literature and Culture* (Stanford, CA: Stanford University Press, 2014), 150.

38. Oller, *La febre*, 28.

39. Oller, *La febre*, 19.

40. In the businessman's self-help guide titled *Tesoro del especulador de bolsa*, the author—"un bolsista retirado" (a retired stockbroker)—asserts that the modern stock market originated in the commerce halls of Ancient Rome (7). He goes on to cite its etymological roots: the surname of the Bruges merchant Van der Beurse ("Van der Bourse") translates to "from the purse" and is still enshrined in the word for stock market in the Romance languages (*Bolsa* [Spanish and Portuguese], *Bourse* [French], *Borsa* [Italian and Catalan]) and echoes in the architectural ornamentation of stock exchanges constructed during the nineteenth century. In the main hall of the Madrid Stock Exchange in the Plaza de la Lealtad, above the decorative aegis of each country that traded on the parquet—from Holland to Japan—one finds small sculptures of change purses, which remind the building's visitors of modern commerce's debts to its medieval or early modern Dutch origins.

41. Oller, *La febre*, 22.

42. See Bolsa de Madrid, "Bolsa de Madrid," accessed December 15, 2021, www.bolsamadrid.es/esp/BMadrid/Palacio/Historia.aspx. Before Constantine's conversion in the fourth century CE, basilicas were used as markets, courthouses, and meeting halls. The palimpsestic ironies inherent in a commerce hall that resembled Catholic architecture rooted in Roman civil architecture was probably not lost on Repullés i Vargas, who also designed basilica-style churches in Madrid.

43. Tsuchiya's recent article "Monuments and Public Memory" contextualizes public sentiment surrounding López y López and the installation and subsequent removals of his statue. Though the monument was celebrated by those who identified in López a motor for imperial might and economic growth, news about his statue and the renaming of the plaza was not universally celebrated. According to an 1884 article in the Catholic journal *La Veu de Montserrat* (The voice of Montserrat), to cite one example, the erasure of Saint Sebastian's name from the plaza worried some members of metropolitan Barcelona's religious community. Akiko Tsuchiya, "Monuments and Public Memory: Antonio López y López, Slavery, and the Cuban-Catalan Connection," *Nineteenth-Century Contexts:*

An Interdisciplinary Journal 41, no. 5 (2019): 479–500.

44. Oller, *La febre*, 41.
45. Lannon, *Privilege*, 97–98.
46. Oller, *La febre*, 32.
47. Oller, *La febre*, 185.
48. Kathleen Davis, "Family Inc.: Corporation and Kinship in *La febre d'or*," *Excavatio*, no. 12 (1999): 187. In Gonzalo Herralde's 1993 televisual adaptation of *La febre d'or*, which aired on the official Catalan-language channel, TV3, Pere's portrait takes on added significance when Gil is shown extracting money from a safe hidden behind it.
49. Oller, *La febre*, 55.
50. Oller, *La febre*, 38.
51. Valis, *Sacred Realism*, 165.
52. Stacy Davis, "'*Hacer las américas*' *es hacer al hombre*: (Re)constructing Spanish Masculinities in the Indianos of Benito Pérez Galdós and Emilia Pardo Bazán" (PhD diss., Washington University in St. Louis, 2016), 4.
53. John Tosh, *Manliness and Masculinities*, 186.
54. Álvarez Junco, *Mater dolorosa*, 503.
55. Surwillo, *Monsters*, 1.
56. Antonio Ferrer del Río, "El indiano," in *Los españoles pintados por sí mismos* (Madrid: I. Boix, 1843–44), 37.
57. Resina, *Barcelona's Vocation*, 15.
58. Schmidt-Nowara asserts that "Columbus performed important ideological work. First, he stood as the starting point of Spain's narration of modernity [. . .] that began [. . .] with Columbus's first voyage in 1492." Christopher Schmidt-Nowara, *The Conquest of History: Spanish Colonialism and National Histories in the Nineteenth Century* (Pittsburgh, PA: University of Pittsburgh Press, 2006), 55. "In this rendering," he continues, "Spain was not the historical laggard but the precocious child of European civilization" (55, 57). Coetaneous monuments to the admiral were raised in Cartagena (1883), Madrid (1886), Las Palmas de Gran Canaria (1892), Granada (1892), and Salamanca (1892–1893) (59).
59. C. Buigas Monrabá, *Monumento a Cristóbal Colón: Honrando a Colón, Cataluña honra a sus hijos predilectos* (Barcelona: Talleres de la Renaixensa), 12.
60. For details about López, see Tsuchiya, "Monuments and Public Memory." For a recent take on Güell's financial contributions to Catalonia, see Andreu Farràs, *Els Güell* (Barcelona: La Butxaca, 2017).
61. Álvarez Junco, *Mater dolorosa*, 503–4.
62. Ángel Bahamonde Magro and José Cayuela, *Hacer las Américas: las élites coloniales españolas en el siglo XIX* (Madrid: Alianza Editorial, 2007), 59.
63. Not all emigrants to the Americas were destined to hold posh or even modestly comfortable positions as clerks and merchants, and illegal travel was common. Davis, "'Hacer las américas,'" 24n3. Most emigrants would have been poor farmers, herders, and soldiers, not all of whom were able to tap into the same transatlantic networks of male homosociality as, for example, the sons, nephews, and friends of magnates like Güell, López, and Xifré.
64. Citing a number of estimates, Stacy Davis reports that millions of men departed the peninsula between 1821 and 1930. "'Hacer las Américas,'" 2. Women also desired to make the journey to the Americas, as reflected in Emilia Pardo Bazán's well-known short story "Las medias rojas" (The red stockings), and they were also victims to transatlantic networks

of sexual trafficking, referred to during the nineteenth century as the *trata de blancas* or "white slavery." Luis Álvarez-Castro, "Transatlantic Sex Trafficking and Imperial Anxiety in Nineteenth-Century Spanish Fiction: *Trata de blancas* (1889) and *Carne importada* (1891)," *Hispanic Review* 86, no. 1 (2018): 26–27.

65. Emigration also had a prominent role to play in the English and French psyche. Numbering in the hundreds of thousands, men from England, Ireland, and Scotland emigrated to the United States of America, Canada, Australasia, and South Africa throughout the nineteenth century. Tosh, *Manliness*, 176. Frenchmen also emigrated in droves during the Second Empire and the Third Republic to the Antilles, Canada, Pacific Islands, and northern Africa. Coetaneous novels attest to the effects such global movements had on the literary imagination. In the denouement of Thomas Hardy's *Far from the Madding Crowd* (1874), for example, Gabriel Oak announces to Bathsheba Everdene his plans—fortunately for the couple, never realized—to leave England for California. Maupassant's *Pierre et Jean* (1888) positions emigration as a last resort for the titular Pierre who, metaphorically and literally dispossessed, no longer feels at home in his native France in the novel's denouement.

66. Pérez Galdós, *Tormento*, 245.

67. Oller, *La febre*, 33–34.

68. Davis, "'Hacer,'" 10, 22.

69. Francesc Cabana, *Bancs i banquers a Catalunya: Capítols per a una història* (Barcelona: Edicions 62, 1972), 9.

70. Oller, *La febre*, 36.

71. Oller, *La febre*, 26.

72. Oller, *La febre*, 26.

73. Oller, *La febre*, 87.

74. In Galdós's novel *El amigo Manso* (My friend Manso), the protagonist's *indiano* brother José María is also accompanied to Madrid by a *negrito* named Rupertico and his mother named Remedios. Although the representation of Rupertico is much less plastic than that of Panxito, the boy is similarly infantilized in that novel and often appears alongside his mother. In Lisa Surwillo's analysis of *El amigo Manso*, and not unlike Panxito in *La febre d'or*, Rupertico emerges as a sort of accessory to the "imperial situation," a figure caught between the "domestic dispute between an *indiano* husband and a Cuban wife." *Monsters by Trade*, 72.

75. Oller, *La febre*, 47.

76. Oller, *La febre*, 48. ("És e papà, que *pota* bobons. [. . .] Dit això, fugí, i encara tingué temps d'apoderar-se de la *papelina*, que el *neguito* li disputava, i entrar amb ella davant de l'estarrufat papà.")

77. Josep M. Fradera, "La figura del negre i del negrer en la literatura catalana del XIX," *L'Avenç*, no. 75 (1984): 57.

78. Oller, *La febre*, 50.

79. Fradera, "La figura," 57. Though Fradera comments on Panxito's fulfillment of his role as narrative decoration in *La febre d'or*, and Surwillo mentions his well-known status within modern Catalan literature, neither provides in-depth readings of the secondary character, nor do they comment on his role in conditioning Gil's "American" or *indiano* brand of middle-class masculinity. Lisa Surwillo, "Passing Counterfeit Whiteness and Mulatta Wealth in *Los misterios de Barcelona*," *Journal of Spanish Cultural Studies* 10, no. 1 (2009): 81.

80. Oller, *La febre*, 54.

81. Buigas Monrabá, "Monumento," 17.

82. The often-Orientalized representations trace a direct genealogy to similar trends in eighteenth-century decorative motifs that ornamented the bureaus and parlors of nobles and monarchs, such as the opulent Porcelain Room of the Royal Palace at Aranjuez (Madrid). See, for example, Tara Zanardi, "Natural History, Porcelain, and 'Mapping' Empire at Aranjuez," *Dieciocho* 43, no. 2 (2020): 241–70.

83. Oller, *La febre*, 50, 157.

84. McClintock, *Imperial Leather*, 214.

85. McClintock, *Imperial Leather*, 209.

86. In a chapter of his memoirs titled "La negra Elo" (Black Elo), Eusebio Güell y López shares the memory of one of his family's black servants: "A person we loved as if she were family was a black woman, purchased by General López de Vega in Cuba when she was twelve years of age, who was handed over to my grandfather when she was sixteen" (Güell y López, *Perspectivas*, 81). Elo's infantilization and the Güell family's love for her mirror Panxito's relationships with Gil and Eudaldet, who symbolically treat the boy as a son and brother, respectively. According to Güell, Elo refused to accept a salary and donated her life's earnings to the Universidad Pontificia, which López, Eusebio's grandfather, founded in Comillas. Güell ends the chapter with a startling anecdote he attributes to Isabel II's youngest daughter:

> Princess Eulalia used to say that one of the most extraordinary things she had seen in her life was when, in the shadows, behind the Japanese screen, she saw my uncle Comillas kissing a black woman. The whole picture was devoid of light: his familiar black suit; the screen's black lacquer; the shadow and Elo's black skin . . . (83).

87. In the previous paragraphs, Mònica includes Blanche, the "franxuta" (frenchie) in her diatribe against the presence of foreigners in the house (Oller, *La febre*, 138), and she later gestures to her discomfort in the company of interstitial houseguests who are neither family nor proper visitors. Oller, *La febre*, 139.

88. Oller, *La febre*, 138.

89. Though abolished in 1820, slave traders and exploitative *indianos* like Xifré continued to sustain the system well past this date (Tsuchiya, "Monuments," 16n2). In the Spanish empire, slavery did not end officially until 1873 in Puerto Rico, and 1880/1886 in Cuba (Schmidt-Nowara, *The Conquest*, 58). Even the United Kingdom, which had abolished slavery earlier, continued to benefit massively from the slave trade. Victorian-era industrial (and industrializing) markets depended on the cheap cotton provided by slavery-based capital until the 1860s.

90. Simon Gikandi, *Slavery and the Culture of Taste* (Princeton, NJ: Princeton University Press, 2011), 2.

91. McClintock, *Imperial Leather*, 222–23.

92. Connell, *Masculinities*, 76.

93. Jeffrey J. Franklin, *Serious Play: The Cultural Form of the Nineteenth-Century Realist Novel* (Philadelphia: University of Pennsylvania Press, 1999), 37.

94. Muñoz-Muriana, "Andando," 181.

95. "Los casinos en España y los clubs en Inglaterra," *La Época (Época Sport)*, June 2, 1891, 1.

96. Cruz, *The Rise*, 198.

97. Cruz, *The Rise*, 198; Mercer, *Urbanism and Urbanity*, 123–25.

98. Oller, *Memòries*, 87.

99. Modesto Lafuente, *Teatro social del siglo XIX* (Madrid: P. Mellado, 1846), 490.

100. Hannah Velten, *Beastly London: A History of Animals in the City* (London: Reaktion Books, 2016), 111.

101. I cite from the letters transcribed in Núria Cabré and Enric Gallén's excellent critical introduction. While Cabré and Gallén situate Rusiñol's letters to Oller in the context of what they have to say about the Catalan painter's awareness of limitations facing Catalan (and Spanish) cultural producers, they do not analyze the epistolary correspondence in the context of an analysis of *La febre d'or* or in light of their implications on male homosocial bonds woven through them.

102. Núria Cabré and Enric Gallén, "Set cartes," 43.

103. Oller, *La febre*, 216.

104. Oller, *La febre*, 215.

105. According to the article by "Jolly Bill" from an 1883 issue of *La Ilustració Catalana*, the lush verdure of a *pelouse* was a mere sparkle in the eye of the beholder: "The ground is low and, consequently, humid and saline, which is why there is no grass on the track and the lawn is no more than a field of rushes and reeds. We understand that improvements of the site's conditions have been planned, but the only remedy we see fit would be to cover it with sod in the style of English gardens." "Hipòdrom de Barcelona," 290. The Hippodrome would have likely received such improvements by the time Oller was writing this chapter during the second half of the 1880s, but his anachronism corroborates the idea that the Catalan novelist viewed himself and Catalan literature as agents of European modernity, while he simultaneously "put the cart before the horse": to compare Can Tunis to more established arenas (an understandable leap, since it was partly sustained by French investors) was to perpetuate the notion that Barcelona was its own version of Paris. The aspirational comparison that emerges corroborates Resina's reflection that "there is a paradox in [such a] self-conscious comparison. Overstatement threw into relief the exaggeration of the claim, for to be a *petit Paris* was to be a *Paris manqué*." Resina, *Barcelona's Vocation*, 43. As Resina summarizes, many visitors to Barcelona recognized its affinities to the French capital, and Emília Llòpis, *La febre*'s precocious demimondaine who speaks Castilian throughout the novel, also sees in Barcelona a *petit Paris* (43).

106. Oller, *La febre*, 216.

107. Erwin, "Fantasies," 549.

108. Oller, *La febre*, 218, 219, 220.

109. Oller, *La febre*, 225.

110. Oller, *La febre*, 228.

111. Oller, *La febre*, 229.

112. Oller, *La febre*, 230.

113. Franklin, *Serious Play*, 4–5.

114. Leo Tolstoy, *Anna Karenina*, trans. Richard Pevear and Larissa Volokhonsky (New York: Penguin, 2004), 196.

115. Oller, *La febre*, 216. This passage foreshadows Gil's and his family's visit to the cemetery to attend the burial of Donya Mònica (the financier's mother-in-law). For an analysis of this scene's engagement with the disconnect between representation and death, see Elisa Martí-López, "Death and the Crisis of Representation in Narcís Oller's *La febre d'or* and Pérez Galdós's *La de Bringas*," in *The Routledge Companion to Iberian Studies*, ed. Javier Muñoz-Basols, Manuel Delgado Morales, and Laura Lonsdale (New York: Routledge, 2017), 357–67.

116. Martí-López, "Death," 360.

117. K. Davis, Mercer, Resina, Dorca, and Martí-López reach similar conclusions, although only Mercer evokes the gendered implications of such ambivalence.

118. Oller, *La febre*, 477. Though I translate "Clavats" (literally "nailed") as "Stupefied," the original term used by Oller is an obvious play with words within the semantic field referencing manual labor and wood.

119. Laureano Bonet, *Literatura, regionalismo y lucha de clases: Galdós, Pereda, Narcís Oller, y Ramón D. Perés* (Barcelona: Edicions de la Universitat de Barcelona, 1983), 68.

120. 1Domingo, "Pròleg," 26.

121. 1Casacuberta, "Dues novel·les," 208.

CHAPTER 4

1. While most scholarship of the last several decades interested in Pereda's literary output focuses to some extent on the patriarchal fantasies he was responsible for crafting, including articles and chapters by Le Bouill, Bonet, Dorca, Iarocci, Valis, and Sinclair with which this chapter dialogues, no study has focused on the explicitly masculine coding of his protagonists, its relevance to mainstream patterns of masculinity, or its reflection of the Cantabrian's own gendered trajectory as a novelist and bourgeois elite.

2. Alison Sinclair, "The Regional Novel," in *The Cambridge Companion to the Spanish Novel from 1600 to the Present*, ed. Harriet Turner and Adelaida López de Martínez (Cambridge: Cambridge University Press, 2003), 50, 62. For Sinclair, the regional novel builds upon "the thematic relation to the idea of a *patria chica*, ambiguity of characterization, and symbolic connotations." The regional novel does not always track realism's paradigms and, as Sinclair also remarks, it would be unproductive to submit the aims of the former to the tenets of the latter (particularly given the heterogeneity of both genres) (50). "If, however, we read [regional] novels as examples of literary and political consciousness, viewing them as vehicles of cultural exchange, even if, at times, their enterprise turns out to be misdirected or failed," Alison Sinclair avers, "then their role in the history of the Spanish novel appears crucial" (50).

3. Nineteenth-century caricatures, such as those included in the pages of anticlerical journal *El Motín* or literary magazine *Madrid Cómico*, tended toward playfulness, irony, or outright mockery in their distorting but not always grotesque representations of human physiognomies. Even though portrait photographs during this time could also be playful and performative, as the introduction to this book illustrates, their high cost and widespread use between men and women alike as genuine tokens of affection—ubiquitous as they were within "the cult of remembrance of dead or absent loved ones" (Benjamin, *Walter Benjamin and Art*, 181)—distance portrait photography from the ambivalent, burlesque, or cheeky aims of caricaturists. Though both visual forms differ in their functions and uses, both are examples of nineteenth-century elite's evolving fascination with new technologies of reproducibility (e.g., daguerreotype, albumen silver printing, photoengraving, etc.), along with their abiding obsession with legacy and self-fashioning via artful representation.

4. In their collection and analysis of data related to the publication and sale of late-nineteenth-century Spanish novels, Elisa Martí-López and Mario Santana argue that "the distinction between commercial and literary authors ignores the fact that both groups

share the same market-oriented publishing strategies." "Spain 1843–1900," 487. Additionally, as we saw to be the case in Oller's novels in Chapter 3, the divide between popular cultural fiction and "serious" literary realism was an artificial one, since realist novelists also absorbed the audience and conventions of *costumbrista* and serialized fiction. Mercer, *Urbanism and Urbanity*, 12. Furthermore, even as they reacted against them, these novelists did little to hide the attachments their own work owed to the earlier, so-called painters of local color like Ramón de Mesonero Romanos, Serafín Estébanez Calderón, Antonio de Trueba, Fernán Caballero and other authors of collections like *Los españoles pintados por sí mismos* and *Los hombres españoles, americanos y lusitanos pintados por sí mismos*. Both Oller and Pereda continued to publish popular local-color sketches or *cuadros de costumbres* well into the 1890s.

5. Cilla was the abbreviated penname of *Madrid Cómico* cartoonist and illustrator Francisco Ramón Cilla y Pérez (1859–1937).

6. His caricatures of authors like Antonio de San Martín (1841–1887) and Luis Taboada (1848–1906) exaggerated their regionalist literary programs (and their own rurality) with recourse to iconography associated with traditional costumes including abdominal sashes and clogs like those depicted in Figure 4.2.

7. Oller describes Pereda in similar terms in his memoirs: "The frankness and warmth with which he treated me from the first instant captivated me immediately." *Memòries*, 65.

8. Lawrence Hadfield Klibbe, *José María de Pereda* (New York: Twayne, 1975), 17. An issue of *El Diario Montañés* (The Santander daily) commemorating Pereda's death in 1906 attests to the public demand for portraits of the Santander native: "Even total strangers were eager to own a portrait of him, and he constantly needed to replenish his reserves and make new ones. Since his robust countenance was an ongoing enticement to painters and photographers, the sheer number of portraits left of the great man from Santander is astonishing." Raquel Gutiérrez Sebastián, "José María de Pereda y la construcción de una imagen," *Ínsula: Revista de letras y ciencias humanas*, no. 772 (2011): 13–15. Madariaga de la Campa and Gutiérrez Sebastián have interpreted the demand for reproductions of his image in the form of caricatures and portraits as an incontrovertible sign of his celebrity status at the turn of the century.

9. Raquel Gutiérrez Sebastián, "José María de Pereda," 13–15.

10. Mecachis (an interjection akin to "Shoot!" in English) was the pseudonym of Eduardo Sáenz Hermúa (1859–1898), a prolific cartoonist for popular magazines including *Blanco y Negro* and *Madrid Cómico*.

11. The *cuévano* (*niñero*) or *cuévana* was first used as a cradle for children by Cantabrian women who were expected to bear their children while they continued to barter, shop, or perform any other activity that required the use of their hands. Typical throughout Cantabria, but specifically associated with the Pas River Valley, these women (*pasiegas*) were also popular sights in Madrid until at least around the middle of the nineteenth century. In cosmopolitan spaces, such women were often contracted by bourgeois families as wet-nurses or caretakers and could sometimes be seen walking around the city in traditional costume. During Théophile Gautier's travels to Spain, recounted for posterity in his *Voyage en Espagne* (1843; Wanderings in Spain), the French author noted the abundance of *pasiegas* as they strolled up and down the Paseo del Prado: "These *pasiegas* are accounted the best wet-nurses in Spain, and their affection for their little charges is as proverbial as is the honesty of the natives of Auvergne in France. [. . .] It is looked upon as a kind of luxury to keep a *pasiega* in full costume." Gautier, *Wanderings*, 78–79. The illustration

accompanying Manuel Bretón de los Herreros's entry on "La nodriza" (The wet-nurse) in *Los españoles pintados por sí mismos* (1843–44; The Spanish painted by themselves) depicts a woman with a covered *cuévano*, and the article corroborates Gautier when it states that the *pasiega*, specifically, represented a special luxury for the affluent family.

12. European doctors like A. Devay were among the many who touted the benefits of "rural settings," for there "a man [could] breathe clean air, eat healthy meals, and get strong by working the land." McKinney, "Enemigos," 98. Eugenia Afinoguénova points out that while the north was indeed advertised as a setting befitting of descriptions like Devay's, local anxieties about contagion that ailing visitors may have brought with them manifest, for example, in Pereda's sketch "El artista": a work in which a tubercular barber causes anxiety among the inhabitants of a northern seaside town. For Afinoguénova, Pereda's tale gives visibility to "the hygienic dangers that such visitors suppose for the community [that] come to the surface when one realizes that this sick character, who came to the beach looking for a cure, works as a barber in a local barbershop, where he can easily infect the clients." Eugenia Afinoguénova, "Beach, Modernity, and Colonial Encounters in Santander and Castro Urdíales in Amos de Escalante and José María de Pereda, 1864–1877," *Mester* 32, no. 1 (2003): 135.

13. Gabino Tejado, "*Don Gonzalo González de la Gonzalera*," *Ilustración Católica*, March 28, 1879, 282.

14. It was not uncommon to use the language of olfaction to characterize an artist or author's rendering of nature during the nineteenth century, but the ubiquity and potentially meaningful coding of such metaphors in Pereda's writings and reviews of them by others warrants closer attention, given the highlander's active hand in the *fin-de-siècle* soap and perfume industries.

15. Madariaga de la Campa, *Pereda*, 172.

16. Jean le Bouill's crucial article highlights Pereda's novels' many connections to nineteenth-century commercial and entrepreneurial networks and sheds light on the debts books like *Don Gonzalo González de la Gonzalera* owe to the novelist's entrepreneurial brothers Juan Agapito and Manuel. For her part, Noël Valis importantly reminds her readers that "the stereotype of Pereda as the hidalgo highlander meditating in solitary splendor in his comfortable house in Polanco has lately given way to a less idealized, less nostalgic image of a Pereda who belonged to a powerful Santander elite of *indianos* and industrialists." *Reading the Nineteenth-Century Spanish Novel: Selected Essays* (Newark, DE: Juan de la Cuesta, 2005), 210. Michael Iarocci has cogently asserted that Pereda's fictions should not be overlooked in the study of the Spanish turn of the century, not least of all because "it is clear that the reading public of 1895," which quickly consumed the first edition of *Peñas arriba* published that year, "continued to anxiously seek [. . .] transcendent, stable meaning in the progressively defamiliarized, alienating modernity wrought by the bourgeois cultural revolution." Michael Iarocci, "On the Ideology of Metaphor in Pereda's *Peñas arriba*," *Revista Hispánica Moderna* 51, no. 2 (1998): 254. As this chapter will show, a focus on masculinity provides yet another reason to reincorporate Pereda and his fiction into the fabric of studies of nineteenth-century culture, gender, and modernity. See Iarocci (236–38) for comprehensive literary reviews of Pereda criticism.

17. Hugh Campbell and Michael Mayerfeld Bell, "The Question of Rural Masculinities," *Rural Sociology* 65, no. 4 (2000): 540. In late nineteenth-century Spain, this was part of the larger trend according to which aristocrats and upper bourgeois folks regularly appropriated the cultural practices associated with the Spanish *pueblo* or lower classes as a way to

distinguish themselves from other Europeans. Smith, "Cultural Capital," 156.

18. Widows and/or their children, for example, often took over family businesses in the event of a husband or father's death. In the printing industry, for example, names such as Tello (one of Pereda's publishers) were carried on by female inheritors together with their children. Additionally, as Cruz shows to be the case between 1750 and 1850, "daughters were [also] a positive resource to establish familial alliances and reinforce the economic strength of the group." *Gentlemen*, 250. Indeed, this is the case in Gil Foix's early intentions to marry off his daughter Delfineta in an effort to unite his family with that of the Balenyàs in Oller's *La febre d'or*. However, in this example, and elsewhere as Cruz points out, commercial firms preferred male heirs for the transmission of capital: "when there was no direct heir, fortunes were usually passed on to a patrilineal nephew." Cruz, *Gentlemen*, 250.

19. To cite an illustrative example in the Restoration context, Gabrielle Miller has recently argued that the "excessive paternal affection" *("¡Mi hijo es mío, puñales!,"* 66) the eponymous protagonist of Galdós's *Torquemada* tetralogy (1889, 1893–95) showers upon his progeny undermines his successful performance of masculine (and fatherly) virtues of moderation. For his part, Bryan Cameron, whose article I dialogue with elsewhere in this chapter, examines the link between nineteenth-century Spanish novelists and the "textual progenies" they engendered via the novel to shed light on liberal authors' allegorization of political stagnation and failure through the "abortive attempts at familial unity" by fictional father figures. In her work on Victorian fiction, Melissa Shields Jenkins demonstrates how English writers "refigure fatherhood" by discovering "another 'way of writing'—a contested ground for paternal authority outside of fiction—that alters the nature of his or her literary output." Melissa Shields Jenkins, *Fatherhood, Authority, and British Reading Culture* (New York: Routledge, 2014), 1. Silke-Maria Weineck reclaims a subject position for the often voiceless father figures of classical and modern German literature by analyzing texts and discourses that show fatherhood to be in a constant state of crisis. Silke-Maria Weineck, *The Tragedy of Fatherhood: King Laius and the Politics of Paternity in the West* (New York: Bloomsbury, 2014), 7.

20. For differences in regional Spanish inheritance practices through the twentieth century, see Llorenç Ferrer-Alòs, "¿Quién hereda?: Desigualdades de género en el acceso a los derechos de propiedad y sistemas hereditarios en España." *AREAS: Revista Internacional de Ciencias Sociales*, no. 33 (2014): 35–47, and David Martínez López, "Sobre familias, élites y herencias en el siglo XIX," *Historia Contemporánea*, no. 31 (2005): 457–80.

21. Madariaga de la Campa, *Pereda*, 57, 171–76.

22. Martínez López, "Sobre familias," 471–72. Daughters could also receive preferential treatment within the inheritance if they were deemed best suited to take care of elderly parents while maintaining the estate. Ferrer-Alòs, "¿Quién hereda?," 45.

23. Ferrer Alòs, "¿Quién hereda?," 45.

24. Martínez López, "Sobre familias," 471–72. Depending on the context, "hermanos" may be translated as brothers, or, alternatively, as siblings (or, in other words, a mixed group of brothers and sisters). Here, Martínez López emphasizes the role played specifically by older brothers, whose agency and freedom of movement within the public sphere made them more proximate surrogates of paternal authority. This is not to say that older sisters did not play a significant part in meaningfully supporting the ambitions of younger siblings. When Benito Pérez Galdós moved from Las Palmas to Madrid in 1862, for example, the material support provided by his sister and brother-in-law helped him to overcome some of the early challenges he faced in his transition to metropolitan living.

25. In an 1892 article for *La Vanguardia*, José Roca contends that Pereda's regionalism was more interested in preserving the local character of Cantabria over the restoration of "anachronistic" regional political and social institutions. Madariaga de la Campa, *Pereda*, 357.

26. Madariaga de la Campa, *Pereda*, 148.

27. Madariaga de la Campa, *Pereda*, 148.

28. Bryan Cameron, "Stillborn Texts and Barren Imaginaries in Leopoldo Alas's *Su único hijo* (1891)," *Revista Hispánica Moderna* 67, no. 2 (2014): 144–45.

29. For example, in Maupassant's *Pierre et Jean*, the divide between polar-opposite brothers is widened by the discovery of their mother Louise's infidelity and the younger brother Jean's related inheritance of a small fortune from a recently deceased family friend.

30. Noël Valis, *Reading the Nineteenth-Century Spanish Novel*, 210.

31. Armando Palacio Valdés, "Discurso del Excmo. Sr. Dr. Armando Palacio Valdés," in *Discursos leídos ante la Real Academia Española en la recepción pública del Excmo. Sr. D. Armando Palacio Valdés, el día 12 de diciembre de 1920* (Madrid: Imprenta de los Hijos de M. G. Hernández, 1920), 5.

32. Emilia Pardo Bazán, *La cuestión palpitante*, ed. Rosa de Diego (Madrid: Biblioteca Nueva, 1998), 290.

33. While the authors of local-color sketches and physiognomies based their studies on what they observed in rapidly urbanizing cityscapes, they were just as likely to depict this world "on the brink of modernity" as they chose to remember or wished to see it, not necessarily as it was in an objective sense. Martina Lauster, *Sketches of the Nineteenth Century: European Journalism and Its Physiologies, 1830–50* (London: Palgrave Macmillan, 2007), 3.

34. Carr, *Spain*, 414.

35. Adrian Shubert, *A Social History of Modern Spain* (New York: Routledge, 1990), 24, 46.

36. Even bourgeois voices from peripheral cities that had not experienced urbanization to the same degree as Madrid, Barcelona, or Bilbao—like Burgos—expressed anxiety about the influx of poor inhabitants of the countryside, which one dubbed "the nursery of mendicity." Shubert, *A Social History*, 52. Still, internal migratory flows before 1950 were smaller and less frequent than those from Spain to the Americas (e.g., Argentina, Cuba, Puerto Rico), northern Africa (e.g., Algeria), and France (44–46).

37. Campbell and Bell, "The Question," 539–40.

38. By using the "the rural in the masculine" or "the masculine in the rural" as lenses through which to better understand Pereda's novels, we may also circumvent narrow appraisals of Pereda that would otherwise overlook his fictions as irrelevant to bourgeois modernity or alternatively as a backward analogue to the allegedly modern or urban narratives by authors like Galdós, Alas, or Pardo Bazán.

39. Alas, *La Regenta*, 2: 499.

40. Carlos Reyero, *Apariencia e identidad masculine: De la ilustración al decadentismo* (Madrid: Cátedra, 1999), 31.

41. Reyero, *Apariencia*, 30–31.

42. McKinney, "How to Be a Man," 148; Reyero, *Apariencia*, 31.

43. Campbell and Bell, "The Question," 536.

44. A pocket-sized album by the Barcelona-based department store El Siglo, printed sometime after the establishment's installation of electric lighting in 1884, depicts a bustling basement-level floor devoted to shipping parcels to provincial destinations. The print and corresponding description reveal El Siglo's mission to be intimately tied to the demand

for fashionable objects beyond Barcelona, ensuring shoppers outside the city of the same prices and quality available to metropolitan residents. *Grandes Almacenes de El Siglo*, Propaganda Comercial, Grans Magatzems, B10.1–C51, Arxiù Històric de la Ciutat de Barcelona, Barcelona, Spain.

45. The Spanish Royal Academy would not admit its first female member until the induction of Carmen Conde in 1979, four years after the death of Francisco Franco.

46. Factors preventing Pereda's earlier consideration for entry into the Spanish Royal Academy were presumably related to his place of residence: members were expected to prove residency in Madrid, a prerequisite for which Marcelino Menéndez Pelayo sought a dispensation for his compatriot, whose residences were in Polanco and Santander.

47. José María de Pereda, "Discurso del Sr. D. José María de Pereda," in *Discursos leídos ante la Real Academia Española en la recepción pública del Sr. D. José María de Pereda, el domingo 21 de febrero de 1897* (Madrid: La Viuda e Hijos de Tello, 1897), 5.

48. The uniform eventually developed for inductees to the Spanish Royal Academy took the form of a tuxedo-style suit with green laurel leaves embroidered into the lapels.

49. Pereda, "Discurso," 9.

50. Pereda, "Discurso," 15.

51. Pereda, "Discurso," 20.

52. Pereda, "Discurso," 15.

53. Pereda, "Discurso," 15.

54. Pereda, "Discurso," 12.

55. Pereda, "Discurso," 25–26.

56. Spain's northern mountains and shoreline had become a major vacation destination for Madrilenian and other European tourists during the second half of the nineteenth century. Eugenia Afinoguénova analyzes the encroachment of tourism on the Cantabrian landscape through the lens of colonialism and suggests that writers like Pereda "experienced modernization of their native lands as a reversed colonial conquest, which stirred old discussions about the role of the Empire, the ownership of lands, and the balance of civilization and barbarity in modern culture." "Beach, Modernity," 130. In *Pedro Sánchez*, Pereda signals this history in the figure of Valenzuela, whose initial reason for traveling to Cantabria—aside from the health benefits for his daughter—included purchasing a summer home.

57. During the 1854 revolution, popular uprisings in Madrid sparked by famine, poverty, and charges of corruption led to the ransacking and burning of ostentatious homes of the moderate politicians then in power and who were deemed most guilty by the crowds. María Zozaya, "'Moral Revenge of the Crowd' in the 1854 Revolution in Madrid," *Bulletin for Spanish and Portuguese Historical Studies* 37, no. 1 (2012): 46. María Zozaya surmises that such little attention has been paid to the popular uprisings in Madrid in 1854 due to a number of historiographical reasons that have either ignored or downplayed its significance for the history of liberalism in Spain. These include the manner in which 1868 was eventually defined as the (only) watershed for Spain's bourgeois revolution, the evasion of liberal historical events by Francoist historians during the mid-twentieth century, and the fact that conservative bourgeois writers during the nineteenth century were themselves guilty of censoring or downplaying the events of July 1854 for fear of reproducing in Spain the so-called liberal revolutions that occurred elsewhere in Europe in 1848 ("Moral Revenge," 20). Viewed through the lens of psychoanalysis, his leadership of the barricades and his concomitant protagonism in the revolutionary uprisings permit readings of Pedro

as an alter ego for Pereda, who was no staunch defender of liberalism even in his youth. See also Toni Dorca, "*Pedro Sánchez*, entre episodio nacional y episodio personal," *Boletín de la Biblioteca de Menéndez Pelayo*, no. 82 (2006): 65n11.

58. José María de Pereda, *Pedro Sánchez*, 2 vols., ed. José María de Cossío (Madrid: Espasa-Calpe, 1958), 3.
59. Pereda, *Pedro Sánchez*, 4.
60. Pereda, *Pedro Sánchez*, 59, 60.
61. Pereda, *Pedro Sánchez*, 63.
62. Pereda, *Pedro Sánchez*, 60.
63. Pereda, *Pedro Sánchez*, 43–44.
64. Pereda, *Pedro Sánchez*, 94.
65. Pereda, *Pedro Sánchez*, 244–45.
66. Pereda, *Pedro Sánchez*, 244.
67. Dorca, "*Pedro Sánchez*," 63.
68. Around the time Pereda was drafting the twenty-first chapter of *Peñas arriba*, his twenty-three-year-old son Juan Manuel took his own life. The eldest of José María's children with Diodora de la Revilla, Juan Manuel worked for the family business (La Rosario) and suffered from crippling social anxiety related to a stutter. The tragic death of Pereda's beloved son was the subject of a number of letters shared between the author and his friends. Indeed, the author's epistolary correspondence had a galvanizing effect on the grieving father's relationships with the likes of Galdós and Oller, among others.
69. Valis, *Reading*, 194.
70. Valis, *Reading*, 198.
71. Valis, *Reading*, 194.
72. Valis, *Reading*, 197.
73. Pereda, *Peñas arriba*, 119.
74. Sarah Sierra, "Time and the Environment: 'Slow Violence' in Benito Pérez Galdós's *Doña Perfecta* and *Marianela*," *Confluencia: Revista Hispánica de Cultura y Literatura* 35, no. 1 (2019): 45, 49.
75. Pereda, *Peñas arriba*, 132–33.
76. Pereda, *Peñas arriba*, 133n22. In his critical edition of *Peñas arriba*, Antonio Rey points out that these authors were well-known during the nineteenth century for their travel novels, a genre to which even nineteenth-century critics like Menéndez Pelayo compared Pereda's novel. Olivier Gloux, born Gustave Aimard and orphaned at a young age, wrote novels inspired by his travels in the Americas and Europe.
77. Pereda, *Peñas arriba*, 134.
78. Iarocci, "On the Ideology," 236.
79. Pereda, *Peñas arriba*, 212.
80. Pereda, *Peñas arriba*, 198–99.
81. Muñoz-Muriana, "*Andando*," 181.
82. Luis Benito García Álvarez, "Moda masculina y distinción social: El ejemplo de Asturias desde la Restauración hasta la Segunda República," *Vínculos de Historia*, no. 6 (2017): 167.
83. Labanyi, *Gender*, 336.
84. Pereda, *Peñas arriba*, 378.
85. Pereda, *Peñas arriba*, 390, 383.
86. Pereda, *Peñas arriba*, 384.
87. Pereda, *Peñas arriba*, 389.

88. The connection to Hercules's victory against the Nemean lion is heightened by the fact that Chisco and Chorcos recommend that Marcelo imagine the "lions" they will encounter as hares in order to bolster the urbanite's confidence prior to their approach to bear's den. Pereda, *Peñas arriba*, 386.

89. Pereda, *Peñas arriba*, 401.

90. Melchor de Palau, "Acontecimientos Literarios: 1895, *Peñas arriba*," *Revista Contemporánea*, no. 97, January 1895, 502.

91. In between the publication of *Pedro Sánchez* and *Peñas arriba*, Pereda appears to have endeared himself to readers who were eager to embrace a cosmovision in which wrongs were righted and moral ambiguities were always resolved: "in 1890, a women's weekly magazine *La Última Moda* [The latest fashion] undertook a survey and Pereda earned the top place among the primary Spanish and foreign authors read at the time. He was the best-suited for a target audience who demanded literature with moralizing themes." Madariaga de la Campa, *Pereda*, 264, 266.

92. Iarocci, "On the Ideology," 252.

CODA

1. Hashtags on Instagram aggregate images tagged with certain labels, thus allowing the user to include the content they post as part of a larger community or group (e.g., #19thcenturyart, #muscleboys), while allowing one to search for images by label. The use of hashtags like #muscleboys in posts about nineteenth-century figures like a nude by Fortuny inevitably throws Victorian-era men into relief against their twenty-first century analogues, which range from the casual beachgoer or gym rat to scantily clad celebrities.

2. Of course, this process began in the late nineteenth century in Spain, when figures like Emilia Pardo Bazán, Concepción Arenal, Faustina Sáez de Melgar, and Víctor Català, among many others, paved the way for future feminist movements. See Christine Arkinstall, "Forging Progressive Futures for Spain's Women and People: Sofía Tartilán (Palencia 1829–Madrid 1888)," in *Modern Spanish Women as Agents of Change: Essays in Honor of Maryellen Bieder*, ed. Jennifer Smith (Lewisburg, PA: Bucknell University Press, 2019), 34–55, and Jennifer Smith, introduction to *Modern Spanish Women as Agents of Change: Essays in Honor of Maryellen Bieder* (Lewisburg, PA: Bucknell University Press, 2019), 5–7.

3. Breward, *The Suit*, 168.

4. John Harvey, *Men in Black* (Chicago: University of Chicago Press, 1995), 23. Collin McKinney's homonymous essay gestures to the relationship between this myth and nineteenth-century Spanish cultural products. Several recent books and essays challenge or refute scholars' overemphasis on nineteenth-century men's use of black clothing. See especially Christopher Breward and Alison Matthews David, both of whom convincingly demonstrate the plurality of ways men adorned themselves during the mid- to late nineteenth century in England and France.

5. McKinney, "Men in Black," 85. There is also a plethora of examples illustrating twentieth-century men's enthusiastic embrace and consumption of fashion and fashionable merchandise in the cultural mainstream. Take, for example, Ramón Gómez de la Serna's playful use of nineteenth-century sartorial aesthetics in his own performances and literary output (e.g., *Greguerías*) or twentieth-century Spanish brands like Varón Dandy, which mainstreamed Victorian-era notions of dandyism in its marketing and sale of cologne. Wolters, "Outfitting."

6. Rubén Darío, *España contemporánea* (Madrid: Biblioteca Rubén Darío, 1900), 222.

7. Darío, *España*, 239.

8. At least since the foundational work of Peter Gay, the word Victorian has been used as shorthand to refer to aesthetics and values associated with the nineteenth-century bourgeoisie in the Americas as well as in Europe. Cruz, *The Rise*, 10.

9. Greenblatt, *Renaissance*, 2.

10. See Alejandro Gómez Palomo, *Palomo Spain* (Barcelona: Grijalbo Ilustrados, 2019).

11. Gómez Palomo, *Palomo Spain*, 169–70. Although Gómez Palomo received his training as a designer in London, he chooses to reside in Posadas (Córdoba), not unlike Pereda, whose formative years in Madrid undoubtedly contributed to his later ability to reside in Polanco (Cantabria) and Santander.

12. For example, Dorota Heneghan has shown some of the ways Leopoldo Alas "Clarín" wrote critically of fashion as a historical phenomenon and industry. *Striking*, 11–13.

13. Benito Pérez Galdós, "El elegante," in *Fisonomías sociales: Obras inéditas*, vol. 1 (Madrid: Renacimiento, 1923), 241.

14. Rita Felski, *The Gender of Modernity* (Cambridge, MA: Harvard University Press, 1995), 99.

15. James Eli Adams, *Dandies and Desert Saints*, 23.

16. See Beth Wietelmann Bauer, "Narrative Cross-Dressing: Emilia Pardo Bazán in *Memorias de un solterón*," *Hispania* 77, no. 1 (1994): 23–30.

Bibliography

Adams, James Eli. *Dandies and Desert Saints: Styles of Victorian Masculinity.* Ithaca, NY: Cornell University Press, 1995.

Afinoguénova, Eugenia, "Beach, Modernity, and Colonial Encounters in Santander and Castro Urdíales in Amos de Escalante and José María de Pereda, 1864–1877." *Mester* 32, no. 1 (2003): 127–54.

Alas, Leopoldo. "El Doctor Centeno." *El Día* [Madrid], August 5, 1883.

———. *His Only Son.* Translated by Margaret Jull Costa. New York: New York Review of Books, 2016.

———. "Introducción." In *Los heroes: El culto de los héroes y lo heroico en la historia*, 2 vols., by Thomas Carlyle, translated by Julián G. Orbón, 1–38, 7–31. Madrid: Manuel Fernández y Lasanta, 1893.

———. *La Regenta.* 2 vols. Edited by Gonzalo Sobejano. Madrid: Clásicos Castalia, 1981.

———. *La Regenta.* Translated by John Rutherford. Cambridge, UK: Penguin, 2005.

———. *Sermón perdido.* Madrid: Librería de Fernando Fé, 1885.

Alcalá Galiano, Antonio. *Memorias de D. Antonio Alcalá Galiano: Publicadas por su hijo.* Madrid: Imprenta de E. Rubiños, 1886.

Albertí, Elisenda. *Un passeig per la moda de Barcelona: Modistes, sastres, botigues . . . del mirinyac als anys vint.* Barcelona: Albertí Editor SL, 2013.

Álvarez-Castro, Luis. "Transatlantic Sex Trafficking and Imperial Anxiety in Nineteenth-Century Spanish Fiction: *Trata de blancas* (1889) and *Carne importada* (1891)." *Hispanic Review* 86, no. 1 (2018): 25–44.

Álvarez Junco, José. *Mater dolorosa: La idea de España en el siglo XIX.* Madrid: Taurus, 2017.

Arbaiza, Diana. "The Marketing of Cecilia Böhl von Faber: Gender, Economy, and the Professionalization of the Artist." *Revista Hispánica Moderna* 72, no. 1 (2019): 1–23.

———. "Valores fluctuantes: Crédito, consumo e identidad nacional en *Lo prohibido* de Galdós." *Decimonónica* 11, no. 1 (Winter 2014): 1–13.

Arencibia, Yolanda. *Galdós: Una biografía.* Barcelona: Tusquets, 2020.

Aresti, Nerea. "La hombría perdida en el tiempo: Masculinidad y nación española a finales del siglo XIX." In *Hombres en peligro: Género, nación e imperio en la España de cambio de siglo (XIX–XX)*, edited by Mauricio Zabalgoitia Herrera, 19–38. Madrid: Iberoamericana, 2017.

Arkinstall, Christine. "Forging Progressive Futures for Spain's Women and People: Sofía Tartilán (Palencia 1829–Madrid 1888)." In *Modern Spanish Women as Agents of Change:*

Essays in Honor of Maryellen Bieder, edited by Jennifer Smith, 34–55. Lewisburg, PA: Bucknell University Press, 2019.

Armon, Shifra. *Masculine Virtue in Early Modern Spain*. Farnham, UK: Ashgate Publishing, 2015.

Arranz Herrero, Manuel, and Ramon Grau Fernández. "Problemas de inmigración y asimilación en la Barcelona del siglo XVIII." *Revista de Geografía* 4, no. 1 (1970): 71–80.

Bahamonde Magro, Ángel, and José Cayuela. *Hacer las Américas: Las élites coloniales españolas en el siglo XIX*. Madrid: Alianza Editorial, 2007.

Bakhtin, Mikhail. "The Bildungsroman and Its Significance in the History of Realism (toward a Historical Typology of the Novel)." In Speech Genres and Other Late Essays, translated by Vera W. McGee, edited by Caryl Emerson and Michael Holquist, 10–59. Austin: University of Texas Press, 1986.

Balzac, Honoré de. *Père Goriot*. Translated by Burton Raffel and edited by Peter Brooks. New York: Norton Critical Editions, 1994.

Barlow, Jennifer. "Love and War: Male Friendship and the Performance of Masculinity in the Poetry of Garcilaso de la Vega (1501–1536)." *Bulletin of Hispanic Studies* 95, no. 4 (2018): 383–98.

Barthes, Roland. *The Fashion System*. Translated by Matthew Ward and Richard Howard. Berkeley: University of California Press, 1990.

Beckert, Sven. *Empire of Cotton: A Global History*. New York: Vintage, 2015.

Benjamin, Andrew. *Walter Benjamin and Art*. London: Continuum, 2005.

Benjamin, Walter. *The Arcades Project*. Translated by Howard Eiland and Kevin McLaughlin. Cambridge, MA: Belknap Press of Harvard University Press, 1999.

———. "The Paris of the Second Empire in Baudelaire." In *The Writer of Modern Life: Essays on Charles Baudelaire*, translated by Howard Eiland, Edmund Jephcott, Rodney Livingston, and Harry Zohn, and edited by Michael W. Jennings, 46–133. Cambridge, MA: Belknap Press of Harvard Univeresity Press, 2006.

Berkowitz, H. Chonon. *Pérez Galdós: Spanish Liberal Crusader*. Madison: University of Wisconsin Press, 1948.

Beser, Sergio. *Leopoldo Alas, crítico literario*. Madrid: Editorial Gredos, 1968.

———. *Leopoldo Alas: Teoría y crítica de la novela española*. Barcelona: Editorial Laia, 1972.

———. "Les limitacions narratives de Narcís Oller." In *Actes del Quart Colloqui Internacional de Llengua i Literatura Catalanes: Basilea, 22–27 de març de 1976*, 333–47. Montserrat: Abadia de Montserrat, 1977.

Bhabha, Homi. *Nation and Narration*. New York: Routledge, 1990.

Bieder, Maryellen. "En-Gendering Strategies of Authority: Emilia Pardo Bazán and the Novel." In *Cultural and Historical Grounding for Hispanic and Luso-Brazilian Feminist Literary Criticism*, edited by Hernán Vidal, 473–95. Minneapolis, MN: Institute for Study of Ideologies and Literature, 1989.

———. "'El escalpelo anatómico en mano femenina': The Realist Novel and the Woman Writer." *Letras Peninsulares* 5, no. 2 (1992): 209–25.

———. "Gender and Language: The Womanly Woman and Manly Writing." In Culture and Gender in Nineteenth-Century Spain, edited by Lou Charnon-Deutsch and Jo Labanyi,

98–119. Oxford: Clarendon Press and Oxford University Press, 1995.

———. "Imágenes visuales de Emilia Pardo Bazán en la prensa periódica." In *Literatura hispánica y prensa periódica (1875–1931)*, edited by Javier Serrano Alonso and Amparo de Juan Bolufer, 221–35. Santiago de Compostela: Universidad de Santiago de Compostela, 2009.

———. "Sexo y lenguaje en Emilia Pardo Bazán: La deconstrucción de la diferencia." In *Actas del XII Congreso de la Asociación Internacional de Hispanistas, IV: Del romanticismo a la guerra civil*, edited by Derek W. Flitter, 92–99. Birmingham, UK: University of Birmingham, Department of Hispanic Studies, 1998.

Blaisdell, Bob. *Creating Anna Karenina: Tolstoy and the Birth of Literature's Most Enigmatic Heroine*. Cambridge, UK: Pegasus Books, 2020.

Blanco, Alda. "Gender and National Identity: The Novel in Nineteenth-Century Spanish Literary History." In *Culture and Gender in Nineteenth-Century Spain*, edited by Lou Charnon-Deutsch and Jo Labanyi, 120–36. Oxford: Clarendon Press and Oxford University Press, 1995.

Blanco Carpintero, Marta. "La indumentaria en las novelas contemporáneas de Galdós a la luz de las nuevas estructuras sociales y económicas." *Isidora*, no. 8 (2008): 21–32.

Bloom, Harold. *The Anxiety of Influence: A Theory of Poetry*. Oxford: Oxford University Press, 1997.

Bly, Peter Anthony. *The Wisdom of Eccentric Old Men: A Study of Type and Secondary Character in Galdós's Social Novels, 1870–1897*. Montreal: McGill-Queen's University Press, 2004.

Bolsa de Madrid. "Bolsa de Madrid." Accessed December 15, 2021. www.bolsamadrid.es/esp/BMadrid/Palacio/Historia.aspx.

Bolsista Retirado, Un. *Tesoro del especulador de bolsa y nuevo sistema de ganar siempre en ella*. Madrid: Baena Hermanos, 1895.

Bonet, Laureano. "Galdós visto por Clarín, Narcís Oller y Pereda: Los mil matices de una conversación." In *La hora de Galdós: Actas*, edited by Yolanda Arencibia and Germán Gullón et al., 1015–26. Las Palmas: Cabildo Insular de Gran Canaria, 2018.

———. *Literatura, regionalismo y lucha de clases: Galdós, Pereda, Narcís Oller, y Ramón D. Perés*. Barcelona: Edicions de la Universitat de Barcelona, 1983.

Botrel, Jean François. "Producción literaria y rentabilidad: El caso de 'Clarín.'" In *Hommage des hispanistes français à Noël Salomon*, 123–33. Barcelona: Editorial Laia, 1979.

Bourdieu, Pierre. *The Field of Cultural Production*. Edited by Randal Johnson. New York: Columbia University Press, 1993.

Bowlby, Rachel. *Just Looking: Consumer Culture in Dresier, Gissing and Zola*. Grantham, UK: Methuen, 1985.

Bozal, Valeriano. *La ilustración gráfica del XIX en España*. Madrid: Comunicación, 1979.

Braudy, Leo. *From Chivalry to Terrorism: War and the Changing Nature of Masculinity*. New York: Vintage, 2005.

Breward, Christopher. *The Hidden Consumer: Masculinities, Fashion and City Life 1860–1914*. Manchester: Manchester University Press, 1999.

———. *Fashion*. Oxford: Oxford University Press, 2003.

———. *The Suit: Form, Function, and Style*. London: Reaktion Books, 2016.

Brontë, Charlotte. *Jane Eyre*. Edited by Deborah Lutz. New York: W. W. Norton, 2016.

Buigas Monrabá, C. *Monumento a Cristóbal Colón: Honrando a Colón, Cataluña honra a sus hijos predilectos*. Barcelona: Talleres de la Renaixensa, 1882.

Burdiel, Isabel. *Emilia Pardo Bazán*. Madrid: Taurus, 2019.

Caballero, Fermín. "El clérigo de misa y olla." In *Los españoles pintados por sí mismos*, 72–75. Madrid: Gaspar y Roig, 1851.

Cabana, Francesc. *Bancs i banquers a Catalunya: Capítols per a una història*. Barcelona: Edicions 62, 1972.

Cabré, Rosa, ed. *Escrits autobiogràfics, 1872–1889*. Lleida: Punctum & Grup d'Estudi de la Literatura del Vuit-cents, 2007.

Cabré, Núria, and Enric Gallén. "Set cartes de Santiago Rusiñol a Narcís Oller." *Faig*, no. 11 (1980): 25–50.

Caçadors d'Hermes. *La Barcelona d'Hermes*. Barcelona: Albertí Editor, 2016.

Calefato, Patrizia. *Luxury: Fashion, Lifestyle and Excess*. Translated by Lisa Adams. London: Bloomsbury, 2014.

Callahan, William James. *Church, Politics, and Society in Spain, 1750–1874*. Cambridge, MA: Harvard University Press, 1984.

Cameron, Bryan. "Paternity Tests: Destabilized Authority and Patriarchal Anxiety in Late-Nineteenth-Century Spain." PhD diss., University of Pennsylvania, 2011.

———. "Stillborn Texts and Barren Imaginaries in Leopoldo Alas's *Su único hijo* (1891)." *Revista Hispánica Moderna* 67, no. 2 (2014): 143–61.

Campbell, Hugh and Michael Mayerfeld Bell. "The Question of Rural Masculinities." *Rural Sociology* 65, no. 4 (2000): 532–46.

Cardona, Rodolfo. "Nuevos enfoques críticos con referencia a la obra de Galdós." *Cuadernos Hispanoamericanos*, nos. 250–52 (1970–1971): 58–72.

Carlyle, Thomas. *Los heroes: El culto de los héroes y lo heroico en la historia*. Translated by Julián G. Orbón. Madrid: Manuel Fernández y Lasanta, 1893.

———. *Sartor Resartus*. Oxford: Oxford World Classics, 2008.

Caro Baroja, Julio. *Introducción a una historia contemporánea del anticlericalismo español*. Madrid: Istmo, 1980.

Carr, Raymond. *Spain 1808–1975*. Oxford: Oxford University Press, 1993.

Casacuberta, Margarida. "Dues novel·les per a dues burgesies: Notes per a una comparació entre *La febre d'or* i *L'Argent*." In *El segle romàntic: Actes de Col·loqui Narcís Oller*, 197–209. Valls, Spain: Cossetània Edicions, 1999.

Casal-Valls, Laura. "La figura de la modista i els inicis de l'alta costura a Barcelona: Trajectòria professional i producció d'indumentària femenina (1880–1915)." PhD diss., Universitat de Barcelona, 2013.

Casanova, Pascale. *The World Republic of Letters*. Translated by M. B. Debevoise. Cambridge, MA: Harvard University Press, 2004.

"Los casinos en España y los clubs en Inglaterra." *La Época (Época Sport)*, June 2, 1891.

Cassany, Enric. "Pròleg." In *Memòries: Història de mos llibres i relacions literàries*, edited by Arnau Soler Pejoan and Enric Cassany, 9–26. Valls, Spain: Cossetània Edicions, 2014.

Castaño, Francisco, *Guía-manual del comercio y de la banca, o sea, Tratado completo teórico-*

práctico de operaciones mercantiles, cambios y arbitrajes, y de monedas, pesas y medidas nacionales y extranjeras. Madrid: Imprenta de la Viuda e Hija de Gómez Fuentenebro, 1886.

Castelar, Emilio. "Prologue." In *Los heroes: El culto de los héroes y lo heroico en la historia,* by Thomas Carlyle, translated by Julián G. Orbón, V–XVIII. Madrid: Manuel Fernández y Lasanta, 1893.

Caudet, Francisco. "*El doctor Centeno*: La educación sentimental de Galdós." In *Zola, Galdós, Clarín: El naturalismo en Francia y España,* edited by Francisco Caudet, 199–233. Madrid: Ediciones de la Universidad Autónoma de Madrid, 1995.

Chang, Julia. "Becoming Useless: Masculinity, Able-Bodiedness, and Empire in Nineteenth-Century Spain." In *Unsettling Colonialism: Gender and Race in the Nineteenth-Century Global Hispanic World,* edited by N. Michelle Murray and Akiko Tsuchiya, 173–202. Albany, NY: SUNY Press, 2019.

Charnon-Deutsch, Lou. "Between Agency and Determinism: A Critical Review of Clarín Studies." *Hispanic Review* 76, no. 2 (2008): 135–53.

———. "Gender and Beyond: Nineteenth-Century Spanish Women Writers." In *The Cambridge Companion to the Spanish Novel from 1600 to the Present,* edited by Harriet Turner and Adelaida López de Martínez, 122–37. Cambridge, UK: Cambridge University Press, 2003.

Clough, Patricia Ticineto. Introduction to *The Affective Turn: Theorizing the Social,* 1–33. Durham, NC: Duke University Press, 2007.

Coffey, Mary L. *Ghosts of Colonies Past and Present: Spanish Imperialism in the Fiction of Benito Pérez Galdós.* Liverpool: Liverpool University Press, 2020.

Coffey, Mary L., and Margot Versteeg. Introduction to *Imagined Truths: Realism in Modern Spanish Literature and Culture,* edited by Mary L. Coffey and Margot Versteeg, 3–35. Toronto: University of Toronto Press, 2019.

Connell, R. W. *Masculinities.* Berkeley: University of California Press, 1995.

Copeland, Eva María. "Empire, Nation and the *indiano* in Galdós's *Tormento* and *La loca de la casa.*" *Hispanic Review* 80, no. 2 (2012): 221–42.

Cruz, Jesús. *Gentlemen, Bourgeois, and Revolutionaries: Political Change and Cultural Persistence among the Spanish Dominant Groups 1750–1850.* Cambridge, UK: Cambridge University Press, 1996.

———. "'El hombre fino': Courtesy Books and Male Bourgeois Conduct in Nineteenth-Century Spain." *Bulletin of Hispanic Studies* 89, no. 4 (2012): 347–62.

———. *The Rise of Middle-Class Culture in Nineteenth-Century Spain.* Baton Rouge: Louisiana State University Press, 2011.

Cueto Asín, Elena. "Looking to France from Barcelona: Correspondence and Travel Writing in *La Vanguardia* (1890–1900)." *Journal of Hispanic Cultural Studies,* no. 9 (2008): 268–83.

———. "Santiago Rusiñol in Paris: The Travel/Tourist Writer." *Catalan Review,* no. 16 (2002): 89–101.

Dardé Moreno, Carlos. *Alfonso XII.* Madrid: Arlanza, 2001.

Darío, Rubén. *España contemporánea.* Madrid: Biblioteca Rubén Darío, 1900.

Davidson, Robert. "Barcelona: The Siege City." In *The Barcelona Reader: Cultural Readings of a City,* edited by Enric Bou and Jaume Subirana, 21–42. Liverpool: Liverpool University Press, 2017.

Davis, Kathleen E. "The 'Cosmorama' of Barcelona: Social Mobility in *La febre d'or*." *Catalan Review* 9, no. 1 (1995): 33–46.

———. "Family Inc.: Corporation and Kinship in *La febre d'or*." *Excavatio*, no. 12 (1999): 187–91.

Davis, Stacy. "'*Hacer las américas*' *es hacer al hombre*: (Re)constructing Spanish Masculinities in the Indianos of Benito Pérez Galdós and Emilia Pardo Bazán." PhD diss., Washington University in St. Louis, 2016.

Delgado, Elena, Pura Fernández, and Jo Labanyi. Introduction to *Engaging the Emotions in Spanish Culture and History*, edited by Elena Delgado, Pura Fernández, and Jo Labanyi, 1–20. Nashville, TN: Vanderbilt University Press, 2016.

Dendle, Brian. "Palacio Valdés's 'Un estudiante de Canarias': A Forgotten Article of 1883." *Anales Galdosianos*, no. 24 (1986): 97–101.

Díaz-Marcos, Ana María. *La edad de seda: Representaciones de la moda en la literatura española (1728-1926)*. Cádiz: Universidad de Cádiz, 2006.

Diccionario histórico de la lengua española. "Centón," accessed 8 September 2022, https://www.rae.es/dhle.

Domingo, Josep. "Pròleg." In *La febre d'or*, edited by Roger Roig, 9–29. Valls, Spain: Cossetània Edicions, 2013.

Dorca, Toni. "Al llindar del comparatisme: El regionalisme literari i la teoria de la novella en la crítica de Josep Yxart." In *Comparatistes sense comparatisme: La literatura comparada a Catalunya*, edited by Teresa Rosell and Antoni Martí, 29–46. Barcelona: Edicions de la Universitat de Barcelona, 2018.

———. "Illustrating Pereda: Picturesque Costumbrismo in *El sabor de la tierruca*." *Arizona Journal of Hispanic Cultural Studies*, no. 6 (2002): 97–114.

———. "*Pedro Sánchez*, entre episodio nacional y episodio personal." *Boletín de la Biblioteca de Menéndez Pelayo*, no. 82 (2006): 61–81.

———. "Pereda and the Closure of the 'Roman à Thèse': From *Don Gonzalo González de la Gonzalera* to *Peñas arriba*." *Hispanic Review* 70, no. 3 (2002): 355–72.

———. "The Town and the City in the Narrative of Narcís Oller." *Catalan Review* 15, no. 2 (2001): 61–77.

Dupont, Denise. "Masculinity, Femininity, Solidarity: Emilia Pardo Bazán's Construction of Madame de Staël and George Sand." *Comparative Literature Studies* 40, no. 4 (2003): 372–93.

———. *Whole Faith: The Catholic Ideal of Emilia Pardo Bazán*. Washington, DC: Catholic University of America Press, 2018.

Dwyer-McNulty, Sally. *Common Threads: A Cultural History of Clothing in American Catholicism*. Chapel Hill: University of North Carolina Press, 2014.

Eça de Queirós, Jose María de. *The Crime of Father Amaro*. Translated by Margaret Jull Costa. New York: New Directions, 2003.

———. *The Maias*. Translated by Margaret Jull Costa. New York: New Directions, 2007.

Entwistle, Joanne. *The Fashioned Body: Fashion, Dress and Modern Social Theory*. Cambridge, UK: Polity, 2015.

Erwin, Zachary. "Fantasies of Masculinity in Emilia Pardo Bazán's *Memorias de un solterón*." *Revista de Estudios Hispánicos* 46, no. 3 (2012): 547–68.

Farràs, Andreu. *Els Güell*. Barcelona: La Butxaca, 2017.

Felski, Rita. *The Gender of Modernity*. Cambridge, MA: Harvard University Press, 1995.

"El Flaco," M. F. "Las Américas." *Periódico para Todos*, January 5, 1875.

Fernández Medina, Nicolás. *Life Embodied: The Promise of Vital Force in Spanish Modernity*. Montreal: McGill-Queen's University Press, 2018.

Fernández Sirvent, Rafael. "Biografía de Alfonso XII de Borbón (1875–1885)." Biblioteca Virtual de Miguel de Cervantes, accessed December 15, 2021. http://www.cervantesvirtual.com/portales/reyes_y_reinas_espana_contemporanea/alfonso_xii_biografia.

Ferrer-Alòs, Llorenç. "¿Quién hereda?: Desigualdades de género en el acceso a los derechos de propiedad y sistemas hereditarios en España." *AREAS: Revista Internacional de Ciencias Sociales*, no. 33 (2014): 35–47.

Ferrer del Río, Antonio. "El indiano." In *Los españoles pintados por sí mismos*, 37–46. Madrid: I. Boix, 1843–44.

Flaubert, Gustave. *Madame Bovary*, edited by Thierry Laget. Paris: Éditions Gallimard, 2001.

Fradera, Josep M. "La figura del negre i del negrer en la literatura catalana del XIX." *L'Avenç*, no. 75 (1984): 56–61.

———. *The Imperial Nation: Citizens and Subjects in the British, French, Spanish, and American Empires*. Translated by Ruth MacKay. Princeton, NJ: Princeton University Press, 2018.

Franklin, J. Jeffrey. *Serious Play: The Cultural Form of the Nineteenth-Century Realist Novel*. Philadelphia: University of Pennsylvania Press, 1999.

Frontaura, Carlos. *Barcelona en 1888 y París en 1889*. Madrid: P. Aguilar, 1899.

Fuente, Vicente de la. "El estudiante." In *Los españoles pintados por sí mismos*, 2 vols., 225–37. Madrid: I. Boix, 1843–44.

Gabriel, Narciso de. "Alfabetización, semialfabetización y analfabetismo en España (1860–1991)." *Revista Complutense de Eduación* 8, no. 7 (1997): 199–231.

García Álvarez, Luis Benito. "Moda masculina y distinción social: El ejemplo de Asturias desde la Restauración hasta la Segunda República." *Vínculos de Historia*, no. 6 (2017): 153–70.

Gautier, Théophile. *Wanderings in Spain*. London: Ingram, Cooke, and Co., 1853.

George, David. "'Playing Japanese' in *Fin-de-siècle* Zarzuela." In *Intersections of Race, Class, Gender, and Nation in Fin-de-siècle Spanish Literature and Culture*, edited by Jennifer Smith and Lisa Nalbone, 123–48. New York: Routledge, 2017.

———. "Reterritorialization and Peninsular Space in Eça de Queirós's *A cidade e as serras* and Pereda's *Peñas arriba*." *Hispanófila*, no. 140 (2004): pp. 139–48.

Gifra i Adroher, Pere. "Gil Foix i Silas Lapham: El petitburgès vist per Narcís Oller i William Dean Howells." *Catalan Review* 5, no. 2 (1991): 55–63.

Gikandi, Simon. *Slavery and the Culture of Taste*. Princeton, NJ: Princeton University Press, 2011.

Gilabert, Joan J. "El mito burgués y la literatura catalana de fin de siglo." In *Mythopoesis, literatura, totalidad, ideología: Ofrecido a Joseph J. Duggan por su distinguida aportación a los estudios literarios*. Edited by Joan Ramon Resina, 167–78, Barcelona: Anthropos, 1992.

Gilman, Stephen. *Galdós and the Art of the European Novel. 1867–1887*. Princeton, NJ: Princeton University Press, 1981.

Ginsburg, Madeleine. "Rags to Riches: The Second-Hand Clothes Trade 1700–1978." *Costume* 14, no. 1 (1980): 121–35.

Goethe, Johann Wolfgang von. *The Collected Works: Vol. 9. Wilhelm Meister's Apprenticeship.* Edited and translated by Eric A. Blackall. Princeton, NJ: Princeton University Press, 1989.

Gold, Hazel. "Looking for the Doctor in the House: Critical Expectations and Novelistic Structure in Galdós's *El doctor Centeno*." *Philological Quarterly*, no. 68 (1989): 219–40.

———. *The Reframing of Realism: Galdós and the Discourses of the Nineteenth-Century Spanish Novel.* Durham, NC: Duke University Press, 1993.

Gómez Castellano, Irene. *La cultura de las máscaras: Disfraces y escapismo en la poesía española de la Ilustración.* Madrid: Iberoamericana, 2013.

Gómez-Martínez, José Luis. "Galdós y el Krausismo español." *Nueva Revista de Filología Hispánica* 32, no. 1 (1983): 55–79.

Gómez Palomo, Alejandro. *Palomo Spain.* Barcelona: Grijalbo, 2019.

Grandes Almacenes de El Siglo. Propaganda Comercial. Grans Magatzems, B10.1-C51. Arxiù Històric de la Ciutat de Barcelona, Barcelona, Spain. Accessed July 3, 2019.

Greenblatt, Stephen. *Renaissance Self-Fashioning: From More to Shakespeare.* Chicago: University of Chicago Press, 2005.

Güell y López, Eusebio. *Perspectivas de la vida.* Madrid: Compañía Ibero-americana de Publicaciones, 1930.

Guerra de la Vega, Ramón. *Guía de Madrid: S. XIX.* 2 vols. Madrid: Guerra de la Vega, 1993.

Gullón, Germán. "Unidad de *El doctor Centeno*." *Cuadernos Hispanoamericanos*, nos. 250–52 (1971): 579–89.

Guroff, Gregory. "A Note on Urban Literacy in Russia, 1890–1914." *Jahrbücher für Geschichte Osteuropas Neue Folge* 19, no. 4 (1971): 520–31.

Gutiérrez-Poch, Miquel. "Is There a Southern European Model?: Development of the Pulp and Paper Industry in Italy, Spain, and Portugal (1800–2010)." In *The Evolution of Global Paper Industry 1800–2050: A Comparative Analysis,* edited by Juha-Antti Lamberg, Jari Ojala, Mirva Peltoniemi, and Timo Särkkä, 211–42. London: Springer, 2012.

Gutiérrez Sebastián, Raquel. "José María de Pereda y la construcción de una imagen." *Ínsula: Revista de letras y ciencias humanas,* no. 772 (2011): 13–15.

Gutkin, Len. *Dandyism: Forming Fiction from Modernism to the Present.* Charlottesville: University of Virginia Press, 2020.

Haidt, Rebecca. *Embodying Enlightenment: Knowing the Body in Eighteenth-Century Spanish Literature and Culture.* New York: Saint Martin's Press, 1998.

———. *Women, Work, and Clothing in Eighteenth-Century Spain.* Oxford: Voltaire Foundation / University of Oxford Press, 2011.

Haliczer, Stephen. *Sexuality in the Confessional: A Sacrament Profaned.* Oxford: Oxford University Press, 1996.

Hammarén, Nils, and Thomas Johansson. "Homosociality: In between Power and Intimacy." *SAGE Open* 1, no. 11 (2014): 1–11.

Harden, Faith. *Arms and Letters: Military Life Writing in Early Modern Spain.* Toronto: University of Toronto Press, 2020.

Hardy, Thomas. *Far from the Madding Crowd*. Oxford: Oxford University Press, 2002.

Harpring, Mark. "The Bachelor at the Crossroads of Gender and Class in the Late Nineteenth-Century Spanish Novel." PhD diss., University of Kansas, 2005.

Harvey, John. *Men in Black*. Chicago: University of Chicago Press, 1995.

Hauser, Philip. *Madrid bajo el punto de vista médico-social: Su policía sanitaria, su climatología, su suelo y sus aguas, sus condiciones sanitarias, su demografía, su morbicidad y su mortalidad*. Madrid: Est. Tipográfico "Sucesores de Rivadeneyra" / Impresores de la Real Casa, 1902.

Heffernan, Michael J. "Literacy and the Life-Cycle in Nineteenth-Century Provincial France: Some Evidence from the *Département* of Ille-et-Vilaine." *Journal of the History of Education Society* 21, no. 2 (1992): 149–59.

Heneghan, Dorota. *Striking Their Modern Pose: Fashion, Gender, and Modernity in Galdós, Pardo Bazán, and Picón*. West Lafayette, IN: Purdue University Press, 2015.

Hoddie, James H. "Reexamen de un enigmático texto galdosiano: *El doctor Centeno*." *Cuadernos Hispanoamericanos*, no. 521 (1993): 47–70.

Hooper, Kirsty. "Reading Spain's 'African Vocation': The Figure of the Moorish Priest in Three *Fin de Siglo* Novels (1890–1907)." *Revista de Estudios Hispánicos* 40, no. 1 (2006): 171–95.

Houpt, Stefan O., and Juan Carlos Rojo Cagigal. "The Origins of the Bilbao Stock Exchange, 1891–1936." *Working Papers in Economic History* 10, no. 5 (2010): 1–33.

Howells, William Dean. *The Rise of Silas Lapham*. New York: Penguin, 1986.

Hume, Lynne. *The Religious Life of Dress*. London: Bloomsbury, 2013.

Iarocci, Michael. "On the Ideology of Metaphor in Pereda's *Peñas arriba*." *Revista Hispánica Moderna* 51, no. 2 (1998): 236–56.

Iglesias-Villamel, Elena. "Masculinidades y representación en la novela de la Restauración." PhD diss., University of Wisconsin, 2011.

Jagoe, Catherine, Alda Blanco, and Cristina Enríquez de Salamanca. *La mujer en los discursos de género: Textos y contextos en el siglo XIX*. Barcelona: Icaria Editorial, 1998.

Jameson, Frederick. *The Antinomies of Realism*. London: Verso, 2013.

Johnstone, Pauline. *High Fashion in the Church*. Leeds: Maney Publishing, 2002.

Jolly Bill. "Hipòdrom de Barcelona: Carreras de 1883." *La Ilustració Catalana*, September 30, 1883.

Jutglar, Antoni. *Els burgesos Catalans: Història crítica de la burgesia a Catalunya*. Barcelona: Dopesa, 1972.

Kaiura, Leslie. "Fernán Caballero's Lessons for Ladies: Female Agency and the Modeling of Proper Womanhood in *Clemencia*." *Decimonónica* 9, no. 1 (2012): 17–33.

Klibbe, Lawrence Hadfield. *José María de Pereda*. New York: Twayne, 1975.

Krauel, Javier. *Imperial Emotions: Cultural Responses to Myths of Empire in Fin-de-Siècle Spain*. Liverpool: Liverpool University Press, 2013.

Krauel, Ricardo. *Voces desde el silencio: Heterologías genérico-sexuales en la narrativa española moderna, 1875–1975*. Madrid: Ediciones Libertarias, 2001.

Kronik, John W. "Leopoldo Alas, Krausism, and the Plight of the Humanities in Spain." *Modern Language Studies* 11, no. 3 (1981): 3–15.

Labanyi, Jo. "City, Country and Adultery in *La Regenta.*" *Bulletin of Hispanic Studies* 63, no. 1 (1986): 53–66.

———. "Doing Things: Emotion, Affect, and Materiality." *Journal of Spanish Cultural Studies* 11, nos. 3–4 (2010): 223–33.

———. *Gender and Modernization in the Spanish Realist Novel.* Oxford: Oxford University Press, 2000.

———. *Spanish Culture from Romanticism to the Present: Structures of Feeling.* Cambridge, UK: Legenda, 2019.

Lafarga, Francisco. "Sobre traductoras españolas del siglo XIX." In *Lectora, heroína, autora (La mujer en la literatura española del siglo XIX): III Coloquio de la Sociedad de Literatura Española del Siglo XIX (Barcelona, 23–25 de octubre de 2002),* edited by V. Trueba, E. Rubio, P. Miret, L. F. Díaz Larios, J. F. Botrel and L. Bonet, 185–94. Barcelona: Universitat de Barcelona, 2005.

Lafuente, Modesto. *Teatro social del siglo XIX.* Madrid: P. Mellado, 1846.

Lannon, Frances. *Privilege, Persecution, and Prophecy: The Catholic Church in Spain, 1875–1975.* Oxford: Clarendon Press, 1987.

Lauster, Martina. *Sketches of the Nineteenth Century: European Journalism and Its Physiologies, 1830–50.* London: Palgrave Macmillan, 2007.

Le Bouill, Jean. "El propietario ilustrado o patriarca en la obra de Pereda." In *La cuestión agraria en la España contemporánea: VI Coloquio del Seminario de Estudios de los siglos XIX y XX,* edited by José Luis García Delgado, 311–28. Madrid: Edicusa, 1976.

Lissorgues, Yvan. *Leopoldo Alas, Clarín, en sus palabras (1852–1901).* Oviedo, Spain: Ediciones Nobel, 2007.

Lloyd, Amy J. "Education, Literacy and the Reading Public." In *British Library Newspapers.* Detroit: Gale, 2007.

López Bago, Eduardo. *El Cura (Caso de incesto): Novela médico-social,* edited by Maite Zubiaurre and Luis Cuesta. Miami: Stockcero, 2013.

López, Ignacio Javier. *La novela ideológica (1875–1880).* Madrid: Ediciones de la Torre, 2014.

López, Juan. "El hongo y la cazadora." *La Moda de Madrid,* no. 1, April 1884, 11–12.

Lukács, Georg. *The Theory of the Novel.* Translated by Anna Bostock. Cambridge, MA: MIT Press, 1971.

Lyons, Martyn. *Readers and Society in Nineteenth-Century France: Workers, Women, Peasants.* London: Palgrave Macmillan, 2001.

Machado, Antonio. "Memory from Childhood." In *Times Alone: Selected Poems of Antonio Machado,* translated by Robert Bly, 19. Middletown, CT: Wesleyan University Press, 1983.

Madariaga de la Campa, Benito. *Pereda: Biografía de un novelista.* Santander, Spain: Ediciones de Librería Estudio, 1991.

Mainer, José-Carlos. Introduction to *El Doctor Centeno,* edited by José-Carlos Mainer, 7–56. Madrid: Editorial Biblioteca Nueva, 2002.

Mandrell, James. "Estudios gay y lesbianos: La revelación de un cuerpo masculino: Una mirada gay." In *El hispanismo en los Estados Unidos: Discursos críticos / prácticas textuales,* edited by José M. del Pino and Francisco LaRubia-Prado, 211–30. Madrid: Visor, 1999.

Martí-López, Elisa. "Death and the Crisis of Representation in Narcís Oller's *La febre d'or* and Pérez Galdós's *La de Bringas.*" *The Routledge Companion to Iberian Studies*, edited by Javier Muñoz-Basols, Manual Delgado Morales, and Laura Lonsdale, 357–67. New York: Routledge, 2017.

Martí-López, Elisa, and Mario Santana. "Spain 1843–1900." In *The Novel*, vol. 3, edited by Franco Moretti, 479–94. Princeton, NJ: Princeton University Press, 2007.

Martínez López, David. "Sobre familias, élites y herencias en el siglo XIX." *Historia Contemporánea*, no. 31 (2005): 457–80.

Matthews David, Alison. "Decorated Men: Fashioning the French Soldier, 1852–1914." *Fashion Theory* 7, no. 1 (2003): 3–38.

Maupassant, Guy de. *Pierre et Jean*, edited by Bernard Pingaud. Paris: Éditions Gallimard, 1982.

McClintock, Anne. *Imperial Leather: Race, Gender, and Sexuality in the Colonial Context.* New York: Routledge, 1995.

McKinney, Collin. "Enemigos de la virilidad: Sex, Masturbation, and Celibacy in Nineteenth-Century Spain." *Prisma Social: Revista de Investigación Social* 13 (2014–2015): 72–108.

———. "How to Be a Man." In *Spain in the Nineteenth Century: New Essays on Experiences of Culture and Society*, edited by Andrew Ginger and Geraldine Lawless, 147–73. Manchester: Manchester University Press, 2018.

———. "'Jugamos a la guerra': Boys, Toys, and Military Masculinity in Galdós's *La desheredada.*" *Revista Canadiense de Estudios Hispánicos* 44, no. 2 (2020): 415–36.

———. *Mapping the Social Body: Urbanization, the Gaze, and the Novels of Galdós.* Chapel Hill: University of North Carolina Press, 2010.

———. "Men in Black: Fashioning Masculinity in Nineteenth-Century Spain." *Letras Hispanas* 8, no. 2 (2012): 78–93.

———. "Pogonology, Physiognomy, and the Face of Spanish Masculinity." In *Modernity and Epistemology in Nineteenth-Century Spain: Fringe Discourses*, edited by Ryan A. Davis and Alicia Cerezo Paredes, 61–87. Lanham, MD: Lexington Books, 2017.

McNeil, Peter, Vicki Karaminas, and Cathy Cole. Introduction to *Fashion in Fiction: Text and Clothing in Literature, Film and Television*, edited by Peter McNeil, Vicki Karaminas, and Cathy Cole, 1–8. Oxford: Berg, 2009.

"Memoria esplicativa: Reseña histórica." In *Concurso Nacional Libre: Monumento a Cristóbal Colón, Proyecto del arquitecto D. C. Buigas Monrabá*, 9–31. Barcelona: Talleres de la Renaixensa, 1882.

Menéndez y Pelayo, Marcelino. "Contestación del Excmo: Señor D. Marcelino Menéndez y Pelayo." In *Discursos leídos ante la Real Academia Española en la recepción pública del Sr. D. Benito Pérez Galdós, el domingo 7 de febrero de 1897*, 19–51. Madrid: Impresor de Cámara de S. M., 1897.

Mercer, Leigh. *Urbanism and Urbanity: The Spanish Bourgeois Novel and Contemporary Customs (1845–1925).* Lewisburg, PA: Bucknell University Press, 2013.

Mesonero Romanos, Ramón de. *El antiguo Madrid: Paseos históricos-anecdóticos por las calles y casas de esta villa.* Madrid: Establecimiento Tipográfico de F. de Mellado, 1861.

Miller, Gabrielle. "Contextualizing Prostitution in Benito Pérez Galdós's *La desheredada*

(1881)." *Romance Notes* 58, no. 3 (2018): 403–14.

———. "Disrupting Nineteenth-Century Dichotomies of Gender: Reading and Imagination in Emilia Pardo Bazán's *La Madre Naturaleza*." *Hispanic Review* 83, no. 3 (2015): 317–36.

———. *"¡Mi hijo es mío, puñales!*: Excessive Paternal Devotion in Benito Pérez Galdós's *Torquemada* Novels." *Decimonónica* 17, no. 2 (2020): 65–80.

Mínguez-Blasco, Raúl. "Between Virgins and Priests: The Feminisation of Catholicism and Priestly Masculinity in Nineteenth-Century Spain." *Gender and History* 33, no. 1 (2021): 94–110.

Miranda García, Soledad. *Pluma y altar en el XIX: De Galdós al cura Sta. Cruz*. Madrid: Pegaso, 1983.

Montesinos, José F. *Galdós*. 3 vols. Madrid: Castalia, 1969.

Montoliu, Manuel de. *José Yxart: El gran crítico del renacimiento literario catalán*. Tarragona: Diputación Provincial de Tarragona, 1956.

Moreno Castillo, Gloria. "La unidad de tema en *El doctor Centeno*." In *Actas del Primer Congreso Internacional de Estudios Galdosianos*, 382–96. Las Palmas: Cabildo Insular de Gran Canaria, 1977.

Moretti, Franco. *The Bourgeois: Between History and Literature*. New York: Verso, 2014.

———. *The Way of the World: The Bildungsroman in European Culture*, translated by Albert Spragia. New York: Verso, 2000.

Mosse, George L. *The Image of Man: The Creation of Modern Masculinity*. Oxford: Oxford University Press, 1996.

———. *Nationalism and Sexuality: Middle-Class Morality and Sexual Norms in Modern Europe*. Madison: University of Wisconsin Press, 1985.

Mundi Pedret, Francisco. "Los estamentos eclesiásticos en tiempo de Clarín." In *Clarín y La Regenta en su tiempo: Actas del simposio internacional*, 707–22. Oviedo: Universidad de Oviedo, Servicio de Publicaciones, 1987.

Muñoz-Muriana, Sara. *"Andando se hace el camino": Calle y subjetividades marginales en la España del siglo XIX*. Madrid: Iberoamericana, 2017.

———. "Dime qué llevas y te diré quién eres: Vestido e identidad social en la literatura peninsular del XIX." *Monographic Review / Revista Monográfica*, no. 25 (2009): 71–88.

Murray, N. Michelle, and Akiko Tsuchiya. Introduction to *Unsettling Colonialism: Gender and Race in the Nineteenth-Century Global Hispanic World*, edited by N. Michelle Murray and Akiko Tsuchiya, 1–16. Albany, NY: SUNY Press, 2019.

Nalbone, Lisa. "La mirada masculina en *Tristana*." In *La hora de Galdós: Actas*, edited by Yolanda Arencibia, Germán Gullón, et al., 193–200. Las Palmas: Cabildo de Gran Canaria, 2018.

Navarro Villoslada, Francisco. "El canónigo." In *Los españoles pintados por sí mismos*, 177–81. Madrid: Gaspar y Roig, 1851.

Neal, Derek. "What Can Historians Do with Clerical Masculinity?" In *Negotiating Clerical Identities: Priests, Monks and Masculinity in the Middle Ages*, edited by Jennifer Thibodeaux, 16–36. Basingstoke: Palgrave Macmillan, 2010.

Nieto Sánchez, José A. *Historia del Rastro: Los orígenes del mercado popular de Madrid, 1740–1905*. Madrid: Editorial Visión Libros, 2004.

"Nuestro Grabado." *El Globo*, April 2, 1878.

"Nuestro Grabado." *El Globo*, September 13, 1883.

Oller, Narcís. *L'Escanyapobres*. Edited by Toni Sala. Barcelona: Edicions 62, 2008.

———. *La febre d'or*. Barcelona: Edicions 62, 2012.

———. *La mariposa: El chico del panadero – El trasplantado – Recuerdos de niño – Angustia – Una visita – El bofetón – Mi jardín – La peor pobreza*. Translated by Felipe B. Navarro. Barcelona: Biblioteca 'Arte y Letras,' 1886.

———. *Memòries: Història de mos llibres i relacions literàries*. Edited by Arnau Soler Pejoan and Enric Cassany. Valls, Spain: Cossetània Edicions, 2014.

———. *Vilaniu*. Edited by Roger Roig César. Valls, Spain: Cossetània Edicions, 2008.

Oropesa Márquez, Salvador. *Literatura y comercio en España: Las tiendas (1868–1952)*. Málaga: Universidad de Málaga, 2014.

Outes-León, Brais. "'El Crisóstomo vetustense': Fermín de Pas, el poder de la palabra y la dimensión ética del lenguaje en *La Regenta*." *Bulletin of Spanish Studies*, 87, no. 5 (2010): 595–611.

Palau, Melchor de. "Acontecimientos Literarios: 1895, *Peñas arriba*." *Revista Contemporánea*, no. 97, January 1895, 501–10.

Palacio Valdés, Armando. "Discurso del Excmo. Sr. Dr. Armando Palacio Valdés." In *Discursos leídos ante la Real Academia Española en la recepción pública del Excmo. Sr. D. Armando Palacio Valdés, el día 12 de diciembre de 1920*, 5–54. Madrid: Imprenta de los Hijos de M. G. Hernández, 1920.

Pardo Bazán, Emilia. *La cuestión palpitante*. Edited by Rosa de Diego. Madrid: Biblioteca Nueva, 1998.

———. *"Miquiño mío": Cartas a Galdós*. Edited by Isabel Parreño and Juan Manuel Hernández. Madrid: Turner, 2013.

———. *La revolución y la novela en Rusia (Lecturas en el Ateneo de Madrid)*. Madrid: Imprenta y Fundición de M. Tello, 1887.

———. "La vida contemporánea." *Ilustración Artística*, no. 847, March 12, 1898.

"Parte política." *La Época*, November 28, 1875.

Pasalodos-Salgado, Mercedes. "Algunas consideraciones sobre la moda durante la *Belle Époque*." *Indumenta* 00 (2007): 107–12.

———. "Ir de compras por Madrid: Los grandes almacenes y sus catálogos ilustrados." *Datatèxtil*, no. 27 (2012): 6–21.

———. *De la geometría a los pespuntes: Tratados, manuales y sistemas de corte y confección en la BNE*. Madrid: Biblioteca Nacional de España, 2015.

Pattison, Walter T. "Verdaguer y Nazarín." *Cuadernos Hispanoamericanos*, nos. 250–252 (1970–71): 537–45.

Pena González, Pablo. "Indumentaria en España: El período isabelino (1830–1868)." *Indumenta* 00 (2007): 95–106.

———. *El traje en el Romanticismo y su poryección en España, 1828–1868*. Madrid: Ministerio de Cultura, 2008.

Penrose, Mehl. *Masculinity and Queer Desire in Eighteenth-Century Spanish Literature and Culture*. Farnham, UK: Ashgate, 2014.

Pereda, José María de. "A las Indias." *Escenas montañesas*. Biblioteca Virtual de Miguel de Cervantes, https://www.cervantesvirtual.com/obra/escenas-montanesas-coleccion-de-bosquejos-de-costumbres-tomados-al-natural--0. Accessed December 15, 2021.

———. "Discurso del Sr. D. José María de Pereda." *Discursos leídos ante la Real Academia Española en la recepción pública del Sr. D. José María de Pereda, el domingo 21 de febrero de 1897*, 5–28. Madrid: Viuda e Hijos de Tello, 1897.

———. *Pedro Sánchez*. 2 vols. Edited by José María de Cossío. Madrid: Espasa-Calpe, 1958.

———. *Peñas arriba*. Edited by Antonio Rey. Madrid: Cátedra, 2011.

———. *El sabor de la tierruca*. Barcelona: Biblioteca 'Arte y Letras,' 1882.

Pereira Muro, Carmen. *Género, nación, y literatura: Emilia Pardo Bazán en la literatura gallega y española*. West Lafayette, IN: Purdue University Press, 2013.

Pérez de Andrés, Carmen. "Una visión global sobre aspectos de conservación, restauración y montaje." *Indumenta* 00 (2007): 23–31.

Pérez Galdós, Benito. *La desheredada*. Edited by Germán Gullón. Madrid: Cátedra, 1999.

———. "Discurso del Sr. D. Benito Pérez Galdós." In *Discursos leídos ante la Real Academia Española en la recepción pública del Sr. D. Benito Pérez Galdós, el domingo 7 de febrero de 1897*, 5–16. Madrid: Impresor de Cámara de S. M., 1897.

———. *El Doctor Centeno*. Madrid: Alianza Editorial, 2012.

———. *La de San Quintín; Electra*. Edited by Luis F. Díaz Larios. Madrid: Cátedra, 2002.

———. "El elegante." In *Fisonomías sociales: Obras inéditas*, vol. 1, 231–42. Madrid: Renacimiento, 1923.

———. *La familia de León Roch*. Madrid: Imprenta y Litografía de La Guirnalda, 1878.

———. *Marianela*. Madrid: Mestas Ediciones, 2001.

———. *Memorias de un desmemoriado*. Valencia: El Nadir, 2012.

———. *Mendizábal*. Madrid: Alianza Editorial, 2010.

———. *Misericordia*. Edited by Luciano García Lorenzo. Madrid: Cátedra, 2006.

———. *Las novelas de Torquemada*. Madrid: Alianza Editorial, 2004.

———. *Lo prohibido*. Edited by James Whiston. Madrid: Cátedra, 2001.

———. "Observaciones sobre la novela contemporánea en España." In *Ensayos de crítica literaria*, edited by Laureano Bonet, 115–32. Barcelona: Península, 1999.

———. "Prólogo." In *La Regenta*, by Leopoldo Alas, 2 vols. Edited by Gonzalo Sobejano, 79–92. Madrid: Clásicos Castalia, 1981.

———. "La sociedad presente como materia novelable." Madrid: Est. Tipografía de la Viuda e Hijos de Tello, 1897.

———. *Tormento*. Madrid: Alianza Editorial, 2012.

Pérez Gutiérrez, Francisco. "¿Por qué *Pedro Sánchez*? (La salida de Pereda hacia dentro)." In *Nueve lecciones sobre Pereda*, edited by J. M. González Herrán and Benito Madariaga, 91–118. Santander: Instituto Cultural de Cantabria, 1985.

Pérez Vidal, José. "Las pensiones madrileñas del estudiante Benito Pérez Galdós (años de aprendizaje)." In *Philologica hispaniensia: In honorem Manuel Alvar*, 323–36. Barcelona: Gredos, 1983.

Pinós Guirao, Gabriel. "De *sportsman* a *motorman* (parte I): Descripción detallada de los vehículos de dos ruedas de Ramon Casas." In *Ramon Casas: Catálogo Completo, vol. I*, edited by Gabriel Pinós Guirao, 127–45. Barcelona: Gothsland, 2018.

Pointon, Marcia. "Enduring Characteristics and Unstable Hues: Men in Black in French Painting in the 1860s and 1870s." *Art History* 40, no. 4 (2017): 744–69.

Pope, Randolph. "Cambio, progreso y transformación: Releyendo *Doña Perfecta* de Galdós." *Anales de la Literatura Española Contemporánea* 38, no. 1–2 (2013): 277–92.

Prado y Sánchez, Manuel. "Revista de modas." *El Arte Español*, no. 8, September 1, 1871.

Pratt, Mary Louise. *Imperial Eyes: Travel Writing and Transculturation*. New York: Routledge, 2008.

Proulx, François. *Victims of the Book: Reading and Masculinity in Fin-de-Siècle France*. Toronto: University of Toronto Press, 2019.

Ramírez López, Marco A. "*El doctor Centeno* de Benito Pérez Galdós: Aspectos autobiográficos." *Fuentes Humanísticas* 28, no. 54 (2017): 157–71.

Ramón y Cajal, Santiago. *Recuerdos de mi vida*. Edited by Juan Fernández Santarén. Barcelona: Editorial Crítica, 2006.

Ramos Pérez, Rosario. *Ephemera: La vida sobre papel*. Madrid: Biblioteca Nacional / Ministerio de Educación, Cultura, y Deporte, 2003.

Reeser, Todd. *Masculinities in Theory: An Introduction*. Oxford: Wiley-Blackwell, 2010.

Reeser, Todd, and Lucas Gottzén. "Masculinity and Affect: New Possibilities, New Agendas." *NORMA: International Journal for Masculinity Studies* 13, no. 3–4 (2018): 145–57.

Rementería y Fica, José. *El hombre fino al gusto del día, Manual completo de urbanidad, cortesía y buen tono, con las reglas, aplicaciones y ejemplos del Arte de presentarse y conducirse en toda clase de reuniones, visitas, etc.; en el que se enseña la etiqueta y ceremonial que la sensatez y la costumbre han establecido; con la Guía del tocador y un tratado del Arte cisoria*. Translated by Don Mariano de Rementería y Fica. Madrid: Imprenta del Colegio de Sordo-Mudos, 1837.

Resina, Joan Ramon. *Barcelona's Vocation of Modernity: Rise and Decline of an Urban Image*. Stanford, CA: Stanford University Press, 2008.

Reyero, Carlos. *Apariencia e identidad masculine: De la ilustración al decadentismo*. Madrid: Cátedra, 1999.

Ridao Carlini, Inma. *Rich and Poor in Nineteenth-Century Spain: A Critique of Liberal Society in the Late Novels of Benito Pérez Galdós*. Suffolk, UK: Boydell & Brewer, 2018.

Ringrose, David. *Spain, Europe, and the 'Spanish Miracle,' 1700–1900*. Cambridge: Cambridge University Press, 1998.

Ríos-Font, Wadda. *The Canon and the Archive: Configuring Literature in Modern Spain*. Lewisburg, PA: Bucknell University Press, 2004.

———. "'How Do I Love Thee': The Rhetoric of Patriotic Love in Early Puerto Rican Political Discourse." In *Engaging the Emotions in Spanish Culture and History*, edited by Luisa Elena Delgado, Pura Fernández, and Jo Labanyi, 39–55. Nashville, TN: Vanderbilt University Press, 2016.

———. *Rewriting Melodrama: The Hidden Paradigm in Modern Spanish Theater*. Lewisburg, PA: Bucknell University Press, 1997.

Roig César, Roger, ed. *Àlbum Narcís Oller*. Valls, Spain: Cossetània Edicions, 2010.

Rodríguez-Galindo, Vanesa. *Madrid on the Move: Feeling Modern and Visually Aware in the Nineteenth Century*. Manchester: Manchester University Press, 2021.

Sanabria, Enrique A. *Republicanism and Anticlerical Nationalism in Spain*. London: Palgrave Macmillan, 2009.

Santiáñez-Tió, Nil. "La dimensión intertextual en *Pedro Sánchez* (Notas sobre la fortuna literaria de Balzac y Hugo en España)." *Romanische Forschungen* 107, no. 3 (1995): 343–67.

San Martín, Antonio de. "La pantalla de velón." *El Periódico para Todos*, January 16, 1875.

Sawa, Alejandro. *Criadero de curas*. Edited by Andreu Navarra Ordoño. Madrid: Libros de la Ballena, 2014.

Scanlon, Geraldine M. "*El doctor Centeno*: A Study in Obsolescent Values." *Bulletin of Hispanic Studies*, no. 55 (1978): 245–53.

———. "Problemas sociales y Krausismo en *Marianela*." In *Actas del Tercer Congreso Internacional de Estudios Galdosianos*, vol. 1, 81–95. Las Palmas: Cabildo Insular de Gran Canaria, 1990.

Schmidt-Nowara, Christopher. *The Conquest of History: Spanish Colonialism and National Histories in the Nineteenth Century*. Pittsburgh. PA: University of Pittsburgh Press, 2006.

Schnepf, Michael. "A Different View of Isidora Rufete as the Symbol of Spain and a Brief Comment on Reader Sympathy." *Romance Notes* 40, no. 3 (2000): 325–33.

Sedgwick, Eve Kosofsky. *Between Men: English Literature and Male Homosocial Desire*. New York: Columbia University Press, 1985.

Shields, David. *Civil Tongues and Polite Letters in British America*. Chapel Hill: Omohundro Institute and University of North Carolina Press, 1997.

Shields Jenkins, Melissa. *Fatherhood, Authority, and British Reading Culture*. New York: Routledge, 2014.

Shoemaker, William H. "Una amistad literaria: La correspondencia epistolar entre Galdós y Narciso Oller." *Boletín de la Real Academia de Buenas Letras*, no. 30 (1963–1964): 247–306.

———. *The Novelistic Art of Galdós*, vol. 2. Valencia: Albatros Hispanófila, 1980.

Shubert, Adrian. *A Social History of Modern Spain*. New York: Routledge, 1990.

Sierra, Sara. "The Anthropological Effect: Cultural Hierarchies and Nationalization in Pérez Galdós' *Doña Perfecta* and Pereda's *De Tal Palo, Tal Astilla*." *Neophilologus*, no. 95 (2011): 565–77.

———. "Time and the Environment: 'Slow Violence' in Benito Pérez Galdós's *Doña Perfecta* and *Marianela*." *Confluencia: Revista Hispánica de Cultura y Literatura* 35, no. 1 (2019): 41–56.

El Siglo: Órgano de los grandes almacenes de este título. Hemeroteca. R 1884 8 Varia III. Arxiu Històric de la Ciutat de Barcelona, Barcelona, Spain. Accessed July 3, 2019.

Sinclair, Alison. "Masculine Envy and Desire in *La Regenta*: The Skull and the Foot." *Tesserae* 1, no. 2 (1995): 171–90.

———. "The Regional Novel: Evolution and Consolation." In *The Cambridge Companion to the Spanish Novel from 1600 to the Present*, edited by Harriet Turner and Adelaida López de Martínez, 49–64. Cambridge: Cambridge University Press, 2003.

Smith, Jennifer. "Cultural Capital and Social Class in Emilia Pardo Bazán's 'La mujer española' and *Insolación*." *Anales de la Literatura Española Contemporánea* 41, no. 1 (2016): 143–69.

———. "Female Masculinity in *La Regenta*." In *Modern Spanish Women as Agents of Change: Essays in Honor of Maryellen Bieder*, edited by Jennifer Smith, 189–204. Lewisburg, PA: Bucknell University Press, 2019.

———. Introduction to *Modern Spanish Women as Agents of Change: Essays in Honor of Maryellen Bieder*, edited by Jennifer Smith, 1–14. Lewisburg, PA: Bucknell University Press, 2019.

Smith, Jennifer, and Lisa Nalbone. "Introduction: Intersections of Race, Class, Gender and Nation in Fin-de-Siècle Spain." In *Intersections of Race, Class, Gender and Nation in Fin-de-Siècle Spanish Literature and Culture*, edited by Jennifer Smith and Lisa Nalbone, 1–19. New York: Routledge, 2017.

Sousa Congosto, Francisco de. *Introducción a la historia de la indumentaria en España*. Madrid: Ediciones Istmo, 2007.

Souto Rumbo, Ismael. "'¡Ay, si en vez de santo fuera hombre . . .!': Religión y masculinidad en *Nazarín* (1895)." In *Hombres en peligro: Género, nación e imperio en la España de cambio de siglo (XIX–XX)*, edited by Mauricio Zabalgoitia Herrera, 155–72. Madrid: Iberoamericana, 2017.

———. "Masculinidad, sexualidad y domesticidad en *Tormento* de Benito Pérez Galdós." In *Sexualidades periféricas: Consolidaciones literarias y fílmicas en la España de fin de siglo XIX y fin de milenio*, edited by Nuria Godón and Michael J. Horswell, 121–49. Madrid: Editorial Fundamentos, 2016.

———. "La medida de un hombre: Las representaciones de la masculinidad en las novelas de Benito Pérez Galdós." PhD diss., Stony Brook University, 2015.

Surwillo, Lisa. *Monsters by Trade: Slave Traffickers in Modern Spanish Literature and Culture*. Stanford, CA: Stanford University Press, 2014.

———. "Passing Counterfeit Whiteness and Mulatta Wealth in *Los misterios de Barcelona*." *Journal of Spanish Cultural Studies* 10, no. 1 (2009): 75–87.

Sussman, Herbert L. *Victorian Masculinities: Manhood and Masculine Poetics in Early Victorian Literature and Art*. Cambridge: Cambridge University Press, 1995.

Tang, Wan Sonya. "Sacred, Sublime, and Supernatural: Religion and the Spanish Capital in Nineteenth-Century Fantastic Narratives." In *The Sacred and Modernity in Urban Spain: Beyond the Secular City*, edited by Antonio Córdoba and Daniel García-Donoso, 21–40. London: Palgrave Macmillan, 2016.

———. "'Yo no soy un hombre': Masculinity, Monstrosity, and Gothic Conventions in Galdós's *La sombra* (1871)." *Hispanic Review* 88, no. 3 (2020): 243–63.

Tejado, Gabino. "*Don Gonzalo González de la Gonzalera*." *Ilustración Católica*, March 28, 1879.

Thompson, John B. Introduction to *Language and Symbolic Power*, by Pierre Bourdieu. Edited by John B. Thompson, translated by Gino Raymond and Matthew Adamson, 1–31. London: Polity, 1991.

Tolstoy, Leo. *Anna Karenina*. Translated by Richard Pevear and Larissa Volokhonsky. New York: Penguin, 2004.

Tortella, Gabriel. *The Development of Modern Spain: An Economic History of the Nineteenth and Twentieth Century*. Translated by Valerie J. Herr. Cambridge, MA: Harvard University Press, 2000.

Tosh, John. *Manliness and Masculinities in Nineteenth-Century Britain*. London: Pearson Education Limited, 2005.

———. "What Should Historians Do with Masculinity?" *History Workshop*, no. 38 (1994): 179–202.

Trenc Ballester, Eliseo. *Las artes gráficas de la época modernista en Barcelona*. Barcelona: Gremio de Industrias Gráficas, 1977.

Tsuchiya, Akiko. *Images of the Sign: Semiotic Consciousness in the Novels of Benito Pérez Galdós*. Columbia: University of Missouri Press, 1990.

———. *Marginal Subjects: Gender and Deviance in Fin-de-siècle Spain*. Toronto: University of Toronto Press, 2011.

———. "Monuments and Public Memory: Antonio López y López, Slavery, and the Cuban-Catalan Connection." *Nineteenth-Century Contexts: An Interdisciplinary Journal* 41, no. 5 (2019): 479–500.

Turner, Harriet. "The Realist Novel." In *The Cambridge Companion to the Spanish Novel*, edited by Harriet Turner and Adelaida López de Martínez, 81–101. Cambridge: Cambridge University Press, 2003.

Valis, Noël. *The Culture of Cursilería: Bad Taste, Kitsch, and Class in Modern Spain*. Durham, NC: Duke University Press, 2003.

———. *The Decadent Vision in Leopoldo Alas: A Study of* La Regenta *and* Su único hijo. Baton Rouge: Louisiana State University Press, 1981.

———. *Reading the Nineteenth-Century Spanish Novel: Selected Essays*. Newark, DE: Juan de la Cuesta, 2005.

———. *Sacred Realism: Religion and the Imagination in Modern Spanish Narrative*. New Haven, CT: Yale University Press, 2010.

Valuy, Benoît. *Directorum Sacerdotale: A Guide for Priests in Their Public and Private Life; with an Appendix for the Use of Seminarists*. Dublin: M. H. Gill, 1907.

Varela Cabezas, Rodrigo. "La educación en *El doctor Centeno*." *Bulletin of Spanish Studies* 82, no. 6 (2005): 773–92.

Vázquez García, Francisco. "La patologización del celibato en la medicina española (1820–1920)." *ASCLEPIO: Revista de Historia de la Medicina y de la Ciencia* 70, no. 2 (2018): 1–12.

Velten, Hannah. *Beastly London: A History of Animals in the City*. London: Reaktion Books, 2016.

Vialette, Aurélie. *Intellectual Philanthropy: The Seduction of the Masses*. West Lafayette, IN: Purdue University Press, 2018.

Vidal Tibbits, Mercedes. "La 'memoria' como apología: *Memòries literàries*, de Narcís Oller." *Romance Notes* 39, no. 3 (1999): 231–40.

Viñao Frago, Antonio. "The History of Literacy in Spain: Evolution, Traits, and Questions." *History of Education Quarterly* 30, no. 4 (1990): 573–99.

Weineck, Silke-Maria. *The Tragedy of Fatherhood: King Laius and the Politics of Paternity in the West*. New York: Bloomsbury, 2014.

Wietelmann Bauer, Beth. "Narrative Cross-Dressing: Emilia Pardo Bazán in *Memorias de un solterón*." *Hispania* 77, no. 1 (1994): 23–30.

Willem, Linda. *Galdós's Segunda Manera: Rhetorical Strategies and Affective Response*. Chapel Hill: University of North Carolina Press, 1998.

Wolters, Nicholas. "'Debajo de la sotana': (Re)Dressing Clerical Masculinity in *La Regenta*." *Revista de Estudios Hispánicos* 53, no. 1 (2019): 329–52.

———. "Men of the Cloth: Fashioning the Priest in the Restoration Novel in Spain." PhD diss., University of Virginia, 2016.

———. "Secondhand: The Used Clothing Trade and Narrative Ragpicking in Galdós's *El Doctor Centeno*." *Anales Galdosianos*, no. 53 (2018): 55–75.

———. "The Spanish Cut: Tailoring Men's Fashion and National Identity in Nineteenth-Century Spain." *Journal of Spanish Cultural Studies* 21, no. 3 (2020): 313–33.

———. "Unholy Perversions: Clerical Deviance and Precarious Youth in Nakens, Sawa, and López Bago." In *Perversiones decimonónicas: Literatura y parafilia en el siglo XIX*, edited by Jorge Avilés-Diz, 273–89. Valencia: Albatros Ediciones, 2018.

Wynne, Deborah. "Reading Victorian Rags: Recycling, Redemption, and Dickens's Ragged Children." *Journal of Victorian Culture* 20, no. 1 (2014): 34–49.

Yates, Alan. "The Creation of Narcís Oller's *La febre d'or*." *Bulletin of Hispanic Studies* 52, no. 1 (1975): 55–77.

Yxart, Josep. *Escrits autobiogràfics, 1872–1889*. Edited by Rosa Cabré. Lleida: Punctum & Grup d'Estudi de la Literatura del Vuit-cents, 2007.

———. *La descoberta de la gran ciutat: París, 1878*. Edited by Rosa Cabré. Tarragona: Institut d'Estudis Tarraconenses Ramon Berenguer IV, 1995.

Zakim, Michael. "Customizing the Industrial Revolution: The Reinvention of Tailoring in the Nineteenth Century." *Winterthur Portfolio* 33, no. 1 (1998): 41–58.

Zamora, Andrés. *El doble silencio del eunuco: Poéticas sexuales de la novela realista según Clarín*. Madrid: Fundamentos, 1999.

Zanardi, Tara. *Framing Majïsmo: Art and Royal Identity in Eighteenth-Century Spain*. University Park: Pennsylvania State University Press, 2016.

———. "Natural History, Porcelain, and 'Mapping' Empire at Aranjuez." *Dieciocho* 43, no. 2 (2020): 241–70.

Zola, Émile. *L'Argent*. Edited by Philippe Hamon and Marie-France Azéma. Paris: Le Livre de Poche, 1998.

———. *Nana*. Edited by Henri Mitterand. Paris: Éditions Gallimard, 2002.

Zozaya, María. "'Moral Revenge of the Crowd' in the 1854 Revolution in Madrid." *Bulletin for Spanish and Portuguese Historical Studies* 37, no. 1 (2012): 18–46.

Zubiaurre, Maite. *Cultures of the Erotic in Spain, 1898–1939*. Nashville, TN: Vanderbilt University Press, 2012.

Zuelow, Eric. *A History of Modern Tourism*. New York: Palgrave Macmillan, 2016.

Index

Page numbers in *italic* indicate figures.

www.ingramcontent.com/pod-product-compliance
Lightning Source LLC
Chambersburg PA
CBHW031403270326
41929CB00010BA/1302